Legal Pluralism in Muslim Contexts

Studies in Islamic Law and Society

VOLUME 49

The titles published in this series are listed at *brill.com/sils*

Legal Pluralism in Muslim Contexts

Edited by

Norbert Oberauer
Yvonne Prief
Ulrike Qubaja

BRILL

LEIDEN | BOSTON

Library of Congress Cataloging-in-Publication Data

Names: Oberauer, Norbert, editor. | Prief, Yvonne, editor. | Qubaja, Ulrike, editor.
Title: Legal pluralism in Muslim contexts / edited by Norbert Oberauer, Yvonne Prief, Ulrike Qubaja.
Description: Leiden ; Boston : Brill, 2019. | Series: Studies in Islamic law and society ; volume 49 | Includes bibliographical references and index.
Identifiers: LCCN 2019010461 (print) | LCCN 2019018853 (ebook) | ISBN 9789004398269 (ebook) | ISBN 9789004398214 (hardback :alk. paper)
Subjects: LCSH: Legal polycentricity—Congresses. | Islamic law—Congresses. | Islamic law—Non-Islamic countries—Congresses. | Muslims—Legal status, laws, etc.—Congresses.
Classification: LCC K236 (ebook) | LCC K236 .L445 2019 (print) | DDC 340.9—dc23
LC record available at https://lccn.loc.gov/2019010461

Typeface for the Latin, Greek, and Cyrillic scripts: "Brill". See and download: brill.com/brill-typeface.

ISSN 1384-1130
ISBN 978-90-04-39821-4 (hardback)
ISBN 978-90-04-39826-9 (e-book)

This book is printed on acid-free paper and produced in a sustainable manner.

Contents

Notes on Contributors VII

Introduction 1
Norbert Oberauer

Muslim Legal Practice in the United Kingdom: the Muslim Arbitration Tribunal 12
Yvonne Prief

Unregistered Muslim Marriages in the United Kingdom 43
Vishal Vora

Muslims of Greece: a Legal Paradox *and* a Political Failure 63
Konstantinos Tsitselikis

Islamic Law as Indigenous Law: Sharīʿa Courts in Israel from a Postcolonial Perspective 84
Ido Shahar

Nation Building, Islamic Law and Unofficial Legal Pluralism: the Cases of Turkey and Pakistan 109
Ihsan Yilmaz

Constitutional Recognition of Islamic Family Law and Shariʿa Courts in Ethiopia: Governmental Strategies to Co-regulate the Plural Family Law Arena 139
Katrin Seidel

Legal Pluralism in the Southern West Bank: the Impact of Honour as a Factor on Developments towards an Increased Consideration of Rule-of-Law Principles in Clan-Based Justice 172
Ulrike Qubaja

Legal Pluralism in Indonesia: the Case of Interfaith Marriages Involving Muslims 199
Judith Koschorke

Contextualising Malaysia's Islamic Law: a Nuanced Perspective 230
Karen Meerschaut and Werner de Saeger

Index 255

Notes on Contributors

Judith Koschorke
obtained her master's degree in Arabic/Islamic Studies with a special focus on Islamic Law at Göttingen University, Germany and she is currently a research assistant at the aforementioned department. In her PhD project, she analyses the actualisation and codification of Islamic law in Muslim majority countries, focussing on Indonesia and the Islamic concept of lineage. Judith Koschorke has a special research interest in Islamic law in the modern context between the discursive poles of authenticity, disruption and flexibility.

Karen Meerschaut
graduated with a Law degree at the Vrije Universiteit Brussel and holds a PhD in Law (Vrije Universiteit van Brussel). She is currently a legal attaché at the Supreme Administrative Court of Belgium. She is equally a postdoctoral researcher at the Faculty of Law and Criminology of the Vrije Universiteit Brussel, in the research groups Metajuridica and Fundamental Rights & Constitutionalism (FRC). Her academic work is situated in the field of law and diversity, with a clear focus on fundamental freedoms, minority rights, questions of accommodation of cultural diversity, Islamic law, and the multiculturalism-debate in legal theory. She focuses on the relation between religion and state/law (including legal pluralism), in particular in the Malaysian legal system.

Norbert Oberauer
is a Professor at the Institute of Arabic and Islamic Studies of the University of Münster. His main areas of research include Islamic contract law, Islamic legal theory, pious endowments (*waqf*) and Islamic theology.

Yvonne Prief
holds a magister degree in Islamic Studies, Public Law and Political Science from the University of Münster and is working on her PhD dissertation on Muslim legal practice in the United Kingdom. She was part of the project "Legal Pluralism in Muslim Context – Conflict Regulation in Muslim Communities on the Basis of Customary and Islamic Law and its Relation to their Legal Environment", funded by the Gerda Henkel Foundation. She is currently an academic researcher at the Higher Administrative Court for the State of North Rhine-Westphalia.

Ulrike Qubaja
obtained her magister degree in Islamic Studies, Political Studies and Iranian Studies at Hamburg University. She is working on her PhD dissertation on clan-based customary law in the Southern Westbank against the background of legal pluralism in Palestinian society. Her project has been funded by the Gerda Henkel Foundation as part of the project "Legal Pluralism in Muslim Context – Conflict Regulation in Muslim Communities on the Basis of Customary and Islamic Law and its Relation to their Legal Environment". From 2013 to 2017 she was a Junior Researcher at the Cluster of Excellence for Religion and Politics at the University of Münster.

Ido Shahar
is a senior lecturer at the Department of Middle Eastern and Islamic Studies, University of Haifa. He is a legal anthropologist and a social historian, specialising in the study of Sharīʿa courts and of Palestinian society. He has published extensively on legal pluralism, on Sharīʿa courts in Israel, and on Palestinians in Israel.

Katrin Seidel
is a post-doctoral research fellow in the Law & Anthropology Department of the Max Planck Institute for Social Anthropology, a former fellow at Käte Hamburger Kolleg/Centre for Global Cooperation Research (2015/16), and was the Academic Coordinator of the Joint Network Rule of Law support at Freie Universität Berlin, in collaboration with the German Federal Foreign Office (2017). Based on her interdisciplinary background (Law and African/Asian studies), her research is situated at the intersection of legal pluralism, heterogeneous statehood and governance. Seidel's studies are concerned with interdependent relationships between plural normative and judicial orders at different levels of regulations, and with the intertwinings of respective social actors involved. Her current research is a comparative analysis of post-conflict constitution making in South Sudan and Somaliland.

Konstantinos Tsitselikis
is a Professor in Human Rights and International Organizations at the University of Macedonia (Greece). He has taught at the Universities of Thrace and Bilgi (Istanbul). He has authored several books, studies and articles on human rights, focused on minority and migrants rights and has worked for the Council of Europe (1992–95), the OSCE, the UN and the EU (1997–1999) in human rights and democratisation field missions. He is a member of the board of the Research Centre for Minority Groups (KEMO, www.kemo.gr,

1996–2014) and chairman of the Hellenic League for Human Rights (www.hlhr.gr) (2011–2017).

Vishal Vora
is a research fellow at the Department of Law and Anthropology, Max Planck Institute for Social Anthropology in Halle (Saale), Germany. His current research focuses on the maturing British Hindu community, examining the relationship between religion and state, in particular the community's search for its identity in multicultural Britain. He completed his PhD in Law at the School of Oriental and African Studies, University of London. His thesis was entitled: The Islamic Marriage Conundrum: register or recognise? The legal consequences of the nikah in England and Wales. He was Called to the Bar of England and Wales in 2007 and maintains links with legal professionals, often providing expert witness reports for the courts in family law cases. Prior to his legal education and training, Vishal completed a science degree at University College London.

Werner de Saeger
graduated in theology from Harvard University; in religious studies from the University of Cambridge; in law from the University of Brussels (VUB) and Hebrew University of Jerusalem; in canon law from the Catholic University of Louvain (KU Leuven); and in philosophy of law from the University of Leiden. His research focuses on Islamic law, both from a historical perspective and within its current-day context. He teaches at the University of Cambridge, PXL University of Applied Sciences and Arts in Hasselt, and does research at the Vrije Universiteit Brussel.

Ihsan Yilmaz
is Research Chair of Islamic Studies and Intercultural Dialogue at Deakin University, Australia. He was professor of political science at Istanbul Fatih University between 2008 and 2016, lecturer in law at SOAS, University of London between 2001 and 2008 and research scholar at the University of Oxford between 1999 and 2001. He completed his PhD at the School of Law and Social Sciences, SOAS, University of London in 1999. He has a BA in Political Science and International Relations from the Boğaziçi University (1994). He is the author of (2005, reprinted in 2016) *Muslim Laws, Politics and Society in Modern Nation States*: Dynamic Legal Pluralisms in England, Turkey and Pakistan and has published his work in various international scholarly journals.

Introduction

Norbert Oberauer

The concept of legal pluralism looks back on a history of heated debate.[1] To a large extent, the intensity of this controversy results from the fact that legal pluralism is a subject of different disciplines representing both normative and descriptive approaches. From the perspective of normative legal scholarship, legal pluralism may be interpreted as a challenge to the state's monopoly to establish legal rules. Since the state is typically seen as the guarantor of fundamental values – such as equality, freedom of religion or the rule of law – legal pluralism may be regarded as a threat to those values. Seen from this angle, the concept appears to be an ill-advised compromise of one of the most highly esteemed achievements of modernity.

From a sociological and anthropological perspective, legal pluralism is simply a fact, and its denial is sometimes denounced as a kind of ideological delusion.[2] Legal pluralists argue that in any given society there are multiple normative frames of reference, which should all be equally recognised as "law". In their opinion, it is arbitrary to apply this term only to state law, because this implies a prerogative of the state – which is an ideological claim rather than a scholarly premise.

The cleavage between normative and descriptive approaches to legal pluralism often correlates with another opposition rooted in disciplinary traditions: Legal anthropologists very often study societies with rather weak state

---

1 On the controversy over legal pluralism, see Dupret, "Legal Pluralism"; Woodman, "Ideological Combat"; Tamanaha, "The Folly of Legal Pluralism." For an overview of the development of the concept, see Tamanaha, "Understanding Legal Pluralism"; Merry, "Legal Pluralism"; Benda-Beckmann, "Rechtspluralismus." Further important contributions to the discussion of legal pluralism include Pospisil, *An Anthropology of Law*; Moore, *Law as a Process*; Griffiths, "What is Legal Pluralism"; Vanderlinden, "Return to Legal Pluralism"; Hooker, *Legal Pluralism*; Bearman, "The New Legal Pluralism." Studies of legal pluralism in Muslim contexts include Dupret (ed.), *Legal Pluralism in the Arab World*; Kemper/Reinkowski (eds.), *Rechtspluralismus in der Islamischen Welt*; Benda-Beckmann, F. v./Benda-Beckmann, K. v., "Balancing Islam, Adat, and the State"; "Sartori/Shahar, "Legal Pluralism in Muslim-Majority Colonies"; Shahar, "Legal Pluralism and the Study of Sharīʿa Courts"; id. *Legal Pluralism in the Holy City*; id. "Forum shopping between Civil and Religious Courts"; Sezgin, "Nation-Building and Regulation of Pluri-Legal Jurisdictions"; Turner and Arslan, "Shari'a and Legal Pluralism in the West"; Possamai, Richardson and Turner (eds.), *Legal Pluralism and Shari'a Law*; Oberauer, *Waqf im kolonialen Sansibar* (especially chapter III).

2 See for instance Griffiths, "What is Legal Pluralism", 2 f.

 | DOI:10.1163/9789004398269_002

structures, whereas (western) normative legal studies typically focus on societies with strong states. Thus, the relevance of the concept of legal pluralism tends to be more obvious to anthropologists than to representatives of normative legal scholarship.

However, over the last decades legal pluralism has gained much in relevance even from a normative perspective. Globalisation and, particularly, large-scale migration have intensified interaction between different legal frames of reference. In many western societies, there are large ethnic and religious minorities who sometimes draw on their own normative concepts, including customary and religious laws. Muslim minorities are a case in point. Their representatives sometimes demand some degree of official recognition of Islamic legal practices. Often, those minorities implement religious or customary norms on an informal basis. This has stirred a heated debate in many western countries about whether "parallel justice" should be condoned and to what extent religious norms may be accommodated within a secular legal order without compromising its basic tenets. Thus, legal pluralism has become a challenge to normative legal science in a very real sense.

There is also a reverse effect of globalisation: State law has made its way into virtually all societies over the world, even though it has in some cases remained marginal. This expansion of state law goes along with a global presence of many concepts that are historically related to the idea of state law, such as the rule of law, but also fundamental human-rights concepts. In other words, the advance of Islamic law and other religious or customary laws into the normative discourses of western societies is paralleled (and was in fact preceded) by the global expansion of the concept of state law. As a consequence, conflict and interaction between Islamic and state law are not a recent phenomenon confined to western societies. Most societies in the Muslim world have a long experience with the coexistence of religious and state law. It is true that the social and political conditions of those societies – which are very diverse – differ from those of European societies (which are not homogenous either). Nonetheless, there are many parallels and the editors of the present volume believe that much can be learned from a comparative outlook on western and non-western societies, on weak and strong states, and on Muslim minority and majority societies.

Such a comparative approach renders some features of legal pluralism more visible. For instance, it reveals that legally pluralist settings often involve an imbalance of power. The interacting legal orders are often represented and supported by different power elites, and typically one of them is hegemonic. For this reason, legal pluralism often involves a negotiation not only of legal concepts, but also of political influence or recognition, and the competing legal frames of reference may be highly charged with political symbolism. These features of legal pluralism become very obvious when looking at colonial societies,[3] but in more subtle ways they also characterise contemporary settings of legal pluralism. Thus Ido Shahar argues, in his contribution to the present volume, that Shariʿa courts in Israel have become sites of resistance against the policies applied by Israeli authorities towards the Palestinian population. Ihsan Yilmaz, in his chapter on legal pluralism in Turkey and Pakistan, argues that the official family laws in those countries are the product of a "civilising mission" on the part of modernising power elites. This mission has provoked resistance from "counter-hegemonic" forces within society, who disregard the legal codes, applying their own interpretation of Islamic law instead. The chapters on Ethiopia (by Katrin Seidel), Indonesia (by Judith Koschorke) and Malaysia (by Karen Meerschaut) show that legal pluralism in these three countries is intricately related to the power struggles of specific groups in the respective societies. In Indonesia, the precarious political balance has induced official decision makers to refrain from clarifying the legal situation, which has resulted in a considerable degree of legal uncertainty. In Ethiopia, the relative weakness of the state has prevented official agents from effectively enforcing control over the legal practices of Muslim citizens in the field of family law. Ethiopian state representatives largely content themselves with *de jure* sovereignty, accepting that official law has little impact on actual practice. All those case studies vividly illustrate that it is a dangerous delusion to conceive of state-law as a tool to enforce loyalty to norms that are not rooted in popular sentiment.

There is another insight that can be gained from a comparative perspective on legal pluralist settings – an insight that challenges the very usefulness of legal pluralism as an analytical category: There may be common features to the legal pluralisms of different societies, but the case studies in this volume also reveal that legal pluralisms are very unique settings, each characterised by a singular blend of historical, political, religious, demographic and other circumstances. In other words: legal pluralisms are very specific contexts and one must be careful with generalisations. This is especially relevant when it comes to propositions about how people act within legal pluralist environments. People's choices between different legal forums may be driven by a wide range of motives, not all of them readily conspicuous to an observer unfamiliar with the local framework. If, for example, actors in Turkey and the United Kingdom

3 Cf. Sartori/Shahar, "Legal Pluralism in Muslim-Majority Colonies", 641f.; for case studies, see the works cited therein and the other contributions to JESHO 55/3–4 (2012), a special issue on Muslim legal pluralism under colonial rule, as well as Oberauer, *Waqf im kolonialen Sanisbar*, especially 179–232.

avoid the registration of their marriages, they might do so for very different reasons. Agents may be driven by ideological motives or by plain loyalty to tradition, but also by very rational and pragmatic considerations. Ulrike Qubaja's contribution to this volume, which focusses on the concept of honour in the southern West Bank and its role in clan-based conflict resolution, provides a good example of how intricate the motives of agents can be. This observation brings to mind that the theoretical discussion of legal pluralism should always be grounded in thorough empirical research.

The present volume includes studies from different disciplinary perspectives, representing both normative and descriptive science, and focussing on societies both inside and outside Europe, with Muslim majority and minority populations.

IDO SHAHAR's contribution analyses the operation of Shariʿa courts in Israel. In principle, those Courts apply Islamic Law as codified in the Ottoman Law of Family Rights of 1917 (OLFR), which was largely adopted by the British Mandate authorities and later by the Israeli government. The latter, however, passed additional legislation penalising polygamy, unilateral repudiation of a spouse, and marriage under the age of 18. As Shahar points out, this legislation created a complex legal situation with some inherent contradictions. Thus, for example, unilateral repudiation is now a punishable offence, but it is nonetheless legally valid under the OLFR.

Shahar argues that this intricate situation reflects the general policy of the Israeli state towards Islamic law: On the one hand, state officials are eager to safeguard certain human rights such as equality between the sexes. On the other hand, they refrain from directly intervening into substantive religious law. According to Shahar, this policy is reminiscent of the line of action typically followed by colonial administrators, who – for political reasons – generally admitted indigenous law so long as it was not abhorrent to essential normative concepts of their own legal orders.

The reluctance of the state to interfere with Islamic law has resulted in a relatively autonomous position of the Shariʿa court judiciary, who has assumed a quasi-legislative function within the field of their jurisdiction. Thus, the former president of the Shariʿa Court of Appeals issued no less than twelve "judicial circulars" (*marsūmāt qaḍāʾiyya*) addressing a wide range of issues and initiating a number of legal reforms. In the absence of state legislation in the field of Islamic law, these circulars – which were drawn up with the approval of other acting qāḍīs – have become an important instrument to shape and develop the law.

IHSAN YILMAZ's contribution to the present volume is a comparative study of family law in Turkey and Pakistan. In principle, those countries represent different legal policies: Turkish family law was thoroughly secularised as part of the Kemalist policy, whereas Pakistani family law is based on a reform-oriented interpretation of Islamic law. However, Yilmaz points to a common element in the legal policies of the two states: In both countries, the official family laws resulted from an effort of western-oriented power elites to "construct a new citizen identity of modern Muslims". Thus, state law was utilised as an instrument for "social engineering". Based on an analysis of case law, statistical data, and field research, Yilmaz demonstrates that in both countries this policy has had only limited success. To a considerable degree, family law practice in Turkey and Pakistan remains informal, bypassing state regulations and following a traditional interpretation of Islamic law.

Yilmaz shows that courts and other state institutions often tolerate informal legal practices, such as unregistered marriages, polygamy or marriage under age, and that some institutions even support those practices, referring to Islamic law for justification. Thus, the conflict between official and informal norms is to some extent being negotiated within the institutional structures of the state itself. According to Yilmaz, this negotiation has generated what he calls "hybrid" laws, namely normative constructs that result from the interaction of official and informal law. For example, Turkish courts do not recognise unregistered marriages as valid, but in some cases, they have held that women in unregistered wedlock enjoy insurance claims after the death of their (informal) husbands.

JUDITH KOSCHORKE's contribution is a study on interfaith marriages in Indonesia. Dutch colonial legislation in Indonesia had provided that such marriages must be solemnised according to the husband's religion, but do not require the wife's conversion. This met with resistance from Muslims who held that Islamic law proscribes a marriage between a Muslim woman and a non-Muslim man (or, according to a strict interpretation popular in Indonesia, between Muslims and non-Muslims in general). When a new Marriage Law was drafted in the early 1970s, political pressure induced the legislator to avoid an explicit regulation of interfaith marriages. Instead, an ambiguous provision was passed which has since become the object of an ongoing dispute over interpretation. As Koschorke demonstrates, the state institutions involved in this dispute do not always act in concert. Even Supreme and Constitutional Court jurisdiction has failed to clarify the matter. This has resulted in a considerable degree of legal uncertainty, combined with the invention of legal loopholes to which couples resort in order to facilitate interfaith marriages.

The contribution of KAREN MEERSCHAUT and WERNER DE SAEGER portraits the changing position of Islamic law within the legal system of Malaysia. The country's constitution, passed in 1957, provides that Islam is the state religion. However, up to the 1990s this provision had hardly any impact on the Malaysian legal system as a whole. Since the end of this decade, however, the country experiences an increasing debate over its Islamic identity, combined with a growing trend towards more conservative interpretations of the law. As in many other countries, Islamic legal norms have become the object of political power struggles between competing groups within society.

KATRIN SEIDEL's contribution analyses the position of the Shariʿa courts in Ethiopia, a country with a strong Muslim minority. Shariʿa courts have existed in Ethiopia for centuries, but in 1942, under the rule of Haile Selassie I, they became officially recognised and integrated into the state system, as courts with jurisdiction in personal status matters. De jure, this recognition was withdrawn in 1960 when a new Civil Code expressly repealed all previous written and customary law. However, this had no practical effect on the Shariʿa courts which continued to operate as before.

The current constitution, passed in 1994, re-established the de jure basis of the courts, while at the same time reframing it: In principle, the qāḍīs are expected to apply uncodified Islamic law, but in matters of adjective law, they are bound by the Ethiopian Civil Procedure Code. Moreover, parties must give their express consent to the adjudication of their case by a Shariʿa court instead of a civil court. However, as Seidel demonstrates, those regulations have little effect on the practice of the qāḍīs, who regularly apply Islamic laws of evidence and who often take the parties' consent to their jurisdiction for granted rather than ascertaining it. Many Shariʿa court decisions also appear to contradict constitutional principles, such as the equality of the sexes and the freedom of religion. There is a debate among legal practitioners though whether Shariʿa jurisdiction is in fact subject to constitutional review, and in practice the decisions largely remain unchallenged. Seidel attributes this state of affairs to the relatively weak position of state institutions within society. The state's recognition of the Shariʿa courts is driven by the motivation to retain at least minimal control over legal practices. For the same reason, state actors are reluctant to openly challenge the courts' legal decisions.

ULRIKE QUBAJA's contribution analyses legal pluralism in the southern West Bank. In that region, the relevant legal frames of reference include not only state law and Islamic law, but also clan based customary law (a constellation which, according to Qubaja, is typical for weak states with a predominantly Muslim population). Qubaja shows that during the last decades, this customary law has been increasingly challenged by normative concepts originating from a global discourse on rule-of-law principles. Thus, an increasing number of local agents have adopted a critical stance toward certain practices of customary law, such as vigilante justice, retaliation by attacking a perpetrator's relatives, exiling the perpetrator's family or forcing victims of sexual assault to marry the offender. In many areas of the law, this critical attitude has resulted in a change of practice. However, in cases where the concept of "honour" (*ʿirḍ/ sharaf*) is involved, the influence of rule-of-law principles remains very limited. The data presented by Qubaja indicate that the restoration of honour is so paramount in the eyes of agents that they resort to customary law practices to achieve it, even if they consider those practices unjust and wrong. This observation suggests that the choice between various legal frames of reference is often determined by strategical considerations rather than conviction.

Konstantinos Tsitselikis' contribution is a study of the legal situation of the Turkish-Muslim minority in Thrace (Greece), which presents a very special case of legal pluralism. Owing to certain provisions of the Treaty of Lausanne, the said minority enjoys a partial legal autonomy comprising inter alia the jurisdiction of Muftis in matters of family and inheritance law. The Muftis, who are appointed by the state, apply an interpretation of Islamic law that is neither codified nor standardised in any other formal way. This situation has drawn severe criticism from a human rights perspective. Critics claim *inter alia* that the Muftis' decisions often infringe on women's or children's rights and that it is unpredictable which interpretation of the law the Muftis shall apply. In defence, state officials have stressed that members of the Turkish-Muslim minority are free to choose between the Mufti's jurisdiction and that of civil courts. However, the established case law is not unanimous on this point: According to Tsitselikis, civil courts sometimes deny Muslims the application of civil law, insisting that Islamic law must be applied. Thus for example, some courts have refused to accept wills drawn up by Muslim testators, arguing that the bequests did not comply with Islamic law, and that civil law was not applicable to the case. Tsitselikis criticises this position, arguing that it amounts to a discriminatory and segregationist legal treatment of citizens who should be effectively equal before the law.

Vishal Vora's contribution is a critical analysis of the marriage law of England and Wales. Vora argues that this law reflects a Christian conception of marriage, which results in discrimination towards Muslim and other non-Christian religious groups. The law provides that a marriage must be conducted in a church, in another place of worship registered for that purpose, or on premises approved for civil marriage ceremonies. Since British Muslims do not consider a mosque a natural setting for marriages, they often marry in other places, with the result that their marriages do not meet the formal requirements of the law.

Vora presents case law suggesting that the courts take a very strict attitude towards such marriages: They do not simply declare them void, but insist that they are "non-marriages", a legal category that excludes financial remedies for the affected parties (remedies which are still available in a void marriage). This strict attitude is particularly detrimental for women, because it is usually them who take the economically weaker position within the marriage.

Based on field research, Vora demonstrates that Muslim couples (and particularly women) are often surprised to learn that their marriage is non-existent in the eyes of the law. Vora's analysis suggests that in the case of British Muslims, non-compliance with legal provisions does not stem from an intention to evade state intrusion into religious marriage practices, but rather from the fact that the law makes it unduly difficult for Muslims to obtain a valid marriage. In particular, the requirement that marriages must be conducted in specific places – a concept that seems to reflect the Christian tradition – presents an obstacle for Muslims on the way towards a legal marriage.

To substantiate his argument, Vora takes a comparative look at Scottish law, which is much more flexible regarding marriage ceremonies. According to that law, a marriage may be conducted at any place, the only requirement being the presence of witnesses and a celebrant, who must hold a licence to conduct marriages and who is responsible for handling registration formalities. Statistical data show that 7% of the applicants for such licenses are Muslims, a figure that – according to Vora – suggests that the Scottish system has been well received within Muslim communities. The author does not present any data regarding Muslim marriages in Scotland, but it seems reasonable to assume that the Scottish approach results in a higher rate of legally valid marriages among Muslims.

YVONNE PRIEF's contribution focusses on the Muslim Arbitration Tribunal (MAT), an institution in the United Kingdom which during the last years has sparked a heated public controversy. MAT operates under the Arbitration Act 1996, which grants citizens the right to freely choose any tribunal they wish in order to seek arbitration, and to determine any law of their choice as the relevant basis for the tribunal's decision. Critics have pointed out that this enables MAT to apply Islamic law of evidence, which discriminates against women, since it does not treat the testimony of female witnesses on a par with that of males. The representatives of MAT, while admitting that they apply Islamic law of evidence, point out that parties who seek the tribunal's services do so voluntarily, submitting to Islamic rules of procedure by their own choice.

MAT has also been accused of obstructing criminal prosecution in cases of domestic violence: In family matters, the Tribunal does not offer arbitration, but merely mediation and counselling. Critics have pointed out that in the course of such procedures, victims of domestic violence may be persuaded or even pressurised not to press charges. Again, representatives of MAT point out that the decision whether to press charges rests entirely with the victim and that the latter – far from being pressurised – is in fact supported by the Tribunal in doing so if necessary. In addition, they argue that in most of the cases in which the Tribunal gets involved, there is no need to press charges, because pressure and surveillance exerted on the offender by the community turn out to be sufficient to stop violence.

The case of MAT highlights a dilemma that is typical of legal pluralist settings. The dilemma results from the fact that the law cannot prevent its subjects from waiving their legal rights. Women who choose to submit to tribunals that grant them less legal protection than courts or other forums cannot be legally prevented from that choice. Arguably, the state encourages that choice by providing a legal framework for institutions like MAT. At the same time, however, this framework allows some degree of control, which would be lost if citizens turned to unofficial conflict resolution instead. Structurally speaking, this dilemma is the same as that faced by countries such as Turkey or Pakistan: The attempt to "prescribe" secular legal rights "from above" has limited success, because the legal subjects often turn to unofficial law rather than operating within the official legal framework. This forces legal policy makers to compromise.

The contributions to this volume are based on papers presented at the workshop "Interdisciplinary Approaches to Legal Pluralism in Muslim Contexts", convened on 6–7 October, 2016 at the Westfälische Wilhelms-Universität Münster, with the generous support of the Gerda Henkel Foundation and the Cluster of Excellence "Religion and Politics". We wish to express our gratitude to Theo Riches, who proofread the contributions and to Abdulmuhsin Daş, who carried out the indexing of the volume and other editorial tasks. The editors hope that the volume will be a valuable contribution to the empirical study of legal pluralism from different disciplinary perspectives, and that it will enhance our understanding of legal phenomena in Muslim contexts.

Bibliography

Benda-Beckmann, Franz von. "Rechtspluralismus. Analytische Begriffsbildung oder politisch-ideologisches Programm." *Zeitschrift für Ethnologie* 119 (1994): 1–16.

Benda-Beckmann, Franz von, and Keebet von Benda-Beckmann. "Balancing Islam, Adat and the State: Comparing Islamic and Civil Courts in Indonesia." In *The Power of Law in the Transnational World. Anthropological Enquiries*, edited by id., 216–35. New York: Berghahn Books, 2009.

Berman, P.S. "The New Legal Pluralism." *Annual Review of Law and The Social Sciences* 5 (2009): 225–42.

Dupret, Baudouin. "Legal Pluralism, Plurality of Laws, and Legal Practices: Theories, Critiques, and Praxiological Re-Specification." *European Journal of Legal Studies* 1, no. 1 (2007): 296–318.

Dupret, Baudouin et al., eds. *Legal Pluralism in the Arab World*. The Hague et al.: Kluwer Law International, 1999.

Griffiths, John. "What is Legal Pluralism?" *Journal of Legal Pluralism and Unofficial Law* 24, no. 1 (1986): 38.

Hooker, B.M. *Legal Pluralism: An Introduction to Colonial and New-Colonial Laws*. Oxford: Clarendon Press, 1975.

Kemper, Michael, and Maurus Reinkowski, eds. *Rechtspluralismus in der Islamischen Welt. Gewohnheitsrecht zwischen Staat und Gesellschaft*. Berlin: de Gruyter, 2005.

Merry, S.E. "Legal Pluralism." *Law and Society Review* 22 (1988): 869–896.

Moore, Sally Falk. *Law as a Process. An Anthropological Approach*. London: Routledge & Kegan Paul, 1978.

Oberauer, Norbert. *Waqf im kolonialen Sansibar. Der Wandel einer islamischen Stiftungspraxis unter britischer Protektoratsherrschaft*. Würzburg: Ergon, 2012.

Pospisil, Leopold. *An Anthropology of Law: A Comparative Theory*. New York: Harper & Row, 1971.

Possamai, Adam, James T. Richardson and Brian S. Turner (eds.). *Legal Pluralism and Shari'a Law*. London and New York: Routledge, 2014.

Sartori, Paolo and Ido Shahar. "Legal Pluralism in Muslim-Majority Colonies: Mapping the Terrain." *JESHO* 55 (2012): 637–663.

Sezgin, Yüksel. "Theorizing Formal Pluralism: Quantification of Legal Pluralism for Spatio – Temporal Analysis", *Journal of Legal Pluralism* 50 (2004): 101–118.

Sezgin, Yüksel. "The Israeli Millet System: Examining Legal Pluralism through Lenses of Nation-Building and Human Rights." *Israel Law Review* 43, no. 3 (2010): 631–654.

Sezgin, Yüksel. "Nation-Building and Regulation of Pluri-Legal Jurisdictions: The Case of the Israeli Millet System." In *The Everyday Life of the State: A State-in-Society Approach*, edited by Adam J. White, 91–105. Seattle: University of Washington Press (2013).

Shahar, Ido. "Legal Pluralism and the Study of Sharīʿa Courts." *ILS* 15 (2008): 112–141.

Shahar, Ido. "Legal Pluralism Incarnate: An Institutional Perspective on Courts of Law in Colonial and Postcolonial Settings." *Journal of Legal Pluralism* 65 (2012): 133–162.

Shahar, Ido. "Forum shopping between Civil and Religious Courts: Maintenance Suits in Contemporary Jerusalem" In *Religion in Dispute*, edited by F. Benda Beckmann et. al, 147–164. New York: Palgrave Macmillan, 2013.

Shahar, Ido. *Legal Pluralism in the Holy City. Competing Courts, Forum Shopping and Institutional Dynamics in Jerusalem*. Aldershot: Ashgate, 2015.

Tamanaha, Brian Z. "The folly of legal pluralism." *Journal of Law and Society* 20 (1993): 192–217.

Tamanaha, Brian Z. "A Non-Essentialist Version of Legal Pluralism" *Journal of Law and Society* 27 (2000): 296.

Tamanaha, Brian Z. "Understanding Legal Pluralism: Past to Present, Local to Global." *Sidney Law Review* 30 (2008): 375–411.

Turner, Brian S. and Berna Zengin Arslan. "Shari'a and Legal Pluralism in the West." In *European Journal of Social Theory* 14, no. 2 (2011): 139–159.

Vanderlinden, J. "Return to Legal Pluralism." *Journal of Legal Pluralism* 28 (1989): 149–157.

Woodman, Gordon R. "Ideological Combat and Social Observation: Recent Debate About Legal Pluralism." *Journal of Legal Pluralism* 42 (1998): 21.

Woodman, Gordon R. "The Idea of Legal Pluralism." In *Legal Pluralism in the Arab World*, edited by Baudouin Dupret et al., 3–20. The Hague et al.: Kluwer Law International, 1999.

Muslim Legal Practice in the United Kingdom: the Muslim Arbitration Tribunal

Yvonne Prief

1 Introduction

In 2008 the former Archbishop of Canterbury, Rowan Williams, held a speech at the Royal Courts of Justice on the usage of different systems of law in the UK. He aimed to tackle, "the question of whether there should be a higher attention to religious identity and communal rights in the practice of law" and considered "a delegation of certain legal functions to the religious courts of a community",[1] explicitly focusing not only on Muslim, but also on Christian and Orthodox Jewish communities. Williams discussed the fact that individuals were able to be members in "different but overlapping sets of social relationship"[2] and argued that one could imagine "a scheme in which individuals retain the liberty to choose the jurisdiction under which they will seek to resolve certain carefully specified matters", which could, "include aspects of marital law, the regulation of financial transactions and authorised structures of mediation and conflict resolution".[3] He acknowledged that such a, "scheme allowing for supplementary jurisdiction will [not likely] be simple", but "seems unavoidable"[4] in a pluralistic state in which individuals should not have to choose whether to be loyal to their state or their culture.

Following this speech there was an agitated, public debate fuelled by the media and featuring statements by public persons including politicians, representatives of the judiciary and clerics, women's rights groups and others. The media used dramatic wording: a BBC headline on the day following Williams' complex and long speech – of which only brief excerpts were quoted by the media and often out of context – read "Sharia law in UK is 'unavoidable'".[5] The Daily Mirror published an article stating that "[t]he Muslim tribunals are exploiting a loophole in the Arbitration Act 1996".[6] Its author, Jason Beattie, furthermore claimed that judgements arrived at in "Islamic courts" in the

1 Williams, "Civil and Religious," 267.
2 Ibid., 269.
3 Ibid., 274.
4 Ibid.
5 "Sharia law," *BBC News*.
6 Beattie, "Secret Sharia Law Courts," 19.

 | DOI:10.1163/9789004398269_003

UK "are then enforced through county courts or the High Court",[7] giving the impression – at least in name – that these institutions were real courts, acting somewhat in the shadows of English law but at the same time being acknowledged insofar as their "judgements" were already and unconditionally enforced by English courts. The media repeatedly wrote about "sharia courts"[8] or "Islamic courts",[9] sometimes meaning shariʿa councils, sometimes the Muslim Arbitration Tribunal (MAT), sometimes not making clear which institutions they were actually talking about. The institutions are accused of acting ultra vires by handling cases involving domestic violence, of preventing criminal proceedings and of discriminating against women.[10] Since 2008, MAT as well as shariʿa councils have repeatedly been subject of political discussions.[11] The Casey Review, commissioned in July 2015 by the then Prime Minister, David Cameron, and Home Secretary, Theresa May, and published by Dame Louise Casey in December 2016, summarises that "Sharia Councils and other parallel legal systems" are using "discriminatory practices against women which, in some cases, are causing serious harm" and furthermore allowing or condoning forced marriage, beating and rape.[12] Muslim Arbitration Tribunals are also said to be "arbitrating on issues outside of their jurisdiction, such as child custody and domestic violence."[13]

Five months into the public debate the then Lord Chief Justice, Lord Phillips of Worth Matravers made a public statement backing Williams' position in which he stressed that, as English law itself offered the opportunity to choose a law other than the law of the land, there was "no reason why principles of sharia law or any other religious code, should not be the basis for mediation or other forms of alternative dispute resolution".[14]

While politicians in the House of Lords have been discussing amendments to the relevant legislation and thus facilitating or prohibiting such alternative dispute resolution based on religious principles, the Muslim Arbitration Tribunal carries on with its business. The unique feature of MAT in comparison with shariʿa councils, which mainly handle cases of Islamic divorce, is that

7 Ibid.
8 E.g. Edwards, "Sharia courts."
9 "Sharia court" and "Islamic court" are used interchangeably here: Beattie, "Secret Sharia Law Courts," 19.
10 See e.g. Edwards, "Sharia courts."
11 See e.g. Grillo, Muslim Families, 29–31.
12 Casey, *The Casey Review*, 132 f.
13 Ibid., 133.
14 Statement by Nicholas Phillips, Baron Phillips of Worth Matravers, video originally available on BBC News, "Top judge backs sharia 'role'." Also see Wintour & Butt, "Sharia law could have UK role."

MAT defines itself through the ability to also perform arbitrations and engaging English legal professionals such as solicitors and barristers, as well as trained mediators and arbitrators.[15] This chapter focuses on the MAT's eponymous feature of offering arbitration compliant with Islamic principles. One central question is about how MAT deals with and uses the two legal systems – English law as the law of the land that actually sets a frame for arbitration, and Islamic law, which obviously is what distinguishes it from other arbitration tribunals and defines its main clientele. Does MAT manage to integrate the two systems into each other? How does the institution react to possible contradictions? This chapter will look into the main aspects of criticism and accusations made against MAT. Is the criticism appropriate? Are there aspects in MAT's procedures and conduct that are problematic from the point of view of English law? Would attempts to enact new legislation like the Arbitration and Mediation Services (Equality) Bill procure the benefits intended by its supporters and actually force MAT to change their practice accordingly?

First-hand information on the institution and its procedures was gathered in interviews with its chairman, Faizul Aqtab Siddiqi, and another member of staff.[16]

2 The Muslim Arbitration Tribunal

The Muslim Arbitration Tribunal (MAT) was set up in Nuneaton in 2007 as a "unique Alternate Dispute Resolution organisation which deals with Islamic Sacred Law within the context of the English Legal System".[17] It features a number of branches all over the country; of those especially Bradford, Manchester and London were said by Faizul Aqtab Siddiqi, chairman of MAT, to be facing increasing numbers of cases.[18] Tanya Walker and John Bowen stress that public statements giving the impression that a number of Muslim arbitration tribunals or MAT branches already existed all over the UK have to be considered carefully, as this assumption only arose out of the chairman's activities in different cities.[19] Siddiqi himself explained that their branches are basically facilities on demand, which are set up in mosques, community centres or hotel rooms around the country as and when needed, with arbitrators travelling

15 Siddiqi, interview 2012.
16 Ibid.; Siddiqi & member of staff, interview 2015.
17 Muslim Arbitration Tribunal, "History."
18 Siddiqi, interview 2015.
19 Walker, *Shari'a councils*, 51; Bowen, "Sanctity and Shariah," 132.

there for the occasion. Their number was given as eleven in 2012 by Siddiqi himself, but was said to be increasing.[20]

MAT headquarters are based at "Hijaz Manor", large premises formerly known as "Higham Grange", built as a hunting lodge and later on used as a rehabilitation centre,[21] located near Nuneaton in the Midlands and thus in a remote but nonetheless central spot within the United Kingdom. It houses "Hijaz College", an "Islamic University" which, according to its website, is not recognised as such in the UK but still offers classes in Islamic law and theology from basic levels up until MA level.[22] Hijaz College was founded by Allama Muhammad Abdul Wahab Siddiqi, who was born and educated in Pakistan and came to the UK at the age of 30 in 1972.[23] He died in 1994, the year of the establishment of Hijaz College,[24] and is buried in a mausoleum on the premises. His son Faizul Aqtab Siddiqi, who is a barrister at law at the same time as being an Islamic scholar, is the principal of Hijaz College and chairman of MAT as well as being head or founder of several other Muslim institutions and networks. He has inherited the position of "Head of the Naqshbandi Hijazi Spiritual Sufi Order" from his father.[25] During the two interviews I conducted with Siddiqi and another scholar at MAT, not once did they refer to being Sufi or mention the relevance of spirituality to their work directly – whereas Bowen clearly marks the "spiritual dimension"[26] as a paramount factor distinguishing MAT from other institutions. Walker further explains that some of MAT's cases emerge from spiritual meetings which "appear to provide the context in which much of the family and marital mediation and dispute resolution occurs."[27] She describes as a "common misconception" that MAT's work is usually supposed to consist mainly of official procedures of alternative dispute resolution and mediation; this public impression ist not being put straight but rather further promoted by MAT.[28] In line with this, Bowen confirms what I have found in the interviews as well: "[t]o non-Sufis and, more importantly, non-Muslims, Siddiqi underlines his status as barrister and his role as arbitrator, and most people know of his activities under the rubric of MAT."[29]

20 Siddiqi, interview 2012; Siddiqi, interview 2015.
21 Weddington Castle, "Higham Hall."
22 Hijaz College, "Courses."
23 Hijaz College, "History – The Founder." Also see Bowen, *British Islam*, 145.
24 Hijaz College, "Formation."
25 See Hijaz College, "The Principal."
26 Bowen, *British Islam*, 155.
27 Walker, *Shari'a councils*, 51 fn 17.
28 Ibid., 52.
29 Bowen, *British Islam*, 155.

Siddiqi says that MAT understands itself as an institution offering a service to Muslims in the UK in line with halal food, mosques and Quran classes. He argues that in a civilised, pluralistic society, citizens need and should have access to "their institutions" whether they are religiously or otherwise motivated, in order to feel "at home" – as long as they do not affect other people.[30] But he also stresses that they, as an institution, "are here as a service, not [...] to spread Islam or to glorify Islam".[31] Their aim, he says, is "to help the community and our young people who are suffering."[32]

In order to do so MAT offers a range of services, including dispute resolution through mediation or arbitration, Islamic divorces, drawing up Islamic wills and interpreting existing wills according to Islamic principles, advice, counselling and mentoring. In 2015, Siddiqi and his assistant estimated the amount of cases of dispute resolution they handle at 30–60 a month, of which about 20% are related to matrimonial or divorce issues, 10% are arbitrations and the rest are cases involving mediation.[33] Given the fact that matrimonial and divorce cases can also include mediation and because of a lack of statistics, I suggest to take these numbers as an only rough estimation of the ratio of the different cases and types of procedures. Walker states that while most of MAT's family and marital dispute resolution work happened in the context of the community's spiritual events and meetings, arbitration appears to constitute only the smallest amount of MAT's cases. Furthermore, the total number of cases did "not form the basis of the profile the organisation has had in the press and in the political sphere."[34]

MAT relies on solicitors and barristers – Siddiqi being a barrister and two of his brothers and his brother-in-law being practising solicitors[35] – as well as on trained or at least experienced mediators and arbitrators.[36] It can even count an English District Judge amongst its staff, who was officially given permission to act as an arbitrator for MAT.[37] Siddiqi, while explaining their organisational setup, at times referred to the non-administrative staff as "judges", which underlines that he aims at depicting the status of his institution as an arbitration

30 Siddiqi, interview 2012.
31 Ibid.
32 Siddiqi, interview 2015.
33 Siddiqi & member of staff, interview 2015.
34 Walker, *Shari'a councils*, 53.
35 See Bowen, *British Islam*, 147.
36 Siddiqi, interview 2015.
37 This was revealed and discussed by the media, e.g. Gilligan, "Judge." Judge Shamim Ahmed Qureshi, born 1960, has been a District Judge at Magistrates' Court since 2004. See Courts and Tribunals Judiciary, "District Judges." Also see Oxford Index, "Qureshi, Shamim Ahmed."

tribunal. He stresses that the majority of staff are third and fourth generation Muslims, having grown up in the UK, and hence understand the needs of their mostly young clients. Procedures are usually carried out in English, but most staff is at least bilingual and interpreters are used, should this become necessary in a case. Some of the "judges" – Siddiqi calls these (and himself) "hybrids" – are trained both in English law and as Islamic scholars.[38] He says that about 40% of staff at MAT are women, which he proudly states is better than in the English courts.[39] All mediators and arbitrators are volunteers and only paid their expenses.[40] This might in part explain the relatively low fees MAT charges for its services. The institution's website gives the costs for a *khulʿ*, an Islamic divorce applied for by the wife, at £ 300, drafting and executing a will at £ 200. Siddiqi specifies that a mediation or arbitration would cost about £ 50 to £ 500, depending on how complex the case is.[41] MAT claims to be a non-commercial organisation,[42] being – as is Hijaz College – part of Jamia Islamia (Islamic Studies Centre) Trust, which is a registered charity. When studying the two institutions, the charity and the persons involved, it also becomes clear that they are closely intertwined – two of Siddiqi's brothers being members of the Board of Trustees of Hijaz College as well as of Jamia Islamia Trust.[43]

3 Using Islamic Legal Principles and Terms of Alternative Dispute Resolution

As an institution for Muslims in the UK, MAT uses Islamic legal principles and at the same time claims to adhere to the framework of English law in order to legitimise the procedures on offer. The former Archbishop of Canterbury spoke about "supplementary jurisdictions",[44] thus alluding to the debate on parallel

38 Siddiqi, interview 2012.

39 Ibid. The percentage of female judges in the English courts has increased over the last years but is in fact only 22–28% in the different courts, in the tribunals it is 45%, however. Figures as at 1 April, 2017. See Courts and Tribunals Judiciary, "Judicial Diversity Statistics 2017."

40 Siddiqi, interview 2012; Siddiqi, interview 2015.

41 See Muslim Arbitration Tribunal, "Frequently Asked Questions;" Siddiqi, interview 2015.

42 Siddiqi, interview 2012.

43 The charity affiliation is stated on the bottom of the Websites of the Muslim Arbitration Tribunal and of Hijaz College. Jamia Islamia (Islamic Studies Centre) Trust is registered to the chairman of MAT and principal of Hijaz College, Faizul Aqtab Siddiqi with the public address for the charity given as Hijaz College. See Charity Commission, "Jamia Islamia Trust." Also see Hijaz College, "Board of Trustees."

44 Williams, "Civil and Religious Law," 274.

or competitive justice. Jack Straw, the then Lord Chancellor and Secretary of State for Justice, referring to this debate emphasised in a public speech in 2008 that the existing possibilities of applying Islamic principles in the UK through arbitration or other forms of dispute resolution had not been changed since 1996. This means that parties to a dispute could always voluntarily use such alternative forums or likewise refer their case to an English court, "particularly if they feel pressured or coerced to resolve an issue in a way in which they feel uncomfortable."[45] Straw did not see any reasons to prevent religious tribunals or councils from using Islamic principles when solving disputes, "provided they do not come into conflict with English law."[46] Accordingly, he said, it was the government's position that, "English law will always remain supreme, and religious councils subservient to it."[47] Straw thus negates parallel legal systems and stresses that the existing legal situation does ensure equality before the law.

Similarly, Ian Edge considers the, "recognition of such [i.e. religious] practices by the state and [...] their inclusion within laws promulgated by the state"[48] as the only option for the use of Islamic law in the UK, whereas any form of legal pluralism was not acceptable. He states that by facilitating the use of Islamic law – the Arbitration Act 1996 speaks about, "the law chosen by the parties [i.e. to a dispute] as applicable to the substance of the dispute, or [...] such other considerations as are agreed by them or determined by the tribunal"[49] – "English law already incorporates aspects of Islamic law into state law."[50] Therefore, Edge does not see English and Islamic law as two parallel systems existing in the UK separately, but as a hierarchy, in which the law of the land grants individuals the possibility to deviate from its rules in a specified area of law and to adhere to a different set of norms instead. In my opinion, the fact that the Arbitration Act 1996 enables disputants to choose in this way is an example of what Merry subsumes under the definition of "new" legal pluralism, namely, the existence of relations and interdependencies between the legal system of the state and unofficial "forms of ordering".[51] Many researchers today likewise agree that, "plural normative orders are found in virtually all

45 Straw, speech 2008.
46 Ibid.
47 Ibid.
48 Edge, "Islamic finance," 119.
49 Arbitration Act 1996, Part I, 46 (1) (a), (b).
50 Edge, "Islamic finance," 119.
51 Merry, "Legal Pluralism," 872 f.

societies,"[52] and that legal pluralism in this sense is a fact and as such "impliedly accepted to a certain extent".[53]

Disputants approaching the Muslim Arbitration Tribunal have made their choice to contact a "Muslim" institution and thus most likely expect a solution that is in accordance with Islamic principles. In fact they can ask for MAT to apply the principles of their favoured school of law. Siddiqi says they can take the four Sunni schools as well as the Jaʿfari school of law into account, with the Hanafi school being the prevalent one if no other was chosen and for Non-Muslims.[54] At the same time he mentions that rather than drawing upon "the actual letter", i.e. drawing on the sources of Islamic law, scholars at MAT would "look at the principles, the spirit of the law".[55] He states that "everything in Islamic commercial law is based on common sense and fairness and sharing"[56] and highlights that principles of moral value like the ineffectiveness of unethical clauses such as usury are what distinguishes an Islamic ruling from the decision an English judge would take.[57] Other than that, he claims, there were no main differences in finding solutions in any of the law systems, whether it is Islamic or English law, as they were all in fact basically the rules of natural justice.[58]

The procedures for the various cases received and handled by MAT carry English terms rather than classical Arabic ones. MAT uses different mechanisms of alternative dispute resolution (ADR) according to the nature of each case. While commercial and financial disputes usually go to arbitration which leads to binding awards, matrimonial as well as other personal or family disputes tend to go into mediation, where disputants will find help to solve their disputes amongst themselves. The procedure leading to an Islamic divorce or marriage dissolution by a panel of scholars can include mediation at some point but does not necessarily do so.[59] English labelling of dispute resolution procedures by MAT clearly aims at underlining the institution's statement to be dealing "[...] with Islamic Sacred Law within the context of the English Legal System."[60] This claim seems to implement what Werner Menski and David Pearl called "Angrezi Shariat" in 1998 already – a new form of Islamic law

52 Ibid., 873.
53 Menski, "Plurality-Conscious Rebalancing," 39.
54 Siddiqi, interview 2012.
55 Ibid.
56 Ibid.
57 Ibid.
58 Siddiqi, interview 2015.
59 Siddiqi, interview 2012; Siddiqi & member of staff, interview 2015.
60 Muslim Arbitration Tribunal, "History."

developed in the UK that aims at complying with the requirements of both normative systems.[61] In practice, MAT uses English terminology for mechanisms of alternative dispute resolution and also draws upon English law directly, namely, the Arbitration Act 1996 for arbitration cases. Bowen thinks that while at MAT, mainly consisting of law experts, they "know the difference between arbitration and other forms of mediation quite well",[62] the fact that all procedures – whether arbitration or other – are performed by the institution under the name Muslim *Arbitration* Tribunal leads to constant misunderstandings.[63] This is most evident in the media coverage following Williams' speech in 2008: different newspapers claimed that "Islamic sharia law courts" would use the Arbitration Act 1996 to make their decisions on "cases including divorce, financial disputes and even domestic violence"[64] legally binding.

4 Family Disputes and Islamic Divorce

In fact, cases involving matrimonial disputes or other personal or family matters are solved in procedures the institution calls mediation.[65] This label determines that the outcomes of family dispute resolution at MAT are not legally binding and thus not enforceable in the English courts under the Arbitration Act 1996. Siddiqi stresses that the arbitration procedures at MAT are not applicable to marriage and divorce cases and that MAT uses different procedures to treat such cases.[66]

Like shariʿa councils, MAT offers a service for ending Islamic marriages through divorce or dissolution, using similar procedures to do so.[67] Siddiqi explains that Islamic law gave them "the power [...] to do that", to "give the woman relief".[68] Here he uses the Islamic terms: *khulʿ*, i.e. a divorce at the request of the wife, given by the husband and thus obtained through negotiation

61 See Pearl and Menski, *Muslim Family Law*, 75–77.
62 Bowen, *British Islam*, 155.
63 Ibid., 156.
64 E.g. "Islamic Sharia Courts," *Huffington Post*.
65 Siddiqi, interview 2012; Siddiqi & member of staff, interview 2015.
66 Siddiqi, interviews 2012 & 2015.
67 I observed this similarity of procedures while conducting research on MAT and several shariʿa councils in the UK including the Islamic Shariʿa Council and the Muslim Law (Shariah) Council in London, the Sharee Council at Dewsbury as well as the Family Support Service & Counseling Clinic and Shariah Council at Birmingham Central Mosque. Also see Walker, *Shariʿa councils*, 53 f.
68 Siddiqi, interview 2012.

or mediation with the help of MAT, as Siddiqi puts it;[69] and *faskh*, the dissolution of an Islamic marriage "through findings",[70] which would – in classical terms – be decided upon and pronounced by a Muslim judge. In the absence of an Islamic court system, shariʿa councils and MAT have made Islamic divorce and marriage dissolution their business and offer it to Muslims in the UK. The chairman of MAT and his colleague estimate that they do more *khulʿ* procedures than *faskh*, probably amounting to a ratio of 60% *khulʿ* and 40% *faskh*.[71]

Siddiqi stresses that if "reconciliation has been attempted",[72] there is no need to prolong matters by insisting on any further discussion about saving the marriage. In many cases, however, misunderstandings or problems that could be solved if they were only clearly revealed led to conflicts which then resulted in the wish for divorce. As an example Siddiqi quotes a common situation, as he says, in which the wife was not happy about living together with her in-laws – Siddiqi's exemplary solution being a conversation with the husband and the in-laws, convincing them of the need for the married couple to get their own home.[73] Such problems with in-laws seem to be a frequent cause for domestic quarrel and are mentioned in divorce applications of Muslim women at shariʿa councils, as well.[74]

While the mere issuing of the *khulʿ* or the pronunciation of *faskh* are a religious act and as such not recognised by English law, there may be mediation involved prior to a divorce or marriage dissolution by MAT in case, "the people [had not yet] given themselves the right opportunity and forum to consider reconciliation",[75] and the scholars see the possibility of solving the dispute and saving the marriage.

In the case of a divorce application being filed and where there is no possibility of reconciliation between the spouses, mediation remains an option for settling organisational questions around the clients' separation.[76] Siddiqi explains that at MAT they cannot perform "court mediation", however, and were not registered to hold, "mediation information and assessment meetings" (MIAM).[77] For parties to family disputes about child arrangements, parental

69 Siddiqi, interview 2015.

70 Ibid.

71 Siddiqi & member of staff, interview 2015.

72 Siddiqi, interview 2015.

73 Ibid.

74 Such a case was witnessed by myself on 15 April, 2014 at the shariʿa council of Birmingham Central Mosque.

75 Siddiqi, interview 2015.

76 Member of staff (MAT), interview 2015.

77 Siddiqi, interview 2015.

responsibility, guardianship as well as financial disputes, for example about maintenance provisions or questions relating to property or pension sharing, attending a MIAM is mandatory before a court order can be obtained.[78] In such a meeting an authorised mediator informs the disputants about ADR, including mediation, and evaluates whether mediation or another form of ADR is suitable for the case.[79] Exemptions from the MIAM requirement include domestic violence, child protection concerns and urgency, as immediate access to court is important in such cases,[80] but also the participation, "in another form of non-court dispute resolution relating to the same or substantially the same dispute"[81] during the four months prior to or at the time of making the application to the court. This means that disputants who went through mediation before – which should not exclude a mediation procedure at an Islamic institution – and in the aftermath desire a court order to be made, would not have to attend a MIAM anymore. In fact, "[t]he court [...] must take into account [...] whether the parties attempted mediation or another form of non-court dispute resolution and the outcome of that process."[82] This does not mean that the outcome of mediations at MAT or shariʿa councils will be "legally binding" automatically, but it does mean that the court is meant to take any agreements made by the disputants in such procedures into account and can then either approve of them or judge differently.

Facilitating this, every mediation process at MAT ends with writing up the results, Siddiqi says. He confirms that questions around the separation of a couple, like money, property, care and maintenance of children (these, as mentioned above being exactly the applications listed in the English family procedure rules) can be agreed upon by the parties at MAT through mediation. A "joined consent order" can then be presented in the presence of both parties' lawyers in front of a judge who may or may not approve of the arrangements and accordingly declare them legally binding and enforceable or not.[83] Siddiqi claims that getting such a consent order was a common outcome of mediations at MAT and that judges usually agreed with the arrangements the parties arrived at.[84] A solicitor working for MAT, however, told Bowen in an interview that at least in divorce cases consent orders were in fact rarely made, because the parties to such disputes were usually angry, not prepared to

78 See Ministry of Justice, "Practice Direction 3A," No. 2.

79 See ibid., No. 3, 9 & 10.

80 For these see Ministry of Justice, Procedure Rules "Part 3," No. 3.8 (1) (a), (b) & (c).

81 Ibid., No. 3.8 (1) (d).

82 Ibid., No. 3.3 (1) & (2) (c).

83 See GOV.UK, "Money and property."

84 Siddiqi, interview 2015.

agree on matters in a mediation procedure – and thus eventually went to court for litigation.[85]

5 Implementing the Arbitration Act 1996

The Muslim Arbitration Tribunal primarily became the focus of media attention because of its name, combining "Muslim" with "Arbitration Tribunal", since its arbitral awards can be enforced in British courts under the Arbitration Act 1996. As mentioned above, however, arbitration constitutes only about 10% of MAT's cases.[86] These cases are commercial or debt disputes, issues around contracts, leases, collaborations, joint ventures, etc.,[87] but not family matters.[88] In order to make the awards in cases labelled as arbitrations by MAT legally enforceable under English law, the procedures as directed in MAT's procedure rules and described by Siddiqi – assuming these are in fact carried out accordingly – have to conform to the Arbitration Act 1996.

The Arbitration Act 1996 states in its general principles, that the purpose of arbitration is a, "fair resolution of disputes by an impartial tribunal without necessary delay or expense".[89] This establishes some basic principles including the necessity of a "tribunal" of some sort, its impartiality, the quick and inexpensive execution of the process, as well as the underlying principle of fairness. The Act furthermore reads that, "the parties should be free to agree how their disputes are resolved, subject only to such safeguards as are necessary in the public interest".[90] This gives the parties a relatively large scope of arranging the arbitration procedure according to their needs and wishes. There are some "mandatory provisions" laid down in the Arbitration Act, however, that cannot be overruled by any contrary agreements. All the clauses of the Act also hold provisions for when the parties do not come to any agreement.

The authorisation to choose, "a law other than the law of England and Wales or Northern Ireland as the applicable law in respect of a matter",[91] and the admittance that, "[t]he arbitral tribunal shall decide the dispute in accordance with the law chosen by the parties as applicable to the substance of the dispute, or if the parties so agree, in accordance with such other considerations as

85 Bowen, *British Islam*, 160.
86 Siddiqi & member of staff, interview 2015.
87 Siddiqi, interview 2012.
88 Ibid. Siddiqi, interview 2015.
89 Arbitration Act 1996, Part I, 1 (a).
90 Ibid., Part I, 1 (b).
91 Ibid., Part I, 4 (5).

are agreed by them or determined by the tribunal,"[92] is crucial: this gives MAT leave to apply Islamic law. The parties do not even have to explicitly agree on this, as "an applicable law [...] which is objectively determined in the absence of any express or implied choice, shall be treated as chosen by the parties".[93] It can be presumed that people who turn to MAT are aware of and likely request the usage of Islamic principles.

According to the Arbitration Act, the composition of the arbitral tribunal can be decided on by the parties as well. They can appoint any number of arbitrators and may or may not nominate a chairman or umpire – this being a requirement, however, in the case of an even number of arbitrators unless otherwise agreed by the parties. If the parties do not specify a number of arbitrators, one arbitrator is sufficient.[94] MAT usually forms a tribunal consisting of at least one Islamic scholar and one solicitor or barrister, i.e. someone trained in English law. This being the minimum established in MAT's procedure rules,[95] an arbitral tribunal will sometimes consist of three or four persons, whereas mediations are usually carried out by only one or two persons. Siddiqi explains that "hybrids" like he himself, who are trained in both legal systems, can also arbitrate alone.[96] The Arbitration Act holds that the arbitrators need to be impartial, qualified according to the specifications possibly defined in the arbitration agreement and physically and mentally capable of conducting the arbitration procedure.[97] MAT's policy that all arbitrators must be experts in English or Islamic law or both is not a direct provision of the Arbitration Act but a requirement that MAT set for its own arbitration procedures. The parties can, according to the Arbitration Act, also decide on the procedure for appointing the arbitrators,[98] as well as the roles of the arbitrators and a possible chairman or umpire.[99] MAT's standard constitution of tribunal meets these requirements, as long as the parties agree to it.

If no chairman or umpire is appointed, the Arbitration Act further reads, "[...] the parties are free to agree how the tribunal is to make decisions, orders and awards. If there is no such agreement, decisions, orders and awards shall

92 Ibid., Part I, 46 (1).
93 Ibid., Part I, 4 (5).
94 Ibid., Part I, 15 (1)–(3).
95 Muslim Arbitration Tribunal, "Procedure Rules," No. 10 (1).
96 Siddiqi & member of staff, interview 2015.
97 See Arbitration Act 1996, Part I, 24 (1).
98 Ibid., Part I, 16 (1).
99 Ibid., Part I, 20 (1) & 21 (1).

be made by all or a majority of the arbitrators."[100] This seems to be the regular case at MAT.

Furthermore, the arbitration tribunal, "may rule on its own substantive jurisdiction"[101] and, "[a]ny such ruling may be challenged by any available arbitral process of appeal or review".[102] An award can be challenged, "as to its substantive jurisdiction"[103] or, "on the ground of serious irregularity affecting the tribunal, the proceedings or the award"[104] and which causes, "substantial injustice".[105] The Arbitration Act also includes the opportunity to, "appeal to the court on a question of law arising out of an award made in the [arbitral] proceedings", unless the parties agreed not to include this right or, "to dispense with reasons for the tribunal's award".[106] According to the procedure rules MAT has set up, "[w]here the Tribunal determines a case it must serve on every party a written determination containing its decision and the reasons for it".[107] This rule complies with the Arbitration Act,[108] so that an appeal is not made impossible by dispensing with reasons for the award. MAT has, however, explicitly excluded appeals in its procedure rules, only leaving the possibility of judicial review through application to the High Court which has supervisory jurisdiction and would survey the decision process and whether the tribunal acted within its competences.[109] This exclusion of the right of appeal to the English courts which parties will agree on by signing MAT's procedure rules does meet the requirements of the Arbitration Act.

The parties can, however, also apply to the court in various other situations according to the Arbitration Act, whether they have questions as to the jurisdiction of the tribunal, desire an arbitrator to be removed from the tribunal, or wish the award to be enforced.[110] "An award made by the tribunal pursuant to an arbitration agreement may, by leave of the court, be enforced in the same manner as a judgement or order of the court to the same effect."[111] This sentence is the main aspect highlighted in the media, as it gives legal power to tribunals working in line with the Act *de jure*. Siddiqi confirms that an arbitration

100 Ibid., Part I, 22.
101 Ibid., Part I, 30 (1).
102 Ibid., Part I, 30 (2).
103 Ibid., Part I, 67 (1) (a).
104 Ibid., Part I, 68 (1).
105 Ibid., Part I, 68 (2).
106 Ibid., Part I, 69 (1).
107 See Muslim Arbitration Tribunal, "Procedure Rules," No. 8 (3).
108 See Arbitration Act 1996, Part I, 52 (3), (4); 55 (2).
109 See Muslim Arbitration Tribunal, "Procedure Rules," No. 23.
110 Arbitration Act 1996, Part I, 32 (1); Part I, 24 (1) & Part I, 66 (1).
111 Ibid., Part I, 66 (1).

award pronounced by MAT is binding on the parties who have to agree to abide by it beforehand and that it could also be enforced in a County Court or High Court, depending on the amount in dispute.[112] The court would always have to evaluate whether an award corresponds to public policy and public interest before enforcing it.[113] Siddiqi adds that an enforcement of an arbitration award made by MAT has not yet been necessary, however, as they, "have a good track record."[114]

The Arbitration Act also gives the tribunal the power, "to decide all procedural and evidential matters",[115] including the time and place of the proceedings, the languages of proceedings as well as required translations of any documents and, "whether and if so what form of written statements of claim and defence are to be used".[116] It can furthermore decide how to proceed with relevant documents, that is, "whether and if so which documents [...] should be disclosed between and produced by the parties and at what stage",[117] set time limits,[118] etc. The tribunal is furthermore granted the authority to decide, "whether to apply strict rules of evidence (or any other rules) as to the admissibility, relevance or weight of any material"[119] and, "whether and to what extent there should be oral or written evidence or submissions".[120] The tribunal has to act according to its "general duty", specified in the Arbitration Act as,

> act[ing] fairly and impartially between the parties, giving each party a reasonable opportunity of putting his case and dealing with that of his opponent, and adopt[ing] procedures suitable to the circumstances of the particular case, avoiding unnecessary delay or expense [...][121]

– a duty which also applies to procedural and evidence matters.[122]

MAT makes use of these options and has standardised its procedures accordingly. In fact Siddiqi claims that the institution's established standards and procedures were similar to those used by British courts, while at the same time

112 Siddiqi, interview 2015.
113 Also see Edge, "Islamic finance," 122.
114 Siddiqi, interview 2015.
115 Arbitration Act 1996, Part I, 34 (1).
116 Ibid., Part I, 34 (2) (c).
117 Ibid., Part I, 34 (2) (d).
118 Ibid., Part I, 34 (3).
119 Ibid., Part I, 34 (2) (f).
120 Ibid., Part I, 34 (2) (h).
121 Ibid., Part I, 33 (1).
122 Ibid., Part I, 33 (2).

being quicker and more cost efficient.[123] Any client approaching MAT about a dispute and wanting it settled by arbitration is first sent an application form, which has to be completed and complemented with a detailed statement laying out the main aspects of the dispute as well as what is expected from MAT's involvement. After examining these papers, MAT will contact the party in order to ask for any details or documents that might be missing and send out a letter to the other party to the dispute in order to find out about their view on the matter. In many cases, Siddiqi says, both parties approach MAT together wanting the institution to settle their dispute, or will at least have spoken about contacting MAT in advance. Before the actual arbitration starts, both parties have to sign an arbitration agreement, which can be amended according to their needs or wishes but in any case safeguards that the parties will abide by the arbitral award.[124] The written form of the arbitration agreement is furthermore necessary for the Arbitration Act 1996 to apply to an arbitration procedure.[125] As soon as all the relevant information, statements of both parties giving their positions and necessary documents forming a picture of the whole dispute situation as well as the agreement to arbitration are assembled and examined by the tribunal, a hearing will be scheduled. If the case turns out to be clear, the tribunal may be able to decide after one hearing, whereas more complex disputes may require a second or third hearing. During the joint hearing both parties will be given the opportunity to state their position and the tribunal will be able to cross-examine them.[126] MAT's rules of procedure show that the tribunal, "may allow oral, documentary or other evidence"[127] including witnesses. One brief sentence in MAT's procedure rules then reveals what distinguishes it from other, non-religious tribunals: "All witnesses must testify in the form and manner prescribed by Islamic Sacred Law."[128] If this is considered to relate to classical rules of the Sunni schools of law, it means that a witness would have to meet the requirement of *ʿadāla*, i.e. being a Muslim and a "person of good morals"[129] adhering to religious rules of conduct, being of clear mind and having attained full age.[130] This provision would also bring with it the requirement of two male witnesses or one male and two female

123 Siddiqi, interview 2012.

124 Siddiqi & member of staff, interview 2015.

125 Arbitration Act 1996, Part I, 5 (1).

126 Siddiqi & member of staff, interview 2015.

127 Muslim Arbitration Tribunal, "Procedure Rules," No. 14 (1).

128 Ibid., No. 14 (3).

129 Tyan, "ʿAdl," 209 f.

130 See e.g. Peters, "Shāhid," 207; and for the Hanafi school of law e.g. al-Kāsānī, *Kitāb Badāʾiʿ*, Vol. 9, 122.

witnesses as a rule of evidence based on the Quran and stipulated by all four Sunni schools of law.[131] This is one main point of criticism levelled against MAT, e.g. in the debate on the Arbitration and Mediation Services (Equality) Bill, carried out in the House of Lords in January 2017, where Baroness Caroline Cox demurred, "that the value of a woman's testimony is deemed to be just half that of a man's."[132] Siddiqi generally confirms that they use Islamic principles when it comes to rules of evidence – but only in arbitration cases.[133] Thus, it may be argued that the parties involved submit to discriminatory rules of evidence by their own choice. It is disputable, however, whether this provision meets the abovementioned requirement of a fair and impartial arbitration procedure as well as the principle of equality declared by MAT itself on its website: "All matters will also be considered without any prejudice to [...] gender [...]."[134]

After having gathered all statements and evidence, the tribunal will withdraw for deliberations and afterwards give the arbitral verdict, which will be final and binding on the parties.[135] Bowen describes that this decision is usually accompanied by spiritual guidance.[136] He argues that all the legal terminology and appearance is rather theoretical and but a framework, "for what is really an age-old process of seeking guidance from a spiritual guide",[137] with Siddiqi's spiritual status legitimising his resolutions. Bowen describes him as playing "the role of spiritual and also business advisor" and Hijaz as a "spiritual center" that offers far more than dispute resolution through MAT.[138] While this may well be the case, arbitration at MAT at least externally appears as being a process largely regulated by English legal provisions.

6 Attempting to Alter the Legal Framework: the Arbitration and Mediation Services (Equality) Bill

The Arbitration and Mediation Services (Equality) Bill was first introduced in the House of Lords by Baroness Cox in 2011 and has repeatedly been on the agenda of the House of Lords, receiving first and second readings since then. The Bill made it into a third reading at the House of Lords as well as a first

131 See Quran 2, 282. Also see e.g. Peters, "Shāhid," 207.
132 Statement by Cox, House of Lords, "Arbitration Bill. Second Reading," 2017, Column 892.
133 Siddiqi, interview 2015.
134 Muslim Arbitration Tribunal, "Values and Principles."
135 Siddiqi & member of staff, interview 2015.
136 Bowen, *British Islam*, 164 f.
137 Ibid., 166.
138 Bowen, "Sanctity and Shariah", 136.

reading at the House of Commons once in 2016, but was not passed – so that Baroness Cox started over with a first reading at the House of Lords in May 2016 and a second hearing in January 2017.[139]

Cox emphasises that her Bill, "seeks to address [...] the suffering of women oppressed by religiously sanctioned gender discrimination, and a rapidly developing alternative quasi-legal system which undermines the fundamental principle of one law for all."[140] The phrase "One law for all" is utilised in various contexts and serves as a title for the "Campaign against Sharia law in Britain",[141] which together with other "[s]upporters of the Bill actively lobbied in Parliament and elsewhere."[142] The campaigners declare that they, "call on the UK government to bring an end to the use and institutionalisation of Sharia and all religious laws and to guarantee equal citizenship rights to all."[143] While in 2008 the National Secular Society, which supports the Bill and the One Law for All campaign,[144] listed Cox as a supporter to the campaign,[145] she is not on the list of prominent supporters published on the campaign's own website in 2016.[146] She does, however, frequently refer to the, "principle of One Law for All"[147] and supporters of the One Law for All campaign are quoted as informants in discussions in the House of Lords.[148]

The fact of the Bill being read in the House of Lords over the course of several years shows that it hit a sore spot. The Bill has found a growing number of supporters,[149] including the Council of Ex-Muslims of Britain, feminists, Christian clerics, secularist pressure groups, think tanks and right-wing

139 The bill has not made any further progress in the 2016–2017 session of Parliament. See Parliament.uk, "Arbitration Bill 2016–17." In October 2018 the bill was not listed amongst the Bills before Parliament 2017–19. See Parliament.uk, "Bills before Parliament 2017–19."

140 Statement by Cox, House of Lords, "Arbitration Bill. Second Reading," 2017, Column 891.

141 One Law for All, "About."

142 Grillo, *Muslim Families*, 150.

143 One Law for All, "About."

144 See Grillo, *Muslim Families*, 173–177.

145 National Secular Society, "Campaign against Sharia law."

146 One Law for All, "List of Prominent Supporters."

147 See e.g. Cox, "Letter to the Chairman;" or statement by Cox, House of Lords, "Arbitration Bill. Second Reading," 2015, Column 875.

148 E.g. the Iranian and Kurdish Women's Organisation, whose director is amongst the prominent supporters of the campaign. See the statement of Baroness O'Loan, House of Lords, "Arbitration Bill. Second Reading," 2012, Column 1691. Also see "Diana Nammi", One Law for All, "List of Prominent Supporters."

149 The number of Lords and Baronesses speaking out in favour of the bill has increased noticeably over the course of years. See House of Lords, "Arbitration Bill. Second Reading," 2012 & 2017.

organisations and political parties.[150] Ralph Grillo shows that there is "evidence that anti-Islam/anti-Muslim sentiments are growing in the UK, across the spectrum" and that "the Cox Bill [...] is one of a series of events which have given Muslims cause to believe they are increasingly under siege from a hostile 'West'."[151] On the other hand, the Bill has numerous critics and opponents, politicians and organisations representing different faiths,[152] who mainly question whether the Bill could in fact effectively serve its designated purposes and who point out that the existing legislation is sufficient to ensure equal rights and opportunities for all citizens irrespective of their religion or gender.[153]

The drafted Arbitration and Mediation Services (Equality) Bill aims at averting parallel justice. Alternative dispute resolution offers disputants the opportunity of getting quick and cheap decisions out of court and – if they want – according to principles of a law other than the English. Baroness Cox and her supporters say that institutions like shariʿa councils and MAT use alternative dispute resolution to exercise Islamic jurisdiction in the UK. While the Bill, "recognises legitimate forums for arbitration, including Muslim arbitration tribunals" which adhere to the provisions of the Arbitration Act, Cox is concerned that, "some [tribunals] are practising sex discrimination" and, "acting outside their remit; for example, by deciding cases relating to criminal law".[154] This is why the Bill intends making, "further provision about arbitration and mediation services and the application of equality legislation to such services",[155] and thus aims to eliminate any potential breeches of basic rights. Accordingly, it includes potential amendments to the Equality Act 2010, the Arbitration Act 1996, the Family Law Act 1996 and the Courts and Legal Services Act 1990.

Since the prevention of gender discrimination is one of its central aspects, the Bill would, by amending the Equality Act 2010, prohibit "anything that constitutes discrimination, harassment or victimisation on grounds of sex"[156] when providing arbitration services. It would furthermore define that amongst such actions were unequal acceptance of men and women as witnesses as well

150 See very detailed Grillo, *Muslim Families*, 163–212.

151 See Ibid., 244, 245.

152 See Ibid., 212–226.

153 E.g. the Lord Bishop of Manchester, Nigel McCulloch, House of Lords, "Arbitration Bill. Second Reading," 2012, Column 1693. Also see Grillo, *Muslim Families*, 152–159.

154 Statement Cox, House of Lords, "Arbitration Bill. Second Reading," 2015, Column 877.

155 Preamble to the latest version of the "Arbitration and Mediation Services (Equality) Bill [HL]," 2016.

156 Ibid., Part 1, 1 (2) (11).

as awarding men and women unequal shares of estate or property.[157] The same provisions would be introduced into the Arbitration Act 1996.[158] The possibility of letting the arbitrator(s) decide on evidence rules would thus be reduced, as the classical Islamic combination of two female witnesses replacing one male witness would surely count as "unequal acceptance" of the two sexes. The prohibition to award male and female parties unequal shares on grounds of sex would be relevant in inheritance disputes, as the Islamic law of succession often privileges to male heirs.[159] On its website, however, MAT does not list inheritance cases under the heading of arbitration and states that their, "decision regarding the shares of the various parties concerned according to Islamic law" could be placed, "before the civil court as evidence of what the deceased would have known and intended."[160] Accordingly, a decision of MAT concerning an inheritance is not legally binding under the Arbitration Act 1996 and thus the Bill would not be effective in this particular matter.

Siddiqi severely criticises the Bill as being illogical, which is why in his opinion the government cannot accept the Bill. If it was enacted, however, this would not necessarily affect MAT's work, he says. Instead, he stresses that any procedure at MAT was voluntarily entered into and that if a woman wished to attain full recognition of her rights under English law, she was always free to go to a different tribunal – MAT being only one of about 300 – or seek litigation through an English court. However, if a woman came and entered into a procedure at MAT in the first place, she was convinced that she wanted matters settled according to the principles of her religion. Siddiqi asks how you could stop her wanting to do that, as denying her a solution in accordance with her religion would mean limiting her civil rights.[161]

Another regulation of the draft Bill is laid down as an amendment to the Courts and Legal Services Act 1990, making, "[f]alsely claiming legal jurisdiction"[162] "an offence and liable on conviction on indictment to imprisonment for a term not exceeding 7 years."[163] MAT has always been clear about its nature as an arbitration tribunal, with only the media calling it a "sharia court". When acting under the Arbitration Act 1996, MAT does not claim to be anything else but an arbitration tribunal. However, other services such as mediation and counselling are offered by the institution under the name of

157 Ibid., Part 1, 1 (2) (12).
158 See Ibid., Part 2, 3 (2).
159 See Schacht, "Mīrāth," 107 f.
160 Muslim Arbitration Tribunal, "Inheritance disputes."
161 Siddiqi, interview 2012 & Siddiqi, interview 2015.
162 "Arbitration and Mediation Services (Equality) Bill [HL]" 2016, Part 4, 5.
163 Ibid., Part 4, 5 (2).

"Muslim Arbitration Tribunal", and this seems to be confusing the media, who apparently misapprehend those as being procedures of "jurisdiction" although they do not generate legally binding effects. The fact that Siddiqi at times refers to their non-administrative staff as "judges"[164] may be misleading, too. Moreover – as access to hearings could not be obtained – it is unclear to me whether clients always understand what the different procedures mean and if they are aware of the competences MAT's scholars have or do not have. It seems that Siddiqi solves many disputes "incidentally", as Bowen says, without keeping records or categorising them explicitly as an official ADR procedure.[165] If people rather experience such procedures as guidance from a spiritual leader, then this could rather be called "not claiming mundane jurisdiction".

As to the accusation that MAT was handling cases relating to criminal law, MAT announces on its website: "MAT is unable to deal with criminal offences as we do not have jurisdiction to try such matters in the UK."[166] This rather means that it cannot prosecute and punish offenders, as the police and English courts can, and Siddiqi is very clear about this. But it does not mean that MAT could or would simply not act if addressed in a case involving domestic violence. This issue shall be addressed in the following section.

7 Further Critique: Cases Relating to Criminal Law

As indicated above, one major allegation against MAT as well as shariʿa councils which is made not only by the media[167] but also by members of the House of Lords and primarily Baroness Cox, is that these institutions are, "deciding cases relating to criminal law, such as those involving domestic violence and grievous bodily harm."[168] Cox addresses the abovementioned concern against, "Muslim arbitration tribunals" in one sentence and in the next quotes the Home Secretary in that there was evidence of women being forced to stay in abusive marriages by "Sharia councils"[169] – again not differentiating between the institutions.

The Muslim Arbitration Tribunal did not deny handling cases which involve domestic violence. In 2012 Siddiqi stressed that in such cases they work

164 Siddiqi, interview 2012. During the second interview, he did not use "judges", but "arbitrators" and "mediators" only. Siddiqi, interview 2015.

165 See Bowen, *British Islam*, 166, 168 f.

166 Muslim Arbitration Tribunal, "Services."

167 See e.g. Beattie, "Secret Sharia Law Courts," 19.

168 Cox, House of Lords, "Arbitration Bill. Second Reading," 2015, Column 877.

169 Ibid.

together with the police and get social services involved, but that it was always up to the victim to press charges against the offender. MAT would help and empower a victim to do so and ensure that it has full, "option to pursue the criminal proceedings".[170] Siddiqi claimed, however, that most women did not want to go to the police or had already been there but would prefer not to press charges because they knew this was going to end their relationship including possible disruptions of further family ties. They would instead ask a solution from MAT, wanting the domestic violence to stop. On that account, MAT would use mediation in such cases which could be shuttle mediation, i.e. featuring separate meetings. They would furthermore support the victim personally and by facilitating and ensuring the acceptance within and backing of the community. At the same time MAT would use community pressure and control on the offender in order to prevent further violence.[171] In an interview with Elham Manea, Siddiqi further stated that they would not only try to monitor the situation themselves, but ask the community in the area of the clients to watch victim and especially offender in order to make sure that no further violence occurred. In 95% this was successful, he claimed.[172] By informing the offender about his or her religious duties and obligations as well as the spiritual consequences of such violent behaviour, Siddiqi also aims at, "putting a fear of God in that person"[173] and thus changing the dynamics of the relationship between victim and offender by involving God. This is a service, Siddiqi states, which is not provided elsewhere.[174]

At the end of 2017, MAT could according to its website – after helping victim and offender to reach reconciliation – pass on, "[t]he terms of such a reconciliation [...] to the Crown Prosecution Service (CPS) through the local Police Domestic Violence Liaison Officers with a view to reconsidering the criminal charges."[175] Although obviously, "the final decision to prosecute always remains with the CPS",[176] this was one of the points that could raise further criticism for being an obstruction of punishment. It thus seemed odd that MAT claimed to be neutral and empowering victims to stand up to the wrong they suffer and on the other hand offered to get involved with the CPS aiming to possibly avert criminal charges, even if they were acting upon the explicit and voluntary request of the victim. In October 2018 the respective statement had vanished

170 Siddiqi, interview 2015.
171 Siddiqi, interview 2012 & Siddiqi, interview 2015.
172 See Manea, *Women and Shari'a Law*, 224.
173 Siddiqi, interview 2012.
174 Ibid.
175 Muslim Arbitration Tribunal, "Services."
176 Ibid.

from MAT's website, which now clearly stated that "[i]ssues relating to domestic violence are dealt with by the Crown Prosecution Service (CPS) through the local Police Domestic Violence Liaison Officer. MAT offers mediation to parties wishing to find solutions to their problems."[177]

The decision to prosecute is in any case dependent on the evidence and on public interest as well as the interests of the victim. According to the Code for Crown Prosecutors, "prosecutors should take into account the views expressed by the victim about the impact that the offence has had. In appropriate cases, this may also include the views of the victim's family."[178] For this reason it would be important to assure that victims are not under pressure when giving evidence. The CPS has published guidelines for their prosecutors stating:

> Cultural or religious beliefs may also be a deterrent for victims coming forward; victims may feel ashamed by their community, or may fear isolation by the community. Additionally, community leaders or faith leaders in some cultures or ethnic groups may play the role of a mediator and discourage the victim from reporting. Prosecutors should be sensitive to cultural issues which may take the form of mediation, as well as certain practices which some cultures exercise. Cultural and religious practices should be respected to a point; however, they should not be seen as an 'excuse' to cover domestic abuse between partners or family members.[179]

Although it is not known whether and to what extent MAT actually got or may still get involved with the police or the CPS in this sense, the latter are prompted to be alert as well as respectful to the practices of institutions like MAT.

Furthermore Siddiqi is very clear that in "extreme" cases, where they see no chance that the violent behaviour is going to stop, they would urge the victim to press charges or at least free themselves of the situation by leaving the offender. The same applies for violence against minors, especially if executed by a family member, where MAT would get social services involved in order to assure immediate prevention of further violence.[180]

In cases where a court order is in place, parties, "should not even be here",[181] Siddiqi says. The only service provided by MAT in such cases would be an

177 Ibid., accessed 15 October, 2018.
178 The Crown Prosecution Service, "The Code for Crown Prosecutors. The Full Code Test," No. 4.12, 3.
179 The Crown Prosecution Service, "Domestic Abuse Guidelines."
180 Siddiqi, interview 2012.
181 Siddiqi, interview 2015.

Islamic divorce or marriage dissolution which would be done without any further consideration, as reconciliation was unthinkable per se.

8 Concluding Remarks

The debate around "sharia courts" – including the criticism of their actions by the media and the discussions held in the House of Lords – tends not to differentiate between the various institutions involved and the wide range of cases, procedures and situations of the clients that the institutions work with.

In fact the Muslim Arbitration Tribunal – just like shariʿa councils – facilitates Islamic divorces or marriage dissolutions. Questions that arise around family and matrimonial issues really constitute most of MAT's daily tasks.

Religious marriages are not recognised by the English state, unless they are performed at registered places in the UK,[182] in which case they are equally regarded as civil marriages. Any couple without a civil marriage counts as cohabitees and thus Islamic divorces or the dissolution of Islamic marriages have no legal impact from the point of view of English law. Muslim wives often wish to end their religious marriage according to their religious beliefs, however, which enables them to gain the acceptance of their family and community. Facilitating Islamic divorces and marriage dissolutions does hence constitute a valuable service for Muslim wives who have no other authority in the UK to turn to in these matters but shariʿa councils or MAT.

Domestic violence often plays a role in marital disputes brought before such institutions and is one main reason given by clients wanting MAT to dissolve their Islamic marriage. Alongside shariʿa councils, MAT is accused of taking these cases on at all – which it does, as Siddiqi freely admits and explains. Arbitration is not used in these cases, he says. But according to English legal principles any form of alternative dispute resolution may be inappropriate, as immediate access to court shall be facilitated. MAT says that it does not handle "extreme" cases and leaves these to the police and English courts. But the institution is vague as to what constitutes an extreme case, and the decision as to whether a case is taken on or refused rests entirely with the scholars on duty. One major advantage over shariʿa councils is that scholars at MAT are trained in English law and may thus better assess the prospects of prosecution in the individual case and whether it was not better for the victim and in the public

182 A religious marriage carried out abroad will usually be recognised by the English state as a legally valid marriage if it meets the requirements of a legal marriage in the country in which it was conducted.

interest to hand over the case to police and courts. In the "less extreme" cases MAT aims at stopping the violence and use spiritual as well as community pressure to assure this. While this may be possible within its direct community, I am not sure as to how far the institution can reach.

Another accusation against "sharia courts" by the media and some politicians is that they were giving victims the impression as though prosecution of domestic violence was not an option or not likely to be successful and that these institutions were thus frustrating criminal prosecution. The fact that MAT has erased the offer to ask the Crown Prosecution Service to drop charges after having managed to reconcile a couple, when domestic violence was an issue in the relationship, from its website appears in keeping with the values and principles publicly promoted by MAT.

As shown above, "falsely claiming legal jurisdiction" is an aspect that could be relevant if MAT did not clarify the nature of procedures to its clients. The Muslim Arbitration Tribunal is the only Muslim institution in the UK that claims to perform arbitrations in accordance with both Islamic principles and the requirements of the Arbitration Act 1996. The institution acts under the name Muslim "Arbitration" Tribunal in all its cases although only about 10% of those are actually determined by arbitration, the rest being mediation, matrimonial issues and Islamic divorce and marriage dissolution. Siddiqi and his colleague were not able to give exact numbers of how many cases have in fact been arbitrated or mediated there or how many divorces they facilitate. And due to the lack of empirical evidence, it is unclear whether parties using the various services of MAT always understand the differences regarding procedure and legal effect, especially in view of accounts by Bowen and Walker that many disputes are dealt with incidentally during spiritual meetings.

MAT strives to present itself as an institution working with young experts of English and Islamic law alike. It says it endures being criticised by the community's own elders for advocating women's rights,[183] which mainly relates to divorce and marriage dissolution procedures. The institution makes an effort of showing that it respects and applies English law. Its website gives the full text of the Arbitration Act 1996 as well as MAT's own procedure rules, so that clients can inform themselves in advance about what they are going to agree to. Most of the procedure rules and standards that Siddiqi and his staff elaborated on during the interviews meet the provisions and requirements of English legislature on alternative dispute resolution. But there are also some aspects which seem problematic and have been subject to heavy criticism.

---

183 Siddiqi, interview 2015.

One of these issues usually criticised about MAT's arbitration cases concerns the rules of evidence which MAT only specifies as being those of Islamic law. While according to the Arbitration Act 1996, any decision concerning evidential matters lies with the tribunal, MAT introduces by using evidence rules of Islamic law a provision that actually holds male and female testimony unequal – which is clearly discriminatory against women. MAT argues that using their services is voluntary, so that no woman has to submit to its arbitral jurisdiction. In my opinion, however, denying women the capability of being accurate in their testimony, likewise if they are not personally affected by the results of a decision when acting as a witness and only being third party to a dispute, generally contradicts MAT's attempts at being a modern and educated institution established in the UK, accrediting English law, and wanting to be an integral part of the country's infrastructure: how can MAT – as it proudly does – employ women as scholars, lawyers or mediators, deciding on arbitration cases or helping clients mediate their disputes alongside their male colleagues, when at the same time their own testimony would not be deemed sufficient in financial and business disputes? While provisions against any discrimination on grounds of sex are well positioned in the Equality Act 2010, it does not list arbitration tribunals or mediators amongst the authorities to which it applies.[184] The Arbitration and Mediation Services (Equality) Bill could, by introducing the prohibition of such discrimination in the context of arbitration and mediation procedures into the Equality Act 2010 as well as the Arbitration Act 1996 make a statement to underline its importance. Whether this is entirely necessary, is a different question. The Arbitration Act 1996 requires the tribunal to "act fairly and impartially as between the parties"[185] and "comply with that general duty [...] in its decisions on matters of procedure and evidence"[186] – which should in fact already preclude discrimination on grounds of sex.

On the whole, MAT's procedure rules seem somewhat abstract to me – which could result from the fact that observation was denied by MAT and the actual course of procedures and hearings is hardly exemplified by real cases. The institution lets researchers come in for interviews, and interview time was generously given. However, they did not facilitate for me (and other researchers) to witness any hearings or see any case files, as these were said to be confidential and clients usually not prepared to have any third persons attend.[187]

184 Equality Act 2010, Part 1, 1 (3).
185 Arbitration Act 1996, Part 1, 33 (1) (a).
186 Ibid., Part 1, 33 (2).
187 Also see Manea, *Women and Shari'a Law*, 224.

The restrained reaction of Siddiqi's assistant to my request on seeing some case files lets me share Bowen's view that for many cases, there simply are no regular case files. Especially if cases come in as mere consultations and then turn out to need an arbitral decision, this is most likely done informally, without the parties having filed an application form, although definitely featuring a written arbitration agreement.[188] Bowen managed to interview some clients, but was not himself allowed into their hearings, either.[189] Siddiqi claims to be very open and transparent, though, criticising in fact that many articles and programmes about MAT are created without even talking to them. In line with this, MAT did agree to let the BBC do a programme including filming on the premises and in Siddiqi's office. Apart from that, MAT has been hugely discussed about, but not appeared in the media very often. It is also noticeable that to the best of my knowledge no decision by MAT has ever been taken to court either for judicial review or for enforcement. Therefore, there is no evidence to be found in court records either.

Based on this state of information, the evaluation of the combination of Islamic and English law by MAT rests on a dissatisfying empirical foundation. At the same time it seems questionable whether the highly emotional debate on the legal effects of MAT's actions was worthwhile, given the assumption that arbitration procedures are just a minor part of its business.

Bibliography

Primary Sources

Arbitration Act 1996.

"Arbitration and Mediation Services (Equality) Bill [HL]", 25 May, 2016.

Cox, Caroline. "Letter to the Chairman from Baroness Cox", Review of select committee activity and proposals for new committee activity – Liaison Committee Contents, Appendix 5: Committee proposals from members of the house, 22 November, 2012, https://publications.parliament.uk/pa/ld201213/ldselect/ldliaison/135/13510.htm.

House of Lords (HL). "Arbitration and Mediation Services (Equality) Bill [HL]. Second Reading", London, 19 October, 2012, https://www.publications.parliament.uk/pa/ld201213/ldhansrd/text/121019-0001.htm.

House of Lords (HL). "Arbitration and Mediation Services (Equality) Bill [HL]. Second Reading", London, 23 October, 2015, https://publications.parliament.uk/pa/ld201516/ldhansrd/text/151023-0001.htm.

188 Bowen, *British Islam*, 166, 168 f.

189 Ibid., 169.

House of Lords (HL). "Arbitration and Mediation Services (Equality) Bill [HL]. Second Reading", London, 27 January, 2017, https://hansard.parliament.uk/Lords/2017-01-27/debates/CB7A1173-F802-42CE-89F8-16B26FF5DFE0/ArbitrationAndMediationServices(Equality)Bill(HL).

Ministry of Justice. "Practice Direction 3A–Family Mediation Information and Assessment Meetings (MIAMS)," updated 9 June, 2017, https://www.justice.gov.uk/courts/procedure-rules/family/practice_directions/pd_part_03a#para3.

Ministry of Justice. Procedure Rules "Part 3 – Non-court dispute resolution", updated 30 January, 2017, https://www.justice.gov.uk/courts/procedure-rules/family/parts/part_03.

Siddiqi, Faizul Aqtab (Muslim Arbitration Tribunal). Interview by author. Nuneaton, 20 September, 2012.

Siddiqi, Faizul Aqtab & member of staff (Muslim Arbitration Tribunal). Interviews by author. Nuneaton, 3 November, 2015.

Straw, Jack. Speech to the Islamic Finance and Trade Conference. London, 29. October, 2008. https://webarchive.nationalarchives.gov.uk/20081105155115/http://www.justice.gov.uk/news/sp301008a.htm.

The Crown Prosecution Service. "Domestic Abuse Guidelines for Prosecutors: Minority ethnic communities." Accessed 15 October, 2018. https://www.cps.gov.uk/legal-guidance/domestic-abuse-guidelines-prosecutors.

The Crown Prosecution Service. "The Code for Crown Prosecutors." Accessed 26 June, 2017. https://www.cps.gov.uk/publication/code-crown-prosecutors.

Books and Articles

Bano, Samia. "Multicultural interlegality? Negotiating family law in the context of Muslim legal pluralism in the UK." In *Law and anthropology*, edited by Michael D. A. Freeman, 408–429. Oxford: Oxford University Press, 2009.

Bowen, John. "Sanctity and Shariah: Two Islamic Modes of Resolving Disputes in Today's England." In *Religion in Disputes. Pervasiveness of Religious Normativity in Disputing Processes*, edited by Franz von Benda-Beckmann et al, 129–145. New York: Pelgrave Macmillan, 2013.

Bowen, John. *On British Islam: Religion, Law and Everyday Practice in Shariʿa Councils.* Princeton: Princeton University Press, 2016.

Casey, Louise. The Casey Review: A review into opportunity and integration. London: Department for Communities and Local Government, 2016. Accessed 8 June, 2017. https://www.gov.uk/government/uploads/system/uploads/attachment_data/file/575973/The_Casey_Review_Report.pdf, 132.

Edge, Ian. "Islamic finance, alternative dispute resolution and family law." In *Islam and English law*, edited by Robin Griffith-Jones, 116–143. Cambridge/New York: Cambridge University Press, 2013.

Grillo, Ralph. *Muslim Families, Politics and the Law. A Legal Industry in Multicultural Britain*, Farnham/Burlington: Ashgate, 2016.

al-Kāsānī, ʿAlāʾ ad-Dīn Abū Bakr b. Masʿūd. Kitāb Badāʾiʿ aṣ-ṣanāʾiʿ fī tartīb aš-šarāʾiʿ. Bayrūt: Dār al-Kutub al-ʿIlmīya, 1997, 10 Vol.

Manea, Elham. *Women and Shariʿa Law: The Impact of Legal Pluralism in the UK*. London/New York: I.B. Tauris, 2016.

Menski, Werner. "Plurality-Conscious Rebalancing of Family Law Regulation in Europe." In *Family, Religion and Law: Cultural Encounters in Europe*, edited by Prakash Shah, Marie-Claire Foblets and Mathias Rohe, 29–48. Farnham/Burlington: Ashgate, 2014.

Merry, Sally Engle. "Legal Pluralism." *Law & Society Review* 22, no. 5 (1988): 869–896.

Pearl, David and Werner Menski. *Muslim Family Law*. Third edition. London: Sweet & Maxwell, 1998.

Peters, Rudolph. "Shāhid." In *Encyclopaedia of Islam*, edited by P. Bearman et al, 2nd. edition, Vol. 9, 207 f. Leiden: Brill, 1997.

Schacht, Joseph. "Mīrāth." In *Encyclopaedia of Islam*, edited by Bearman et al, 2nd edition, Vol. 7, 106–111. Leiden: Brill, 1993.

Tyan, Emile. "ʿAdl." In *Encyclopaedia of Islam*, edited by. P. Bearman et al, 2nd edition, Vol 1, 209 f. Leiden: Brill, 1960.

Walker, Tanya. *Shariʿa councils and Muslim women in Britain: Rethinking the role of power and authority*. Leiden/Boston: Brill, 2016.

Williams, Rowan. "Civil and Religious Law in England: A Religious Perspective," *Ecclesiastical Law Journal* 10 (2008), 262–282.

Websites and Online Resources

Charity Commission. "Jamia Islamia (Islamic Studies Centre) Trust." Accessed 9 June, 2017. http://beta.charitycommission.gov.uk/charitydetails/?subid=0&regid=517456.

Courts and Tribunals Judiciary. "District Judges (Magistrates' Courts)." Last updated 4 April, 2017. https://www.judiciary.gov.uk/about-the-judiciary/who-are-the-judiciary/list-of-members-of-the-judiciary/dj-mags-ct-list/.

Courts and Tribunals Judiciary. "Judicial Diversity Statistics 2017." Accessed 9 June, 2017. https://www.judiciary.gov.uk/about-the-judiciary/who-are-the-judiciary/diversity/judicial-diversity-statistics-2017/.

GOV.UK. "Money and property when a relationship ends." Accessed 26 June, 2017. https://www.gov.uk/money-property-when-relationship-ends/apply-for-consent-order.

Hijaz College. "Courses." Accessed 7 June, 2017. http://www.hijazcollege.com/courses.php.

Hijaz College. "Formation of Hijaz College." Accessed 7 June, 2017. http://www.hijazcollege.com/formation_hijaz.php.

Hijaz College. "History – The Founder." Accessed 7 June, 2017. http://www.hijazcollege.com/history.php.

Hijaz College. "The Principal." Accessed 7 June, 2017. http://www.hijazcollege.com/the-principle.php.

Hijaz College. "Hijaz College." Accessed 9 June, 2017. http://www.hijazcollege.com/index.php.

Hijaz College. "Board of Trustees." Accessed 9 June, 2017. http://www.hijazcollege.com/board-of-trustees.php.

Muslim Arbitration Tribunal. "Muslim Arbitration Tribunal." Accessed 9 June, 2017. http://www.matribunal.com/.

Muslim Arbitration Tribunal. "History." Accessed 7 June, 2017. http://www.matribunal.com/history.php.

Muslim Arbitration Tribunal. "Frequently Asked Questions." Accessed 26 June, 2017. http://www.matribunal.com/faqs.php.

Muslim Arbitration Tribunal. "Inheritance Disputes and Islamic Wills." Accessed 26 June, 2017. http://www.matribunal.com/inheritance-disputes.php.

Muslim Arbitration Tribunal. "Procedure Rules of Muslim Arbitration Tribunal." Accessed 26 June, 2017. http://www.matribunal.com/rules.php.

Muslim Arbitration Tribunal. "Services: Islamic Divorce & Family Disputes." Accessed 26 June, 2017. http://www.matribunal.com/family-dispute-cases.php. Updated website accessed 15 October, 2018.

Muslim Arbitration Tribunal. "Values and Principles." Accessed 26 June, 2017. http://www.matribunal.com/values-and-principles.php.

National Secular Society. "Campaign against Sharia law in Britain to be launched at the House of Lords." Updated 5 December, 2008. http://www.secularism.org.uk/104288.html.

One Law for All. "About." Accessed 26 June, 2017. http://onelawforall.org.uk/about/.

One Law for All. "List of Prominent Supporters." Updated 01 June, 2016. http://onelawforall.org.uk/about/prominent-signatories/.

Oxford Index. "Qureshi, Shamim Ahmed." Accessed 9 June, 2017. http://oxfordindex.oup.com/view/10.1093/ww/9780199540884.013.U10000404.

Parliament.uk. "Arbitration and Mediation Services (Equality) Bill [HL] 2016–17." Accessed 1 December, 2017. https://services.parliament.uk/bills/2016-17/arbitrationandmediationservicesequality.html.

Parliament.uk. "Bills before Parliament 2017–19." Accessed 15 October, 2018. https://services.parliament.uk/bills/#a.

Weddington Castle. "Higham Hall & Higham Grange (later Hijaz College)." Accessed 7 June, 2017. http://www.weddingtoncastle.co.uk/higham-hall--grange.html.

Newspaper Articles

Beattie, Jason. "Secret Sharia Law Courts Already Used in UK Cases." *Daily Mirror*, 15 September, 2008.

Edwards, Richard. "Sharia courts operating in Britain." *The Telegraph*, 14 September, 2008. http://www.telegraph.co.uk/news/uknews/2957428/Sharia-law-courts-operating-in-Britain.html.

Gilligan, Andrew. "Judge allowed to sit on sharia court set up by Hebdo protest cleric." *The Telegraph*, 1 January, 2016. http://www.telegraph.co.uk/news/uknews/law-and-order/12090591/Judge-allowed-to-sit-on-sharia-court-set-up-by-Hebdo-protest-cleric.html.

Hickley, Matthew. "Islamic Sharia Courts in Britain now 'legally binding'." *Huffington Post*, 15 October, 2008. http://www.huffingtonpost.com/2008/09/14/islamic-sharia-courts-in_n_126323.html.

Phillips, Nicholas. "Top judge backs sharia 'role'." *BBC News UK*, 4 July, 2008. http://news.bbc.co.uk/2/hi/uk_news/7488960.stm.

"Sharia law in UK is 'unavoidable'." *BBC News*, 7 February, 2008. http://news.bbc.co.uk/2/hi/uk_news/7232661.stm.

Wintour, Patrick, and Riazat Butt. "Sharia law could have UK role, says lord chief justice." *The Guardian*, 4 July, 2008. Accessed 7 June, 2017, https://www.theguardian.com/uk/2008/jul/04/law.islam.

Unregistered Muslim Marriages in the United Kingdom

Vishal Vora

1 Marriage Is Still an Important Aspiration

Marriage is an important milestone in one's life and moreover, many members of the British South Asian communities continue to hold marriage as a mandatory requirement in adulthood, despite the increasing trend of cohabitation in wider British society. This importance on marriage can be demonstrated by the lack of open cohabitation, for the vast majority of self-classifying observant Muslims. This is not permitted by their faith and not acceptable under any circumstances. In order for a British Muslim couple to live together and be accepted by their community as such, they must marry. As will be examined in due course, the type of marriage they typically enter has changed and in some cases it lacks legal recognition in the jurisdiction of England and Wales. This will be illustrated by the reported legal cases of the family court, discussed further in this chapter.

2 The Law of Marriage – *Brief History*

Whilst this chapter does not purport to give a comprehensive historical narrative of the development of English marriage law, a brief overview does serve as a good starting point. The first statutory provision governing the law of marriage was the Act for the Better Preventing of Clandestine Marriages 1753, which sought to provide when and how a marriage will be deemed valid or void by setting out the requirements for marriage. Before its enactment, there was a trade in irregular marriages known as Fleet marriages, as they were performed in and around the Fleet Prison in London with little regulation. Such clandestine marriages were considered problematic for the personal interests of the elite as they endangered their eligible young men, who would otherwise end up with inappropriate spouses.[1] There have been incremental changes to the statutory provisions but these have been carried out on a piecemeal basis and thus the current Marriage Act 1949, as a whole, still carries its eighteenth

1 Probert, *Marriage Law and Practice in the Long Eighteenth Century*, 212.

 | DOI:10.1163/9789004398269_004

century legacy. This legacy is embodied in the double requirement that the marriage ceremony be conducted (a) in particular registered buildings and (b) by an authorised person. Both requirements remain vitally important and it is clear to see they stem from a Christian template of marriage; marriages taking place in a chapel and being conducted by a priest.

There are three routes into marriage. One leads via a religious Anglican ceremony and the required preliminaries, of which there are three: either the calling of banns on three successive Sundays, obtaining a common licence or obtaining a special licence. The second option is a civil marriage, which can be held either in a traditional register office, or on approved premises[2] preceded by the civil formality of giving noticing. The third option is a combined procedure, viz. compliance with civil preliminaries, which are giving notice by each party in the registration district where he or she has been resident for at least seven days[3] and the production of a considerable amount of documentary evidence followed by a religious marriage at an authorised place of worship that is officially registered for that purpose, within 12-months.

There are exceptions for Jewish and Quaker marriages, there are no formal legal restrictions on the place of marriage, so legally binding marriage ceremonies can take place anywhere, including private homes.

Other religious groups are restricted to conducting marriage ceremonies in places of religious worship,[4] which must also be registered for the solemnisation of marriages. In addition to this double restriction to place, the presence of an authorised person is required to record the marriage. You can see there are several routes into legal marriage in England and Wales with different options based upon whether a religious or civil ceremony is chosen and furthermore, different religions are treated quite differently, with the differences being measured against a Christian guide of how marriage can be entered into.

The regulation of marriage is important, the state should play a role in such regulation, deciding when to enforce and when to deny marital obligations, however what should happen if and when marriages are entered into, without completing all the required steps?

The law has not been specified to define this very question, as obvious as it may seem, especially in the present day. There seems to be very little guidance in place to provide the threshold requirements of a valid marriage. What exactly makes a marriage, in the eyes of the law, void? Furthermore, a void

2 Venues such as hotels, restaurants and stately homes, but to name a few are the sorts of places eligible to be licensed for civil ceremonies.

3 Marriage (Scotland) Act 1977, section 27.

4 *Places of Worship Registration Act* 1855.

marriage, contrary to the dictionary definition of the word, still enables one party to apply for a decree under section 11 of the Matrimonial Causes Act 1973. Furthermore financial remedies under sections 23 and 24 of the same act remain available in void marriage situations. In short, there is no real difference between a void and valid marriage as the same financial remedies are open to both categories.

The current Act[5] fails to have taken into account the changes in society, the plural and diverse nature based on migration. It is useful to note the 1949 Marriage Act is a consolidating Act; it has been amended many times on a piecemeal basis. The exceptions made for particular religious groups seem to add complication, different rules for different groups.

Although the freedom to have a religious marriage that is legally recognised is longstanding and applies across religions in England and Wales, there is a puzzling disconnection between, the applicable law and social reality. The law in England and Wales provides for buildings to be certified as places of worship. Such buildings may then additionally be registered for the solemnisation of marriage. As such, the law makes provision for religious celebrants to solemnise legally recognised marriages in these buildings. Couples can and do celebrate a religious marriage in their mosque, temple or other place of worship, and it will be legally recognised if the requirements of the law are met. If religious celebrants or individual couples do not wish to take advantage of this provision, a couple have the option of a separate civil ceremony of marriage in order to have a legally valid marriage.

However based on customary practices of British Muslims, it is apparent that for many, a religious building like a mosque is not the natural setting for marriages to be conducted. This can be seen from the relatively (relative the British Muslim population as a whole) low numbers of registration of religious buildings to obtain the relevant status to conduct marriages. As of January 2018 there were 395[6] Islamic religious buildings registered for the solemnisation of marriage but this is an increase from 263[7] reported three years earlier.

Therefore it is often necessary for them to 'marry twice', once in accordance with the civil law and then again via their faith. But what happens if they fail to do so, completing the legal stage, that is: if they marry only via the faith? How does the current law of England and Wales treat marriages that have failed to meet the required civil formalities, either regarding the preliminaries to civil marriage or the marriage ceremony itself, or both?

---

5 *Marriage Act 1949*.

6 "Places of Worship Registered for Marriage – GOV.UK."

7 HL Deb. (6 July 2015) Col 88.

3 Failures to Meet Formalities of Marriage

Based on the reported legal cases, why are British Muslims falling short of completing the final step of civil registration? Since 2001, with the conception of judicial 'non-marriage', it will be shown that informal *nikah* ceremonies of marriage are more likely to be held to be deemed non-existent. A non-existent marriage is one that bears little or no resemblance to an ordinary marriage; it has never existed in the eyes of the law and thus has no legal consequences at its dissolution. Conversely as mentioned above, a void marriage carries financial repercussions, despite void meaning 'not valid or legally binding'.[8]

This failure of British Muslims to complete the marriage process is not a new issue, the community itself has been long aware of this fact; this was one of the main reasons for the establishment of Shari'a councils in the mid-1980s.[9] This lack of compliance with marriage formalities has been in issue for a significant period of time now, although it has been only since the legal creation of non-marriage that the harsh and unfair consequences have been really felt, to the detriment of informally married British Muslim women. In terms of rate in incidence of unregistered marriage, not much is known about the precise numbers. The most recent and largest empirical survey was commissioned by Channel 4[10] and involved 901 Muslim women on their experiences about getting married and the procedures they have undertaken. Whilst a survey of this nature, methodologically speaking, will not give a definitive answer, it is worth noting that it found only 16 to 17 per cent[11] of this 901 cohort were not aware that their *nikah* marriages were not actually valid under English law, and therefore would not be recognised by the courts.

4 *Nikah*-Only Marriage Is Non-marriage

It is surprising that the English law should consider an internationally recognised form of religious marriage, at least in Islamic countries, as not capable of being a marriage and giving rise to some consequences upon dissolution. As explained above, to effect a valid marriage compliance with the formalities as set out the 1949 Act must be followed. The statute deals with those marriage ceremonies that fall short of some of the formalities, giving rise to a void

8 "Void | Definition of Void in English by Oxford Dictionaries."

9 http://www.shariahcouncil.org/?page_id=23.

10 Hall, "The Truth About Muslim Marriage."

11 Shah, "Does Channel 4's Documentary Provide the Truth about Muslim Marriage?"

marriage over a valid one. But what the minimum requirements are in order for a ceremony to have created a legal marriage is still unknown, and this question has become an urgent one following the supposed increase in informal Muslim marriages being conducted in this jurisdiction.

Nikah-only marriages when conducted in England or Wales are not only not capable of being valid marriages, they are now not even considered void marriages either, but are subsumed under the newly created category of "non-marriage". As set out above, a void marriage carries the same financial consequences as a valid one. A non-marriage however has profound consequences on the parties. Unlike a void marriage, there are no financial orders available to non-marriage parties, although it is a serious question what exactly the differences are between a void marriage and non-marriage. To answer this question, the next section provides case analysis on two key cases in this area of law.

5 Judicial Guidance – *Hudson v Leigh*

In the case of *Hudson v Leigh*[12] the court provided some much needed judicial guidance on how and where to draw the dividing line between a void marriage and a non-marriage. This case concerned a cohabiting couple with one child. The wife was a devout Christian and the husband identified himself as an atheist Jew. Approximately two years following the birth of their child, they decided to get married. The wife wished to have a religious marriage but the husband wanted a civil one. The couple therefore decided after much discussion, to be married through a religious ceremony in South Africa where the wife had mainly lived for a period of the relationship, which would then be followed by a civil marriage in England.

A Christian minister celebrated the South African wedding and it followed the typical order of a wedding, complete with ceremony, reception, sit-down dinner, speeches and dancing.[13] During the religious ceremony the Minister, as instructed by the couple, omitted the legal formalities from his service and there was no signing of the marriage register and he did not complete the appropriate registration that would be normally required to effect a legal marriage in South Africa.[14] However there was an exchange of rings followed by the words, "I give you this ring as a sign of our marriage".[15] On the morning of

12 *Hudson v Leigh* (Status of Non-Marriage) [2009] EWHC 1306 (Fam).

13 Ibid., paragraph 20.

14 Ibid., paragraph 22.

15 Ibid., paragraph 21.

the religious marriage ceremony the parties signed a pre-nuptial agreement stipulating the intention of the marriage to effectively have two distinct parts, the South African religious ceremony followed by the London civil marriage approximately six weeks later. Before the date for the civil marriage in London was fixed however, the relationship broke down. The matter proceeded to court to ascertain the legal effect of the South African religious ceremony and whether or not the wife was entitled to claim financial relief, the usual financial orders available to divorcing couples, via either a valid or void marriage or in the alternative by a decree of nullity (which allows an applicant to obtain the financial remedies to which s/he would have been entitled if the marriage had been valid in the first place).

The court was persuaded by the positive intention of all three key participants, the wife, the husband and the minister in not wishing to have a legal marriage.[16] The formal validity of the marriage was governed by South African law and it was held that if the ceremony was to have effected a marriage at all, it would result in a void marriage. This was due in part for failing to comply with all the formalities. The husband's expert called this 'compound non-compliance'.[17] It was held, however, that the marriage ceremony in South Africa had not created the status of marriage at all between the parties and following this there was no application for financial relief arising from this non-marriage.

In reaching this decision, the court offered some limited guidance to the matter of such non-marriage but refused a general test, as the judge remained unconvinced there could be such a single formulation. The four factors[18] of guidance were to ask the following questions in such matters:

(a) Whether the ceremony or event set out or purported to be a lawful marriage;
(b) Whether it bore all or enough of the hallmarks of marriage;
(c) Whether the three key participants (most especially the officiating official) believed, intended and understood the ceremony as giving rise to the status of lawful marriage; and
(d) The reasonable perceptions, understandings and beliefs of those in attendance.

The court was careful to set down a broad disclaimer along with these four factors. In particular, it was said "the factors listed should be taken account of but

16 Ibid., paragraph 76.
17 Ibid., paragraph 39.
18 Ibid., paragraph 77.

not exhaustively"[19] and the issues in the case should be taken in account on a case-by-case basis, merely as a framework to begin evaluation of the specific circumstances of a case. Such limitations (of the factors) can only mean that they should be considered as judicial guidance and not broad guidance or for that matter, clarification of the law regarding the concept of non-marriage.

The four factors in determining whether a marriage ceremony is capable of giving the status of marriage on the parties reveal pressure points of the ceremony and the actions of the parties. Nonetheless, judging whether the marriage can be deemed to have complied with enough or all of the requirements of marriage, as set down by English law can be problematic, especially when making such assessments of non-Anglican Christian forms of marriage, as the law predominately follows the Christian marriage tradition as a benchmark.

6 Harsh and Inequitable Consequences – Application of the 'Four Factors'

The judgment in *Hudson v Leigh* should have led to better outcomes and protections for those minority ethnic women who undertake a religious ceremony of marriage without completing, erroneously, the necessary legal formalities. However the case of *Dukali v Lamrani*[20] demonstrates the harsh realities such women can face. In this case a Moroccan couple, both of the Muslim faith entered into what they both believed to be a civil ceremony of marriage at the Moroccan Consulate in London. A notary conducted their marriage, as they specifically wanted a legal marriage and not a religious one. Following this marriage ceremony a property, the matrimonial home, was purchased and conveyed in the husband's sole name. The couple had a child shortly after marriage. The relationship broke down about seven years later and the wife petitioned for divorce. Her action prompted the husband to issue a parallel petition for divorce in Morocco. The Moroccan divorce made a very modest financial provision for the wife. The wife argued that she had a right to apply for financial relief following an overseas divorce under Part III of the Matrimonial and Family Proceedings Act 1984 (the 1984 Act).

The husband opposed her application for two reasons, first because there was no marriage capable of recognition in England and Wales and secondly because the Moroccan divorce should not be recognised in this jurisdiction. The court's judgment had to decide if the wife could establish that there had

19 Ibid., paragraph 79.

20 *Dukali v Lamrani* (Attorney General Intervening) [2012] EWHC 1748 (Fam).

been a marriage within the wording of section 12(1)(a) of the 1984 Act and if so, whether the Moroccan divorce was recognisable in England and Wales as required by s12(1)(b).

The court found the marriage was not valid due to the wholesale failure to comply with the formal requirements of English law.[21] The marriage was not void due to it not being a marriage under the 1949 Act and therefore it was declared to be a non-marriage.[22] Accordingly the wife was refused leave to apply for any financial orders under Part III of the 1984 Act because the marriage, being a non-marriage, did not meet the requirements of section of the 1984 Act.

7 Discussion of Dukali

Examining the four factors stemming from *Hudson v Leigh*, it was unexpected that the Court was not minded to deem the marriage ceremony in Dukali as at least void because on the face of it, there is compliance with the four factors. The ceremony set out to be lawful, it bore hallmarks of marriage, those three persons involved in the ceremony believed, intended and understood the ceremony to be lawful, as did their guests. In this case therefore, why despite the judicial guidance given the case of *Hudson v Leigh*, did Dukali did not escape being declared a non-marriage?

Although the four factors was a non-exhaustive list, there was no explicit hierarchy, as presented by the judge in Hudson, it was interpreted to mean that they all held equal or similar weight when determining the existence of a marriage, without focus on the external appearance of a ceremony. However in *Dukali v Lamrani*[23] this does not appear to be the case. Despite the alleged legality of the ceremony, intention of both the parties and the staff of the Consulate where the marriage took place[24] (factor c) was side-lined, despite evidence to the contrary.

In applying the non-exhaustive factors that came from *Hudson v Leigh*, there seems to be difficulty in overcoming the external factors, (a) and (b) of

21 Ibid., paragraph 27.

22 Although provisions of the Vienna Conventions on Diplomatic and Consular Relations 1963 states that marriages conducted in embassies or consulates are valid and recognised by countries hosting the diplomatic or consular representations, under English law (*Radwan v Radwan* 1973 Fam 24) it has been firmly established that the premises of a consulate are part of the territory of the receiving State, not the sending State.

23 *Dukali v Lamrani* (Attorney General Intervening) [2012] EWHC 1748 (Fam).

24 Ibid., paragraph 23.

such marriages. It has been hypothesised that these factors have in fact created a hierarchy.[25] The first tier of the hierarchy examines the purported compliance with the legal formalities under the Marriage Act and the second tier scrutinises the intention of the parties, officiating officers and those present at the ceremony. In irregular marriage ceremonies, the Court will first look to see if there has been compliance with the Marriage Act 1949, the form of the marriage, in the event there has not been so, then intention of the parties cannot override this initial failure to comply. This observation demonstrates that if a marriage ceremony differs from the Christian template of marriage (the external appearance of marriage), it is likely to be regarded as a non-marriage. As the vast majority of such cases coming to court are conducted in accordance with Islamic rites of marriage, this is problematic and potentially discriminatory, as already mentioned above, the law of marriage does not define the threshold of when a marriage is valid or void.

In determining the existence of a marriage, should the law focus on the external appearance (compliance with formalities) of the marriage or instead focus on the intention of the parties?[26]

The judgment from Dukali[27] and other English cases[28] would seem to support the proposed hierarchy model solely because intention of the petitioner(s) was rejected. In Dukali,[29] confirming the parties' intentions and beliefs regarding the validity of their marriage, the ceremony took place in an official building, the Moroccan Consulate in London. The wife said in her statement dated 23 December, 2011:

> ... The venue for the marriage was always agreed by me, [the husband] and both our parents and was intended to be a proper civil marriage in the fullest sense. I would not have agreed to the marriage if it had been a religious only marriage ... I can confirm that as far as either of our families were aware as was I and [the husband] that the marriage was a valid civil ceremony ...[30]

It could be argued that the intention of both parties in the Dukali case was very clear, as the formality involved indicates that the purported marriage was considered to be a lawful one and took place in an official and subjectively

25 Bevan, "The Role of Intention in Non-Marriage Cases Post *Hudson v Leigh*", 91.
26 Probert, "When Are We Married?," 398.
27 *Dukali v Lamrani* (Attorney General Intervening) [2012] EWHC 1748 (Fam).
28 *El Gamal v Al Maktoum* [2011] EWHC B27 (Fam).
29 *Dukali v Lamrani* (Attorney General Intervening) [2012] EWHC 1748 (Fam).
30 Ibid., paragraph 15. Wife's statement paragraph 5.

relevant building, not at home or in secret. The ceremony itself was a very public affair. The husband only became aware of the potential to evade his marital responsibilities upon receiving legal advice calling into doubt the legal nature of the marriage.

Despite the facts in the Dukali case meeting a somewhat higher threshold in terms of the external *Hudson v Leigh* factors, still little, if indeed any weight was given to the intentions of both the parties. The hierarchy model can account for this finding, in assessing questionable marriage ceremonies; the first question the court examines is the compliance with the 1949 Act. Only if there has been compliance, then party intention becomes a relevant factor. Because it was held in Dukali "manifold non-compliance with every requirement of the Marriage Acts"[31] the role of intention was outweighed by the external factors, namely the formal validity of the marriage ceremony.

Looking at the four factors arising from the Hudson case, the crucial point is this: factor (a), viz. the "purported lawfulness", is being interpreted as compliance with formal requirements as laid down in the 1949 Act. In addition, this compliance is set on top of a hierarchy, or rather: It is made a *conditio sine qua non*, rather than one of several points to be considered.

It is therefore argued the guidance offered in *Hudson v Leigh*[32] has been subject to judicial shift in application to case law. Following Chris Bevan's analysis and model of hierarchy, it becomes strikingly clear that if a ceremony marriage fails to comply with the formal requirements of the 1949 Act – i.e. the external factors arising from *Hudson v Leigh* override the other internal ones. In fact it could be said the internal factors are not given any consideration when classifying the ceremony as a non-marriage, if appearance is not familiar to a Christian form of marriage.

This result seems to indicate for those of the minority ethnic groups, which the vast majority of non-marriage cases seem to concern, the default position is that marriage ceremonies that fail to comply with the statutory framework of marriage will be non-marriages based on appearance alone. The judicial shift, instead of offering protection seems to disproportionately disadvantage certain groups causing injustice and hardship through non-marriage. Is such judicial shift appropriate or should non-marriage be limited to those circumstances in which one could not have seriously considered a ceremony to create the legal status of marriage?

Rebecca Probert, a legal historian specialising in the law of marriage agrees that non-marriage is a judicial creation however argues that upon working

31 Ibid., paragraph 36.

32 *Hudson v Leigh* (Status of Non-Marriage) [2009] EWHC 1306 (Fam).

through the neglected terms of the current marriage act and their logical implications for different situations, non-marriage can be marked out as a 'relatively narrow scope'.[33]

The law is does not compel judges to come to this conclusion of non-marriage, there is no mention of non-marriage in the current Marriage Act, the concept of non-marriage remains a judicial creation that has been confirmed by the Court of Appeal[34] as being correctly applied in the case of *Dukali v Lamrani*.[35]

This author argues the current law on non-marriage is discriminatory and a disproportionately large number of British citizens will be adversely affected by the denial of financial relief upon the breakdown of their marriages. Already there has been an alarmingly high number of non-marriage cases reported arising from Islamic marriages conducted in this jurisdiction. The Marriage Act 1949 reflects the interests of the early nineteenth century and requires reform to account for the significant changes that have occurred in society.

8 Respondent Accounts

This author's doctoral research focused on the narrative accounts of British Muslim respondents, shedding light on the wider socio-legal realties they faced, upon the realisation that their *nikah*-only marriages were not legally enforceable. Extracting with great care their stories also revealed their impression of the law, how it ought to have applied to their cases and how it failed to protect them, as British citizens. Presented below are two contrasting case studies from my doctoral research dating from 2013. All names are pseudonyms.

Cyra is a British born Pakistani who was raised in London. She was brought-up with a strong sense of her cultural heritage although was not particularly religious, akin to her parents. Following her university studies she began working in the financial sector and met her husband on a matrimonial dating website for South Asians. The couple got engaged very quickly after meeting and then dated during this period for 18 months. The *nikah* took place at Cyra's parents' home and was conducted by am imam. The marriage broke down within 12 months. No religious divorce has been either given by the husband or sought by Cyra.

33 The Evolving Concept of Non-Marriage [2013] CFLQ 314.

34 *Sharbatly v Shagroon* [2012] EWCA Civ 1507 raised the question where the Dukali decision was rightly decided.

35 [2012] EWHC 1748 (Fam).

Dalia is a British born Pakistani who was also raised in London. Her family is religious although culturally liberal. Dalia worked in the higher education sector (non-academic) and then went on to set up her own high street business. She met her husband through mutual friends and they got engaged within a month of meeting. Their *nikah* marriage took place a restaurant, conducted by an imam. The restaurant was an approved premises, therefore an approved building for the purposes of celebrating a legal marriage. The couple had one child and their marriage broke down after 10 years. The matter proceeded to the High Court and the *nikah* marriage was declared a non-marriage. Following this Dalia began civil proceedings and received a modest financial settlement after two years of litigation.

9 Why a *Nikah*-Only Marriage?

Both respondents self-identified as British Muslims, they were proudly British and yet acutely aware of their inherited identity. Being British they felt at ease when it came to exercising their cultural and religious freedoms as British Muslims, it was right for them to get married through a ceremony that was relevant for them. Cyra and Dalia held the nikah marriage in high esteem and for them; it was clearly the only-way to enter the institution that is marriage. On the other hand, when questioned about civil registration of marriage, in a town hall setting, they both reported it being an administrative process, simply a piece of paper.

Both Cyra and Dalia said very clearly that it was the *nikah* that gives them the feeling of being married and importantly being accepted as such by their families and the wider community. The *nikah* itself is a meaningful ceremony that the civil registration cannot complete with.

10 Impression *Nikah* Marriage Was Valid, in Law

Both respondents demonstrated confusion between international and domestic law when it came to marriage formalities and requirements, as explained above; compliance with the civil formalities of marriage, giving notice and getting married in a prescribed building. Cyra and her husband were married following a two-year engagement. The marriage took place at her parents' house although Cyra reported that she would have preferred to have done it at the local mosque, which was undergoing repairs at the time. But regardless she said, it is very normal to have a *nikah* done at home. Following their home *nikah* the couple were clearly told they needed to register their marriage by the imam. On the face of it, there could be little confusing here, the couple were clearly instructed to follow an additional step, that of registration. Cyra had in fact complied with some of the civil preliminaries required of marriage prior to the *nikah*, however she was mistaken about the notice she had given, and hence the actions, post *nikah* that were still required of her and her husband. She understood, following the imam's clear statement concerning registration, that she needed to undertake a rubber-stamping (registration) of the ceremony that had taken place, and not an entirely separate and additional (civil) ceremony of marriage. As far as she was concerned, she had done her bit, now the husband needed to do his bit, post-*nikah*. There was a two-fold false sense of belief, firstly in what she had done and what it meant and secondly, what registration of marriage, post-*nikah* meant.

She did all she could, giving notice for the marriage but was unable to get her husband to do the same. When pressed on this point it was revealed that she thought this notice she had given was somehow connected to her *nikah* ceremony, and the fact the imam had told them both, you need to 'register' your marriage, she thought this only applied to her husband, as she has already done this by completing the form and paying the appropriate fee.

The plausibility of Cyra's explanation initially seemed doubtful however on reflection it seemed the confusion regarding post-*nikah* steps stemmed from the use of the word 'register', and she did not appreciate this meant undertaking an entirely separate civil marriage ceremony, instead it was just a formality which, according to her (mis)understanding, simply required the completion of a form and payment of a small fee.

Cyra reported that her *nikah* marriage was witnessed by over 20 high-ranking professionals at her parents' home, and she was confused upon the realisation that it was legally valid, how can this not be legal? Following the *nikah* ceremony she described a lavish event organised by her parents with over 200 guests in attendance. Wedding invitations were printed and sent out, it looked like a wedding.

Dalia's marriage on the other hand took place at a wedding venue, and when she was searching for appropriate setting, she was told by the venue manager 'we are registered for marriages'. Although Dalia did not really understand what this [legally authorised to solemnise a civil wedding] meant at the time, she took it to be a positive and thought by doing the *nikah* there, it would be legally binding by default. She accepted that she did not give this much thought at the time. At the time of making the wedding arrangements, the legality of marriage did not feature much in the process, although Dalia made it clear she always intended for her marriage to be legal and compliant with English law:

> All the 130 guests present believed we were entering into a formal wedding ceremony and that we were married.... I signed it [the *nikahnama* contract] in three places but that was it. All I was concerned about was getting in the car and starting my married life as a wife.

Again Dalia's wedding was attended by a large number of guests, an imam conducted the ceremony and to all present, it looked like a wedding. At every stage of proceedings it was clear that Dalia wanted a legally binding marriage. She made it very clear even saying during the course of our interview, had my parents realised we were not properly married, they would not have allowed me to sit next to him on the sofa, let alone have a child together! Legal validity was important not just for Dalia but her family.

Furthermore it is important to note that both respondents, as well as the majority interviewed for the doctoral research, only behaved as married, that is to engage in intimate relations, following their *nikah* ceremonies, and not before. Complying with the law of the land was important to them.

On reflection, the narratives captured demonstrate an imbalance of power in both of these relationships. Not only was this seen during the time of the marriage, there being a somewhat clearer understanding on the husband's side about the consequences of non-registration but also as in virtually all cases, it was the husband who held the assets in his sole name.

Both these respondents were under the impression that their respective marriages were legally valid, even though their reasons for this belief differed. Dalia was under this impression due to the place where her *nikah* was conducted; she was told the venue was licensed to hold weddings, but she did not appreciate that such a licence only granted the celebration of civil marriages, with an appropriate person. Cyra's interchange with her local town hall lead her to believe, wrongly, that she had completed all that was required of her, and her husband must complete the same. In neither case did the respondents consider that they needed to have an entire and distinctly separate ceremony of marriage, the "civil registration". The term civil registration is highly confusing in this context as very few respondents appreciated it to mean another wedding. And such a belief was seen in the majority of the other respondent case studies collected for the author's doctoral research.[36]

---

36 Vora, "The Islamic Marriage Conundrum: Register or Recognize? The Legal Consequences of the Nikah in England and Wales."

11 Feelings of Injustice: a Need to Protect Families

Of the two cases presented in this section, only Dalia's proceeded to court, and at the time of interview her case had been heard and judgment handed down. A High Court judge of the family division declared her *nikah* marriage to be a non-marriage, as she had wilfully closed her eyes to the issues under the 1949 Act and was not therefore entitled to rely on her own ignorance. In essence, she was being held to a far higher standard that the average person; it was held that she should have known the precise requirements of the marriage act at the time of her *nikah* marriage ceremony. This was in part because Dalia's siblings, it was heard, had experience of their own marriages and been able to engage with the law and get married, properly. The fact her *nikah* marriage took place on 'approved premises' although was somewhat coincidental; she felt it should have been given more weight. From what Dalia told reported of the court proceedings, it was as if this fact was almost used against her because she did not specifically choose the venue because it held this status, instead she chose it because of the excellent catering.

Dalia said during the High Court hearing the judge asked her what is meant to be a British Muslim. She said:

> I am British, I was born in Britain and I was brought up in Britain, I was educated here, that makes me British. This is my home … my son is more British that me. I don't have a Pakistani passport but some of my family do.

Dalia felt that her hearing got off on the wrong foot and she was said to be defensive in giving evidence, especially when discussing the validity of the marriage. Dalia was keen to stress in court her belief that of the *nikah* marriage being legal this was not accepted. It was found that Dalia was not reasonably entitled to hold the view that her *nikah* marriage would be good in law.

Dalia explained that she felt many unnecessary elements were raised against her during the High Court case, matters like her higher education, her work and her alleged lack of knowledge regarding marriage law, and they were used to contradict her case. She reported during the interview that such matters were raised by the judge, as he felt she should have known better. Dalia felt it was unfair because she was expected to know the law owing the actions of her siblings and how they arranged their marriages. There was a further sense of unfairness because Dalia felt conflicting elements were not raised against the husband in the same way. The fact that the husband had married twice under shariʿa law but was also British did not seem to matter. Following the breakup with Dalia, the husband re-married via a *nikah* again. Dalia said the judge was fully aware he had remarried and there seemed to be no repercussions to such behaviour or his choice of law.

"As I had falsely believed my nikah was legal, it seemed that it was my fault. This did not seem fair." The final blow came following this fact:

> My [ex] in-laws have washed their hands of me and my son, their grandchild. He wants to know who is in his dad's family and asks 'don't they love me?' There have been no birthday cards for him. The father doesn't have contact with his son and has not asked for it.

In conclusion Dalia felt let down by the justice system, from her perspective her husband was able to walk away from his marriage obligations, after bearing a child, without any adverse consequences or penalty. The judge commented that she was alone in thinking the *nikah* would result in a legally binding marriage but she clearly explained that this was the belief of her family and it was very important, especially to her parents that she be married in accordance with the law of the land, English law. The judge did not think the husband had misled her in the *nikah* marriage. Although the matter got to the High Court and benefited from being heard by an experienced family division judge, from the information Dalia presented during the course of the initial interview, her case would appear to have been poorly managed by the legal professionals, and she appeared to have received poor legal advice on the likely chances of success from the outset.

12 Tackling Discrimination

This author's position on the discriminatory and unfair nature of non-marriage is a minority point of view. The majority take the stance that non-marriage must exist as there will be situations, created by marriage acts that can neither be valid or void, hence based on this, a third category must exist. While this may be true, it is the liberal application of non-marriage that causes the present issue of discrimination against British Muslims.

The case law shows non-marriage being applied to factual situations where a couple has lived together, for a significant period of time, bearing children and completing the commonly associated things that married couples do. The judiciary has enough previous experience for the 'correct' determination of such cases and has had the opportunity, several times now, to clarify the law in this area, but have not done so.[37]

With so much turning on whether a marriage is void or non-existent, and with it being made clear the current law is discriminatory towards British Muslims and possibly other minority ethnic groups, reform of the Marriage Act 1949 is required so as to provide a clear and comprehensive set of rules that result in certain and predictable outcomes.

Case law in this area places a great deal of emphasis on the form of ceremony, the place it is celebrated and who conducts the ceremony. To recap, this approach is unsatisfactory as the court is led to make a 'value judgment'[38] as to what is an English ceremony of marriage. In the case of British Muslims, the chances of an Islamic marriage closely resembling an 'English ceremony of marriage' is unlikely, for the external appearance of the two are unlikely to be matched. In the two cases discussed above, the decisive issue was the lack of registration. As has been shown throughout this chapter, the current law of marriage in England and Wales requires non-Anglican Christian groups to take additional steps, beside their religious ceremony to be "really married", and it is this that seems to be at the root cause of unregistered Muslim marriages. Compounded with the relatively recent creation on non-marriage means that non-compliant minority ethnic marriage ceremonies are more likely to be deemed non-marriages than their mainstream counterparts and as such this is discriminatory. Furthermore there is also a gender imbalance given that more often than not, as demonstrated by the case law, the losing party is the female partner. Marriage breakdown, across the society adversely affects women over men.[39]

13 The Scottish System

In Scotland effecting a legal marriage is governed by the Marriage (Scotland) Act 1977. Scotland accepts that religious marriage ceremonies vary greatly and as such, only seek to ensure the following two conditions[40] are met:

37 The law is discriminatory in its consequence, it is not suggested that any of the judges who have delivered judgments in this area intended their judgments to be discriminatory.

38 Supra n26, 403.

39 Fisher and Low, "Who Wins, Who Loses and Who Recovers from Divorce?," 254.

40 http://www.nrscotland.gov.uk/registration/getting-married-in-scotland/marriage-ceremonies-in-scotland.

A declaration by the parties, in the presence of each other, the celebrant[41] and two witnesses, that they either accept each other as husband and wife or accept each other in marriage, or make both declarations; and

A declaration by the celebrant, after the foregoing declaration, that the parties are then husband and wife or are then married, or make both declarations.

There is no legally prescribed form of words to be used in relation to 'marriage vows'. The ceremony may be conducted in either English or any other language so long as all the parties, including the celebrant can understand the language, with the services of a translator if required. There are no restrictions as to place of solemnisation, so private homes are included, as are outdoor venues. Registration formalities are handled by the celebrant performing the marriage.

The Scottish system is flexible and open-ended, the *nikah* ceremony under this mechanism need not be amended yet it would still satisfy the legal burden as well as the faith requirements, according the wishes and beliefs of the parties.

The English mechanism of obtaining the relevant registration to solemnise marriages has been said to be complex and often difficult to obtain. The Scottish system not only offers a three year licence to members of almost all faith and belief groups to become their own celebrants, it also offers a temporary registration system,[42] allowing essentially anyone who is considered fit and proper,[43] from a recognised faith group to apply and solemnise a marriage. Perhaps the most interesting factor in this system is the uptake of registration. It is not surprising to see the vast majority of those holding such registration are those from the non-Church of Scotland group, however it is telling to see that seven per cent of all registrations are held by those of the Islamic faith groups. Compare this figure to the number, or lack thereof re mosques in England and Wales that are registered for the solemnisation of marriage, and it is clear to see this celebrant based system is has been well received.[44]

41 Marriage (Scotland) Act 1977, section 9.

42 Ibid., section 12.

43 There seems to be no legal requirement to becoming a religious marriage celebrant though the Registrar General will reject any nominee not a fit and proper person to solemnize a marriage, see Marriage (Scotland) Act 1977 section 9(2).

44 Data was obtained from the National Records Scotland office, Registration of Approved Celebrants Rolling Programme 1 January 2015, (11 June, 2015) *record on file with the author.*

14 Conclusion

The legal cases discussed in this chapter along with the presentation of two contrasting case studies have endeavoured to show the discriminatory application of law, when it comes to the formalities of marriage, and the need for law reform starting with an implementation of celebrant based system. Failure to do so will mean continuing down the path of value judgments on any marriage ceremony, in particular Islamic ones, that do not conform to a Christian template.

The celebrant based marriage system in Scotland is a simple mechanism by which many of those British Muslims who experienced difficult with their informal marriages in England and Wales would have received the legal recognition and hence financial relief upon divorce.

The law concerning non-marriage might change, by a decision of the Supreme Court, or law reform of the Marriage Act 1949. This author's PhD fieldwork study has shown the majority of *nikah* marriages take place in a private setting, usually the bride's home. In terms of providing a fresh approach to this issue, it will be shown the implementation of a celebrant based marriage system, similar to the system in Scotland, may be successful in removing the requirement for British Muslims to marry twice and in a particular marrying within an approved or registered building. By placing the responsibility of registration on a celebrant and removing the need for the ceremony to follow a particular form, giving freedom of choice when it comes to the language the ceremony is conducted in, such measures would give the best platform for British Muslims to engage with the system and would lead to a reduction in the number of informal marriages, and the injustices suffered as a result.

Bibliography

Bevan, Chris. "The Role of Intention in Non-Marriage Cases Post *Hudson v Leigh*." *Child and Family Law Quarterly* 25, no. 1 (2013): 80–95.

Dukali v Lamrani (Attorney General Intervening), EWHC 1748 (Fam) (2012).

El Gamal v Al Maktoum, EWHC B27 (Fam) (2011).

Fisher, Hayley, and Low, Hamish. "Who Wins, Who Loses and Who Recovers from Divorce?" In *Sharing Lives, Dividing Assets: An Inter-Disciplinary Study*, edited by Joanna Miles and Rebecca Probert, 227–56. Oxford Portland: Hart Pub, 2009.

Hall, Anna. "The Truth About Muslim Marriage," 2017. https://truevisiontv.com/films/details/295/the-truth-about-muslim-marriage.

HL Deb. (6 July 2015) Col. 88.

Hudson v Leigh (Status of Non-Marriage), EWHC 1306 (Fam) (2009).

Marriage Act (1949).

Marriage (Scotland) Act 1977.

"Places of Worship Registered for Marriage – GOV.UK." Accessed 16 January, 2018. https://www.gov.uk/government/publications/places-of-worship-registered-for-marriage.

Places of Worship Registration Act (1855).

Probert, Rebecca. "When Are We Married? Void, Non-Existent and Presumed Marriages." *Legal Studies* 22, no. 3 (1 September, 2002): 398–419. https://doi.org/10.1111/j.1748-121X.2002.tb00199.x.

Probert, Rebecca. *Marriage Law and Practice in the Long Eighteenth Century: A Reassessment.* Cambridge: Cambridge University Press, 2009.

Shah, Prakash. "Does Channel 4's Documentary Provide the Truth about Muslim Marriage?" *Areo* (blog), 7 December, 2017. https://areomagazine.com/2017/12/07/does-channel-4s-documentary-provide-the-truth-about-muslim-marriage/.

"Void | Definition of Void in English by Oxford Dictionaries." Oxford Dictionaries | English. Accessed 6 March, 2018. https://en.oxforddictionaries.com/definition/void.

Vora, Vishal. "The Islamic Marriage Conundrum: Register or Recognize? The Legal Consequences of the Nikah in England and Wales." PhD thesis, SOAS, University of London, 2016.

Muslims of Greece: a Legal Paradox *and* a Political Failure

Konstantinos Tsitselikis

1 More Than an Introduction: Old and New Islam in Greece

The present chapter attempts to examine the legal position of Muslims in Greece, focusing on persistent legal paradoxes and political failures that violate the principles of equal citizenship and human rights. Some basic considerations regarding Muslims in Greece have been already presented in previous studies.[1] However, the position of Shari'a law within the Greek legal order as currently challenged before the European Court of Human Rights[2] may change the way the personal status of Muslims in Greece (Greek citizens) is perceived by the courts.

Muslims in Greece do not form a homogenous group, neither on the social or economic level, nor regarding language, national or ethnic identity or legal status. First of all, Muslims of Greek citizenship belonging to the minority of Thrace (and the Dodecanese islands) constitute a separate group with a minimum degree of internal coherence (*Old Islam*), despite ethnic and linguistic differences within the community. Special legal status attributed by the Treaty of Lausanne and implemented by a series of legal acts have contributed to this cohesion. Other Muslim groups of traditional settlement, such as the Muslims of the Dodecanese islands, do not have real social bonds with Muslims of Thrace. The second category of Muslims, the immigrants (*New Islam*), who settled mostly in urban areas and especially in Athens, create a network of Islamic society apart, segregated through the national affiliation of each community. Recently arrived asylum seekers are forming a new branch of New Islam in Greece. Alongside these categories, Islam creates a common denominator, ideological, legal and political, which renders all Muslims a distinct 'minoritised' group.

1 Tsitselikis, *Old and New Islam*, 410–411; Tsitselikis, "Seeking To Accommodate Shari'a," 119–120.

2 ECtHR, *Molla Sali v Greece*, application No 20452/2014; Judgment, Grand Chamber, 19 December 2018.

 DOI:10.1163/9789004398269_005

2 The Genealogy of Old Islam

The Greek revolution of 1821 which led to the independence of Greece (1830) from the Ottoman Empire was the first successful national movement in the Balkans, and it established a pattern that was followed by similar national revolts on the part of other nations based on the belief that the 'Christian nations' had 'awakened' and thrown off the 'Ottoman yoke'. In this ideological, political, and institutional context, Muslims became a minority subjected to differentiated legal treatment well before the establishment of the minority protection system by the League of Nations during the Inter-War period.

In 1830, Muslims constituted a very small group within the then borders of Greece with almost no special institutional protection. By 1881, with the annexation of Thessalia-Arta (1881), Muslim communities (numbering about 40,000 at that time) acquired protection as a minority by the Treaty of Constantinople (1881). In effect, the Ottoman *millet* system (ethno-religious communal institutional autonomy) was preserved and the local muftis acquired quasi-judicial authority in personal status matters. Muslim schools and religious foundations (*vakif*) were recognised in Greek law and were administered by local Muslim Community Councils. By the end of the Balkan Wars (1912–13) and with the annexation of the New Territories by Greece, the same status was extended to more than 500,000 Muslims who became Greek citizens. With the Treaty of Athens, signed between Greece and the Ottoman Empire in 1913, the legal status of the Muslim communities was consolidated. Community schools and the *waqfs* were kept under their authority, and the muftis acquired advisory jurisdiction on personal matters. It is worth noting that Crete, too, before its union with the Greek Kingdom in the same year and during its political autonomy from the Ottoman Empire, offered a sophisticated legal framework to the Muslim community of the island which was elaborated mostly by Eleftherios Venizelos, future predominant political figure of Greece.[3]

After the Greek-Turkish war of 1919–1922, a compulsory population exchange took place under the Lausanne Convention of January 1923 and 450,000 Muslims left Greece for Turkey. According to the Convention, 92,000 Muslims of Western Thrace (Turkish-speakers and Bulgarian-speakers or Pomaks) were exempted from the population exchange, as a counter weight to the Greek Orthodox population of Istanbul, Imvros and Tenedos who were also exempted from the exchange. Another 25,000 Albanian-speaking Muslims in Epirus and Macedonia were extra-conventionally exempted. Being sympathisers of the Italian/German occupation forces after 1940, Muslims of Epirus (Chams)

3 Tsitselikis, *Old and New Islam*, 36–46.

were forced to flee to Albania in 1944/45. In 1947, when the Dodecanese Islands were annexed by Greece, a population of about 12,000 Muslims (Greek and Turkish speaking) became Greek citizens.

Today, Muslims of Greek citizenship of Thrace (about 85,000) are the only recognised minority in Greece. They are mostly Turkish-speakers and many express Turkish national feelings. About 20,000 of them have Pomak (a Bulgarian dialect) as their mother tongue, partly expressing an ethnic Pomak identity, often along with a Turkish (national) identity, and about 5,000 speak Romany (partly expressing an ethnic Roma identity), although most of the Muslim Roma are monolingual Turkish speakers. As religion and mother tongue ceased to be asked after in the national census after 1951, all the above figures are rough estimates. Minority Muslims are all Sunni except for 2,000 or 3,000 who are Bektashi. Today, Muslims from Thrace also live in Athens (15,000) and Thessaloniki (4,000), where they have migrated for economic reasons. In the Dodecanese Islands (Rodos and Kos) about 2,000 live on each island. During the Greek-Turkish confrontations of 1960s and 1970s, a wave of Muslims emigrated from Thrace to Turkey, Germany and other countries for political and economic reasons.

3 The Formation of New Islam

By the late 20th century, Muslims migrated to Greece as part of a broader migration wave triggered by the collapse of the USSR, the wars in the Middle East, Iraq, Afghanistan and the extreme poverty and environmental disasters which struck Asia and Africa. As a result, a 'New Islam' brought by immigration gradually enriched Greece's Islam with new elements. Migrant Muslims belong to a series of different communities, and to a certain extent their population is variable as undocumented immigrants and asylum seekers tend to leave Greece after a short or long period of residence.

Muslim immigrants come mostly from African and Asian countries. Sunnism is the most widespread form of Islam and is followed by immigrants from Africa, Bangladesh, Pakistan and most Arab countries. Shi'ism is far less widespread, existing mainly among Kurdish, Pakistani and Iranian communities, while Alevism is found mostly among Turks and Kurds. There are no reliable statistics according to the 2011 census about the number of immigrants in Greece. They could be about 8% of the overall population, totalling 1,000,000. Around 200,000–300,000 of them are presumed to be Muslims, not including Albanians, the majority of whom are of Muslim background, but without expressing affinities with Islam. By 2017, among the immigrants with an Islamic affiliation, the Afghani community numbers 20,000, the Pakistani 50,000, the Bangladeshi 30,000, Palestinians and Jordanians 12,000, Egyptians 15,000, Iraqis more than 40,000 and Syrians more than 50,000. They are mostly settled in Athens, except for those who, as asylum seekers, are scattered in camps and urban settlements all over the country. However such figures are highly unreliable, as there is a large number of clandestine immigrants and constant population mobility. Moreover, leaders of Muslim associations are tempted to exaggerate community figures in support of political and social claims.

4 A Legal Paradox: All Equal? All Different?

Both "Islams" coexist but have considerably different characteristics. Yet, citizenship (being a Greek citizen or alien) draws a rigid distinction, according to which immigrants (aliens) and minority Muslims (Greek citizens) have access to different rights and obligations. Moreover, they live apart, share different ethnic and linguistic identities and confront different challenges vis-à-vis the Greek state, law and society. However, minority and immigrant Muslims are seen by Greek national ideology as outsiders to the Greek *genos* or race that determines the Greek nation or *Hellenism*.[4] Moreover, the identity issue in Thrace has remained a highly controversial issue insofar as Greek and Turkish nationalisms confront each other in the field. Symptomatic of the situation is the transfer of the diplomatic controversy, which invests the term "Turk/Turkish" with conflict-laden ideological meaning, into the Greek courtrooms, distorting the legal content of the relevant right to association. The respective judgements of the Greek courts and the European Court of Human Rights[5] are indicative of an astonishing and persistent ideological use of law.

The major dividing factor as far as the legal treatment of Muslims in Greece is concerned is the Treaty of Lausanne. The treaty places only the Muslims of Greek citizenship of Thrace under a special minority protection framework and not other minorities or Muslims outside of Thrace. Since 1923, the minority of Thrace is governed by the chapter of the Treaty of Lausanne on minority protection (art. 37–45) which creates mirror obligation for Turkey and Greece regarding non-Muslims and Muslims respectively. This legal protection system

4 Christopoulos and Tsitselikis, "Impasses of treatment regarding minorities and *homogeneis* in Greece," 81.

5 See the cases before the European Court of Human Rights regarding the 'Turkish Union of Xanthi' (*Tourkiki Enosi Xanthis and Others v. Greece*, no. 26698/05), and the 'Turkish women's association' of Komotini (*Emin and others v. Greece*, no. 34144/05) both judgments of 27 March, 2008.

reflects once again a *millet*-like precept regarding the attribution of religious and linguistic rights and is put into effect via religion. Since early on, and especially after 1964 and 1974, until the mid-1990s, minority protection suffered from Greek-Turkish antagonisms through the notorious principle of (negative) reciprocity. However, the 'Lausanne system' survived unchanged after the new era that brought in the United Nations system for minority protection, and the post-1991 new multi-lateral minority protection system established in Europe. Thus the status of the Turkish/Muslim minority of Thrace encompasses specific minority rights regarding religious freedom and linguistic rights in parallel to the nexus of rights that (Greek) citizenship entails in the following way:

a. Three muftis appointed by the government are based in Thrace. They are the religious authority in their respective region and exert special jurisdiction over Muslims on family and inheritance matters.[6] The selection of the muftis became an issue of major political importance and a field of national (Greek-Turkish) confrontation and legal controversy:[7] Today in parallel to the three government-appointed muftis, another two are elected by part of the minority and are operational in Thrace. In many cases until October 2018 the mufti's jurisdiction had become *obligatory to Muslims* – with no option to choose – raising a series of contradictions (see Section 4, hereinafter).

b. Minority schools offer bilingual education to Muslim students. The latter also attend Greek public school. Christian teachers teach the Greek curriculum and Muslims the Turkish curriculum. There are about 165 elementary schools, and four high schools (gymnasia/lycea). Two of them are religious seminaries (*medrese*). By 1997 a special quota for Muslims from Thrace to enter Greek university has been adopted, thus facilitating social integration.

c. Muslim community property (*vakif/vakoufia*) is administered by councils, which are not elected but appointed by the government since the times of the junta in 1967. The relevant Act 3647/2008 is not implemented. *Vakif* properties

6 Ktistakis, *Charia, Tribunaux religieux et droit grec*; Tsitselikis, *Old and New Islam*, 367.

7 ECtHR, cases related to the penal prosecution of the elected muftis: *Serif v Greece*, Application No 38178/97, judgment of 14 December, 1999; *Agga v Greece (No 2)*, judgment of 17 October, 2002, applications nos. 50776/99 and 52912/99, *Agga v Greece (No 3)*, judgment of 13.7.2006, application no. 32186/02 and *Agga v Greece (No 4)*, judgment of 13 July, 2006, application no. 33331/02. In a similar case concerning the mufti of Bulgaria, the Court held that "In democratic societies the State does not need to take measures to ensure that religious communities are brought under a unified leadership," ECtHR, *Hasan and Chaoush v Bulgaria*, application No 30985/96, judgment of 6.10.2000, par. 78.

also exist in the Dodecanese islands (both community and private),[8] placed under a special law, not linked to the Treaty of Lausanne.

The members of the minority enjoy all rights safeguarded by the Constitution and the international human rights treaties in the same way as any other Greek citizen. A series of minority associations operate in Thrace (and outside Thrace). Other community organisational structures or prerogatives have been lost through time, such as the election of community councils, special quota for political representation to the parliament, or exemption from military service. A few (1–4) minority deputies from Thrace are normally elected to the Parliament as candidates of the main political parties. Muslims also participate in the elected boards of local authorities throughout Thrace. A series of newspapers and journals are published in Turkish (one in Pomak) and radio programmes are broadcast in Turkish by members of the minority. As far as places of worship are concerned, there is a sufficient number of mosques in Thrace (more than 250, and another four in the Dodecanese islands) functioning for everyday ritual needs. Muslim cemeteries also are operational in Thrace and the Dodecanese islands.

The further a Muslim goes from Thrace, the fewer special rights he/she enjoys: The Treaty of Lausanne is not applicable outside Thrace, but in addition no mosque or cemetery is available. It follows that a Muslim wedding cannot be registered outside Thrace. Therefore Muslims of Greek citizenship and migrant Muslims, as long as they live outside Thrace (and Rodos and Kos), enjoy general human rights in the same way as any other citizen, but they do not have access to the special rights nor to general rights pertaining to freedom of religion. The one and only mosque scheduled to be erected in Athens has still not been built due to technical 'problems' that have a political and islamophobic flavour to them.[9] In Athens, Thessaloniki and some other towns, about 80 *masjits* do exist and they are operated by immigrant Muslim communities mostly without official permits. Only three worship halls have acquired an official permit (in Piraeus, Athens and Thiva). The rest of them have not applied or cannot meet the criteria required by the law. The non-availability of a Muslim cemetery outside Thrace (Rodos and Kos)[10] adds one more dimension to the bi-zonal legal framework (in/out of Thrace) that applies to Muslims in Greece.

8 Two more groups of vakif exist in Greece. Egypt owns vakif properties in Kavala and Thasos. Last, a vakifonce owned by Albanian Muslims is set under sequestration in Thessalia (Tsitselikis, *Old and New Islam*, 327–365).

9 Sakellariou, "Islamophobia in Greece," 200–18.

10 Tsitselikis and Sakellariou, "Greece," 334.

TABLE 1 Muslims and access to rights

	Access to mosques/ cemetery	Special schools	Community properety (waqf)	Shari'a law/ courts	Registration of Muslim marriage
Muslims of Thrace (Greek citizens)	Y	Y	Y	Y	Y
Muslims of Dodecanese (Greek citizens)	Y	N	Y	N	Y
Muslims everywhere else in Greece (Greek citizens)	Only in private prayer houses	N	N	N	N
Migrant Muslims	Only in private prayer houses	N	N	N	N
Refugee Muslims	N [very limited]	N	N	N	N

The application of Shari'a law reveals certain aspects of conflict that test the balance between minority rights and human rights.

5 Personal Status for the Muslims of Thrace: Is Something Missing?

As stated above, the mufti is not only a religious leader but also a judge: According to article 5 of Law 1920/1991, "The mufti has jurisdiction over Muslim Greek citizens of his region in matters of marriage, divorce, minors' emancipation, custody, Islamic wills and ab intestat succession as far as these legal relations are governed by the Sacred Law of Islam". Shari'a law can be directly applied only by the mufti, the sacred courts of Thrace or taken into consideration by a civil court while testing the constitutionality of the sacred court's decision. In practice, most of the mufti's field of jurisdiction concerns divorce. The Muslims of Thrace settle their will through donations in life to their heirs before a notary. The First Instance Courts have also curtailed the muftis' jurisdiction over children's custody.[11]

11 Among others, see First Instance Court of Rodopi, judgment No 129/2016, according to which the term "custody" regarding the right to communication of divorced parents with their child is a matter governed by the Civil Code (art. 1510 and 1518) and not the Shari'a.

The contact between Shariʿa law and civil law can be seen at three different instances: a. when applied by the mufti in the framework of his special jurisdiction according to art. 5 of Law 1920/1991; b. When the First Instance Court has to review the constitutionality and the competence exerted by the sacred court; and c. When a civil court remands a case to the sacred court denying the application of civil law (Law 4511/2018 reduced seriously this possibility). In all three cases, compatibility between Shariʿa law and human rights standards are at stake.

In theory, the mufti's decision should not contravene the Constitution as far as the free will of the litigant is concerned. The judicial competence of the mufti should be preferential and supplementary in the sense that Muslims are free to choose between the Civil Court and Islamic jurisdiction. If the mufti's jurisdiction was obligatory it would be a legally imposed segregation among Greek citizens on the ground of religion, a situation which would contradict the Constitution, and international human rights law (art. 9, 14 of the Convention and Convention on the Elimination of All Forms of Discrimination against Women, art. 1, 2, 15, 16). Most of the muftis' decisions infringe women's (equality of sexes) and children's rights as endorsed by the Constitution or the Convention. The applicable Shariʿa law is neither standardised nor codified and is left to the broad interpretation of the judge. Two more questions in relation to the procedures taking place at the Mufti Court regard: a) right to fair trial, under article 6 of the ECHR, when equality of the litigants is not safeguarded, nor representation through a lawyer or predictability and visibility of the applicable law is provided; b) lack of efficient remedy for the review of the merits of the mufti's decision, and lack of effective means to review its constitutionality.[12]

It is not surprising that all relevant international and national monitoring bodies have repeatedly expressed their strong concerns about the issue and addressed their recommendations to align the way Shariʿa law is applied in Greece with the principles and norms of fundamental human rights. The Greek National Commission for Human Rights stated in 2016 that it is concerned because, "the Greek civil law does not apply to the Thrace Muslim minority regarding marriage and inheritance" while reporting to the ICERD.[13] The

---

12 Ktistakis, *Charia, Tribunaux religieux et droit grec*, 127.

13 Greek National Commission for Human Rights, Written Information submitted by the Greek National Commission for Human Rights (GNCHR) in relation to the implementation of the International Convention on the Elimination of all forms of Racial Discrimination (ICERD) in Greece, July 2016.

Committee on the Elimination of Discrimination against Women, in their concluding comments and remarks (of 2007 and 2013), expressed concerns about the non-application of the general law of Greece to the Muslim minority on matters of marriage and inheritance, as Muslim communities can choose to be governed by Muslim law:

> The Committee is concerned about the situation of women in the State party in the area of marriage and inheritance. It is concerned that this situation leads to discrimination against Muslim women, in contravention of the Greek Constitution and article 16 of the Convention,

and called the Greek government

> to fully harmonise the application of local Shari'a law and general law in the State party with the provisions on non-discrimination of the Convention, in particular with regard to marriage and inheritance.[14]

The Committee recommended that the government

> train the legal profession, including the judiciary, as well as ethnic communities' and religious leaders on the Convention and the Committee's General Recommendations and encourage them to refer to the Convention and the norms and standards contained therein.[15]

The UN Committee on Human Rights of the International Covenant on Civil and Political Rights expressed its concern about the problems Muslim women could face because general Greek law in the field of marriage and inheritance did not apply to the Muslim minority in Thrace. It strongly urged Greece "to increase the awareness of Muslim women of their rights and the availability of remedies, and to ensure that they benefit from the provisions of Greek civil law".[16] Lastly, the most recent report on Islam in Europe, presented before the

---

14 Committee on the Elimination of Discrimination against Women, Concluding observations on the seventh periodic report of Greece adopted by the Committee at its fifty fourth session (1 March, 2013), CEDAW/C/GRC/CO/7.

15 Committee on the Elimination of Discrimination against Women, Concluding comments on of the Committee on the Elimination of Discrimination against Women: Greece (2/2/2007), CEDAW/C/GRC/CO/6.

16 Human Rights Committee, 2005, (ICCPR) 'Greece', Concluding observations, 25/04/2005, CCPR/CO/83/GRC, Geneva: United Nations, paragraph 8.

Parliamentary Assembly of the Council of Europe, upholds that "the application of Shari'a law in Western Thrace is prejudicial to women".[17]

Despite the above-mentioned critique from a human rights viewpoint, the Greek government fell short in attempting to reform the sacred courts and the applicable law, although they never expressed an overt support to the mandatory applicability of Shari'a or the subordination of the principle of non-discrimination to Shari'a. In 2009 and 2013 two Ministers of Justice publicly stated that: a. All Muslims have the right to opt for civil law instead of Shari'a law, and b. Further to the applicability of Shari'a law, the implementation of Greek law does not depend on religious convictions of the citizens.[18] In a report to the UN Human Rights Committee in 2014, the Greek government depicts the situation as fully compliant with human rights standards, although – as we shall see – actual court practice does not always live up to what the report professes (my emphasis):[19]

59. The law provides for the potential application of the Shari'a law in matters of family and inheritance law among members of the Muslim minority in Thrace. *The choice whether to use the Shari'a or the Greek Civil Code in the above mentioned matters is made by the members of the Muslim minority themselves.* As shown over the last years, by cases involving women from the minority, this option is a fact of life in Thrace.

60. *Members of the Muslim minority in Thrace are completely free to address themselves either to the civil courts or the local Muftis. Whenever they choose the former, general legislation is applied.* Whenever they choose the latter, the Shari'a law is implemented to the extent that its rules are not in conflict with the fundamental values of the Greek society and the Greek legal and constitutional order. The law provides that the courts shall not enforce decisions of the Muftis which are contrary to the Greek Constitution. In this respect, derogations from civil law provisions are minor: concepts such as polygamy, marriage below legal age without court permission, marriage by proxy, repudiation, etc. are not allowed, on the basis of the aforementioned principle.

---

17 Meritxell Mateu, Introductory memorandum, *Compatibility of Sharia law with the European Convention on Human Rights: can States Parties to the Convention be signatories of the 'Cairo Declaration'?*, Committee on Legal Affairs and Human Rights, Parliamentary Assembly, Council of Europe, AS/Jur (2016), 7.10. 2016, 9–10. Finally Resolution 2253 (2019) adopted a clear stance against the application of shari'a in Greece.

18 Minister of Justice, Answer to parliamentary question on Shari'a law, Athens 23.12.2009 and Minister of Justice, Answer to parliamentary question on Shari'a law, Athens 25.1.2013.

19 UN, Human Rights Committee Consideration of reports submitted by States parties under article 40 of the Covenant Second periodic reports of States parties due in 2009. Greece. [23 January, 2014] CCPR/C/GRC/2 [pp. 13–14].

63. Finally, it is important to clarify that *in Greece there are no "parallel legal orders" or "separate societies", dependant on the religious affiliation of Greek citizens*. Muslim women of the minority are fully included in gender equality policies and participate in relevant programs implemented by the competent authorities.

Despite these declarations made by the Greek government, the Greek civil courts often deny justice to Muslim litigants and remand the case to the mufti or uphold that the mufti's judgments do not breach the constitutional principle of equality of sexes. In some other cases, Muslim testators were not allowed to draft public wills. The courts held that only Shariʿa law was applicable and therefore only Islamic will or intestate succession were available to them. The established case-law on the applicability of Shariʿa law, mostly endorsed by the Court of Cassation (*Areios Pagos*), renders Islamic law mandatorily applicable and the civil code inaccessible to Muslims of Thrace.

6 Between Legal Pluralism and Discrimination

Bearing in mind the above mentioned mapping of Islam in Greece, the generally applicable human rights law and the special jurisdiction of the mufti in Thrace, one question comes up: Does this variety of regimes represent a successful strategy to cope with legal pluralism, or does it embed the seeds of discriminative treatment? The case of the application of Shariʿa law by the mufti in Thrace is of key importance to this discussion.

A successful approach to dealing with legal pluralism ensures a balance between the legal orders involved, taking into account different ethno-religious particularities. It thereby allows for the accommodation of different social realities in the same legal order. The coexistence of different legal systems could be seen as a laudable case of pluralism of law, *so long as it ensures everyone a choice to opt for one or the other legal system*. In a case brought by a Roma woman from Spain, whose relationship was not considered a legal marriage by the authorities, the ECtHR[20] said that that "the force of the collective beliefs of a community that is well-defined culturally cannot be ignored". The Court also upheld that, while belonging to a minority does not create an exemption from the need for compliance with marriage laws, it may have an effect on the manner in which those laws must be applied. However, the special jurisdiction of

20 ECtHR, *Munoz Diaz v Spain*, 49151/07 judgment of 8 December, 2009, para 19. See also *Serife Yigit v Turkey*, 3976/05, Grand Chamber, 16 December, 2009.

the mufti in Greece provides such a possibility to Muslims of Thrace and thus one can say that in principle (unless a non-compliance to fundamental human rights is detected) it fits what the Court accepts as legal pluralism within a homogenous European legal order of human rights. On the other hand, the imposition by law of a certain jurisdiction -with no option to choose- is also highly problematic, especially when the latter is not compatible with fundamental human rights values and norms. As the Court said, if a certain juridical system is *imposed* on the individual on the basis of religious affiliation, it would contradict the general principles and values of the European legal order and democratic society.[21] Therefore two issues need to be tackled: a. the mandatory imposition of a special legal system which contradicts the universal one; b. the implementation of certain legal norms that breach public policy (*ordre public*) and thus cannot be tolerated.

Considering the status of the mufti within the Greek and European legal order inevitably touches upon the issue of how to accommodate non-liberal laws of a minority in a liberal legal context. To move forward, this discussion must manoeuvre between the demands for integration, preservation of minority identity, and the relationship between individual and collective identity as potential fields of normative action.[22]

Applying Islamic law within the framework of a European legal order seems to result in contradictions between individual rights and principles of equality, on the one hand, and religious freedom on the other. In short, *Shariʿa* law, when seen through the prism of human rights law, includes discriminatory provisions against women. In practice then, legal pluralism, as experienced within the Greek legal order, entails a paradox in which the violation of fundamental principles of a democratic society is retained in the name of respect for the minority's religious specificity. This tension means that what may seem multicultural today, or is presented as an aspect of Greece's multiculturalism, is just a persisting legacy of the Ottoman period, which entails elements that contradict current European human rights standards regarding equality of the sexes and the right to a fair trial. On the other hand, adjudication by the mufti is seen as of major importance for the preservation of minority identity for a part of the minority of Thrace. Yet each member of the minority, in accordance with his or her freely formulated wishes, should be given a real opportunity to choose whether they wish to live according to the 'juridical traditions' of the group or not. According to the Court, legal categorisation according to one's religion reduces the role of the state as of guarantor of human rights and

21 ECtHR, *Refah partisi v Turkey*, par. 126–128.

22 Tsitselikis, "Seeking To Accommodate Shari'a," 119–120.

freedom of religion in a democratic society, as the individuals are obliged to conform to religious jurisdiction.[23] If the individual is given no choice, direct discrimination is applied: Muslims of Thrace are deprived of their right to submit their case before the same courts (civil courts) as anyone else because of an objective and mandatory definition of their religious adherence which imposes a given jurisdiction (the mufti's courts) and a given law (Shariʿa).

What is of prevailing importance for the rule of law is to guarantee all Greek citizens access to courts under the same law. The protective treatment of Muslims under special law can be attributed only on the condition that it remains optional. The imposition of a system of law that is, by the standards of the ECHR, inherently discriminatory has no place in a modern European state and undermines any legal protection of the free development of the personality (Art. 5.1, Constitution). Article 14 ECHR does not prohibit distinctions in treatment: on the contrary, it allows for different treatment in different situations,[24] but it does not impose differentiation in treatment at the expense of universal human rights. The law has to handle equal situations with equal means: the right to bring a case before civil courts is accorded by the Greek Civil Code to all with no exception.

The criterion of being under the Lausanne minority protection framework is membership to the Muslim minority. Consequently, religion is discerned objectively and by default by the state authorities. However, religion can be held as a criterion only when a special right is granted, which is activated according to the desire of the bearer of the right, not the reverse, namely the discretion of the state. Minority rights constitute positive measures, which means that the bearer of the said rights enacts them according to his/her wish. Any mandatory referral by the courts on the basis of religion to special law, instead of the universal civil law, introduces differentiated treatment and therefore constitutes discrimination according to Article 14. Imposing Muslim law on those who have already opted for civil law is a disproportionate legal technique that cannot comply with the freedom to choose his/her jurisdiction (*forum shopping*).

7 Abolish, Maintain or Reform Shariʿa Law?

The Greek National Commission for Human Rights, along with the bar associations of Greece recommended the abolition of Shariʿa law as it contravenes art. 20 of the Greek constitution (right to effective legal protection), and art. 6 of

23 ECtHR, *Refah partisi v Turkey*, 13.2.2003, par. 119 and Tsitselikis, *Old and New Islam*, 410–411.

24 ECtHR, *Thlimmenos v Greece*, 343469/97, 6.4.2000.

the Convention and called the government to cooperate with the chairperson of the Court of Cassation in order to educate the judiciary about the position of Shari'a law within the Greek legal order.[25] The Parliamentary Assembly of the Council of Europe linked the abolition of Shari'a law to the selection mode of the muftis. The Assembly urged the Greek authorities to

> allow the Muslim minority to choose freely its muftis as mere religious leaders (that is, without judicial powers), through election or appointment, and thus to abolish the application of Shari'a law– which raises serious questions of compatibility with the European Convention on Human Rights – as recommended by the Commissioner for Human Rights.[26]

Greek scholars also proposed the abolition of Shari'a.[27] Others propose the amendment of Shari'a in order to embody human rights principles through evolution from within the mufti courts and the community.[28]

In considering proposals for the abolition or the maintenance of Islamic law, one has to carefully evaluate the social and political factors that make up the "minority question" of Thrace, free of any preconceptions of the past. A development that could resolve the tension between religious minority rights and Western democratic standards may be the internal reform of Islamic law. The written sources of Shari'a could be interpreted through the critical hermeneutic endeavour of jurists to analyze and comprehend them in a way that meets human rights standards.[29] If that were to happen, Shari'a law, reformed from within, could comply with fundamental human rights principles; and Western law could accommodate Islamic law. Needless to say, the consultation of those

25 Greek National Commission for Human Rights, *Recommendation on religious freedom issues*, 1.3.2001, 10–11. The plenary of the Presidents of the Bar Associations in Greece (Press Release, 2 May, 2009) proposed the abrogation of article 4 of Act 141/1914 and article 5 of Act 1920/1991.

26 PACE, Resolution 1704 (2010) Parliamentary Assembly, Council of Europe, par 18.5 and PACE, Michel Hunault, Report (Doc 11860) on *the 'Lausanne minorities' in Turkey and Greece*, Strasbourg: Council of Europe, 2009, par. 48.

27 Ktistakis, *Charia, Tribunaux religieux et droit grec*, Kotzabasi, *The family legal relations of the Greek Muslims*.

28 Kalambakou, "Equality confronting religious pluralism;" Tsitselikis, *Old and New Islam in Greece*.

29 "After carefully digesting what these new giants of *Shari'a* law [of the university of Cairo] wrote, I am fully convinced that the *corpus-juris* elaborated by the jurists of the past is not a closed book, but an open one which can be brought to life and rejuvenated in order to cope with the requirements of the modern world." El Kosheri, "Islamic Schools of Law," 43.

who are directly involved, namely the religious courts and the local society of Thrace, is a must. The need for an open dialogue on the issue has been stressed by the Commissioner for Human Rights of the Council of Europe who also expressed strong opinions on the implementation of Muslim law in Greece:[30]

III. The Commissioner takes note of the very serious concerns that have been expressed by competent national and international organisations about the application to Muslim Greek citizens in Thrace of the Shariʿa Law in family and inheritance law matters by Muftis who are appointed by the Greek state. Given the issues of incompatibility of this practice with European and international human rights standards, the Commissioner recommends its review by the authorities, institutionalizing at the same time an open and continuous dialogue with representatives of the Muslim minority on all matters affecting their everyday life and human rights, in accordance with the Council of Europe standards. Any amendment of the current legal framework should be carried out with the direct involvement of the minority concerned that should be fully enabled to participate effectively in cultural and social life and in public affairs. In the meantime, the Commissioner urges the Greek authorities to ensure an effective review and control by domestic civil courts of the judicial decisions which are rendered by Muftis.

8 A Court Case That Challenges the Position of Shariʿa Law in Greece

A case adjudicated by the European Court of Human Rights[31] raised legal questions regarding the validity of the public will drafted by a Muslim Greek citizen, resident of Thrace, and the right of his heir to enjoy the right to property. The Court of Cassation upheld that a public will, drafted by a Muslim Greek citizen, is not valid, as Shariʿa law is *mandatorily* applicable. The Court quashed the Court of Appeal's judgment (No 392/2011, which upheld the First Instance Court judgment No 50/2010) that said that any citizen has access to civil courts and that civil law is applicable to all.

In effect, the Court of Cassation deprived the testator of his right to dispose his property to his wife, because a bequest in favour of close relatives is not valid under Islamic law. By the same judgment the Court of Cassation denied to his wife (the Applicant) access to (non-Shariʿa) civil law. It upheld this inflexible stance, thus violating fundamental rights stemming from both

30 Hammarberg, *Report*.

31 See above note No 2.

the Greek Constitution and the Convention regarding a fair trial related to a civil dispute (Art. 6, par. 1). In other words, the Court of Cassation declined to apply the relevant universal civil law which is (or should be) applicable to all: According to Art. 20 par. 1 of the Constitution anyone has the right to "legal protection" *by the courts*, and according to Art. 94 par. 3 "civil disputes are submitted to the civil courts".

The case raises general issues of compatibility of Shariʿa law within the Greek constitutional order, and human rights norms set by the ECHR and other international instruments, all of which ought to have precedence according to art. 28 par. 1 of the Constitution. The core issue of this case pertains to the position of a series of judgments that denied Muslims of Thrace access to the Greek Civil Code.

It has to be stressed that Muslim sacred law is not a source of law for civil courts, but applicable only by the Shariʿa courts, according to article 5 of Law 1920/1990. Moreover, no law provides that Shariʿa law can be applied to any litigant who takes recourse to the civil courts. Indeed there has been a long discussion of whether the jurisdiction of the mufti should be mandatory or concurrent. In a series of cases the Court of Cassation has ruled that the sacred law has to be applied mandatorily to Muslims.[32] On the other hand, the Court of Appeal of Thrace, in his decision no. 642/2009, upheld that a Muslim can draft a public will, just like any other Greek citizen. It appears that the Court of Cassation has been protecting the status quo of so-called 'minority protection' by not allowing the very minorities the protection of their choice, namely Greek Civil law. Under this restrictive and segregational approach, the Shariʿa law and the mufti's jurisdiction are being interpreted as exclusive. The Commissioner for Human Rights of the Council of Europe also made reference to the strict implementation of Muslim law in Greece:[33]

The Commissioner is aware that the decision to proceed to the application of Shariʿa Law in family and inheritance law matters may be taken by members of the Muslim minority in Thrace, who have, in principle, the right to choose between Greek civil law and Shariʿa Law. It is to be noted, however, that exceptions occur in matters relating to inheritance law where the Shariʿa Law is strictly applied.

---

32 Court of Cassation, judgments 1097/2007, 1497/2013, 1862/2013 and Court of Appeals of Thrace judgment 245/2015, among others. For a critical overview of the jurisprudence see Kalambakou. "Equality confronting religious pluralism," 297–302. On the recent case law see Pantelidou, "Regulations on inheritance relations of the Greek Muslims," 809.

33 Hammarberg, *Report*, par. 41.

What is striking is that the Court of Cassation asserts that Muslims have no right to draft any will except those acknowledged by Shari'a law and article 5, Law 1920. In other words, they cannot choose to come under the jurisdiction of Greek Civil law. This interpretation cannot be founded on any legal norm, as there is no law that forbids Muslims to draft any other will except those that the mufti would have jurisdiction upon. If there was such a law, it would certainly be considered segregationist. The jurisdictional practice that imposed this segregation should be reviewed for being discriminatory.

The mandatory division of jurisdiction between Muslims and others (namely mostly Christians) is often presented by the Court of Cassation as stemming from international obligations. However there are no such international legal obligations. None of the relevant legal instruments (namely the Treaty of Athens, 1923, the Treaty of Sevres 1920/1923 and the Treaty of Lausanne, 1923) provides for a *compulsory* jurisdiction of the mufti or for the *mandatory* applicability of Shari'a law, even *against the express wish of the members of the minority* themselves. Even if such an interpretation was valid in the beginning of the 20th century until 1945, the new international law of human rights stemming from the Universal Declaration of Human Rights (1948) and all relevant legal instruments (UN and Council of Europe), created a new legal order within which all previous engagements have to be interpreted accordingly. There is no need to make detailed reference to treaty international law and the *clausula rebus sic stantibus*, according to article 62 of the Convention of Vienna (1969). In that sense, Article 4, Law 147/1914 and Law 1920/1991 have to be interpreted under contemporary human rights law, which has been introduced into the Greek legal order. Therefore the mandatory implementation of Shari'a *does not comply* with fundamental legal principles and norms.

9 The Failed Citizenship

Equality before the law and the principle of non-discrimination are pillars of democracy and rule of law. A pluralistic society also demands special treatment for those who have special needs. Minority rights are granted when minority characteristics, such as language, national belonging or religion are not just tolerated but require positive action from state authorities. However, the enjoyment of minority rights cannot contravene the substance of general human rights.

The jurisdiction of the mufti for Muslim personal status in Thrace, as it is applied by the Greek juridical authorities, has a mandatory character for all Muslims which results in denial of justice for those who would otherwise opt to submit their cases before the general civil courts. In the case presented above (*Molla Sali v Greece*), the freedom of a Muslim of Thrace to opt for one or the other law in accordance to international human rights law is essential for the whole political program that civic citizenship entails: Namely, a global equality of citizens before the law, beyond origin or religion.[34] The prevailing judicial practice that breaches the human rights of the members of the Muslim minority fragments the uniform citizenship and undermines/frustrates the legitimate expectation that fundamental norms of rule of law are universally applicable. It can be also asserted that the Court of Cassation by upholding that Shari'a law has to be applied even against the wish of the testator brought severe interference with the right of all Muslims of Greek citizenship to have fair proceedings.

The mandatory referral to Shari'a law by the Greek courts against the wishes of the litigant and the elimination of the legal effects already produced by the civil courts rulings annul the context of 'active citizenship' that presupposes active civic membership within a given society and legal order. It also contravenes international human rights law. The special position of the Shari'a law within the Greek legal order stems from international obligations of Greece, dating from 1913 and 1923, as part of the minority protection framework granted to Muslims of Thrace. These international obligations have to be seen in light of human rights law that has evolved after 1945 and constitutes the corner stone of the present Greek constitutional legal order. Minority rights have a place within this legal order to the extent that there is no breach of fundamental rights granted to all, with no discrimination. As the Commissioner for Human Rights put it,

> any obligations that may arise out of the 1923 Lausanne Peace Treaty, or any other early 20th century treaty, should be viewed and interpreted in full and effective compliance with the subsequent obligations undertaken by the ratification of European and international human rights instruments.[35]

Then, as already said, the non-discrimination principle has to be tested: The restrictions against Muslim (female) plaintiffs from having access to Civil Courts systematically undermines the equality of individual Muslim women when Shari'a law is applied. It is also worth noting that, while women have the choice to appeal to the civil court, in practice they face social pressures to

34 Christopoulos, *Who is a Greek citizen?*

35 Hammarberg, *Report*, para. 41.

appeal before the mufti. The UN Human Rights Committee commented on this issue, urging Greece "to increase the awareness of Muslim women of their rights and the availability of remedies, and to ensure that they benefit from the provisions of Greek civil law".[36]

The ECtHR adopted most of these comments: It upheld that there was violation of the right to property in conjunction to the prohibition of discrimination. Most important, the Court said "Refusing members of a religious minority the right to voluntarily opt for and benefit from ordinary law amounts not only to discriminatory treatment but also to a breach of a right of cardinal importance in the field of protection of minorities, that is to say the right to free self-identification" (para. 157).

An amendment to the Mufti's law, anticipating the ECtHR judgment, was submitted in December 2017 before the Parliament and finally adopted by Law 4511/2018. It made clear that the civil courts will have competence by default for all civil disputes, unless both of the litigants make an agreement to have their case adjudicated by the mufti. Moreover, all wills drafted by a Muslim can be subject to civil law. By a Presidential Decree the mufti's court procedure will be also regularised. After the implementation of the new law which commenced in October 2018 through a new amendment to the law, it is expected that the number of cases brought before the mufti will be considerably decreased. However, the questions of incompatibility of the content of the applicable law by the Mufti will be still remaining open.

10 Conclusions

The era after the population exchange of 1923 was marked by a drastic decrease of the Muslim population in Greece and the minoritisation of the Muslims of Thrace (and after 1947 of the Muslims of the Dodecanese islands). Hence, the Muslim minority became part of a political balance of bilateral relations between Greece and Turkey and its welfare is safeguarded by an old-fashioned legal status stemming from the Treaty of Lausanne. On the other hand, the arrival in Greece after the 1990s of hundreds of thousands of Muslim immigrants seeking political asylum or economic prosperity has created a 'new Muslim minority' which struggles for a better future within the Greek society. Today, the legal position of Muslims in Greece is governed by a fragmented legal framework, outside and inside Thrace. As far as the latter is regarded, the

36 Human Rights Committee, 2005, (ICCPR) 'Greece', Concluding observations, 25/04/2005, CCPR/CO/83/GRC, Geneva: United Nations, par. 8.

jurisdiction of the mufti is one of the most ambivalent characteristics of minority protection, insofar as it contradicts fundamental human rights.

For long the Greek law did not provide for the application of Shari'a law by civil courts. Often, the Court of Cassation was introducing exemptions to the universal applicability of the Civil Code based on a segregation of 'Greek' and 'Muslim' law. Citizens are seen as belonging to closed communities, subject to different legal orders. Human rights standards are bent according to religious affiliation. This situation amounted to an imposed division between Greek citizens on religious grounds, contradicting the Constitution and the Convention under the scope of discrimination on the ground of religious identity (ECHR, Art. 14). Yet Islam is still perceived as incompatible with the prevailing Christian/Greek identity, which makes it difficult for Muslims to fully enjoy Greek citizenship. Although the new regulations will settle several issues of incompatibility with fundamental human rights principles, the Greek governments seem to suffer from inertia, as they remain reluctant to acknowledge and incorporate the transformations which in the near future, if not today, will characterise Greek Islam.

Bibliography

Christopoulos, Dimitris. *Who is a Greek citizen?* Athens: Vivliorama, 2011 [in Greek].

Christopoulos, Dimitris and Konstantinos Tsitselikis. "Impasses of treatment regarding minorities and *homogeneis* in Greece." *Jahrbücher für Geschichte und Kultur Südosteuropas* 5 (2003): 81–93.

El Kosheri, Ahmed Sadek. "Islamic Schools of Law" In *Islamic Law and its reception by the courts in the West*, edited by Christian v. Bar, 43. Köln/Munich: Karl Heymanns Verlag KG, 1999.

Hammarberg, Thomas. *Commissioner for Human Rights of the Council of Europe, Report following his visit to Greece on 8–10 December 2008, Issue reviewed: Human rights of minorities*, CommDH(2009)9. Strasbourg: Council of Europe, 2009.

Hunault, Michel. *Freedom of religion and other human rights for non-Muslim minorities in Turkey and for the Muslim minority in Thrace (Eastern Greece)*, Parliamentary Assembly, Committee on Legal Affairs and Human Rights, Report, Doc 11860, 21.4.2009. Strasbourg: Council of Europe, 2009.

Kalambakou, Eleni. "Equality confronting religious pluralism: exceptions from general and neutral laws due to religion." PhD diss., Aristotle University of Thessaloniki, 2014 [in Greek].

Kotzabasi, Athina. *The famity legal relations of the Greek Muslims.* Thessaloniki: Paratirirtis, 2003 [in Greek].

Ktistakis, Yannis. *Charia, Tribunaux religieux et droit grec.* Istanbul: Istos, 2013.

Pavlou, Miltos and Dimitris Christopoulos. "Introduction." In *Greece of migration* edited by Dimitris Christopoulos and M. Pavlou, 29–38. Athens: Kritiki, 2004 [in Greek].

Pantelidou, Kalliroi. "Regulations on inheritance relations of the Greek Muslims." *Efarmoges Astikou Dikaiou* 10–11 (2014): 809–822.

Sakellariou, Alexandros. "Islamophobia in Greece. National Report." In *European ispamophobia report,* edited by E. Bayrakli and F. Hafez. 200–18. Istanbul: SETA, 2015.

Tsitselikis, Konstantinos. "Citizenship in Greece. Present challenges for future changes." In *Multiple Citizenship As A Challenge To European Nation-States,* edited by D. Kalekin-Fishman and P. Pitkänen, 45–170. Rotterdam: SensePublishers, 2006.

Tsitselikis, Konstantinos. "Seeking To Accommodate Shari'a Within A Human Rights Framework: The Future Of The Greek Shari'a Courts." *Journal of Law and Religion,* XXVII (2012): 341–360.

Tsitselikis, Konstantinos. *Old and New Islam in Greece. From traditional minorities to immigrant newcomers.* Leiden/Boston: Martinus Nijhoff, 2012.

Tsitselikis, Konstantinos and Alexandros Sakellariou. "Greece" In *Yearbook of Muslims in Europe,* vol. VIII, edited by Oliver Scharbrodt et al., 324–335. Leiden/Boston: Brill, 2017.

Islamic Law as Indigenous Law: Sharīʿa Courts in Israel from a Postcolonial Perspective

Ido Shahar

1 Introduction[1]

During the past three decades, legal historians and anthropologists have devoted much attention to the connection between law and colonialism.[2] Their main focus has been the development of legal systems in a colonial context. Laura Nader, Sally F. Moore, and Martin Chanock, among many others, have written monographs about the mechanisms and processes that led to the consolidation of "customary law," or "indigenous law," alongside – or, to be more precise, under – European colonial law.[3] Their main argument is that customary/indigenous law is not an authentic or original remnant of a traditional legal system. Rather, it is the outcome of the asymmetrical power relationship between the (colonial) ruler and the ruled. Therefore, the attempt to present customary/indigenous law as a "pure" legal system reflecting the values and points of view of the colonised society is to be regarded as ideological rhetoric.

These studies are founded on three premises. The first is that "law" constitutes the "cutting edge of colonialism,"[4] so to understand the nature of colonial rule and the ideological concepts underlying it, the legal systems developed by it must be studied. Second, indigenous legal systems, being a product of asymmetrical power relations and colonisation, are necessarily anchored in the colonial and postcolonial legal context and cannot be viewed as autonomous or

---

1 This chapter is a revised version of an article that was published by *Journal of Levantine Studies*: "Islamic law as indigenous law: The shari'a courts in Israel from a postcolonial perspective," *Journal of Levantine Studies* 5, no. 1 (December 2015): 83–106. I am grateful for the editors of JLS and for the Van Leer Institute in Jerusalem for granting the permission to republish it in this volume.

2 The concept "colonialism" is here defined broadly as "unequal relationships between two or more groups, characterised not only by one group controlling the other group/s, but also by an attempt by the controlling group to force its own cultural order on the other group/s." Merry, "Law and Colonialism," 894. For a comprehensive survey of research studies on the development of legal systems in colonial contexts, see Benton, *Law and Colonial Cultures*.

3 See Nader, *Harmony Ideology*; Moore, *Social Facts and Fabrications*; Chanock, *Law, Custom and Social Order*.

4 Chanock, *Law, Custom and Social Order*, 4.

 | DOI:10.1163/9789004398269_006

as representing continuous, unchanging tradition.[5] The third premise is that despite the asymmetrical power relationship characteristic of the colonial reality, indigenous courts subjected to colonial legal systems frequently developed into sites of opposition where indigenous peoples succeeded in challenging old and new power structures.[6]

Indeed, as shown by a great number of studies published since 1990, colonial legal systems, which incorporated indigenous legal systems, "constituted a vehicle simultaneously of governmentality and of its subversion, of subjection and emancipation, of dispossession and reappropriation."[7] In recent years this perspective has also been employed in research into the development of the legal systems in the Middle East.[8]

Despite the significant colonial chapter in the history of Israel/Palestine (the period of the British Mandate, 1918–1948), and despite the quasi-colonial arrangements introduced in the State of Israel into family law (expanded on below), the functioning and condition of the sharīʿa courts in Israel have yet to be methodically analysed in the context of the postcolonial paradigm.[9] Accordingly, this chapter intends to show that studying this system through the postcolonial prism of legal history and anthropology provides interesting insights into the characteristics and functioning of the sharīʿa courts in Israel.

To avoid the debate regarding whether Zionism is a colonial movement and whether Israel is a colonial state,[10] the situation of the sharīʿa courts in Israel is here defined as a quasi-colonial reality. The chapter aims to demonstrate that, as in other colonial contexts, the space of these "indigenous" courts in Israel is Janus-faced and paradoxical: it constitutes a site of state intervention and control and, simultaneously, a site of agency, autonomy, and opposition. Indeed, as illustrated recently by Moussa Abou Ramadan, the sharīʿa courts in

5 Sierra, "Indian Rights and Customary Law in Mexico," 229.

6 Merry, "Law and Colonialism," 895.

7 Comaroff, "Colonialism, Culture and the Law," 307. See also, for example, the articles published in Lazarus-Black and Hirsch, *Contested States*.

8 See, e.g., Christelow, *Muslim Law Courts and the French Colonial State in Algeria*; Fluehr-Lobban, *Islamic Law and Society in the Sudan*; Messick, *The Calligraphic State*; Weiss, *In the Shadow of Sectarianism*.

9 This lacuna is even more marked in light of the considerable attention devoted in recent years to the study of various legal issues during the British Mandate period. See, for example, Likhovski, *Law and Identity in Mandate Palestine*; Likhovski, *Tax Law and Social Norms in Mandatory Palestine and Israel*; Shamir, *The Colonies of Law*.

10 In the 1980s and 1990s, quite a heated debate raged on this issue. See, for example, Shafir, "Zionism and Colonialism."

Israel constitute hybrid institutions that merge not only legal cultures but also ideological agendas.[11]

The chapter opens with a brief review of the status of the sharīʿa courts in the Ottoman Empire, expanding on the ramifications of the administrative and legal reforms (*tanẓīmāt*) carried out in the empire in the second half of the nineteenth century. This will be followed by a short discussion of developments in the sharīʿa court system in Palestine during the Mandate period. The chapter will conclude by looking at the status of the sharīʿa courts in the State of Israel and discussing similarities between these courts and other customary/indigenous court systems that developed in colonial realities.

2 Reforming the Sharīʿa Courts at the Close of the Ottoman Empire: an Ottoman Project in the Spirit of Western Colonialism

A broad review of the status and functioning of sharīʿa courts (or sharīʿa councils, as they were called) in the Ottoman Empire prior to the modern era is beyond the scope of this chapter. For our purposes, suffice it to say that these institutions, which enjoyed far-reaching judicial and administrative authority before modern times, had seen dramatic transformations during the nineteenth century. Throughout the second half of that century, the Ottoman authorities embraced ambitious reforms, with the aim of centralizing the power structure of the empire and increasing its efficiency. As part of these reforms, modernised administrative mechanisms that left a deep imprint on political, social, and economic life in the empire were implemented. The Ottoman legal system in particular underwent extensive transformations: its structure was changed as new judicial institutions (*nizamiye* courts) of different types (civil, criminal, commercial, and so on) were set up alongside the sharīʿa courts. These courts were provided with designated codices, which were formulated along the lines of Western examples.[12]

Following the establishment of nizamiye courts, the sharīʿa courts were turned, in practice, into family courts whose jurisdiction was restricted to matters of personal status and the regulation of endowments (*awqāf*). Although the substantive law applied by the sharīʿa courts was officially reformed only in 1917, on the eve of the dissolution of the Ottoman Empire, even prior to the publication of the new code of personal status (the Ottoman Law of Family

11 Abou Ramadan, "Islamic Legal Hybridity."

12 See Rubin, *Ottoman Nizamiye Courts*.

Rights of 1917, henceforth OLFR),[13] the sharīʿa courts were greatly affected by the reforms implemented in other areas of the law.[14] Some of the new codices that were promulgated, such as the *Mejelle*,[15] were also implemented in sharīʿa courts. In addition, as part of the efforts at modernisation, rationalisation, and standardisation, new operating practices were also implemented in all aspects of the activity of the sharīʿa courts: court hearing procedure, documentation, *qāḍī* training, *qāḍī* term of office, payment of court levies, and so forth.[16]

The tanẓīmāt have been revisited in recent years by scholars studying the Ottoman Empire. These wide-reaching reforms are no longer perceived as a simple process of "Westernisation" but rather as a pronounced "Ottoman project" that occurred against the background of a longstanding, rich tradition of implementing administrative reforms and amendments.[17] This new perspective aims to show that even if the tanẓīmāt reforms were carried out under Western inspiration, they assumed an "Ottoman guise": the models were processed and adapted to the circumstances, cultural perceptions, and social, economic, and political structures that existed in the empire.[18]

Even if we accept this new approach to understanding the tanẓīmāt reforms (which this writer does), it cannot be disputed that they were effected under Western inspiration and that practices and perceptions that were prevalent in the colonial space were also prevalent in the nineteenth-century Ottoman Empire.[19] The reformers, who belonged to the empire's intellectual elite – most of whom were educated in the West – had internalised Western perceptions of the sharīʿa as being an outdated, anachronistic legal system. As a result, when taking on the task of modernising sharīʿa law, they tended to imitate Western models. As has been noted by many postcolonial scholars, these models were based on notions of modernisation – and even more so, on *practices* of modernisation – that were conceived, developed, tested, and applied in the colonial context.[20]

In the spirit of postcolonial scholarship, I would like to further argue that the process the sharīʿa underwent during the tanẓīmāt reforms is to a large

13 Ottoman Law of Family Rights [OLFR] (1917) – *Dustur*, 2nd series, vol. 9, 762–783.

14 Agmon, "Batey ha-din ha-sharyim be-Falastin be-sof ha-tkufa ha-Otomanit."

15 Mejelle (1869–1876) – *Mecelle-i Ahkam Adliye* (Istanbul: Mahmut Bey, 1909).

16 See Agmon, "Recording Procedures;" Agmon, *Family and the Courts*.

17 Agmon, "Recording Procedures," 334.

18 See, for example, Deringil, "'They Live in a State of Nomadism and Savagery';" Evered, *Empire and Education under the Ottomans*.

19 See, e.g., Ozbek, "Policing the Countryside;" Makdisi, "Ottoman Orientalism." See also Messick, *The Calligraphic State*, 54–72.

20 See, e.g., Dirks, *Castes of Mind*.

extent reminiscent of the modernisation, codification, and bureaucratisation processes experienced by other customary legal systems under colonial rule. The attitude of Western policymakers toward Islamic law was essentially similar to their attitudes toward other non-Western legal systems. Brinkley Messick notes the following:

> The attribution of an ossified character to Islamic law fit general Western conceptions of non-Western societies as either dormant (simple societies) or stagnant (traditional civilizations) until the enlivening moment of Western contact or colonization.[21]

A detailed examination of the processes that led to the shaping of "modern" sharīʿa law, as reflected in the Ottoman codes promulgated during the period of the reforms, shows a parallelism with that of "customary" laws being studied by legal anthropologists. Thus, for example, the colonial officials who participated in the codification of the customary legal system in Tanganyika perceived the results of their labour as

> not a new system invented by us, but a continuation of the judicial functions of native authority, which have existed ever since the emergence of those units possessing a common language, a single social system.[22]

In like manner, the Mejelle commission was of the frank opinion that "there was no need to establish a civil law in the Ottoman Empire, because such a law was already in existence, and all it needed was a convenient and orderly reediting."[23] As Messick shows, the Mejelle in fact diverged fundamentally from sharīʿa law prior to its promulgation and brought about deep, far-reaching changes in the way in which knowledge, justice, and law were perceived.[24] That being the case, one sees that the creation of the Mejelle and of customary law in Tanganyika shared a marked common denominator: legislators produced codes of laws that were, by and large, a "new creation" that changed prevailing customs and imparted new cultural perceptions, while viewing and presenting it as an old, unchanged legal system. Put differently, it was a matter of an "invention" of a new tradition presenting itself as an ancient one.[25]

---

21 Messick, The Calligraphic State, 59.

22 Moore, "Treating Law as Knowledge," 16.

23 Quoted in Goitein and Ben Shemesh, *Ha-mishpat ha-Muslemi bi-Medinat Yisrael*, 110 (my translation).

24 Messick, The Calligraphic State.

25 On the invention of tradition, see Hobsbawm and Ranger, *The Invention of Tradition*.

I do not seek to argue that the sharīʿa is a new creation that was shaped only in the nineteenth or twentieth century. Such an assertion would be as absurd as contending that the African tribes did not possess mechanisms for the resolution of conflicts and the maintenance of social order prior to their territories being occupied by the colonial powers. Furthermore, legal codes do not appear out of nowhere, neither in Tanganyika nor in Istanbul nor even in Jerusalem. Obviously, traditions cannot be presented as ancient if they have nothing in common (both procedurally and substantively) with the conventions and norms prevailing prior to their creation. Nonetheless, following in the footsteps of Messick, I would like to argue that Ottoman reformers approached sharīʿa law in a "colonial state of mind," and this largely shaped the characteristics of the reforms they introduced.[26]

Thus, the code designated for the sharīʿa courts, the OLFR of 1917 (which was promulgated together with the new Ottoman Code of Sharīʿa Procedure),[27] was based on the eclectic expedient embraced by the Ottoman legislators in order to "adapt it to the spirit of the time."[28] It drew from the four major schools of religious law within Sunni Islam, as well as from minority opinions that at times were chosen arbitrarily from various schools,[29] and hence constituted a revolutionary code of Muslim family law. As Messick shows, this closed formal code, which was promulgated with the sultan's signature, replaced the open flexible religious law developed by Islamic legal jurists. Statutory law thus came to replace jurists' law, and abstract analytical categories replaced the analogical case-specific thinking that had previously characterised the sharīʿa.

Furthermore, the OLFR was revolutionary from another perspective: the Ottoman reformers who compiled it aspired to turn it into a general family law that would apply to all the subjects of the empire, both Muslim and

26 Here it is also appropriate to emphasize the differences between the codification undergone by the Sharīʿa in the Ottoman Empire and that undergone by customary legal systems in Africa and elsewhere. In the latter case, the codification and "ascertainment" of customary law occurred in various populations and territories under the direct colonial rule of European powers. In contrast, the Ottoman Empire was never subjected at any stage to direct colonial rule. At the same time, as Messick shows, its economic, military, and technological inferiority to the West contributed to the adoption of "colonial" states of mind by its legislative elites.

27 Law of Procedure for Sharīʿa Courts (1917) – Dustur, 2nd series, vol. 9, 783–94.

28 As stated by the drafting committee of the Mejelle in the introduction to the codex (my translation).

29 This practice went even further than in the case of the compilation of the *Mejelle*, which was mostly grounded on Ḥanafī jurisprudence. It is no wonder, therefore, that Schacht described this expedient as "unrestrained eclecticism." See Schacht, *An Introduction to Islamic Law*, 106.

non-Muslim. Indeed, out of a total of 157 articles, about 30 relate specifically to Jews and Christians. Article 155 of the law explicitly declares that any provision of the law that is not specified as an exception is applicable to *all* the subjects of the empire. Moreover, Article 156 revokes the legal authority of "spiritual leaders" (i.e. "non-Muslim religious functionaries") in the matters of personal status of the members of their communities. It transpires, therefore, that the promulgation of the OLFR constituted a first step on the path to dissolving the Ottoman *millet* system and replacing it with a uniform family law applicable to all subjects of the empire.

Under the Ottoman Empire, the OLFR was never implemented in Palestine. It was, however, adopted in 1919 by the British Mandate authorities as the code that bound sharīʿa courts. Because the process of reforming family law was not completed by the Ottoman reformers prior to the dissolution of the empire, this – together with the development of relevant judicial mechanisms – became the inheritance of its successors, the colonial regimes and the nation-states that were established on its ruins. As shall be elaborated below, the British authorities in Palestine chose to implement some of the principles of the reform, while ignoring others.

3 The Legacy of the British Mandate: Islamic Law Encounters Colonial Politics

Although the British forces only completed their conquest of Palestine in September 1918, they began instituting colonial administrative mechanisms prior to that date (Jerusalem was captured in December 1917). Drawing on their rich experience in the field, they developed a strategy to consolidate their rule in Palestine without arousing the animosity of the local populations, especially that of the Muslims.[30] As they did in their other colonies, they proceeded to gain the support of the local elites, extending benefits and wide authority to them within their communities.[31] A key element in this process was the integration of the customary/religious/indigenous law of local communities into the colonial legal system while changing and adapting them to the needs of the "modern state." Such moves were always made with the active assistance of the representatives of those elites, who thereby attained great power both within their own communities and with the colonial administration.[32]

30 Kupferschmidt, *The Supreme Muslim Council*, 17; McTague, *British Policy in Palestine*, 2–3.
31 Hooker, *Legal Pluralism*, 56.
32 See Hooker, *Legal Pluralism*; Sartori and Shahar, "Legal Pluralism in Muslim Majority Colonies."

In Palestine the British came up against an especially complex reality. The millet system, an institutional legal arrangement that perfectly suited the principles of British colonial rule, was about to be revoked and replaced by a general family law (the OLFR). As a result the mandatory government faced a difficult dilemma. On the one hand, it could implement the ready-made codex received from the Ottoman legislature: a clear, accessible, formal code that was in keeping with Western judicial principles advocated by the British themselves. The temptation was obviously great. On the other hand, and perhaps no less tempting, there was the option to maintain the existing millet system that continued to function in actual practice and that apparently enjoyed the approval of all the religious communities in Palestine.[33]

The British Mandate authorities in Palestine were hesitant about the OLFR, as is illustrated by their initial decision, revoked a few months later, not to implement it.[34] The solution they eventually adopted reflects, perhaps, the complex political reality in which they were forced to function in Palestine: they chose "to have their cake and eat it." An ordinance published on 25 September, 1919, decreed that the OLFR would be implemented in Palestine, but solely in sharīʿa courts, and it would only apply to Muslims.[35] Stated differently, the British decided to adopt the OLFR in a very partial manner while continuing to maintain a millet-like system that granted legal autonomy in matters of personal status to the different religious communities. Accordingly, the articles in the OLFR relating to non-Muslims were abolished, and the sharīʿa courts were stripped of the redundant jurisdiction they had over members of these communities. This governmental move led, in practice, to the integration of the sharīʿa courts in the millet-like system and to the relegation of Muslim law (in its codified modern version) from the level of state law to that of indigenous law.

After taking the decision to preserve the quasi-millet structure of personal status law, the British were careful – during the entire period they ruled Palestine (1918–1948) – not to intervene in the religious laws of the various communities in general, and of the Muslims in particular. Nonetheless, the new political reality led to several essential changes. First, the British Mandate authorities stepped into the shoes of the Ottoman Ministry of Justice and of the Waqf Ministry and started managing Islamic religious matters in Palestine. They appointed Muslim clergy to supervise the sharīʿa courts and nominated new *qāḍīs* to hear cases. Furthermore, since all ties with the Ottoman Empire had been severed, and it was no longer possible to appeal against rulings given by the sharīʿa courts to the grand mufti (*Sheikh-al-Islam*) or to the court of

33 Eisenman, *Islamic Law in Palestine and Israel.*

34 See Abou Ramadan, "Islamic Legal Hybridity," 45.

35 Goadby, *International and Inter-Religious Private Law in Palestine*, 115.

cassation in Istanbul, a sharīʿa court of appeals was established in Jerusalem (1918). The appellate court replaced the Ottoman institutions of appeal, and it therefore had competence to review any decision made by any sharīʿa court in Palestine since the date of the occupation.[36] The Sharīʿa Court of Appeals had three members – a president and two permanent members.

Second, following the riots that erupted during the Nabī Mūsā celebrations of 1920,[37] the British wanted to appease the Muslims in Palestine. After consulting with several Muslim senior leaders, they decided to establish a new entity, the Supreme Muslim Council, which would enjoy wide competences in the management of Muslim religious matters in Palestine, including in the appointment of all the employees of the sharīʿa courts and waqf institutions (such as *qāḍīs*, supervisors, muftis, and waqf commissioners).[38] Although these appointments indeed required the authorisation of the Mandatory government, the establishment of the Supreme Muslim Council in fact granted the Muslim community in Palestine the autonomy in the management of its religious matters that it had previously lacked.

The intention of the British in establishing the Supreme Muslim Council was to create an apolitical administrative body in which the management of all Muslim religious affairs would be concentrated. Soon, however, it gained enormous political power under the charismatic leadership of its president, the grand muftī of Jerusalem, Hajj Amīn al-Ḥussaynī. The British initially acquiesced to this situation, but in 1937, following the publication of the Peel Commission Report, which described the Supreme Muslim Council as a "State within a State," they dismissed al-Ḥussaynī, expelled him from Palestine, and began closely monitoring the activities of the Council.[39]

There is no doubt that the policy employed by the Mandate authorities toward the sharīʿa courts had an enormous impact on the manner in which they developed. The code of law implemented through them during the British Mandate was indeed formulated and promulgated by the Ottoman reformers, not by British colonial officials. However, since it had never been applied in Palestine under the Ottomans, it was the British Mandate that transformed it from abstract words into a binding legal code. The authority of the sharīʿa

36 Kupferschmidt, The Supreme Muslim Council, 18–19.

37 The Nabī Mūsā celebrations (*mawsim*) were the most important popular Islamic event held in Palestine, attracting tens of thousands of believers from all over the country to the *makām* (the grave) of the prophet, adjacent to Jerusalem. In 1920 anti-British and anti-Zionist riots erupted during the celebrations. See al-Kayyālī, *Taʾrīkh Filasṭīn al-ḥadīth*, 148–149.

38 Vitta, *The Conflict of Laws in Matters of Personal Status in Palestine*, 102–104.

39 Peled, *Debating Islam in the Jewish State*, 6.

courts over non-Muslims was revoked, and the sharīʿa was relegated to the level of religious law, or of indigenous law applying solely to Muslims. At the same time, it appears that the authority of the sharīʿa courts in matters of Muslim personal status was broadened in comparison with the late Ottoman period.

The sharīʿa courts maintained their preeminence relative to that of other communities' courts[40] and even benefited from state allocations, again in contrast to the latter, which were funded independently by their communities.[41] The establishment of the Sharīʿa Court of Appeals in Jerusalem was a move of far-reaching legal and administrative significance, reflecting a process of localisation and reinforcement of the autonomy of the sharīʿa court system in Palestine during the Mandate period. The establishment of the Supreme Muslim Council also contributed to the furtherance of this trend. Moreover, the politicisation undergone by the council and the key role it played in the political struggle against Zionism turned the council and the sharīʿa courts it handled into important political institutions that were perceived as a symbol not only of values and of Islamic identity but also of Arab/Palestinian national identity.

To summarise, the British policy toward the sharīʿa courts in Palestine was ambivalent: it reflected the subordination of the sharīʿa courts to the colonial power structure, yet it undoubtedly incorporated many empowering elements that not only preserved the independence of the sharīʿa courts but also helped them develop into monopolistic institutions in the realm of the personal status of Muslims, and hence, into institutions with great community influence. As alluded to in the introduction, this ambivalence, so typical of indigenous legal systems in colonial contexts, would continue under Israeli rule, the period with which we shall now deal.

4 Islamic Law as Indigenous Law: the Sharīʿa Courts under Israeli Rule

The 1948 War and the establishment of the State of Israel also marked the destruction of the local Palestinian community. When the roar of the cannons subsided and the ceasefire agreements were signed, the dimensions of the catastrophe (*Nakba*) that had befallen the Palestinian community became clear:

40 The competences of the sharīʿa courts were determined in Article 52 of the Palestine Order in Council, 1922, and included exclusivity in matters of personal status of all Muslims in Palestine. In contrast, the competences of the rabbinical and Christian courts, determined in Articles 53 and 54, respectively, of the Palestine Order in Council included exclusive competence solely in some matters, and equal competence in others.

41 See Kupferschmidt, *The Supreme Muslim Council*, 87–88.

thousands had been killed in the fighting and clashes; approximately 450 villages (of the roughly 550 located in the area where the State of Israel was established) had been destroyed and ceased to exit; and about 700,000 Palestinians had fled or were exiled and had become refugees.[42]

The 150,000 Palestinians who remained within the boundaries of Israel discovered practically overnight that they had become aliens in their own motherland, an Arab-Palestinian minority in the newly established Jewish state. This population consisted mainly of fellahin and urban workers. The vast majority of the community's elite – including the members of the Supreme Muslim Council, *qāḍīs*, and other religious officials – had hurriedly left the country when the fighting began, leaving the community's social structure and political (and religious) leadership almost completely destroyed. The sharīʿa courts, which remained without functionaries, also stopped operating during the war. The renewal of jurisdiction in matters of the personal status of Muslims in the new Jewish state was left, therefore, to Israeli policymakers, who started searching for methods of assuming the management of the Muslim institutions in Israel even before the war was over.[43]

Accordingly, the newly established Israeli Ministry of Religion revived the activity of the sharīʿa courts in Nazareth and Acre as early as August 1948, appointing *qāḍīs* on its behalf. Steps were also taken to protect sites sacred to Islam, and an updated list of waqf assets in Israel was drawn up.[44] The Law and Administration Ordinance, the first act of legislation to be enacted by the Knesset, determined that the laws and regulations in force prior to 15 May, 1948, would continue to apply.[45] Thus, when the sharīʿa courts resumed activity, they continued to implement the Ottoman laws previously approved by the British mandatory government (the Mejelle, the OLFR, and the 1917 Ottoman Code of Sharīʿa Procedure). In 1950 two additional sharīʿa courts were established in Jaffa and Taybe, and a court of appeals was established in Jerusalem in 1953. When the pressure of work mounted in the first four sharīʿa courts, two further courts were established in 1971, in Haifa and Beersheba.[46] A seventh court was founded in Jerusalem in 1988, and another court was established in Bāqa al-Gharbiyya in 2006, bringing the number of regional sharīʿa courts in Israel to eight.

42 Morris, *The Birth of the Palestinian Refugee Problem*, 1.

43 Peled, *Debating Islam in the Jewish State*, 18.

44 Ibid., ch. 2.

45 Law and Administration Ordinance, no. 1 (5708–1948) – Laws of the State of Israel, vol. 1, 9.

46 Shaashua, *Batey ha-din ha-Muslemim bi-Medinat Yisrael*, 15–20.

Israeli legislators adopted Article 52 of the Palestine Order in Council, 1922–1947, granting the sharīʿa courts exclusive authority over all matters relating to the personal status of Muslims in the country.[47] Nevertheless, in 1965 the jurisdiction of the sharīʿa courts (and of other religious courts) was diminished by the Law of Succession, which required the advance agreement, in writing, of all parties involved in an inheritance case.[48] The Succession Law determined that without such an agreement, the case would be dealt with according to civil rather than religious law.[49] More than thirty-five years later, in November 2001, the Knesset enacted further legislation that had a dramatic effect on the jurisdictions of the sharīʿa courts. Amendment No. 5 of the Family Courts Law conferred on the Knesset equal competence in all matters of personal status of Muslims in Israel, with the exception of marriage and divorce. This amendment limited the previously exclusive jurisdiction of the sharīʿa courts in all matters of personal status, which now became concurrent in most matters.

Besides this direct restriction of the competences of the sharīʿa courts, a significant number of laws passed by the Knesset influenced their activity indirectly. Thus, for example, the Age of Marriage Law, 5710–1950, determined that the marriage of a minor girl under the age of eighteen constituted a criminal offence, and the offender, or whoever abetted such an action, would be liable to imprisonment for two years.[50] Not only was this law incompatible with the OLFR of 1917, which decrees that the legal age of marriage for females is seventeen years, it also transferred to a civil judge the right to allow a girl younger than eighteen to marry.[51]

In like manner, the Women's Equal Rights Law, 5711–1951,[52] prohibits polygamy and unilateral divorces (that is to say, without the consent of the wife), while the OLFR grants husbands both these rights. Be that as it may, it is important to stress that the criminality of a given action (for example, the unilateral divorce of a wife) does *not* invalidate it from the perspective of Islamic religious law. This means that a husband who divorces his wife unilaterally may

47 Palestine Order in Council (1922–1947), *Laws of Palestine*, vol. 3, 2569.

48 Succession Law (5725–1965) – *Sefer ha-hukim* (5725–1965), 446, 63.

49 See Layish, "Muslim Religious Jurisdiction in Israel," 70.

50 Until recently, the minimum age for marriage for girls was seventeen; Amendment no. 6 to the Age of Marriage Law equalized the minimum age of marriage for girls to that of boys, setting it at eighteen. See Age of Marriage Law, Amendment no. 6 (5773–2103) – *Sefer ha-hukim* (5773–2013), 2416, 58.

51 Like the Israeli law, the OLFR also allowed exceptions to the age limit: should the *qāḍī* examine the minor girl and find her grown up enough for marriage, he was authorized to allow it. The Israeli Age of Marriage Law revoked this right and transferred it to a civil judge. See Layish, "Maamad ha-isha ha-Muslemit be-veit ha-din ha-sharʿi be-Yisrael."

52 Women's Equal Rights Law (5711–1951) – *Sefer ha-hukim* (5711–1951), 82, 248.

have committed a criminal offence as well as a tort – and may indeed be liable to criminal charges and a compensation suit – but this does not change the fact that the pronounced divorce is perfectly valid.

In evaluating Israeli legislation concerning personal status matters, we may say that the Knesset was guided, in this field, by three principles: (1) it refrained from directly intervening in substantive religious law; (2) it passed civil laws whose declared purpose was to ensure equality between the sexes and prevent gender discrimination against women. Notably, while these laws were designed to be implemented in both civil and religious courts, they were *not* designed to restrict the authority of the religious courts; and (3) the Knesset determined sanctions in the Israeli Penal Code for specific actions and behaviours, such as the marriage of minor girls, polygamy, and the unilateral repudiation of a wife, even if religious law permitted them. This strategy of indirect legislation created a complex fabric of clearly contradictory religious precepts and civil and criminal laws that coexist without voiding each other. The result is that a heavy burden is placed on the High Court of Justice, which is often required "to put matters in order" and to decide between laws and between disputing courts.[53]

Although the Israeli policy-makers' decision to adhere to the Mandate quasi-millet system had probably very little to do with the status of Muslims in Israel,[54] the outcome of this decision was highly significant for the sharīʿa courts: it provided them with a protective umbrella not only against the threat of their abolition (a threat that materialised in countries such as Egypt and Libya, for example), but also against direct intervention in their applied law and in their rulings. In other words, with this choice Israeli policymakers granted, perhaps unintentionally, far-reaching legal and religious autonomy to the country's Muslims. In the reality of the Palestinian minority in Israel, this is by no means a trivial matter.

When comparing the status of sharīʿa law in Israel with that of indigenous law in colonial Africa and other colonial regions, many points of both similarity and difference emerge. A major point of difference is that in contrast to colonial officers, who busied themselves creating new "indigenous" legal codes, the State of Israel refrained from such an initiative, instead choosing to adopt a foreign code (OLFR), as transformed by the British Mandate. As noted, even when the Israeli legislators initiated far-reaching reforms in civil law, the status quo in substantive religious law was maintained.

In contrast, an important point of similarity between the pluralistic personal status system in place in Israel and that typifying European colonies in

53 See, for example, Woods, *Judicial Power and National Politics*, 29–57.

54 Friedman, "The Structural Foundation for Religio-Political Accommodation in Israel."

Africa and elsewhere is that in both, matters of personal status were precisely those where legal autonomy found expression.[55] Chanock points out that the colonial officers viewed issues of personal status as the most sensitive, reflecting indigenous cultural and moral perceptions more than any other area.[56] Accordingly, they made every effort to instill "British Morals" in the "natives," to make them "more respectable." He argues that matrimonial matters were the area in which colonial intervention in African society was most felt.[57]

As mentioned above, the Israeli authorities did not intervene directly in the Islamic codes. However, indirect legislation by the Knesset in certain matters is very reminiscent of the activity of the colonial administrators. Just as the British in Africa, "generally recognised indigenous law, with the exception of laws that violated British law or were 'repugnant to natural justice, equity or good conscience,'"[58] likewise the State of Israel outlawed certain behaviours and actions that were unacceptable in a "civilised society." This trend was re-affirmed in numerous rulings by the civil courts. Thus, for example, the High Court of Justice determined that polygamy is not a custom that can exist in a state desirous of being modern, and that if,

> a modern country such as the State of Israel saw a need to do away with the existing discrimination and to make polygamy illegal for all residents of the country, it cannot be accused of disregard, as it were, for the religious obligations of its Muslim citizens.[59]

In a similar vein, the District Court expressed a wish that "the *qāḍīs* in Israel would follow in the footsteps of Islamic religious reformers in the Muslim world who advocate for renewed *ijtihād* directed at adapting religion to the needs of modern life."[60]

A pronounced point of similarity between the sharīʿa court system in Israel and indigenous courts that were subordinated to colonial legal systems is the dialectic of control and resistance characteristic of both. As numerous studies in legal anthropology show, indigenous/customary legal systems in colonial contexts have a double, contradictory role: on the one hand, they serve as a

55 Chanock, *Law, Custom and Social Order*, 145; Gluckman, *The Ideas in Barotse Jurisprudence*, 64; Bohannan, *Justice and Judgment among the Tiv*, 72.

56 As has been shown, this perception was also the legacy of the Ottoman reformers.

57 Chanock, *Law, Custom and Social Order*, 145–160.

58 Merry, "Law and Colonialism," 897.

59 HCJ 49/54, quoted in Shaashua, *Batey ha-din ha-Muslemim bi-Mdinat Yisrael*, 41 (my translation).

60 Civil Case 376/59, quoted in Layish, "Ha-shiput ha-dati shel ha-Muslemim be-Yisrael," 32.

tool in the hands of the ruling group (or colonial power) for instilling norms, shaping identities, and gaining command and control; on the other hand, they open a door for the subordinate group to display resistance to the mechanisms of control and co-option of the state.[61]

An examination of the sharīʿa system in the Jewish state shows that it clearly fulfills this double, contradictory function. No doubt the sharīʿa courts in Israel are deprived of any formal autonomy: the state nominates its functionaries, pays their salaries, decides whether to enforce their rulings or not, and decides what in sharīʿa law is lawful and what is "unlawful." The fact that such state control is "mediated" by Muslim courts, where Muslim *qāḍīs* officiate and hand down rulings grounded on (allegedly) Muslim religious law, indeed helps to camouflage this control, but it does not change the basic power structure, and does not undermine the state's hegemony.[62]

And yet, despite this clear function of control that the sharīʿa courts fulfill for the State of Israel, they represent a kind of remote sphere, "out of sight, out of mind" that comes under only scanty surveillance and to which almost no attention is paid.[63] Thus it is perhaps not surprising to find that these courts are poorly supported in terms of budgeting, state-funded positions, and buildings, and that the bureaucratic handling of their needs is characterised by inaptitude and sluggishness.

This neglect, however, also expands the levels of freedom enjoyed by the employees (*qāḍīs* and other functionaries) of the sharīʿa court system. Indeed, the *qāḍīs* at the Israeli sharīʿa courts seem to benefit from the "advantages of marginality" – a term coined by Iris Parush in the context of the education of Jewish women in nineteenth-century Eastern Europe.[64] Parush demonstrates that, paradoxically, in certain situations it is precisely a condition of marginality that enables the weak/cast-off/inferior to improve their status. This contradictory outcome is achieved because socially marginal spheres, to which no importance is attached and no attention paid, are also the very ones where the mechanisms of control and supervision are less stringent.

61 See Lazarus-Black and Hirsch, *Contested States*; Merry, "Law and Colonialism."

62 Abou Ramadan, "Notes on the Anomaly;" Abou Ramadan, "The Sharīʿa in Israel."

63 The State Comptroller's Annual Report for 1995 devotes a whole chapter to the governance of the sharīʿa courts in Israel, presenting grave findings of neglect, irregularities, and lack of supervision. In practice, nothing much was done to change this reality, even after the promulgation of the report. See Ha-doh ha-shnati shel mevaker ha-medina, 46 [State comptroller's annual report 46] (Jerusalem: Official Press of the Government of Israel, 1996).

64 Parush, *Reading Jewish Women*.

Returning to the sharīʿa courts in Israel, it is not surprising to learn that in comparison with judges officiating in other Israeli courts, *qāḍīs* in Israel enjoy extremely broad judicial freedom, enabling them to carry out far-reaching reforms in both substantive and procedural law. In the Israeli context, since there is neither an Islamic legislature nor a sharīʿa council that may introduce changes to the applied sharīʿa law, reforms and changes in the material law employed in the sharīʿa courts are predominantly introduced on the *qāḍīs'* initiative.[65]

This broad judicial level of freedom is best exemplified in the issuance of no less than twelve "judicial decrees" (*marsūmāt qaḍāʾiyya*) by the former president of the Sharīʿa Court of Appeals, *Qāḍī Aḥmad Naṭūr*. With the approval of the other officiating *qāḍīs*, Naṭūr initiated the regulation of diverse topics by means of the dissemination of independent judicial decrees. The decrees covered a wide range of issues, such as the settlement of the will of an orphan grandson (judicial decree No. 3), matrimonial arbitration (judicial decree No. 5), annulment of a betrothal (judicial decree No. 8), and determination of fatherhood (judicial decree No. 10).[66]

As noted by several observers, the decrees were issued by the *qāḍīs* independently of Knesset legislation and of any other governmental ministry/agency/authority.[67] Indeed, as mechanisms of legal reform, the judicial decrees constitute an odd choice: the Israeli *qāḍīs* sought to initiate much-needed legal reforms, but they enacted these reforms neither by issuing court rulings – as judges usually do – nor by instigating legislation amendments. Instead, they took it upon themselves to reform the law independently and to do it by a quasi-legislative act. No wonder that some critics claimed that the issuance of the judicial decrees, being an act of legislation, violates the principle of separation of powers.[68] Putting aside the debate about the validity of the judicial decrees,[69] the very audacity of the Israeli *qāḍīs* in engaging themselves in the self-enactment of self-initiated legal reforms testifies to their sense of judicial autonomy.

65 See Abou Ramadan, "Notes on the Anomaly."

66 For details on all the judicial circulars, see Zahalka, *Batey ha-din ha-shariyim*, 51–59.

67 See, e.g., Abou Ramadan, "Judicial Activism;" Layish, "Adaptation of a Jurists' Law to Modern Times in an Alien Environment."

68 Abou Ramadan, "Judicial Activism," 287 n. 153.

69 The validity of the judicial circulars was recently dealt with by the High Court of Justice (P"D 3094/13, from March 9, 2015), in which it was stated by the Sharīʿa Courts' Administration (and approved by the HCJ) that the ruling according to the circulars is based on agreement among all the *qāḍīs* and that the circulars do not compel the *qāḍīs* to rule in a particular manner.

5 The Sharīʿa Courts in Israel as Sites of Resistance

This concluding section focuses on two particular sharīʿa courts, in Beersheba and in West Jerusalem, where I conducted participant observations.[70] I argue, as mentioned above, that viewed from a postcolonial perspective, these two courts clearly constitute arenas of both control and autonomous action. Since the function of control has been dealt with previously by other writers,[71] I will concentrate here on the function of resistance.

Many of the litigants who appeal to the sharīʿa courts seek support in various matters: spouses finding themselves in matrimonial conflict ask for the court's help in solving their disputes; wives, deserted by their husbands, seek financial help in the form of an alimony decree; minor girls may seek the protection of the court and ask it to prevent their being forced to marry an unwanted husband; and a group of kin may ask for the court's guidance in devising an inheritance in a proper *sharʿī* manner.

All these are quite common appeals that may be dealt with by the sharīʿa courts on a daily basis. The sharīʿa courts in Beersheba and Jerusalem, however, also provide support for different types of distress and need. In Beersheba, for example, the bedouin population of the Negev uses the sharīʿa court for the purpose of maintaining important aspects of their "traditional" way of life. This way of life is threatened in the modern era, and not only in Israel.[72] One way to preserve it is to stick to tribal social logic that emphasises the size of the patrilineal descent group as a criterion for social status.[73]

In other words, it appears that Bedouin men are generally striving to maintain large families with a significant number of offspring.[74] This task is difficult to achieve, however, because state law bans polygamy and criminalises it. How does all this relate to the sharīʿa court in Beersheba? It seems that with the aid of this institution, which turns a blind eye toward certain practices, Bedouin men manage to literally "dance at two weddings at the same time." The Bedouins manoeuvre between customary bedouin law (*ʿurf*), state law, and sharīʿa law, and this manoeuvring allows many of them to maintain large polygamous families without paying the price of legal sanctions. Furthermore,

---

70 Participant observation was conducted in the Beersheba sharīʿa court in 1996: see Shahar, "Trilemma be-veyt ha-din;" and in the Jerusalem sharīʿa court during the years 1998–1999 and 2001–2005. For a detailed description of my field research in the Jerusalem court, see Shahar, *Legal Pluralism in the Holy City*.

71 See, e.g., Abou Ramadan, "The Sharīʿa in Israel"; Dumper, *Islam and Israel*.

72 See e.g., Cole, "Where Have the Bedouin Gone?"

73 See Kressel, *Descent through Males*.

74 Abu Rabia, "Redefining Polygamy among the Palestinian Bedouins in Israel."

they may even find some unexpected benefits in this process: they may become eligible for double and triple allowances of various kinds from the National Insurance Institute.[75]

In Jerusalem, in contrast, where the Israeli-Palestinian conflict has become the organizing principle that shapes all aspects of life in the city, the Israeli sharīʿa court constitutes an important "mechanism of normalisation." This court – which was initially viewed with suspicion and distrust by the Muslim-Palestinian population, who saw its establishment in the late 1980s as just another attempt to marginalise Islamic institutions in the city – has gained considerable legitimacy among this population in recent years. Indeed, the ban on appealing to Israeli courts is still intact in Jerusalem, but it appears that the sharīʿa court has been excluded from it and that Muslim Jerusalemites have flooded this court in recent years with thousands of appeals.[76]

I argue that the recently achieved "popularity" of this court among Muslim Jerusalemites emanates from its perceived functionality. It seems that its presiding *qāḍīs* (and its personnel in general) have made use of their broad agency to turn this court into a friendly arena for this population. They not only went out of their way to facilitate easy access to the court, to litigant-friendly procedures, and to easy-to-use, functional decisions, they also "enlisted" the court, so to speak, for the mission of resisting anti-Palestinian policies employed by the Israeli authorities in Jerusalem.

To briefly illustrate this, I present two short excerpts drawn from an interview I conducted with a Palestinian social worker. This man, who was employed by the Jerusalem municipality, was in charge of social services in one of the neighbourhoods of East Jerusalem and was therefore a frequent visitor in the court. The interview took place in the court's waiting room on 3 October, 2002. The conversation was mainly in Arabic (with a few Hebrew words interlaced in the social worker's discourse):

> We had a request to take care of a family that was residing in al-'Azariyya.
>
> *Who requested that you take care of them?*
>
> Never mind who. A request. They were in a very dire situation: their two children suffered from mental deficiency – the daughter from a severe deficiency, she couldn't take care of herself at all. Neither the mother nor the father could take care of the children. Both were incapable – they didn't work, [were] unable to support themselves. So, we were asked to

75 See Shahar, "Trilemma be-beyt ha-din"; Soffer and Shalev, *Mimusha ba-poal shel tviʿat ha-shiva ha-Falastinit.*

76 Shahar, "A Tale of Two Courts."

help them. The problem was, that they were from al-'Azariyya – a neighborhood just outside of the municipal borders of Jerusalem – and therefore beyond our jurisdiction. I told them: "I cannot help you. You live in al-'Azariyya. My hands are tied."

Did they have blue ID cards?

Yes, they had. However, the ministry of interior affairs refused to register their children on their parents' ID cards, claiming that they live outside of Israel.[77]

Eventually we found a solution: I talked with [he names a sharʿī advocate], and I asked him to file a suit on the wife's behalf here [in the Israeli sharīʿa court in West Jerusalem] claiming that she and her husband are at odds, and that she had left the nuptial house. The advocate first filed a suit for maintenance and permission to rent a house, and the woman was granted that. We then instructed her to rent a house in the Old City. Not a house, a tiny room, two meters by three. Clearly you cannot live with two children in such a place. But after she had a rental contract, the advocate filed another suit – this time for custody.

The qāḍī asked for our review of the matter, and we recommended that the children be in their mother's custody. He [the qāḍī] wanted to speak with the parents, but we explained the situation to him and asked him to run things as quickly as he can, because the children were in such a dire situation. And he did – the whole affair only took a month or so. After the mother had the custody decision, she then went with me to the Ministry of the Interior and we registered her children on her ID card as

77 Since Palestinian residents of annexed East Jerusalem were granted the status of "permanent residents," rather than full-fledged Israeli citizenship, their ID cards – and hence their right to reside in the city (and in Israel) – could be sequestrated if they moved the "centre of their lives" to places outside Israel for a period of longer than seven years. The Ministry of the Interior, in collaboration with Jerusalem's municipal authorities and the National Insurance Institute (NII), therefore conducted a systematic review in the mid-1990s of the places of residence of Jerusalemite Palestinians holding Israeli ("blue") ID cards, in order to facilitate the sequestration of the ID cards of those who did not reside within the Israeli municipal borders of the city. This policy came to be known as "the quiet deportation." Regarding the quiet deportation, see B'Tselem, "The Quiet Deportation: Revocation of Residency of East Jerusalem Palestinians" (1997), accessed 26 June, 2017, http://www.btselem.org/Download/199704_Quiet_Deportation_Eng.doc; B'Tselem, "The Quiet Deportation Continues: Revocation of Residency and Denial of Social Rights of East Jerusalem Palestinians" (1998), accessed 26 June, 2017, http://www.btselem.org/Download/199809_Quiet_Deportation_Continues_Eng.doc; see also Zinc, "A Quiet Transfer."

> residing in her Old City house. Only then could we take the kids out of the house and transfer them to a proper institution.

And the second excerpt:

> We had a wife with a blue ID card married to a husband with an orange ID card.[78] They were living in Ramallah, but both were working in Jerusalem, in professional jobs. They were working all day in Jerusalem, and then traveling late at night back to Ramallah, only to return to Jerusalem very early in the morning after. So, this couple had a baby girl. Her mother wanted to register her on her blue ID card, so that she can get child benefits and national and health insurance. They told her: "NO! You live in Ramallah." What did they do? She allegedly left her husband and went to live with her family in Jerusalem. She then filed a suit for maintenance and custody. After she had her custody order, she registered her baby girl in her ID card. Then they said, "That's it. We have reconciled." [My interviewee said this in Hebrew (zehu, hishlamnu) and then in Arabic (khalas, istalaḥna).] Then they went back to living together.

These two short excerpts illustrate clearly, I believe, that the Israeli sharīʿa court in West Jerusalem has indeed become an important arena for resisting anti-Palestinian policies in Jerusalem. I suspect that the social worker, whom I interviewed, knew very well that such plots, designed to provide remedies for Palestinians who were threatened with denial of their permanent residency status, could only have worked in a court that is sympathetic to their cause. As we have seen, the social worker, the *qāḍī*, and the entire sharīʿa court staff – all Muslim Palestinian citizens of Israel – made use of their position of authority within a state institution or within the municipality to undermine the logic that guides the state's operation. It is this capacity for resistance from within that turned the sharīʿa court in West Jerusalem into such a "popular" institution among Muslim Jerusalemites.

Discussing the political and legal intricacies of unified Jerusalem in depth, or the complex situation of the Bedouin in the Negev, is beyond the scope of this chapter. For our purposes here, the above examples from the sharīʿa courts in Beersheba and Jerusalem should suffice to illustrate that the Israeli sharīʿa courts, like so many other "indigenous courts" studied by postcolonial researchers, are indeed "Janus-faced" institutions that serve opposing functions:

78 This means that he is a denizen of the West Bank and is therefore not entitled to the benefits that come with the blue (Israeli) ID card.

they serve as both mechanisms of colonial control and mechanisms of resistance that strive to undermine this control.[79]

To conclude, although the sharīʿa courts are perceived by Israeli decision makers as less important institutions than other, more pronounced, spheres of control and struggle (such as the labour market, the education system, or the general legal system), it is precisely because of this that their importance, from the point of view of Muslim Palestinians in Israel, is not negligible at all. In the context of the troubled relationships between the State of Israel and its Palestinian subjects – citizens and permanent residents alike – it seems that the sharīʿa courts have come to constitute one of the most effective arenas of autonomous action. No doubt the *qāḍīs* and the other personnel of these courts achieved this status by capitalising not only on their authority but also on the "advantages of marginality."

This conclusion, as this chapter has sought to demonstrate, grew directly from analysis employing a postcolonial framework, which has both provided us with a fresh perspective on an extensively studied institution and brought to light some characteristics of these courts' operations that had not been dealt with previously. I believe the utility of the postcolonial perspective calls, therefore, for further postcolonially informed research into the functioning of the sharīʿa courts in Israel.

Bibliography

Abou Ramadan, Moussa. "Judicial Activism of the Sharīʿa Appeal Court in Israel 1994–2001: Rise and Crisis." *Fordham International Law Journal* 27, no. 1 (2003): 254–303.

Abou Ramadan, Moussa. "The Sharīʿa in Israel: Islamization, Israelization and the Invented Islamic Law." *UCLA Journal of Islamic and Near Eastern Law* 5 (2005–2006): 81–105.

Abou Ramadan, Moussa. "Notes on the Anomaly of the Sharīʿa Field in Israel." *Islamic Law and Society* 15, no. 1 (2008): 84–111.

Abou Ramadan, Moussa. "Islamic Legal Hybridity and Patriarchal Liberalism in the Sharīʿa Courts in Israel." *Journal of Levantine Studies* 4, no. 2 (2015): 39–67.

Abu Rabia, Rawiya. "Redefining Polygamy among the Palestinian Bedouins in Israel: Colonialism, Patriarchy, and Resistance." *Journal of Gender, Social Policy & the Law* 19, no. 2 (2001): 459–493.

Agmon, Iris. "Recording Procedures and Legal Culture in the Late Ottoman Sharīʿa Court of Jaffa, 1865–1890." *Islamic Law and Society* 11, no. 3 (2004), 333–377.

79 John L. Comaroff, "Foreword," ix.

Agmon, Iris. *Family and the Courts: Legal Culture and Modernity in Late Ottoman Palestine.* Syracuse, NY: Syracuse University Press, 2006.

Agmon, Iris. "Batey ha-din ha-sharʿyiim be-Falastin be-sof ha-tkufa ha-Otomanit (ha-meah ha-19) [The sharīʿa courts in Palestine toward the end of the Ottoman Period (19th century)]." In *Lenokhah bait ha-din ha-sharʿi: Tahalikhey shinuy be-maamadan shel nashim Muslemiyot be-Yisrael ve-bamizrah hatichon* [*Facing the sharīʿa court: Processes of change in the status of Muslim women in Israel and the Middle East*] edited by Liat Kuzma, 33–56. Tel Aviv: Resling, 2012.

Benton, Lauren. *Law and Colonial Cultures: Legal Regimes in World History, 1400–1900.* New York: Cambridge University Press, 2002.

Bohannan, Paul J. *Justice and Judgment among the Tiv.* London: Oxford University Press, 1957.

Chanock, Martin. *Law, Custom and Social Order: The Colonial Experience in Malawi and Zambia.* Cambridge: Cambridge University Press, 1985.

Christelow, Allan. *Muslim Law Courts and the French Colonial State in Algeria.* Princeton, NJ: Princeton University Press, 1985.

Cole, Donald P. "Where Have the Bedouin Gone?" *Anthropological Quarterly* 76, no. 2 (2003): 235–267.

Comaroff, John L. "Foreword." In *Contested States: Law, Hegemony and Resistance*, edited by Lazarus-Black, Mindie and Susan F. Hirsch, IV–XI. New York: Routledge, 1994.

Comaroff, John L. "Colonialism, Culture and the Law: A Forward." *Law and Social Inquiry* 26, no. 2 (2001): 305–314.

Deringil, Selim. "'They Live in a State of Nomadism and Savagery': The Late Ottoman and the Post-Colonial Debate." *Comparative Studies in Society and History* 45, no. 2 (2003): 311–342.

Dirks, Nicolas B. *Castes of Mind: Colonialism and the Making of Modern India.* Princeton, NJ: Princeton University Press, 2001.

Dumper, Michael. *Islam and Israel: Muslim Religious Endowments and the Jewish State.* Washington, DC: Institute for Palestine Studies, 1994.

Eisenman, Robert, H. *Islamic Law in Palestine and Israel.* Leiden: Brill, 1978.

Evered, Emine. *Empire and Education under the Ottomans: Politics, Reforms and Resistance from the Tanzimat to the Young Turks.* London: I. B. Tauris, 2012.

Fluehr-Lobban, Carolyn. *Islamic Law and Society in the Sudan.* London: Frank Cass, 1987.

Friedman, Menachem. "The Structural Foundation for Religio-Political Accommodation in Israel: Fallacy and Reality." In *Israel: The First Decade of Independence*, edited by Ilan Troen and Noah Lucas, 51–82. Albany: SUNY Press, 1995.

Gluckman, Max. *The Ideas in Barotse Jurisprudence.* New Haven, CT: Yale University Press, 1965.

Goadby, Frederic M. *International and Inter-Religious Private Law in Palestine.* Jerusalem: Hamadpis Press, 1926.

Goitein, Shmuel, D. and Aharon Ben Shemesh. *Ha-mishpat ha-Muslemi bi-Medinat Yisrael* [*Islamic law in the State of Israel*]. Jerusalem: Hebrew University Faculty of Law, 1958.

Hobsbawm, Eric, T. and Terrance Ranger, eds., *The Invention of Tradition*. Cambridge: Cambridge University Press, 1983.

Hooker, M.B. *Legal Pluralism: An Introduction to Colonial and New-Colonial Laws.* Oxford: Clarendon Press, 1975.

Al-Kayyālī, ʿAbd al-Wahhāb. *Taʾrīkh Filasṭīn al-ḥadīth* [*Modern history of Palestine*]. Beirut: Al-Muʾasasa al-ʿArabiya liʾl-Dirāsāt waʾal-Nashr, 1970.

Kressel, Gidon, M. *Descent through Males: An Anthropological Investigation into the Patterns underlying Social Hierarchy, Kinship and Marriage among Former Bedouins in the Ramla-Lod Area* (*Israel*). Wiesbaden: Harrosowitz, 1992.

Kupferschmidt, Uri, M. *The Supreme Muslim Council: Islam under the British Mandate for Palestine*. Leiden: E. J. Brill, 1987.

Layish, Aharon. "Ha-shiput ha-dati shel ha-Muslemim be-Yisrael." [Muslim religious law in Israel]. *Hamizrakh Hekhadash* [*The new East*] 13 (1963): 19–42.

Layish, Aharon. "Muslim Religious Jurisdiction in Israel." *Asian and African Studies.* 1 (1965): 49–79.

Layish, Aharon. "Maamad ha-isha ha-Muslemit be-veit ha-din ha-sharʿi be-Yisrael" [The status of Muslim women in Israeli sharīʿa courts], In *Maamad ha-isha ba-hevra u-ba-mishpat* [*Women's status in Israeli society and law*], edited by Frances Raday et al. 372–399. Jerusalem: Shoken, 1995.

Layish, Aharon. "Adaptation of a Jurists' Law to Modern Times in an Alien Environment: The Case of the Sharīʿa in Israel." *Die Welt des Islams* 46, no. 2 (2006): 168–225.

Lazarus-Black, Mindie and Susan F. Hirsch, eds. *Contested States: Law, Hegemony and Resistance*. New York: Routledge, 1994.

Likhovski, Assaf. *Law and Identity in Mandate Palestine*. Chapel Hill: University of North Carolina Press, 2006.

Likhovski, Assaf. *Tax Law and Social Norms in Mandatory Palestine and Israel.* New York: Cambridge University Press, 2017.

Makdisi, Ussama. "Ottoman Orientalism." *The American Historical Review* 107, no. 3 (2002): 768–796.

McTague, John. *British Policy in Palestine, 1917–1922*. London: Rowman and Littlefield, 1983.

Merry, Sally E. „Law and Colonialism." *Law and Society Review* 25, no. 4 (1991): 889–922.

Messick, Brinkley. *The Calligraphic State: Textual Domination and History in a Muslim Society*. Berkeley: University of California Press, 1993.

Moore, Sally F. *Social Facts and Fabrications: "Customary" Law on Kilimanjaro, 1880–1980*. Cambridge: Cambridge University Press, 1986.

Moore, Sally F. "Treating Law as Knowledge: Telling Colonial Officers What to Say to Africans about Running 'Their Own' Native Courts." *Law and Society Review* 26, no. 1 (1992): 11–46.

Morris, Benny. *The Birth of the Palestinian Refugee Problem, 1947–1949*. Cambridge: Cambridge University Press, 1987.

Nader, Laura. *Harmony Ideology: Justice and Control in a Zapotec Mountain Village*. Stanford, CA: Stanford University Press, 1990.

Ozbek, Nadim. "Policing the Countryside: Gendarmes of the Late 19th Century Ottoman Empire (1876–1908)." *International Journal of Middle East Studies* 40, (2008): 47–67.

Parush, Iris. *Reading Jewish Women: Marginality and Modernization in Nineteenth-Century Eastern European Jewish Society*. Waltham, MA: Brandeis University Press, 2004.

Peled, Alisa. *Debating Islam in the Jewish State: The Development of Policy toward Islamic Institutions in Israel*. Albany: State University of New York Press, 2001.

Rubin, Avi. *Ottoman Nizamiye Courts: Law and Modernity*. New York: Palgrave Macmillan, 2011.

Sartori, Paolo and Ido Shahar. "Legal Pluralism in Muslim Majority Colonies: Mapping the Terrain." *Journal of Economic and Social History of the Orient* 55, no. 4–5 (2012): 637–663.

Schacht, Joseph. *An Introduction to Islamic Law*. Oxford: Oxford University Press, 1964.

Shaashua, Shlomo. *Batey ha-din ha-Muslemim bi-Medinat Yisrael* [*Islamic Courts in the State of Israel*]. Holon: Faraj Printing, 1980.

Shafir, Gershon. "Zionism and Colonialism: A Comparative Approach." In *Israel in Comparative Perspective: Challenging the Conventional Wisdom*, edited by Michael Barnett, 227–242. Albany: State University of New York Press, 1996.

Shahar, Ido. "Trilemma be-veyt ha-din: Beyt ha-din ha-shari bi-Ver Sheva ki-nekudat mifgash shel shalosh maarakhot hok – Hukey ha-medina, ha-hok ha-shari ve-ha-din ha-bedoui" [Trilemma in court: The sharīʿa court in Beersheba as a convergence point of three law systems – Israeli law, shariʿa law and bedouin ʿurf]. *Jamaa* 1 (1997): 11–40.

Shahar, Ido. "A Tale of Two Courts: How Organizational Ethnography Can Shed New Light on Legal Pluralism." *Political and Legal Anthropology Review* 36, no. 1 (2013): 118–137.

Shahar, Ido. *Legal Pluralism in the Holy City: Competing Courts, Forum Shopping, and Institutional Dynamics in Jerusalem*. Farnham and Burlington: Ashgate, 2015.

Shamir, Ronen. *The Colonies of Law: Colonialism, Zionism and Law in Early Mandate Palestine*. Cambridge: Cambridge University Press, 2000.

Sierra, Maria T. "Indian Rights and Customary Law in Mexico: A Study of the Nahuas in the Sierra de Puebla." *Law and Society Review* 29, no. 2 (1995): 227–254.

Soffer, Arnon and Gil Shalev. *Mimusha ba-poal shel tvi'at ha-shiva ha-Falastinit* [*The application of the actual realization of the Palestinian right of return*]. Haifa: Reuven Chaikin Cathedra for Geostrategy, University of Haifa, 2004.

Vitta, Eduardo. *The Conflict of Laws in Matters of Personal Status in Palestine.* Tel Aviv: M. Shaham's Press, 1947.

Weiss, Max. *In the Shadow of Sectarianism: Law, Shi'ism and the Making of Modern Lebanon.* Cambridge, MA: Harvard University Press, 2010.

Woods, Patricia. *Judicial Power and National Politics: Courts and Gender in the Religious-Secular Conflict in Israel.* Albany: State University of New York Press, 2008.

Zahalka, Iyad. *Batey ha-din ha-shariyim: Beyn ha-shiput la-zehut* [*The sharīʿa courts: Between adjudication and identity*]. Tel Aviv: Israeli BAR Press, 2009.

Zinc, Valerie. "A Quiet Transfer: The Judaization of Jerusalem." *Contemporary Arab Affairs* 2, no. 1 (2009): 122–133.

Nation Building, Islamic Law and Unofficial Legal Pluralism: the Cases of Turkey and Pakistan

Ihsan Yilmaz

1 Introduction

Similar to many others in different parts of the world, modernising "power elites"[1] of Muslim majority countries assigned themselves a civilising mission and imagined[2] their societies as nations following the model of Western modernity. Their hegemonic nation building projects have always given prominent place to state law as an instrument of top-down social engineering. Thus, law has become an ideological and repressive apparatus of the state in the Althusserian sense.[3] In this ideological use, law is not only employed as an instrument of social control but also as a hegemonic mode of organising and even fabricating beliefs and values, in addition to manufacturing the consent of the masses.[4] Law is seen in utilitarian terms as a tool, "an amoral and infinitely plastic device of government".[5] Nation-building legal instrumentalists treat the social space between legislator and individual implicitly as a normative vacuum and envision that the state is more or less autonomous from the social context in which the law is to have its effects, the subjects of the rule are atomistic individuals and the legislator's command is uninfluenced by the social medium.[6] Nevertheless, even a brief perusal of The Journal of Legal Pluralism and Unofficial Law that has been published for the last fifty years would show that an impressive number of socio-legal and social anthropological studies have repeatedly and consistently found that "the state is not

1 Mills, *The Power Elite*.

2 Anderson, *Imagined Communities*.

3 Louis Althusser developed the Marxist theory of the State and distinguished the repressive state apparatuses (RSA) from the ideological state apparatuses (ISAs). RSAs are government, courts, police and armed forces and ISAs are social institutions such as the religious ISA, the educational ISA, the legal ISA, the political ISA, the media ISA, the cultural ISA. The ruling hegemonic class uses the RSAs to dominate the other classes and subordinate them by violent or non-violent coercive means. Instead of repression and coercion, the ISAs reinforces the hegemony through ideology; people submit out of fear of social ridicule, rather than fear of legal prosecution or state violence, Althusser, "Ideology and Ideological State Apparatuses".

4 Gramsci, *Selections from the Prison Notebooks*.

5 Cotterell, *The Politics of Jurisprudence*.

6 Griffiths, "What is Legal Pluralism."

 | DOI:10.1163/9789004398269_007

necessarily the only entity in charge of what goes on, in law and in life".[7] Unlike legal modernists have assumed and legal positivists have argued, "the state in the form of courts is not actually completely in charge of things".[8] Pakistan and Turkey are two remarkable examples of this socio-political phenomenon of unofficial legal pluralism.[9]

These two countries have followed different trajectories in their nation-building endeavours vis-à-vis Islam and Muslim laws. The Kemalist hegemonic elite of Turkey decided to build a new modern nation by manufacturing secularist and nationalist "acceptable citizens".[10] To achieve this aim they have employed a number of Althusserian repressive and ideological apparatuses of the state. Law has been used by the Kemalist state as one of these repressive state apparatuses to modernise and westernise the family unit so that acceptable citizens could be produced.[11] Thus, they decided to replace Muslim laws by transplanting the Swiss Civil Code with a few pro-Islamic[12] and patriarchal[13] modifications. On the other hand, Pakistani social engineers continued the centuries-old personal law system that officially allows different religious personal and family laws to co-exist. This official legal pluralist arrangement is called weak legal pluralism in Griffiths' terminology.[14] But even the Pakistani state wanted to reform its society and construct a new modern nation by reforming Muslim laws in Pakistan. This has not been without resistance from the counter-hegemonic traditionalists, conservatives, religious reactionaries, Salafists and patriarchal power structures in society. Thus, in addition to official or weak legal pluralism, unofficial Muslim legal pluralism, "strong legal pluralism"[15] is a part of daily life. Some sections of society still obey the unofficial religious law as it is understood traditionally and interpreted by conservative *ʿulama*, and not the hegemonic nation state's laws.

Some Muslims in these two countries have developed their own ways of reconstructing the socio-legal arena, paving the way for unofficial dynamic Muslim legal pluralism. Despite the states' social engineering attempts, subalterns have resisted in one way or another to the hegemonic power of the modern nation state. In these contexts, national, international, secular, religious,

7 Menski, "Governance and Governability," 44.
8 Ibid., 56.
9 Yilmaz, *Muslim Laws, Politics and Society*.
10 Yilmaz, "Homo LASTus and Lausannian Muslim" and Yilmaz, "Religious Freedom."
11 Yilmaz, *Muslim Laws, Politics and Society*.
12 Miller, "The Ottoman and Islamic Substratum."
13 Özsu, "Receiving' the Swiss Civil Code."
14 Griffiths, "What is Legal Pluralism."
15 Ibid.

and customary law all interweave[16] and more than one source influences and guides the attitudes and behaviours of individuals.[17] This situation is not static and new hybrid unofficial laws are being continuously constructed by skillful post-modern legal navigators.[18] By looking at the available case law, statistical data, official reports, surveys and field research on age of marriage, registration and solemnisation of marriage, polygamy and divorce, this chapter, which draws on and updates my earlier work,[19] aims to present the current socio-legal picture of Muslim legal pluralisms in Pakistan and Turkey.

2 Pakistani Muslim Legal Pluralism

No country other than Pakistan has made religion the sole basis of Muslim nationality.[20] After Pakistan's independence, the question of whether or not Muslim laws should play a larger role in state, law and society became one of the fundamental issues. As Pakistan was imagined by its founding moderniser elite as a state purely for Muslims, creating a modern Muslim Pakistani national identity has been a central issue for them. The tension between modernists and conservatives in how this identity should be constructed had an impact on political and legal developments.[21] The same Pakistani Constitution drafted by a secular and modernising elite that protects western fundamental rights also elevates Muslim laws.[22]

The modern nation state of Pakistan has produced positive law based on a plural, incoherent and contradictory corpus of Muslim laws. The process is almost chaotic, let alone linear, thanks to tensions and interactions between politics, society, norms and practices.[23] Variation in the enforcement and interpretation of Muslim laws by the courts has intensified this chaotic pluralism, especially when dealing with the delicate regulation of marriage.[24]

16 Santos, *Toward a New Legal Common Sense.*
17 O'Neill and Toktas, "Women's Property Rights," 39.
18 Yilmaz, *Muslim Laws, Politics and Society.*
19 Yilmaz, "Secular Law and the Emergence"; Yilmaz, "Non-Recognition of Post-Modern"; Yilmaz, *Muslim Laws, Politics and Society*; Yilmaz, "Good Governance in Action"; Yilmaz, "Pakistan Federal Shariat Court's."
20 Devji, *Muslim Zion*, 5.
21 Lau, "Sharia and National Law in Pakistan," 423.
22 Yefet, "What's the Constitution," 348.
23 Pearl and Menski, *Muslim Family Law*; Ali, "Testing the Limits of Family"; Mehdi, *The Islamization of the Law*; Shah, *Women, The Koran and*; Ahmad, Batool and Dziegielewski, "State of Inheritance Rights," 7.
24 Yilmaz, "Good Governance in Action," 165; Yefet, "What's the Constitution," 348.

Unofficial Muslim laws have three main functions in Pakistan. First, they provide a point of reference in construing enacted laws and provisions. Secondly, they fill a void in the legal system. Thirdly, they question an existing law or provision in regard to injunctions of Islam.[25] A recent analysis of *fatāwa* (plural of *fatwā*, an unofficial legal injunction of Muslims jurists) in Pakistan shows that *fatāwa* have been used for all these purposes.[26]

The reform of Muslim family laws in Pakistan can be divided into three distinct periods. The first period (1947–77) represents an effort to modernise and reform the family law and make it less gender discriminatory. The second period (1978–99) reversed this trend and conservative, patriarchal, Islamist, Salafist and even repressive interpretations of Muslim laws dominated the state. The amendments in Muslim family laws were influenced by the Islamist and Salafist interpretations. The current period (2000–), similar to the first period, is focused on removing gender discrimination and decreasing inequalities present in family law.[27] Saleem defines each period by a quintessential law: The first period is defined by the Muslim Family Law Ordinance (MFLO), 1961; the second period by the Zina Ordinance, 1979 and the third by the Women Protection Act, 2006.[28]

The main legislation in the area of family law is the Muslim Family Laws Ordinance, 1961 (MFLO). It represents a reformist and modernising interpretation of Muslim family law, restricting the rights of men in the area of divorce and polygamy.[29] The Islamic nature of the MFLO has remained controversial from the very beginning. The ordinance presents a compromise between Islamists and modernists/reformists.[30] The conservative religious groups vehemently protested when it was promulgated but the military government did not compromise. The reformist aspect that endeavoured to improve the plight of women did not sit well with the traditional, conservative, patriarchal, Islamist and Salafist sections of society who converged on their opposition to the reforms. The superior courts have also found several provisions of the MFLO contrary to the traditional and customary interpretations of Islamic law.[31] Thus, as the case law and research that shall be referred to below have

25 Lau, *The Role of Islam*.

26 Cheema, "Fatawa in Pakistani Courts."

27 Saleem, "Effect of Islam's Role," 373.

28 Ibid.

29 Mehdi, *The Islamization of the Law*, 164 and Lau, "Sharia and National Law in Pakistan," 415.

30 Mehdi, *The Islamization of the Law*, 157.

31 Shah, *Women, The Koran and*, 153.

repeatedly shown, the wide gap between the laws of the state and the plurality of legal practices still exists in Pakistan.

2.1 *Registration and Solemnisation of Marriage*

The Pakistani state needed to impose compulsory marriage registration since in both civil and criminal cases questions often arose concerning the existence of a marriage contract and the marital status of the parties involved. In the absence of official documentation, uncertainty and confusion are inevitable.[32]

The MFLO 1961 provided for the compulsory registration of marriages under section 5. However, under the Ordinance the non-registration of marriage does not make the marriage invalid or unlawful, although registration is important in proving the existence of a marriage. The loophole left in the law of registration to satisfy the counter-hegemonic factions is that non-registration does not make a marriage invalid or unlawful.[33] Thus, '(j)udicial relief is not denied to unregistered marriages in Pakistan, if they can be proved by other means'.[34] In many instances, it was found to be difficult to locate the relevant records of marriage registers and to obtain the necessary copies.[35]

Conservatives, Islamists and Salafists conceive compulsory registration as interference in the sacred law by the state.[36] They agree on the importance of registration, but are opposed to criminal sanctions to enforce its implementation. Thus, although this law remains in force, many marriages in Pakistan are still not registered. Moreover, the courts have held that an oral and unregistered marriage is valid.[37]

Counter-hegemonic factions pressured the Federal Shariat Court (FSC) to declare marriage registration a violation of Islamic law and thus of the Pakistani Constitution. But the FSC found this statutory requirement in accordance with Islamic law. It argued that the registration requirement clarifies an individual's marital status, which is helpful in establishing an orderly society and in helping against the denial of women's and children's legal rights. Thus, the FSC held that the statutory marriage registration requirement cannot be termed un-Islamic or opposed to the injunctions of Islam. As a result, the FSC upheld the constitutionality of the registration requirement, and further

32 Patel, *Socio-Economic Political Status*, 139.

33 Mehdi, *The Islamization of the Law*, 159; see also Carroll, "The Muslim Family Laws", 119–121.

34 Mehdi, *The Islamization of the Law*, 159.

35 Patel, *Socio-Economic Political Status*, 143.

36 See in detail Tanzilur-Rahman, *Muslim Family Laws*.

37 Balchin, *A Handbook on Family Law*, 51; Mehdi, *The Islamization of the Law*, 159.

directed the legislature to provide substantial penalties as an effective deterrent against non-registration.[38]

On the other hand, in Allah Rakha v. Federation of Pakistan PLD [2000] FSC 1, the Federal Shariat Court clearly held that unregistered Muslim marriages continue to be accepted and legally recognised by Pakistani law. Thus, the registration of marriage is not necessarily the only proof of marriage, as according to Muslim laws marriage (*nikāḥ*) could be performed by a marriage proposal and its acceptance in the presence of witnesses.[39]

The Prevention of Anti-Women Practices Act of 2011 strengthened women's rights. It criminalised forced marriages and any attempt to stop women from inheriting property. It also eliminated loopholes that were used to reduce the punishment of persons guilty of rape. It also outlawed the patriarchal and tribal custom of "marriage with the Quran" that had no Islamic basis.[40]

2.2 *Age of Marriage: Child Marriages*

Most traditional marriages are still arranged by the families in Pakistan and the opportunity for a boy or a girl openly to get to know and choose their partner seldom occurs. In the process of such marriages being arranged by family members, safeguards in the law are often ignored. Minimum age of marriage and mutual consent requirements are not observed. Despite the National Registration Act 1973, according to one estimate, as of 2010, around 40% of married men and 52% of married women had unregistered marriages in Pakistan.[41] The state has not done much to ensure that marriages are consensual. In many instances, the age of a girl will be changed on her marriage certificate in order to avoid questions over her being underage.[42] The ability of individuals to bypass the law without any fear of repercussions has also perpetuated archaic customary practices of selling girls into "marriage" in exchange for money, settling disputes with the exchange of girls known as *vani* or *swara* and the use of girls as compensation for crimes. While the official laws in Pakistan do not condone these practices, the officials and courts do not properly address and tackle them, allowing informal patriarchal power structures to implement a law of their own.[43] Only in 2011 did the Pakistani legislature pass two pro-woman bills aimed at protecting women from harmful traditional customs, including

---

38 Yefet, "What's the Constitution," 374.

39 Shah, *Women, The Koran and*, 155.

40 Saleem, "Effect of Islam's Role," 390.

41 Nasrullah "Child Marriage," 34.

42 WLUML, *Child, Early and Forced Marriage*, 32.

43 WLUML, *Child, Early and Forced Marriage*; Amnesty, "Child Marriages."

so-called marriage with the holy Quran and forced wedlock, and seeking severe punishments for violators.[44]

Child marriages are theoretically restricted by the Child Marriage Restraint Act, 1929, which prescribed penal sanctions where the bridegroom had not reached the age of eighteen and the bride fourteen.[45] With the promulgation of section 12 MFLO 1961, the age of fourteen was substituted with the age of sixteen. A female under 16 years of age is defined as a 'child' and it is an offence to marry her. A marriage contracted after the attainment of puberty and before the age of 16 years for females and 18 years for males is valid under Pakistani Muslim laws. The Child Marriage Restraint Act does not make such marriages invalid or void. The Act prescribes punishments for the groom who marries a child considered to be under-age for the purposes at hand, for the person who performs, conducts or directs any under-age marriage, and, where a minor contracts such a marriage, for the person in charge of the minor. The law was changed in 2014 and the penalties for child marriage were increased but the state failed to increase the marriage age for girls from 16 to 18.[46] However, traditionalists vehemently oppose the age restriction.[47]

According to the Pakistan Demographic and Health Survey conducted in 2006–2007, over one-third of ever-married women in Pakistan entered into marriage before their 18th, and around 12 to 13 percent before their 15th birthday.[48] In a recent survey, in-depth discussions with the community revealed that the main age for marriage in rural Jacobabad for girls fell between 13 and 14 years and for boys between 14 and 18. In rural Matiari, the age for girls was reported to be around 12 to 13 years in a majority of community discussions and even between 8 and 10 in a few others.[49]

Many men and women believe that Shari'a requires girls to be married after their menarche. In many discussions men said that according to the Holy Quran, if a girl is not married as soon as she reaches puberty, their parents have to bear the burden of this sin.[50]

Overall, 47.8% of currently married women aged 15–24 years in Pakistan were married before the age of 18 years. According to a UNICEF estimate, the

44 Dawn, "Senate Passes Two Pro-Woman"; Saleem, "Effect of Islam's Role", 390.

45 Carroll, "Nizam-i-Islam," 60; Patel, *Socio-Economic Political Status*, 149.

46 Fatimah and Zahir, "Is Child Marriage Associated," 55.

47 See in Tanzilur-Rahman, *Muslim Family Laws*, 291.

48 National Institute of Population Studies (NIPS). Pakistan Demographic and Health Survey 2006–07, 72.

49 Ibid., 11.

50 Ibid., 14.

prevalence of child marriage among all women aged 20–24 years in Pakistan is 24.0%.[51]

New laws have recently been enacted to prevent child marriages. Sindh was the first province to act on this issue. It promulgated the Sindh Child Marriage Restraint Act in April 2014, increasing punishments and fines for those who force children to marry and for officials who register child marriages and for local imams who unofficially solemnise them. In March 2015, the Punjab Child Marriage Restraint Act was passed, again increasing fines and punishments to deter people from supporting/administering child marriages.[52]

2.3 *Polygamy*

Under traditional Muslim laws, women are subject to strict monogamy, yet men may be married to four women at a time. The right of males to plural marriages was entrenched in the Pakistani official law. While the Qur'anic purpose underlying the polygamy license was to establish social justice and protect widows and orphans, this moral duty has turned into a matter of sexual adventure in today's Pakistan.[53]

Section 6 of the MFLO tried to restrict the male's right of polygamy. Under section 6 of the MFLO, polygamy is restricted to the extent that a man who is planning to marry a second or subsequent wife must submit an application for permission to the chairman of the Union Council stating the reasons that justify the proposed marriage and also whether the consent of the existing wife or wives has been obtained. The council may then grant permission if it is satisfied that the proposed marriage is necessary and just.

However, the MFLO does not specifically state that a polygamous marriage entered into without the permission of the Council is illegal, void or voidable.[54] Thus subsequent marriages contracted in contravention of section 6 of MFLO remain valid. This makes the official law less effective against arbitrary and unjustified polygamy.[55]

As case law[56] shows, almost all Muslim polygamists in the country remain unpunished and the second or subsequent marriage is still considered valid. Thus, the official law cannot guarantee a woman that her husband will not

51 Nasrullah, *Child Marriage*, 34.
52 Saleem, "Effect of Islam's Role," 392.
53 Yefet, "What's the Constitution," 369.
54 Mehdi, *The Islamization of the Law*, 164.
55 Balchin, *A Handbook on Family Law*, 77; Mehdi, *The Islamization of the Law*, 160.
56 Cases where the husband contracts a subsequent marriage without the permission of existing wife/wives include: Sana PLD (1967) Pesh 324; Mohd. Zaman PLD (1967) Lah 1109; Abdul Basit (1970) SCMR 753; Zulai Khan PLD (1986) Quetta 290; Sher Muhammed (1986)

bring a co-wife into the house. These regulations appear to be mere formalities rather than effective deterrents. Whatever the official law commands, the practice of polygamy is socially accepted and practiced.

The state's attempt to regulate polygamy faced strong opposition by the anti-Reformists on account of the conditions they place on polygamy. It has been argued that section 6 "must be deleted in toto, for, in its present form, it is totally repugnant and foreign to the words and spirit of the Holy *Qur'an* and *Sunna* and the fundamental principles of Islamic jurisprudence".[57] Nevertheless, in the Allah Rakha v. Federation of Pakistan (PLD 2000 FSC 1) case, the FSC underlined that polygamy is not mandatory or even recommended in Islam. It is only tolerated. It may be restricted or even prohibited if it leads to unlawful consequences or injustice. Accordingly, the FSC advised that authorities must adopt suitable measures to end or at least to minimise the instances of injustice. By upholding the MFLO's limitations on the male polygamy license, and by recommending the enactment of further necessary checks and balances to prevent polygamy's abuse, the FSC took a progressive, anti-Salafist stance with its equitable interpretation of Muslim laws consonant with women's rights.[58]

On the other hand, in 2014, the state's official advisory body, The Council of Islamic Ideology (CII), criticised the MFLO's restrictions on polygamy and also the Child Marriage Restraint Act 1929, which prohibits child marriages.[59]

2.4 *Divorce*

The *right of ṭalāq* is the unilateral right of a/the husband to divorce his wife. In *Hanafi* law, neither the wife nor any witnesses are required to be present at the time and place when a husband is unilaterally divorcing his wife. It is effective orally or in writing. However, Section 7 of the MFLO 1961 has attempted to convert the *ṭalāq al-bid'a* (irrevocable divorce unilaterally declared by the husband) into a revocable divorce. The objective of section 7 is to prevent the hasty dissolution of marriage by *ṭalāq* pronounced unilaterally by the husband. The MFLO mainly relates to procedural aspects of the family laws. It does not touch upon what the substantive laws are, thus leaving it to the courts to rely on the uncodified Muslim personal law. For instance, it does not list the grounds for divorce, its forms and when a wife can ask for it.[60] Although the official

PCrLJ 1510; M. Ashraf PLD (1987) Lah 27; Faheemuddin PLD (1991) SC 1074; Nazar Hussain (1991) CLC Note 238; Tofazal Hussain Shah (1991) PCrLJ 1063.

57 Tanzilur-Rahman, *Muslim Family Laws*, 131.

58 Yefet, "What's the Constitution", 372; see also Yilmaz, "Pakistan Federal Shariat Court's" and Yilmaz, "Good Governance in Action."

59 Shah, "Fresh Controversy over Polygamy."

60 Shah, *Women, The Koran and*, 152.

law aims to reform the traditional Muslim laws to protect women, it fails in practice to restrict the man's right of divorce. As in the case of polygamy, the divorce procedure provided in the official law has become a mere formality instead of deterring and regulating the unilateral use of divorce by the husband.[61]

Divorce in Pakistan is very easy for men. They can divorce their wives, either orally or in writing. They may speak, write, fax, email, or even SMS the word *ṭalāq* three times and get rid of their marital ties. All the MFLO did to restrict this power was to require the divorcing husband to register the divorce with the Union Council and withhold its validity for a period of ninety days. The MFLO threatened an offender with imprisonment and fines but it remained silent as to the validity of unregistered divorce. Some courts have preferred uncodified Islamic legal rules over the express provision of the ordinance. Some others have followed both the ordinance and the unofficial laws: laying down that violation of the ordinance is a punishable act but anything done according to Shari'a would not be invalid. Thus, non-registration of a marriage and notice of divorce to a wife are punishable under the MFLO but, according to un-codified Muslim laws, non-registration will not invalidate the marriage.[62] Some other courts held that compliance with Section 7's registration requirement is a prerequisite to the validity of a divorce.[63]

Two decades after the pro-women, progressive MFLO was enacted, this chaotic situation on the procedural requirement was combined with the Zina Ordinance and became a deadly weapon in the hands of vindictive former husbands.[64] The criminalisation of adultery and fornication as a result of the Zina Ordinance 1979 had an unintended effect on the MFLO procedures that were designed to protect women's rights. After the passing of the Zina Ordinance, abandoned wives who had since remarried were unexpectedly accused of adultery by their former husbands, the latter claiming that they had not followed the procedures contained in Section 7 of the MFLO. Thus, they had never validly been divorced and their (former) wives were guilty of adultery.[65] Because of jealousy, they denied ever having pronounced *ṭalāq* and charged them with *zinā* (adultery), an offence that until very recently could carry the death penalty.[66] In order to protect the women, judges dealing with these cases often decided that the divorce had been valid, despite non-compliance with the MFLO. But this has weakened the obligatory character

61 Mehdi, *The Islamization of the Law*, 171.
62 Shah, *Women, The Koran and*, 162.
63 Yefet, "What's the Constitution," 376.
64 Ibid.
65 Lau, "Sharia and National Law in Pakistan," 417.
66 Yefet, "What's the Constitution," 374–375.

of the mandatory notification. On the other hand, the notification requirement was upheld in cases concerning purely family, not criminal law matters.[67] Later, the FSC invalidated the registration requirement in the Allah Rakka v Federation of Pakistan (PLD 2000 FSC 1) case and severed the dangerous tie between the MFLO and the Zina Ordinance.[68] The Protection of Women Act, 2006 has finally ended this chaos. The law now states that it is sufficient for a woman to believe herself to be validly married to avoid a charge of adultery.[69] Even if the divorce preceding her re-marriage turns out to be invalid, she will not face charges if she can convince the court that she had reasons to believe that her divorce and subsequent marriage were valid.[70]

Besides divorce by the husband, the MFLO recognises other forms of dissolution of marriage: mutual release which may either take the form of *khulʿ* or *mubāraʾa* and the "option of puberty" (if a girl is married in her minority she may dissolve such a marriage on attaining puberty), and delegating the power of divorce to the wife (section 8).[71] Unlike a husband's no-fault based right to divorce (*ṭalāq*) which is not based on the consent of the wife, *khulʿ* requires the consent of the husband. Under traditional Muslim laws, a Muslim wife does not have a no-fault based right to dissolve her marriage equivalent to a Muslim husband's absolute right to divorce his wife without assigning any reason. A Muslim wife could get a divorce only through a court presided over by a Muslim judge after establishing 'fault' on the part of her husband under very limited circumstances.[72]

However, in a remarkable case (Saleem Ahmad v Government of Pakistan PLD 2014 FSC 43), a wife's unilateral right to no-fault based divorce under Muslim laws attained the sanction of the Federal Shariat Court (FSC). In 2002, the legislature amended section 10(4) of the Family Courts Act, 1964, authorising family courts to dissolve a marriage on the basis of *khulʿ* if reconciliation between the spouses fails. This amendment was challenged before the FSC on the ground that it was against the injunctions of Islam. In this case, the FSC did not take into account the strict principles of Hanafi jurisprudence and instead resorted to *ijtihād* by directly referring to the primary sources of Muslim law (Qur'an and Sunnah). As a result, the Court extended to wives the right of *khula* without the consent of their husbands. After reviewing various juristic opinions (*fatāwā*), which unanimously held that a judge does not have any

67 Lau, "Sharia and National Law in Pakistan," 417.
68 Yefet, "What's the Constitution," 376.
69 Lau, "Sharia and National Law in Pakistan," 416.
70 Ibid., 417.
71 Shah, *Women, The Koran and*, 152.
72 Abbasi "Women's right to unilateral," 83.

authority to order the dissolution of a marriage on the basis of *khula* without the consent of the husband, the FSC held that it was not bound by these unofficial juristic opinions. The Court observed that the injunctions of Islam regarding gender are based on equality without any discrimination. Thus, the Court held that Islam does not intend to force a wife to live a miserable life, in a hateful unhappy union, forever. If she is unhappy and reconciliation fails, she should be entitled to get relief.[73] The FSC argued that in the primary sources, there is no express prohibition of granting a woman a divorce without the consent of her husband. The Court also emphasised that marriage in Islam is dependent on (re)conciliation, thus if the wife expresses her unwillingness to continue the marriage, then the conciliation does not exist. The FSC also held that the rights and responsibilities of husband and wife are similar in Muslim laws and that there is no room for discrimination. If men could unilaterally divorce their wives, women could also ask for their release from the same marriage bond.[74]

Despite this development, another state organ, the CII (The Council of Islamic Ideology) declared in 2014 that the Dissolution of Muslim Marriages Act 1939 (DMMA) was not Islamic because it allowed the dissolution of marriage by a wife on grounds of her/the husband entering into another marriage without following the provisions given in the law. Its chairman argued that a woman could not demand divorce if her husband married a second, third or fourth time. Thus, the CII claimed that the relevant provision of the Dissolution of Muslim Marriages Act (DMMA) 1939 was against Shariʿa and it wanted the government to repeal it.[75]

It seems that a Kulturkampf over women and Muslim laws between reformists and Salafists not only in Pakistani society but also within the state institutions will continue in the foreseeable future. All in all, the Pakistani legal system has failed to decisively respond to the socio-cultural bias against women in Pakistan resulting from deep-rooted and problematic hegemonic masculinity and has, willingly or not, enabled masculinist and patriarchal interpretations of Islam at the expense of the women.[76] The FSC's new progressive and reformist pro-women *ijtihāds*[77] and most of the abovementioned recent legislation are promising to tackle this problem that is an unfortunate result of strong legal pluralism in Pakistan.

---

73 Ibid., 88.

74 Saleem Ahmad v Government of Pakistan PLD 2014 FSC 43.

75 Shah, "Fresh Controversy over Polygamy."

76 Hussain, "History, Law and Vernacular," 64–65.

77 See for more details on this, Yilmaz, "Pakistan Federal Shariat Court's" and Yilmaz, "Good Governance in Action."

3 Turkish Muslim Legal Pluralism

Turkey is, like Pakistan, a Muslim majority country. Moreover, it is also a Sunni and Hanafi majority country. Despite the fact that the Civil Code is purely secular and does not recognise any Muslim laws, similar to Pakistan, unofficial Muslim laws have continued to co-exist, defying the staunchly secularist expectations of the Kemalist nation builders.[78]

The pressing aim of the Turkish Republic's modernising and secularising founders, the hegemonic Kemalist elite, was to transform the 'backward', traditional, and religious society into a modern, secular and 'civilised' one. The process of 'civilisation', "took on the character of a cultural revolution aiming to produce radical changes in social mentality, lifestyles and world views".[79] The Kemalists espoused western modernity and its French-type secular model that did not like public expressions and manifestations of Islam and that gradually aimed to secularise society.[80] In other words, unlike the Anglo-Saxon secularism model that is based on "twin tolerations"[81] that safeguard the mutual autonomy of religion and state (wall of separation), the Turkish model aimed to purge Islam from the social domain in the long run. The state has resorted to the instrumentalist use of law,[82] education,[83] and the strict control of religion,[84] media, art and culture. But in the short and medium terms, it has used Islam through the Directorate of Religious Affairs (Diyanet) as a helping hand to manufacture the consent of the masses.[85] In attempting to build a new national identity for Turkey, the secular legal system became the very foundation of the modern Turkish state.[86] State law has been an effective instrument in building the new secular modern Turkish nation. Kemalist legal and judicial reforms were an essential part of the general social engineering project which aimed to westernise/modernise the newly established republic.[87]

Hooker argues that Turkey's experience "is an excellent example of a state undertaking the process of legal importation as a result of fundamental

78 Yilmaz, "Secular Law and the Emergence"; Yilmaz, "Islamic Family Law"; Yilmaz, "Semi-official Turkish Muslim."
79 Özman, "Law, Ideology and Modernization," 70.
80 For different modes of secularism, see Taylor, "Modes of Secularism."
81 Stepan, "The World's Religious Systems."
82 Yilmaz, "Non-Recognition of Post-Modern"; Yilmaz, *Muslim Laws, Politics and Society*; Özman, "Law, Ideology and Modernization."
83 Zorlu-Durukan, "The Ideological Pillars."
84 Yilmaz, "State, Law, Civil Society."
85 Ibid.
86 Starr, "The Role of Turkish Secular Law," 169.
87 Özman, "Law, Ideology and Modernization," 69.

revolution, and under the impetus of that upheaval, attempting to establish a completely clean legal sheet".[88] Thus, the Minister of Justice of the time, Mahmut Esat Bozkurt, "declared that what he desired was not reform but a revolution of Law".[89]

The transformation of society would start with the very smallest unit, the family. Thus, after the proclamation of the Turkish Republic in 1923, radical reforms were introduced in family law matters as well. Because the reforms were primarily legalistic and not the product of grassroots discourses, much remained the same as it was during the Ottoman Empire in the rural areas of the new republic.[90] In the field of family law, all earlier reforms, however extensive they seemed, had not affected the traditional Muslim laws which governed family life.[91] Anthropological and socio-legal studies in Turkey in the 1950s, 60s and 70s, suggested that the goals of the secularists were not completely achieved. This early research repeatedly found that Turkish Muslim women living in rural villages continued to be bound by Islamic and customary traditions.[92]

There are a number of differences between the secular civil law of Turkey and the unofficial Muslim laws. These differences include the secularisation of the marriage ceremony, the ban on polygamy and the secularisation of divorce proceedings. The new law gave both parties an equal right to sue for divorce. *Ṭalāq* was no longer recognised. Divorce could only be granted by an official court.

Nevertheless, Muslim Turks have sought other ways to adapt their unofficial Muslim laws to the modern and secular milieu. They have reconstructed their unofficial laws to meet the demands of both official and unofficial laws.[93]

3.1 *Registration and Solemnisation of Marriage*

Under the official law, civil-only marriages performed by authorised marriage officers are allowed and recognised. A marriage may be solemnised in accordance with any religious rites if the parties desire, but registration of marriage preceding such a solemnisation is necessary. Only after the celebration of the

88 Hooker, *Legal Pluralism*, 306.

89 Bozkurt, "The Reception of Western European," 294.

90 Yildirim, "Gender and Resistance," 360.

91 Bozkurt, "The Reception of Western European," 294; Starr, *Law as Metaphor*, 91.

92 Stirling, *Turkish Village*; Yasa, *Hasanoglan*; Timur, *Turkiye'de Aile Yapisi*; Magnarella, *Tradition and Change*; Starr, *Law as Metaphor* and Starr, "The Role of Turkish Secular Law."

93 Yilmaz, *Muslim Laws, Politics and Society*; Powell, *Shari'a in the Secular State*, 2016).

civil marriage is a religious marriage (*imam nikahı*)[94] permitted and the parties should present their marriage document to the *imam* before the religious marriage. Men and women who perform a religious marriage ceremony without having concluded the legal marriage contract are punishable.

Nonetheless, religious-only marriages have continued to take place. In the late 1980s and earlier 1990s, the State Planning Organization (SPO) conducted a quantitative survey that is representative of the whole of Turkey (SPO 1992). This comprehensive research was done with 18,210 randomly selected households from urban and rural communities. The results were then generalised to apply to all Turkey. According to this research, the percentage of civil-only marriages was 9.56, religious-only marriages was 4.89, and both civil and religious marriages was 84.92.[95] A survey in 1998 based on data from interviews conducted with 599 women in 19 settlements in Eastern and Southeastern Anatolia found that the percentage of civil-only marriages was 5.8, religious-only marriages was 19.6 and both civil and religious marriages was 74.4.[96]

Another quantitative study[97] that surveyed 462 married women aged between 15 and 49 in an East Anatolian city found that while 95% of monogamous women were both officially and unofficially married, only 4.6% of them had a religious-only marriage. As for the polygamists, the figures were respectively 61.5% and 38.5%. 100% of all women had a religious marriage.

An official report from 2014 found that in 2011, 2.6% of marriages in Turkey were conducted with a religious ceremony only, along with 3.4% of marriages conducted with a civil ceremony only, and 93.9% of marriages had both a civil and a religious ceremony.[98] The Turkish Statistics Institute also recently found that 1.1% of marriages in Turkey were conducted with a religious ceremony only. 1.8% of marriages were conducted with a civil ceremony only, and 97.1% of marriages had both a civil and a religious ceremony.[99] In the age group of 15–19, 81.85 of those who are married had both official and unofficial marriages

94 In classical Islamic law, there is no need an imam to solemnise the marriage. Acceptance of both parties at the presence of two witnesses is enough. But in the Turkish culture, it has become a social norm to make sure that an imam or a religious person solemnises the marriage. In the daily use, unofficial Islamic marriage is referred to as "*imam nikahı*" (marriage solemnised by an imam) even though in many cases not an imam but a person who has some religious knowledge solemnises these marriages in informal family gatherings attended by close relatives.

95 SPO, *Türk Aile Araştırması*, 42.

96 İlkkaracan, "Exploring the Context," 69.

97 Gücük et al, "Van İlindeki Çok Eşlilik," 128–129.

98 Yildirim, "Gender and Resistance," 365.

99 TurkStat, "Form of Solemnization by Age."

while 0.5% had civil-only and 17.7% religious-only marriages.[100] Most probably these religious-only marriages were child marriages that could not legally be solemnised. Thus, they were illegally solemnised through an unofficial marriage.

There are some unofficial marriage (*imam*/religious-only marriage) cases dealt with by the secular Turkish courts. Several of these cases have reached the top level of the Court of Cassations (Yargıtay).[101] Case law shows that the Court of Cassations accommodates unofficial religious marriages, "when the matter at hand is not related to giving effect to the marriage but, for instance, to the law of obligations where the Court does not have to go into the issue".[102] For instance, for reasons of justice, the Court of Cassations has, "extended the right to compensation for death in work-related accidents to the unmarried cohabiting woman, albeit on a different basis from the married woman".[103] In these cases, women who were only married with a religious marriage applied to the courts for insurance claims after the deaths of their husbands and the Courts have generally decided for compensation, albeit for lower percentages compared to official wives.[104]

In May 2015, the Constitutional Court annulled the Criminal Code's article that provided that, for an illegal, religious-only marriage ceremony, the bride, groom, and imam who officiated the marriage could be sent to jail for two to six months.[105] The majority (12 to 4) opinion argued that since it is not illegal for two persons to live together without a civil marriage, it would be discriminatory to punish two persons living together after a religious-only marriage.[106] The Constitutional Court had unanimously ruled the opposite in a 1999 case.[107]

---

100 Ibid.

101 For a 2010 Court of Cassation case involving religious only marriage see YHGK 22.12.2010 E.2010/3–634 – K.2010/677.

102 Örücü, "Judicial Navigation," 46.

103 Ibid., 45. See cases: 96/1606; 96/1661; 21.3.1996; 22 Yargıtay Kararları Dergisi 1996, 1291; Yargitay Hukuk Genel Kurulu E. 1997/4–690 K. 1997/893 T. 5.11.1997, For A Similar 2002 Case See T.C. Yargitay Hukuk Dairesi 4 Esas No.2001/13026 Karar No. 2002/3866 Tarihi 01.04.2002; T.C. Yargitay 4. Hukuk Dairesi E. 2001/4849 K. 2001/8843 T. 1.10.2001; T.C. Yargitay 4. Hukuk Dairesi E. 2004/5370 K. 2004/14142 T. 13.12.2004; 02/1153; 03/2380; 6.3.2003; 29 Yargıtay Kararları Dergisi, 2003, 1044; Danıştay 11. Daire, E:2003/121, K:2005/5372.

104 T.C. Yargitay 4. Hukuk Dairesi E. 2004/15423 K. 2005/13451 T. 13.12.2005, Yargitay 21. Hukuk Dairesi E. 2007/289 K. 2007/8718 E. 2007/289 K. 2007/8718 T. 28.5.2007. For Similar Previous Court of Cassation cases see Y. 21. Hukuk Dairesi E. 1996/1604 K. 1996/1661 T. 21.3.1996, Y.21.H.D. 03.02.2000 Gün 2000/711 Esas 2000/637 Karar, Y. 21. Hukuk Dairesi E. 2001/4847 K. 2001/6170 T. 25.9.2001, Y. 21. Hukuk Dairesi E. 1997/2093 K. 1997/2188 T. 25.3.1997.

105 TCC, *Judgment*, 2015/51.

106 Saleem, "Effect of Islam's Role," 370.

107 Asimovic-Akyol, "Turkish Court Stirs Marriage Debate."

The Constitution has not changed on this matter between 1999 and 2015 but the membership structure of the Court did. It is no longer controlled by the Kemalists, since the majority of the members have been appointed by Islamist presidents, Abdullah Gül and R. Tayyip Erdoğan, since 2007.

3.2 *Age of Marriage: Child Marriages*

After the establishment of the Turkish Republic in 1923, the age of marriage was adopted from Swiss law as being 18 years for males and 17 years for females. However, it was later reduced to 17 (15 with the permission of the judge) and 15 (14 with the permission of the judge) respectively in 1938. With the Article 124 of the new Civil Code of 2001, marriage age for both parties is now 17. Article 124 further states that under extraordinary conditions a judge may allow a man or woman who completed their 16th year of age to get married.

The official law is in conflict with traditional Muslim laws. In the eyes of many traditional Muslims, when a girl or boy reaches puberty, he or she can marry whatever his or her age. Quantitative data show that people in many cases do not take into account the provisions of the Civil Code. In these cases, families at first employ only Muslim laws and solemnise marriages according to Muslim laws. Married only by *imam nikahı*, the spouses' cohabitation is legitimate for the community. After reaching the officially permitted age, they register their marriages with the state if they want. Although it is considered a crime of rape to have sexual relations with a child under the age of 15 years, in religious-only marriages such behaviour is usually not reported as a crime, and no criminal action is taken. This is one of the obstacles to the prevention of child marriages.[108]

Even official census data show the reality of under-age marriages. The above-mentioned State Planning Organization survey shows that the percentage of under-age marriages (under 16 years) in Turkey was about 9% in 1991.[109] Only 0.37% of all existing marriages were conducted at or below the age of 12, 0.90% at the age of 13, 2.19% at the age of 14 and 5.38% at the age of 15.[110] In 1994, according to the State Institute of Statistics (TurkStat), in the age group of 12–14, 0.54% of females and 0.88% of males were married.[111] It must be emphasised that these figures are not reflective of the true proportion of experience since most of the time people do not report such illegal marriages.

108 Yüksel-Kaptanoğlu and Ergöçmen, "Early Marriage: Trends," 1711.
109 SPO, *Türk Aile Araştırması*, 39.
110 Ibid.
111 TurkStat, *Marriage Statistics: 1994*, 20.

In 1998, a survey based on data from interviews conducted with 599 women in Eastern and Southeastern Anatolia showed that 16.3% of women living in the region were married under the age of 15 and in a religious ceremony.[112] A decade later, another study underlined that in 2008, 14% of all women in Turkey aged 20 to 24 years were married before the age of 18.[113]

Another quantitative survey that surveyed 462 married women aged between 15 and 49 years, found that, "(t)he percentage with age at first pregnancy of ≤14 years was 11.5% for women in polygamous marriages and 10.2% for women in monogamous marriages".[114] 17.3% of polygamist women were married at or before the age of 14 and the figure for the monogamist women is 20.3%. About 10% of these women had their first pregnancies either at the age of 14 or below.[115]

The European Commission of the European Union reported in 2010 that early and forced marriages remain a cause for concern. There are no reliable figures on the incidence of such marriages. Women's organisations report deterioration in their dialogue and their cooperation with relevant public institutions, at both central and local levels.[116] With regard to gender equality and women's rights, the legal framework is broadly in place but sustained further efforts are needed to turn this legal framework into political, social and economic reality.[117] A report by the United Nations stated in 2014 that child marriage is practiced in all regions of Turkey, but that there is regional variation. Whereas teenage childbearing (taken as a proxy for child marriage) is highest in Central East Anatolia (10%), it is lowest in the East Black Sea Region (3%). Teenagers in rural areas are more likely than teenagers in urban areas to have started childbearing (9% and 5%, respectively).[118] But child marriage is not only a rural phenomenon or limited to uneducated & poor individuals. For instance, former Turkish President Abdullah Gül married his wife when she was fifteen.[119] At the time, he was a PhD student at Istanbul University and his wife was a high school student in Istanbul.

Hacettepe University in Ankara conducts "The Turkey Demographic and Health Survey" every five years. It has a nationally representative sample survey. The target sample size of the TDHS-2013 was set at 14,496 households.

112 İlkkaracan, "Exploring the Context," 66, 69.
113 Yüksel-Kaptanoğlu and Ergöçmen, "Early Marriage: Trends," 1708.
114 Gücük et al, "Van İlindeki Çok Eşlilik", 127.
115 Ibid., 129.
116 EU, *European Commission Turkey 2010 Report*, 26.
117 Ibid., 79.
118 UNFPA, *Child Marriage in Turkey*, 4.
119 Euractiv, "Polygamy Widespread in Turkey."

In TDHS-2013, interviews were completed with 11,794 households and 9,746 women in the 15–49 age group in 641 clusters. The survey found that 0.2% of the females in Turkey gave birth to a child at the age of 16. 0.3% of them were pregnant with first child and 0.5% of them began childbearing at the age of 16.[120] The survey showed that, among women aged 25–49, 22% of women in Turkey married by age 18 and 4% of all women in Turkey got married before their 15th birthday[121] According to the state's Turkish Statistics Institute (TurkStat, TÜİK), 28.2% of women who got married in 2016 in Turkey were underage, while the ratio of men in the same category was 5.6%.[122]

In 2016, the EU repeated its earlier criticisms: early and forced marriage continued to be a major concern, including the situation among the Syrian refugee population.[123]

3.3 *Polygamy*

The 1926 Civil Code rendered polygamy impossible by requiring that both prospective spouses be single at the time they apply for a marriage certificate.[124] When polygamy was abolished by the Civil Code in 1926, the Muslim laws justifying polygamy became officially null and void. The official law does not allow polygamous marriage under any circumstances. If a person is a party to an existing marriage, he or she cannot validly contract a second or subsequent marriage. Articles 92, 113, 114, 115 of the Civil Code 1926 and Article 130 of the Civil Code 2001 provide that no person shall marry again unless he or she proves that the earlier marriage has been dissolved by death, by divorce, or by a decree of nullity. Article 145 of the Civil Code 2001 states that a second marriage is invalid if a person still has a spouse living at the time of the subsequent marriage. In other words, the second marriage is absolutely void, or void ab initio.

Similarly to religious-only marriage cases and child marriages, the solemnisation of polygamous marriages has also unofficially continued in Turkey. A survey that included 599 women aged 14 through 75 in South-eastern and Eastern Turkey showed that while 89.4% of them had monogamous marriages, 10.6% were living in polygamous partnerships.[125]

The Economist reported in 2005 that it is difficult to know how many men have more than one wife in Turkey, because it is illegal. The practice is known to be especially common in Kurdish regions, where life is still largely organised

120 HUIPS, *Turkey Demographic and Health Survey 2013*, 73.
121 Ibid., 107.
122 TurkStat, "Age at First Marriage by Sex."
123 EU, *European Commission Turkey 2016 Report*, 75.
124 Yildirim, "Gender and Resistance," 362.
125 İlkkaracan, "Exploring the Context," 69.

around tribal structures and Islam, and where status and power are measured in numbers. Across rural Turkey, the authorities turn a blind eye to polygamy.[126]

In a 2010 survey that interviewed 462 married women aged between 15 and 49 years, it was found that "while 410 (88.7%) women were in monogamous marriages, 52 (11.3%) were in polygamous marriages".[127] It was also found that 78.2% of women in polygamous marriages and 57.3% of women in monogamous marriages were illiterate, and polygamy significantly decreased with literacy.[128] However, similar to child marriages, polygamy is not confined to rural areas or to uneducated and poor individuals. Mr. Ali Yüksel made the headlines when he was appointed as advisor to the Prime Minister Erdoğan in June 2010. He is married to three women and declared his intentions to marry a fourth. Mr. Yüksel's polygamy already made headlines in 2004, but the Turkish media highlighted the issue of his polygamous lifestyle when appointed by Erdoğan in 2010.[129] The social anthropologist Jenny White who has worked on Turkey since 1970s states that "polygamy is particularly common in the East, although I have encountered several examples in both the poor neighbourhoods of Istanbul and among the educated Islamists".[130] She reports that the legal wives are devastated by the situation but they cannot divorce or leave their husbands. Many of them are poor and do not have credible job prospects after several years of being housewives. For the educated ones, it would be seen as "treason to the cause" (*daʿwa, jihād*) to make a scene about polygamy which is, after all, allowed in Islam. Even educated Islamist women cannot risk losing the protection and goodwill of their community.[131]

A recent study aiming to investigate the sociodemographic characteristics, sexual function, and psychological status of polygamously and monogamously married men surveyed 35 polygamous and 45 monogamous men in Kahramanmaraş Province between April 2011 and February 2014.[132] The main reasons for multiple marriages reported by polygamous men, in descending order, were: 1) decreased satisfaction of sexual desires by a wife (37.1%); 2) falling in love with the second wife (22.8%); and 3) incompatibility with the first wife (17.1%).[133]

126 The Economist, "Turkey and Polygamy."
127 Gücük et al, "Van İlindeki Çok Eşlilik," 127.
128 Ibid., 130.
129 Ynet News, "Erdoğan's Advisor's Polygamy."
130 White, "New Report on Marriage Practices in Turkey."
131 Ibid.
132 Ekerbiçer et al, "A Comparison of Sexual Function."
133 Ibid., 385.

The case law shows that the courts have had to deal with some polygamy cases.[134] In some cases, courts treat the second wife with some recognition despite the fact that she was only married unofficially. In one case, the judge held that the (unofficial) second wife should be paid some compensation from the insurance company because of the death of her unofficial husband at work.[135]

With the increasing authoritarianism and Islamist populism of the ruling AKP, Islamists' attitudes about polygamy have been gradually changing and they find it easier to talk positively about polygamy in the public sphere. For instance, on 18 June, 2016, on pro-AKP TV channel Kanal A, four male panellists discussed if Muslim men are/were free to observe their religion in Turkey. Two of them argued that "No, Muslims are not free. For example, they cannot get married according their religion. The laws of secular Turkey dictate just one wife, so Muslims cannot take a second or third".[136] In another case, an AKP supporter, Hasan Güray Özüyer, advised the AKP supporters to have polygamous marriages with wives of the imprisoned Gülen Movement participants who have resisted AKP's increasing Islamism and authoritarianism. Mr. Özüyer was criticised that his remarks were reminiscent of the practices of the ISIS militants who forcefully take women (already married or not) in the territories they occupy as their second, third and fourth wives. After an outpouring of criticism on Twitter, Mr. Özüyer had to close his Twitter account.[137]

This relaxation has also influenced bureaucrats. Seval Yildirim[138] reports that when she inquired with the Turkish Institute of Statistics (TurkStat) in November 2011 about the official numbers on the rate of polygamy in Turkey, she was told that since polygamy is outlawed in Turkey, there were no official statistics on polygamy. But recently the government started publishing official statistics on the rate of polygamy in Turkey. In 2013, the Turkish Parliament's Committee on Equality for Women and Men released official numbers on women's status, including numbers on polygamy. According to this, as of 2013, 372,000 women were in polygamous marriages across Turkey.[139]

In May 2015, the Islamist-dominated Constitutional Court nullified the law punishing religious-only marriages. Experts raised concerns that this will

134 See for case law: YHGK 26. 03. 1986, E. 2. 751- K. 287; Y2HD 27. 02. 1986, E. 1729- K. 2054; Y2HD 03. 06. 1990 194. 2546.

135 Y21HD 21.03.1996, E. 1604- K. 1661. See for similar cases involving polygamy: Yargitay Genel Kurulu E. 2006/2–558 K. 2006/568 T. 20.9.2006; Yargitay 4. Hukuk Dairesi E.2004/14503 K. 2005/11211 T. 20.10.2005.

136 Tremblay, "Turks worked up over."

137 Turkey Purge, "Turkish Government Official;" TM, "AKP men advised to have."

138 Yildirim, "Gender and Resistance," 364.

139 Ibid.

increase the number of polygamous marriages. Some experts and activists have noted that the influx of Syrian refugees has revived the tradition of polygamy. In nearly 80% of all polygamy cases, financial security and dowry are the main reasons.[140] Another report[141] confirmed that the unfortunate situation of Syrian refugees in Turkey is fuelling a rise in polygamy and argued that the government is turning a blind eye to the problem. Just in the town of Kilis, with its population of 230,000, at least 5,000 religious ceremonies have been performed between 2011 and 2014, wedding already married Turkish and Syrian men to Syrian women. According to Nur Burhan, a Syrian gender researcher with the Centre for Civil Society and Democracy, the majority of second wives are child brides sold to Turkish and Syrian men by their own families. The families get money for having their daughters married. One prosecutor stated that one of the main problems is that, until May, *imams* were not allowed to perform religious marriages before a civil marriage had taken place but that law has been repealed, making it legal for *imams* to conduct "*imam nikahı*" without punishment.[142]

The percentage of polygamous marriages in Turkish society has always been relatively low.[143] The data from the 1885 and 1906 Ottoman Censuses in Istanbul show that 2.29% of all married men in Istanbul were married polygamously. The percentage is 2.51% in the 1885 census and 2.16% in the 1906 Census.[144] It seems that the state's social engineering and modernisation have not made much impact on the rate of polygamy.

3.4 *Divorce*

The Civil Code of 1926 gave husband and wife an equal right to sue for divorce. *Ṭalāq* was no longer recognised. Divorce could only be granted by an official court on the ground that the marriage had irretrievably broken down.[145] The Code did not allow for a divorce by collusion or mutual consent. However, Article 166 of the new Civil Code 2001 makes a divorce by mutual consent possible again.

On the other hand, since marriages are religious, divorces are also made by *ṭalāq* to terminate the religious marriage, the *imam nikahı*. There are also many limping marriage cases in Turkey where a woman obtains a civil divorce, yet she thinks that she is not divorced by her husband in religion and her former

140 Tremblay, "Turks worked up over."
141 Nawa and Sebzeci, "Activists Condemn Turkey's."
142 Ibid.
143 Yildirim, "Gender and Resistance," 363.
144 Behar, "Polygyny in Istanbul, 477; Duben and Behar, *Istanbul Households*.
145 Now, Articles 161–173 of Civil Code 2001.

husband blackmails her or simply prevents her re-marriage by not pronouncing *ṭalāq*.[146] There is another phenomenon regarding unofficial *imam nikahı* marriages and its abuse. In this scenario, young people, generally university students, have an '*imam nikahı*'-only marriage without informing their parents and thus try to legitimise their sexual relationship. It is called hidden (*gizli*) *nikāḥ*. There is no recognition of their *imam nikahı*-only marriage by the official authorities. The community does not know either. If the man walks away, the woman would have no rights whatsoever before the courts under the official law. In the case of other unregistered marriages, the families and community know that the couple are married, albeit unofficially. Thus, there is a Gemeinschaft pressure on the husband and his family to respect the rights of the wife. Nevertheless, in the case of hidden marriages, the woman is left to the whims of the husband.[147]

There are a few cases where the courts have had to deal with *ṭalāq*. In an earlier case, the Court of Cassation did not recognise the *ṭalāq*, stating that there is only one type of dissolution of the marriage under the Civil Code.[148]

In a 2003 case, the Court of Cassation dealt with an under-age marriage. The woman unofficially married a man even though she was not at the legally prescribed age for marriage. They lived for some years as 'husband' and 'wife' with a view to having an official marriage when they reached the legal age. They confirmed before the court that they illegally got married before they reached the legal age limit. Nevertheless, before they could officially register their 'marriage', they were unable to get along with each other and got 'divorced'. The woman asked for financial compensation which the 'husband' rejected. The Court of Cassation held that since the woman had entered the 'marriage' as a virgin, the man's act was unjust, and she deserved some financial compensation. The Court underlined that "the petitioner's unofficial marriage does not exist legally but social values that paved the way for this marriage put a burden of loyalty on an unofficial marriage".[149]

There is abundant data on religious-only marriages (*imam nikahı*) in Turkey but we do not know much about any incidents of religious-only (*ṭalāq*) divorces. Other than anecdotal evidence, newspaper reports and some court cases, there is no field research, survey or statistics on this issue. It is obvious that more research on this subject is needed.

---

146 Yilmaz, "Non-Recognition of Post-Modern."

147 See ibid. in detail.

148 YHGK 08. 06. 1968 E. 1966. 2–1487- K. 425 T.

149 YHGD E. 2003/4–55 K. 2003/100 T. 26.02.2003.

4 Conclusion

Nation-building projects in Sunni Hanafi Muslim majority countries of Pakistan and Turkey have resorted to state law as an ideological apparatus and instrument of top-down social engineering to create modern Muslim citizens. These two Muslim nations had completely different trajectories in their approach to Islamic law. The staunchly secularist Kemalist Turkish state tried to 'cleanse' the public sphere of Muslim laws by transplanting the Swiss Civil Code and completely disregarding Muslim laws. On the other hand, Pakistan's similarly secular civilising elite could not jettison Islamic laws because creating a pure state for Muslims (Pakistan) was the justification of their partition from India. For this and possibly for some other reasons, they decided to continue the centuries-old personal law system. In this official legal pluralist arrangement (the Ottomans also had this system that was called the *millet* system), the state allows different religious personal and family laws to officially co-exist. Nevertheless, being modernising and civilising, the Pakistani power elite also embarked on reforming the majority's personal laws. Their reform attempts, similar to Turkey, have faced resistance from people in rural areas, patriarchal culture, local and tribal traditions, conservatives, some *ʿulama*, Islamists and Salafists.

As a result, regardless of their different trajectories, the instrumental use of law in these two nation states to reform family, to create modern citizens and to empower women has paved the way for unofficial (strong) Muslim legal pluralism. In these two Muslim nation states (one secular and the other an Islamic Republic), some sections of society still obey the unofficial Muslim laws as traditionally understood and practiced for centuries.

This co-existence of official and unofficial laws in the socio-legal sphere is not static. Neither do these laws operate in isolation from each other. They are intermingled and they interact. As a result, new hybrid official and unofficial laws are being continuously constructed. The case law, statistical data, official reports, surveys and field research on age of marriage, registration and solemnisation of marriage, polygamy and divorce in the Pakistani and Turkish contexts show once again that the modern nation state's claim to monopoly over law has been continually challenged in practice. In the socio-legal realm, various official and unofficial laws do not exist in isolation but rather interact in many ways. This interlegality is also a highly dynamic process. Different laws are superimposed, interpenetrated, and mixed in people's minds as much as in their actions.[150] Muslims in these two countries have been subject to

150 Santos, "Law: A Map of Misreading," 298.

competing ethnic, national, cultural, religious and especially legal reference points.[151] Vanderlinden[152] called these types of individuals *'sujets de droits'* about five decades ago. Rather than gradually fading away, it seems that with the increasing globalisation, this phenomenon will be more complex.

As a result, new hybrid formations of laws have been continually constructed. These new hybrid laws are mostly unofficial, but the Pakistani and Turkish cases also show that official laws have been influenced by the unofficial Muslim laws, too. Especially in the Pakistani socio-legal sphere, case law is full of contradicting judgments as a result of this case of strong legal pluralism. With the increase in the authoritarian Islamism of the Turkish government, the judiciary that once was a stronghold of the anti-religious laicism of the Kemalist hegemony has gradually been taken over by Islamists. As a result, early signs of the, "Pakistanisation of Turkish official laws" have started to emerge. Until recently, the state, while turning a blind eye to unofficial Muslim legal pluralism, has resisted legalising it. But it seems that this is slowly changing. Unofficial Muslim laws, similar to Pakistan, may make inroads into the official law.

Bibliography

Abbasi, Muhammad Zubair. "Women's right to unilateral no-fault based divorce in Pakistan and India." *Jindal Global Law Review* 7, no. 1 (2016): 81–95.

Ahmad, Mahtab, Moazma Batool and Sophia F. Dziegielewski. "State of Inheritance Rights: Women in a Rural District in Pakistan." *Journal of Social Service Research*, (2016): 1–8.

Ali, Shaheen Sardar. "Testing the Limits of Family Law Reform in Pakistan: A Critical Analysis of Muslim Family Laws Ordinance 1961." In *International Survey of Family Law*, edited by A. Bainham, 335 ff. Bristol: Jordans, 2001.

Althusser, Louis. "Ideology and Ideological State Apparatuses." In *Lenin and Philosophy and Other Essays*, 127–86. London and New York: Monthly Review Press, 1971.

Amnesty International in the Asia & Pacific. 2012. "Child Marriages." *Stop Violence against Women Campaign*. Available at: http://asiapacific.amnesty.org/apro/aproweb.nsf/pages/svaw_childMarriages.

Anderson, Benedict. *Imagined Communities: Reflections on the Origin and Spread of Nationalism*. London: Verso, 2006.

151 McLellan and Richmond, "Multiculturalism in Crisis," 669.

152 Vanderlinden, "Le Pluralisme Juridique."

Asimovic-Akyol, Riada. "Turkish Court Stirs Marriage Debate." *Al-Monitor*, 1 June, 2015. http://www.al-monitor.com/pulse/originals/2015/06/turkey-top-court-stirs-debate-on-religious-marriage.html#ixzz4lOvxO58T.

Balchin, Cassandra. *A Handbook on Family Law in Pakistan*. Lahore: Shirkat Gah, 1994.

Behar, Cem. "Polygyny in Istanbul, 1885–1926." *Middle Eastern Studies* 27, no. 3 (1991): 477–486.

Bozkurt, Gülnihal. "The Reception of Western European Law in Turkey (From the Tanzimat to the Turkish Republic, 1839–1939)." *Der Islam* 75, (1998): 283–295.

Carroll, Lucy. "The Muslim Family Laws Ordinance, 1961: Provisions and Procedures. A Reference Paper for Current Research." *Contributions to Indian Sociology* 13, no. 1 (1979): 117–143.

Carroll, Lucy. "Nizam-i-Islam: Processes and Conflicts in Pakistan's Programme of Islamisation with Special Reference to the Position of Women." *Journal of Commonwealth and Comparative Politics* 20, no. 1 (1982): 57–95.

Cheema, Shahbaz Ahmed. "Fatawa in Pakistani Courts: An Appraisal." *Al-Adwa* 46, no. 31 (2016): 61–76.

Cotterell, Roger. *The Politics of Jurisprudence*. Austin: Butterworths, 1989.

Dawn. 2011. "Senate Passes Two Pro-Woman Bills Unanimously", *Dawn*, 12 December, 2011. Available at: http://dawn.com/2011/12/12/senate-passes-two-pro-women-bills-unanimously/ last visited on 2 July, 2017.

Devji, Faisal. *Muslim Zion: Pakistan as a Political Idea*. Cambridge, MA: Harvard University Press, 2013.

Duben, Alan and Cem Behar. *Istanbul Households: Marriage, Family and Fertility, 1880–1940*. Cambridge and New York: Cambridge University Press, 1990.

Ekerbiçer, Hasan Ç. "A Comparison of Sexual Function, Psychological Status, and Sociodemographic Characteristics of Turkish Men within Polygamous and Monogamous Marriages". *Balkan Medical Journal* 33 (2016): 383–9.

EU (European Union). 2010. *European Commission Turkey 2010 Report*. Brussels: EC.

EU (European Union). 2016. *European Commission Turkey 2016 Report*. Brussels: EC.

Euractiv. "Polygamy Widespread in Turkey, Study Shows." Accessed February 1, 2017. https://www.euractiv.com/section/social-europe-jobs/news/polygamy-widespread-in-turkey-study-shows/.

Fatimah, Shifa and Zafar Zahir. 2016. "Is Child Marriage Associated with the Survival Status of First Pregnancy? Evidence from PDHS 2012–13", *National Institute of Population Studies, Women Well-Being: A Life in Progress. An in Depth Analysis of Pakistan Demographic and Health Survey 2–12–2013*. 45–58.

Gramsci, Antonio. *Selections from the Prison Notebooks of Antonio Gramsci*. New York: International Publishers, 1971.

Griffiths, John. "What is Legal Pluralism?" *The Journal of Legal Pluralism and Unofficial Law* 18, no. 24 (1986): 1–55.

Gücük, S. "Van İlindeki Çok Eşlilik Oranları ve Etkileyen Faktorler: Kesitsel Çalışma [Polygamy Rates and the Affecting Factors in Van: A Cross-Sectıonal Study]" *J Kartal TR* 21, no. 3 (2010): 127–33.

Hooker, M.B. *Legal Pluralism.* Oxford: Clarendon Press, 1975.

HUIPS (Hacettepe University Institute of Population Studies). *Turkey Demographic and Health Survey 2013*. Ankara: HUIPS, 2014.

Hussain, Mohammed Subhan. "History, Law and Vernacular Knowledge: The Threat to Women's Collective Representation Under the Guise of Androgyny in Pakistan." *The King's Student Law Review* 7, no. 2 (2016): 64–75.

İlkkaracan, Pinar. "Exploring the Context of Women's Sexuality in Turkey", *Reproductive Health Matters* 6, no. 12 (1998): 66–75.

Lau, Martin. *The Role of Islam in the Legal System of Pakistan.* Leiden: Brill, 2006.

Lau, Martin. "Sharia and National Law in Pakistan." In *Sharia Incorporated: A Comparative Overview of the Legal Systems of Twelve Muslim Countries in Past and Present*, edited by Jan Michiel Otto, 373–432. Leiden: Leiden University Press, 2010.

Magnarella, Paul J. *Tradition and Change in a Turkish Town.* New York: John Wiley and Sons, 1974.

McLellan, Janet and Anthony H. Richmond. "Multiculturalism in Crisis: A Postmodern Perspective on Canada." *Ethnic and Racial Studies* 17, no. 4 (1994): 662–83.

Mehdi, Rubya. *The Islamization of the Law in Pakistan.* Richmond: Curzon Press, 1994.

Menski, Werner F. "Governance and Governability in South Asian Family Laws and in Diaspora." *The Journal of Legal Pluralism and Unofficial Law* 45, no. 1 (2013): 42–57.

Miller, Ruth A. "The Ottoman and Islamic Substratum of Turkey's Swiss Civil Code." *Journal of Islamic Studies* 11, no. 3 (2000): 335–361.

Mills, C. Wright. *The Power Elite.* Oxford and New York: Oxford University Press, 1956.

Nasrullah, Muazzam. "Child Marriage and Its Impact on Maternal and Child Health in Pakistan." PhD diss., University of Bielefeld, 2015.

National Institute of Population Studies (NIPS) [Pakistan]. *Pakistan Demographic and Health Survey 2006–07*. Islamabad, Pakistan: National Institute of Population Studies, 2008.

Nawa, Fariba and Ozge Sebzeci. "Activists Condemn Turkey's Polygamous Marriages Targeting Syrian Refugees." *The World Post.* Accessed 25 July, 2016. http://www.huffingtonpost.com/entry/polygamy-inturkey_us_57964212e4b01180b52fae27 last visited on 2 July, 2017.

O'Neil, Mary Lou and Sule Toktas. "Women's Property Rights in Turkey." *Turkish Studies* 15, no. 1 (2014): 29–44.

Örücü, Esin. "Judicial Navigation as Official Law Meets Culture in Turkey." *International School of Law in Context* 4, no. 1 (2008): 35–61.

Özman, Aylin. "Law, Ideology and Modernization in Turkey: Kemalist Legal Reforms in Perspective." *Social Legal Studies* 19, (2010): 67–84.

Özsu, Umut. "Receiving' the Swiss Civil Code: Translating Authority in Early Republican Turkey", *International Journal of Law in Context* 6, no. 1 (2010): 63–89.

Patel, Rashida. *Socio-Economic Political Status and Women and Law in Pakistan*. Karachi: Faiza Publishers, 1991.

Pearl, D. and Menski, Werner F. *Muslim Family Law*. London: Sweet and Maxwell, 1998.

Powell, Russell. *Shari'a in the Secular State: Evolving Meanings of Islamic Jurisprudence in Turkey*. London and New York: Routledge, 2016.

Rutgers. *The Puppet and the Puppeteers: An Account of Consultative Process on Child Marriages Adolescent Girls Empowerment Project*. Islamabad: Rutgers WPF Pakistan, 2012.

Saleem, Raja M. Ali. "Effect of Islam's Role in State Nationalism on the Islamization of Government: Case Studies of Turkey and Pakistan." PhD diss., George Mason University, 2015.

Santos, Boaventura De Sousa. "Law: A Map of Misreading. Toward a Postmodern Conception of Law." *Journal of Law and Society* 14, no. 3 (1987): 279–302.

Santos, B. *Toward a New Legal Common Sense: Law, Globalization and Emancipation*. London: Butterworths, 2002.

Shah, Niaz A. *Women, The Koran and International Human Rights Law: The Experience of Pakistan*. Leiden and Boston: Martinus Nijhoff Publishers, 2006.

Shah, Waseem Ahmad. "Fresh Controversy over Polygamy, Marriage Dissolution." *Dawn*. Accessed 27 October, 2014. https://www.dawn.com/news/1140685.

SPO (State Planning Organization). *Türk Aile Araştırması*. Ankara: DPT, 1992.

Starr, June. *Law as Metaphor: From Islamic Courts to the Palace of Justice*. New York: State University of New York Press, 1992.

Starr, June. "The Role of Turkish Secular Law in Changing the Lives of Rural Muslim Women, 1950–1970." *Law and Society Review* 23, no. 3 (1989): 497–523.

Stepan, Alfred. "The World's Religious Systems and Democracy: Crafting the 'Twin Tolerations." In *Arguing Comparative Politics*, edited by Alfred Stepan, 218–225. Oxford: Oxford University Press, 2001.

Stirling, Paul. *Turkish Village*. London: Weidenfeld and Nicolson, 1965.

Tanzilur-Rahman. *Muslim Family Laws Ordinance: Islamic and Social Survey*. Karachi: Royal Book Company, 1997.

Taylor, Charles. "Modes of Secularism." In *Secularism and its Critics*, edited by Rajeev Bhargava, 31–53. Delhi: Oxford University Press, 1999.

TCC (Turkish Constitutional Court). "Judgment." Accessed 27 May, 2015. http://www.constitutionalcourt.gov.tr/inlinepages/leadingjudgements/ConstitutionalityReview/judgment/2015-51.pdf.

The Economist. "Turkey and Polygamy: Too Much of a Good Thing. Why a Strong Tradition Persists in Defiance of the Law." Accessed 25 December, 2005. http://www.economist.com/node/5328042.

Timur, Serim. *Turkiye'de Aile Yapisi*. Ankara: Hacettepe Universitty Press, 1972.

Tremblay, Pinar. "Turks worked up over wanting more wives." Al-Monitor. http://www.al-monitor.com/pulse/originals/2016/06/turkey-pious-men-demand-polygamy-rights.html.

Turkey Purge. "Turkish Government Official Advises Ruling Party Supporters to Have Polygamous Marriages with Wives of Jailed Gülenists." Turkey Purge. Accessed 14 January, 2017. https://turkeypurge.com/turkish-govt-official-advices-ruling-party-supporters-to-have-polygamous-marriages-with-wives-of-jailed-gulenists.

Turkish Minute (TM). "AKP men advised to have polygamous marriages with wives of jailed Gülen followers." *Turkish Minute*, Accessed 13 January, 2017. https://www.turkishminute.com/2017/01/13/akp-men-advised-make-polygamous-marriages-wives-jailed-gulen-followers/.

TurkStat (State Institute of Statistics Prime Ministry Republic of Turkey). *Marriage Statistics: 1994*. Ankara: SIS, 1996.

TurkStat (State Institute of Statistics Prime Ministry Republic of Turkey). "Form of Solemnization by Age Group, 2016." Family Structure Survey. http://www.tuik.gov.tr/HbGetir.do?id=21869&tb_id=8.

TurkStat (State Institute of Statistics Prime Ministry Republic of Turkey). "Age at First Marriage by Sex, 2016." Family Structure Survey. http://www.tuik.gov.tr/HbGetir.do?id=21869&tb_id=4.

UNFPA (United Nations Population Fund). *Child Marriage in Pakistan: A Taboo. Study Report*. Islamabad, 2007.

UNFPA (United Nations Population Fund). *Marrying Too Young: End Child Marriage*. New York: UNFPA, 2012.

UNFPA (United Nations Population Fund). *Child Marriage in Turkey*. Istanbul: UNPFA, 2012. http://eeca.unfpa.org/sites/default/files/pub-pdf/unfpa%20turkey%20overview.pdf.

Vanderlinden, Jacques. "Le Pluralisme Juridique: Essai de Synthese." In *Le pluralisme juridique*, edited John Gilissen, 19–56. Brussels: Universite de Bruxelles, 1971.

White, Jenny. "New Report on Marriage Practices in Turkey." *Kamil Pasha: Turkey, and the Thoughts and Fiction of Jenny White*, Accessed 2 July, 2017. http://kamilpasha.com/?p=4071.

WLUML (Women Living Under Muslim Laws). *Child, Early and Forced Marriage: A Multi-Country Study. A Submission to the UN Office of the High Commissioner on Human Rights* (OCHCR), London: WLUML, 2013.

Yasa, Ibrahim. *Hasanoglan: Socio-Economic Structure of a Turkish Village*. Ankara: Public Administration Institute, 1957.

Yefet, Karin Carmit. "What's the Constitution Got to Do With It? Regulating Marriage in Pakistan." *Duke Journal of Gender Law and Policy* 16 (2009): 347–377.

Yildirim, Seval. "Gender and Resistance in Turkey: On Myths of Liberty and Salvation." *Transnational Law and Contemporary Problems* 24, no. 2 (2015): 353.

Yilmaz, Ihsan. "Secular Law and the Emergence of Unofficial Turkish Islamic Law." *The Middle East Journal* 56, no. 1 (2002): 113–31.

Yilmaz, Ihsan. "Non-Recognition of Post-Modern Turkish Socio-Legal Reality and Predicament of Women." *British Journal of Middle Eastern Studies* 30, no. 1 (2003): 25–41.

Yilmaz, Ihsan. *Muslim Laws, Politics and Society in Modern Nation States: Dynamic Legal Pluralisms in England, Turkey and Pakistan*. Aldershot: Ashgate, 2005.

Yilmaz, Ihsan. "State, Law, Civil Society and Islam in Contemporary Turkey." *Muslim World* 95, (2005): 385–411.

Yilmaz, Ihsan. "Good Governance in Action: Pakistani Muslim laws on Human Rights and Gender-Equality." *European Journal of Economic and Political Studies* 4, no. 2 (2011): 155–168.

Yilmaz, Ihsan. "Homo LASTus and Lausannian Muslim: Two Paradoxical Social-Engineering Projects to Construct the Best and the Good Citizens in the Kemalist Panopticon." *Turkish Journal of Politics* 4, no. 2 (2013): 107–126.

Yilmaz, Ihsan. "Religious Freedom, the Muslim Identity and the Secularist Social-Engineering Project in Turkey." *Qaderni di Diritto e Politica Ecclesiastica* 22, no. 1 (2014): 197–204.

Yilmaz, Ihsan. "Pakistan Federal Shariat Court's Collective Ijtihād on Gender Equality, Women's Rights and the Right to Family Life." *Islam and Christian-Muslim Relations* 25, no. 2 (2014): 181–192.

Yilmaz, Ihsan. "Islamic Family Law in Secular Turkish Courts." In *Adjudicating Family Law in Muslim Courts: Cases from the Contemporary Muslim World*, edited by Elisa Guinchi, 148–159. London: Routledge 2014.

Yilmaz, Ihsan. "Semi-official Turkish Muslim Legal Pluralism: Encounters Between Secular Official Law and Unofficial Shari'a." In *The Sociology of Shari'a: Case Studies from around the World, Boundaries of Religious Freedom: Regulating Religion*, edited by A. Possamai, Bryan S. Turner and James T. Richardson, 51–65. Springer, 2015.

Yilmaz, Ihsan. *Muslim laws, Politics and Society in Modern Nation States: Dynamic Legal Pluralisms in England, Turkey and Pakistan*. London: Routledge, 2016.

Yıldırak, Nurettin. *Köy Kadınlarının Sosyo-Ekonomik ve Kültürel Konumları*. Istanbul: Friedrich Ebert Vakfı, 1992.

Ynet News. "Erdoğan's Advisor's Polygamy Stirs Debate in Turkey." Ynet News. Accessed 6 August, 2010. http://www.ynetnews.com/articles/0,7340,L-3931164,00.html.

Yüksel-Kaptanoğlu İlknur and Banu Akadli Ergöçmen. "Early Marriage: Trends in Turkey, 1978–2008." *Journal of Family Issues* 35, no. 12 (2014): 21707–24.

Zorlu-Durukan, Şefika Akile. "The Ideological Pillars of Turkish Education: Emergent Kemalism and the Zenith of Single-Party Rule." PhD diss., University of Wisconsin-Madison, 2006.

Constitutional Recognition of Islamic Family Law and Shariʿa Courts in Ethiopia: Governmental Strategies to Co-regulate the Plural Family Law Arena

Katrin Seidel

1 Introductory Remarks

"Legal Pluralism is a fact. Legal centralism is a myth, an ideal, a claim, an illusion".[1] John Griffiths's statement in the mid-1980s has stimulated the longstanding[2] legal debate on how to deal with the discrepancy between legal claims and legal reality, a debate that has lost none of its relevance. The question of whether legal pluralism is an appropriate analytical category to reflect legal realities seems thus to be answered: The central term legal pluralism permits the analysis of the interrelations and interdependencies between different normative orders.[3] A legal pluralist perspective takes into consideration the development of semi-independent networks and authorities of governance and their respective normativities.[4] It allows for analysing the complex governance-actor constellations and their diverse regulative legal practices and structures in order to better understand changing modes of governance.[5] Accordingly, this perspective acknowledges the fact that local and religious authority structures have long been "agents of governance in many states",[6] and that they have been constructed and utilised in the context of various colonial

1 Griffiths, "What is Legal Pluralism," 4.

2 Beginning of the 20th century the debate was fuelled by the legal scholar Eugen Ehrlich and his focus on the "living law" (see Ehrlich, Grundlegung der Soziologie).

3 See Moore, "Certainties Undone," 346–367. In accordance with Ramstedt ("Anthroplogical Perspectives," 53), normative orders can be defined as "orders guaranteed by the reasonable expectation, informed by experience and observation, on the part of the members of the respective normative communities that these orders will be enforced or infringements avenged by teams of experts responsible with upholding the stability of the respective norms as well as the stability of the social orders rooted in them".

4 Normativities refer to so called non-state law in forms of non-juridified customary law and and religious law. (see Ramstedt, "Anthroplogical Perspectives," 53.)

5 Benda-Beckmann, "Rules of Law," 2.

6 Ibid.

 | DOI:10.1163/9789004398269_008

rules of social control.[7] In dealing with legal realities in which religious, local and state normative orders co-exist as well as with the inherent potential for social and legal conflicts when the various interacting normative orders rely on plural sources of law and different bases of legitimacy,[8] contemporary state actors pursue different approaches. The Ethiopian context provides thought-provoking insights for theorizing legal pluralism in terms of pluralist state policies and implementation efforts. As a result of centuries of coexistence, cooperation and conflict between the different 'semi-autonomous'[9] normative orders, partly overlapping permeable normative structures have evolved. Normative pluralism becomes especially visible in the arena of family law where the local laws of the more than eighty local communities[10] and the religious laws of diverse Christian and Muslim communities[11] are the predominant regulating normative tools. This chapter seeks to sketch how Ethiopian governmental actors attempt to deal with the legal realities of the highly contested family arena. The focus is on the Ethiopian version of Islamic family law applied by the Shariʿa courts. These religious courts have existed on the territory of contemporary Ethiopia for centuries and have always played a significant role in the life of Muslim communities – which constitute at least one-third of Ethiopia's population[12] – regardless of their recognition by the state. In order to regulate the legal pluralities and to mediate the relations of diverse normative orders, Ethiopia has developed its own mode of state-recognised legal pluralism. Ethiopian governments, including the current one, have acknowledged local and religious normative orders to different degrees, depending on their respective *devide et impera* policies. As early as 1942, Emperor Haile Selassie I (1892–1975), in an attempt to regulate plurality, proclaimed that "[…] when we established Kadis' Courts by law we did it in order to achieve national unity".[13] Upon first glance it seems paradoxical to achieve 'national unity' through the recognition of pluralism. One may ask to what extent this political claim could be attained in light of the legal realities. Assuming it is possible, how could a legal framework be constructed to reflect Ethiopian legal pluralities and to create space for their different normative orders? Moreover, how could the space where Islamic, local and state normative perceptions overlap be designed

7 Merry, "From Law and Colonialism," 573.
8 See Benda-Beckmann, "Rules of Law"; Kötter and Schuppert, "Normative Pluralität ordnen."
9 Moore, "Law and Social Change," 719–746.
10 PCCE 2008: 16.
11 Ibid., 17.
12 Ibid., 111.
13 Ḫaylä Šellase I., cit. in: Trimingham, *Islam in Ethiopia*, 231.

institutionally? With the adoption of the *Constitution of the Federal Democratic Republic of Ethiopia* of 1995 (FDRE Constitution) a pluralist legal frame was established: Changing socio-political realities[14] have led to a paradigm shift in thinking about law – from a rather monist to a pluralist approach – which becomes visible in the state legal system since the 1990s: Currently, ethno-linguistic and religious diversity have become *de jure* co-organising principles. For the first time in Ethiopian's legal history the application of Islamic Family law by Shariʿa courts was accorded constitutional recognition.[15] The central hypothesis of this study[16] is that a constitutional recognition of Islamic law can create space and a forum for negotiation processes between the various (institutional) actors involved. The FDRE Constitution defines the general conditions and areas of jurisdiction of the Shariʿa courts, while the concrete, substantive definition is in the hands of the federal and regional legislators. In order not to relinquish authority over co-regulating the 'private sphere', governmental actors follow a double strategy. Alongside the introduction of a comprehensive state family law reform, religious and 'customary' laws have been constitutionally recognised. Thus, the Ethiopian Muslim population has been *de jure* given the choice to be adjudicated by Shariʿa courts and Islamic law. This chapter seeks to show that state-recognised legal pluralism (called 'weak legal pluralism' by Griffiths[17]) inherently leads to tensions between normative concepts of Islamic law and state law. Taking into account that "multiple networks of legal orders are forcing us to constant transitions and trespassings",[18] such pluralism also fosters (re-)negotiations and mutual adaptation processes as reactions to divergent normative values and concepts. Accordingly, the focus on the intersections of different normative orders, or on the 'interlegality'[19] to use a term coined by Boaventura de Sousa Santos's, takes into account the processual nature of constant transformations which constitute an inherently uncertain, unstable and uneven intermingling of different normative orders. Before focussing on the Ethiopian state-recognised legal pluralist arrangement and showing how Ethiopian state actors position themselves as 'wardens' of plurality, it is important to briefly sketch the political history of the current plural

14 Aberra Jembere and Woldetensay Woldemelak, *An Introduction to the Legal History; Legal History of Ethiopia.*

15 Art. 27(2), 78 (5), 34(4,5) FDRE Constitution.

16 The study was part of my Ph.D. research and is based on two periods of fieldwork in Ethiopia conducted in 2008 and 2009. Main research foci were on the Shariʿa courts in Addis Ababa, Dire Dawa and Harar.

17 Griffiths, "What is Legal Pluralism," 8.

18 Santos, "Law," 298.

19 Ibid.; Santos, *Toward a New Common Sense*, 114.

legal arrangement by retracing some key dynamics and events which contributed to the changing legal status of Ethiopian Shariʿa courts.

2 Historical Development of the Official Legal Status of Shariʿa Courts

Islamic jurisdiction with its own judicial mechanisms of dispute has existed within the territory of contemporary Ethiopia for centuries, long before becoming recognised in state law by Emperor Haile Selassie I in 1942. Historical accounts show that Kadis courts were established in different Muslim sultanates within the Northern and Eastern territories of contemporary Ethiopia as well as in Ifat, Dawaro, Bali, Mara, Jimma and Harar from the 10th century.[20] Ethiopia's history was characterised by recurrent power struggles between Muslim and Christian political actors. However, a *modus vivendi* of practices of coexistence, exchange and cooperation developed over time as well, mainly based on joint economic activities and on common cultural elements which have shaped the Ethiopian societal structure.[21] However, despite the manifold interlinkages: Islam in Ethiopia has always been a religion with secondary and, in the eyes of many Ethiopian leaders, inferior status; it emerged in the shadow of Christianity and often suffered from suppression and discrimination. This has had its impact on social opportunities, religious and civil rights and the patterns of self-organisation of the Muslims.[22] Changing global political constellations during World War II and its aftermath led to a strengthening of Islam within the Horn of Africa region between 1930 and 1974.[23] Particularly, the Ethiopian Muslims' legal status changed tremendously during the brief Italian occupation (1935–1941). In the course of Italy's colonial *divide et impera* strategies, Muslim political demands were actively promoted since the European invaders depended on local support and local institutions in order to break the resistance of the former ruling elites. Political as well as military interests motivated the Italian governors in Ethiopia to become 'protectors of Islam'.[24] Accordingly, Benito Mussolini proclaimed in Tripoli in 1937 that "Fascist Italy intends to guarantee to Muslim people of […] Ethiopia peace, justice, prosperity, and respect for the laws of the Prophet […]".[25] Thus, the

20 Ibrahim Idris, "Freedom of Religion," 152; Wagner, "Härar History," 1015.
21 Hussein Ahmed, "Islam and Islamic Discourse," 777.
22 Abbink, "A Historical-Anthropological Approach," 113.
23 Trimingham, *Islam in Ethiopia*, 136.
24 Sbacchi, *Ethiopia under Mussolini*, 161.
25 Mussolini, cit. in: Trimingham, *Islam in Ethiopia*, 137.

Italian administration constructed, for instance, mosques, established Shariʿa courts and appointed Kadis throughout the country.[26] In response to the politically strengthened position of the Muslim population during Italian occupation, Shariʿa courts became officially recognised by Haile Selassie I through the *Kadis Proclamation* of 1942, followed by the *Naiba and Kadis Council Proclamation* of 1944. The Proclamations reduced the wide jurisdiction of the former Muslim councils to family and personal law. They established a two- or three-tiered court structure running parallel to the state courts. The Shariʿa courts were empowered to adjudicate family law and inheritance for Muslims. However, this legal status was challenged by the emperor's codification of state family law in 1960 under the political banner of 'modernisation'. Art. 3347 of the *Civil Code of Ethiopia of 1960* (CC) stipulates, "[u]nless otherwise expressly provided, all rules whether written or customary previously in force concerning matters provided for in this Code shall be replaced by this Code and are hereby repealed".

Even though the integration of a specific clause for Islamic law had been discussed during the drafting process of the CC, the final provisions of the CC made no exception for Muslims.[27] Thus, de jure the Shariʿa courts were deprived of their legal basis. However, instead of being abolished, they remained administratively integrated into the state judicial system since the Shariʿa courts in Addis Ababa were de facto established as a branch of the *Supreme Imperial Court*. Over time even more Kadis were appointed.[28] After the ousting of Haile Selassie I in 1974, the policy under the *Provisional Military Administrative Council* (Derg) was not different from that of its predecessor. Despite constant requests from the *Ethiopian Supreme Islamic Council*, the Derg opted for keeping the status quo[29] and for not changing the legal status of the Shariʿa courts.[30] Ibrahim Idris summarises the development of the de jure legal status of the Shariʿa jurisdiction during that time:

> [...] the process of westernization of the Ethiopian legal system that resulted in the codification of the country's law has had no substantial effect on their [the Muslim's] traditional family practices. In view of this

26 Aberra Jembere, *Legal History of Ethiopia*, 220; Sbacchi, *Ethiopia under Mussolini*, 163; Abdul Wasie, "*Shari'a Courts in Ethiopia*," 21; Hussein Ahmed, "Islam and Islamic Discourse," 775–6.

27 Zaki Mustafa, "The Substantive Law," 142; Abdul Wasie, "*Shari'a Courts in Ethiopia*," 24–26.

28 Sedler, *Ethiopian Civil Procedure*, 12.

29 A circular letter of the Ministry of Justice ordered the Shariʿa courts to continue their previous function according to the 1944 Proclamation.

30 Ibrahim Idris, "Freedom of Religion," 153, 156; Hussein Ahmed, "Islam and Islamic Discourse," 789, 792–3.

> circumstance, it may be difficult and even dangerous to repudiate with a stroke of the pen an institution or practice deeply rooted in religion in order to build a uniform system. [...] It is advisable to look into the factual situations in deciding on the status of Islamic law and Shari'a Courts.[31]

Thus, the Shari'a courts continued to operate for more than forty years without a de jure legal basis. Against the backdrop of these conditions, the FDRE Constitution of 1995 has introduced tremendous changes regarding the legal status and function of the Shari'a courts that will be discussed in the following section.

3 Constitutional Recognition of Islamic Family Law and Shari'a Courts

Like Emperor Haile Selassie I, current Ethiopian state actors follow a dual strategy within a broader policy of advocating for 'unity in diversity': They attempt to regulate the application of local and religious laws by constitutional recognition. This legally plural arrangement was the result of an intense debate during the constitution-making process in March 1994. The *Constitutional Assembly* attempted to find an appropriate solution regarding the legal status of Shari'a jurisdiction. In the course of the debate two major camps of opinion could be identified: According to a rather strict secular position, state recognition of religious courts was perceived as an interference into religious matters. Others argued that a decision in favour of non-recognition would deprive the Muslim population of the chance to be guided by their Islamic family law and would intolerably restrict their freedom of religion. Finally, the *Constitutional Assembly* gave priority to integrating the demands of Muslim authorities.[32] Accordingly, the current FDRE Constitution stipulates: "this constitution shall not preclude the adjudication of disputes relating to personal and family laws in accordance with religious or customary laws, with the consent of the parties to the dispute".[33] The constitution empowers the *House of the Peoples' Representatives* (viz. chamber of the Federal Parliamentary Assembly of Ethiopia) as well as *State Councils* (viz. the parliamentary assemblies of

31 Ibrahim Idris, "Freedom of Religion," 155.

32 See Shukria Mohammad, "Sharia Courts of Ethiopia," 44; Dereje Feyissa, "Muslims Struggling," 36–41.

33 Art. 34(5) FDRE Constitution.

the regional states) to establish official religious and '*customary*' courts.[34] In 1999, the *House of People's Representatives* enacted the *Federal Shari'a Court Consolidation Proclamation* (Proclamation 188/1999). This proclamation established Shari'a courts for Addis Ababa and Dire Dawa under federal jurisdiction. Similarly, several *State Councils* have officially recognised Shari'a courts while others have not gone further than adopting a verbal copy of the above mentioned Art. 34(5) FDRE Constitution. As a result, parallel to the regular courts structure, a three-layer Shari'a court structure has been established at federal and at regional levels: the *First Instance Court of Shari'a*, the *High Court of Shari'a*, and the *Supreme Court of Shari'a*, each staffed with its own Kadis.[35] Accordingly, the Shari'a courts are one de jure option within Ethiopian's plural judicial arena where each normative order involves an alternative basis for legal claims. Studies have shown that in legally plural settings people tend to make use of their options in a strategical fashion. The disputants "[...] base their choice on what they hope the outcome of the dispute will be, however vague or ill-founded their expectations may be".[36] Therefore, governmental actors institutionalise and regulate the choice of legal forums which is often described as 'forum shopping'. Moreover, in the course of governmental actors' claims of ensuring 'legal certainty' and procedural justice, the Ethiopian Shari'a courts are supposed to apply solely the *Civil Procedure Code of Ethiopia* (CPC) as procedural law and uncodified Islamic law as substantive law.[37] On the other hand, the FDRE Constitution puts a strong emphasis on 'equality before the law and equal protection of the law' as well as on 'rights of women'.[38] As mentioned above, a broad family law reform promoting gender-equality has been initiated by governmental actors. The *Revised Family Code* (RFC) of 2000 shows tremendous changes in legislation. The RFC Preamble proclaims that it has become necessary to amend the existing law in order to guarantee the comprehensive protection of children and family – based on equality of the spouses during the conclusion, duration and dissolution of marriage. Moreover, any laws, regulations, decisions and practices inconsistent with the RFC shall not be applicable, in particular not the provisions of the *Civil Code of Ethiopia* of 1960 (CC) on persons, family and inheritance.[39] Like its predecessor, the CC, the RFC acknowledges various forms of marriage – the civil,

---

34 Art. 78(5) FDRE Constitution.

35 Art. 3,11, 12 Proclamation 188/1999; HPNRS Proclamation (amendment) 8/1991 e.c. [Nr. 8/1998 g.c.].

36 Benda-Beckmann, K. v., "Forum Shopping," 117.

37 Art. 6 II i.v.m. 5 V Proclamation 188/1999.

38 Art. 25, 35 FDRE Constitution.

39 Art. 319(1) RFC.

the "customary" and the religious marriage – under binding procedural conditions. All marriages shall produce the same legal effects regardless of the form under which it has been celebrated.[40] The CC was and the RFC is de facto implemented mainly through religious and local dispute resolution mechanisms. Moreover, the legal ideas of the RFC have only very limited effects on the life of the subjects of the normative regime, which may clearly be viewed as a weakness of the *top-down*-approach with regard to the implementation of state family law reforms.[41] According to an empirical study, the majority of people in the capital city Addis Ababa is unaware of the existence of the *Revised Family Code* and its fundamental changes.[42] Thus, the enactment of the *RFC* has not significantly narrowed the huge gap between the 'law in the books' and the 'living law'. Since state legal interventions comply only to a marginal extent with the legal reality, state actors have made huge efforts to not entirely relinquish the authority over co-regulating the 'private' sphere. The constitutional recognition of 'non-state' normative orders is one such effort. However, it inherently leads to tensions between normative concepts, as for instance between Islamic law and state law. In the context of constitutionally recognised legal pluralism the general question arises of how to deal with arising legal conflicts between the religious personal laws, the constitutional order, and fundamental principles applicable to all citizens.

3.1 *The 'Supremacy Clause'*

In general, one might ask whether and how state power can be imposed on each normative order without offending their underlying socio-legal logics. In order to avoid a general erosion of the constitutional order, the FDRE Constitution states that, "any law, customary practice or a decision of an organ of state or a public official which contravenes this Constitution shall be of no effect".[43] The question arises whether the 'supremacy clause' is actually enforced. One may further ask whether the religious courts should be considered as part of the state judiciary. The constitutional recognition of Islamic law and Shariʿa courts has provoked a debate among scholars, legal practitioners and politicians about the comparability of substantive religious provisions with basic constitutional principles such as equality of citizens. Some argue that if religious arrangements and the FRDE-Constitution are in conflict, the

40 Art. 2, 4, 26(1) RFC.
41 Trask, "Challenges for Women," 84.
42 Medhanit Legesse, "Major Changes," 88–95.
43 Art. 9(1) FDRE Constitution.

constitution should prevail.[44] Final decisions of the Shariʿa courts should be compatible with the supremacy clause and human rights norms enshrined in the constitution. Others, however, argue that the application of Islamic law in Ethiopia is an exception to the overall legal system, i.e. even if there are deviations from some constitutional principles, the decision of the Shariʿa courts should be considered as constitutional as long as the procedural requirement of mutual consensus is fulfilled. In support of the first position, it is claimed that Art. 9(1) FDRE Constitution, i.e. 'any decision of state organ' comprises any decision made by the executive, legislature, judiciary, or any organ with judicial power. This includes Shariʿa courts as well. However, this would essentially mean a severe limitation of religious norms by state law. One may object that this position ignores the values and essence of religious and local norms as being a source of cultural attributes and social cohesion in the lives of many people. Uncompromising antagonism towards religion can be counter-productive and may trigger counter-measures towards stricter and more rigid interpretations and practices. Another set of arguments focuses on the requirement for litigants' consent that makes Islamic jurisdiction voluntary. It has been argued that "the very act of expressing consent can 'purify' the 'defective' rules in custom and religion".[45] The pluralist arrangement is made to draw a parallel structure between the two different court systems and thereby maintain the non-reviewability of decisions of one by the other. Hence, decisions of Shariʿa courts that may even breach constitutional norms can be treated as an exception to Art. 9(1); even though the Constitution does not explicitly articulate this exception. In order to deal with these conflicting opinions, the current legislation follows a 'procedural approach' which reveals contentious issues as will be shown in the following.

3.2 *State-Funding and Secularism*

The relationship between constitutionally recognised Islamic law including its judicial administration and the claim to be a secular state is a contentious issue: The FDRE Constitution guarantees individual and collective religious freedom as a fundamental right, and, moreover, reflects the concept of a secular state aiming to ensure equal rights and justice including the recognition of minority rights. According to Article 11 FDRE Constitution, state and religion are separated; there shall be no state religion and the state shall not interfere in religious matters and vice versa. If one takes a closer look at the constitutional history of Ethiopia, it becomes obvious that the idea of secularism is a relatively

44 Menberetshai Tadesse, interview (23.03.2008).

45 See Getachew Assefa, "Federalism and Legal Pluralism," 22.

recent development, since a strong bond between the Ethiopian Orthodox Tewahedo Church and the state existed under monarchic rule. Even though the *Imperial Revised Constitution* of 1955 (IRC) already recognised the freedom of exercise of one's religious rites,[46] the Ethiopian Orthodox Tewahedo Church was "the established church of the empire and was, as such, supported by the state. The Emperor shall always profess the Ethiopian Orthodox Faith".[47] This intertwined bond has been summarised by Perham:

> Constitutionally, [...] the Emperor was the unchallenged head of the church and the fortunes of the Solomonic Dynasty were interwoven by historical associations with those of the church and initial interests. Emperor and church, working together as senior and junior partners, provided the unifying elements, which continually countered the centrifugal forces geography, tribalism and aristocracy.[48]

In contrast to the *IRC*, the *Constitution of the People's Democratic Republic of Ethiopia of 1987* (PDRE Constitution) explicitly declared the separation of state and church/ religion, which was a novelty in the history of the country.[49] The PDRE Constitution *de jure* ended the symbiotic interdependency between the state and Ethiopian Orthodox Tewahedo Church that had lasted for more than a century. This trend was generally welcomed by the marginalised Muslim authorities. However, state attempts to push religion out of the public sphere were accompanied by systematically undermining and defaming religious sentiments. Neither the influential religious authorities nor the religious population welcomed this approach to religion on the part of the government. Despite attempts to establish secular values instead, "the only significant change from the draft to the final text [of the PDRE Constitution] which was debated prior to the approval by referendum was a minor concession to religious interests in the removal of the monogamy clause".[50] Ever since, secularism is the preferred stance of the state. One may ask whether the concept of secularism and the acknowledgement of religious courts is actually a contradiction. Regarding the relation between state and religion as well as the question of state intervention in multicultural and multi-religious contexts, Rajeev Bhargava's perspective, which has been derived largely from Indian experiences, might be applicable

46 Art. 40 IRC.

47 Art. 126 PDRE-Constitution.

48 Perham, *The Government of Ethiopia*, 103.

49 Art. 46(3) PDRE-Constitution.

50 Clapham, *Transformation and Continuity*, 95.

to the Ethiopian context. He pleads for a flexible secularist approach that may be characterised as a 'principled distance' of politics from religion: On the one hand, this approach maintains a 'principled distance' of the state from religious institutions in order to secure a form of minimum consensus on the standard of living for all citizens and may contribute to a more peaceful co-existence of different religions. According to Bhargava, secularism should be understood as a strategy which embraces both state intervention as well as restraint towards religious practices. Moreover, he emphasises that the relationship between religion and politics might if anything be guided by non-sectarian principles consistent with a set of values to guarantee a dignified life for all, prevent discrimination on grounds of religious sentiments, and keep an eye on the often totalitarian claim of religion.[51] On the other hand, state intervention displays a certain interference of religion in politics and politicisation of religion. Accordingly, the Ethiopian governmental decision to constitutionally recognise Shariʿa courts corresponds with the idea of 'principled distance' of politics from religion.

However, regarding the degree of mutual interference of religion and politics, the governmental decision to finance the Shariʿa courts remains a contested feature of the legal plural arrangement. The federal Proclamation 188/1999 states that the budget of the Shariʿa Courts shall be drawn from budgetary subsidies to be allocated by the Federal Government as well as from assistance from other sources.[52] State funding certainly implies involvement in religious affairs. From a different viewpoint, the provision of financial resources could be regarded as consistent, given the state's guarantee of ensuring collective freedom of religion. According to the President of the Federal Supreme Court, the financial support should be rather viewed as beneficial, since the Shariʿa courts require budgetary assistance in order to provide proper legal services. Ultimately, however, "the intention of the government is for the Shariʿa courts to stand on their own".[53] Moreover, the federal Proclamation regulates the administrative co-operation of the Shariʿa courts with governmental institutions with regard to the general operation and accountability of the religious courts.[54] In practice, the state courts and the Shariʿa courts cooperate primarily on the level of administration, both formally and informally: The regular courts support the Shariʿa courts not only regarding the recruitment of staff but also regarding the provision of basic facilities. On an administrative basis

51 Bhargava, "What is Secularism for," 515–6.
52 Art. 19 Proclamation 188/1999.
53 Menberetshai Tadesse, interview (23.03. 2008).
54 See. Art. 20, 23 Proclamation 188/1999.

there are regular meetings where challenges which have arisen are discussed and where conflict resolution strategies are jointly found. Even though the state has to refrain from interfering, the *Federal Supreme Court* (FSC) is involved in disciplinary matters and examines complaints against Kadis of the Shariʿa courts.[55] Moreover, the established *Federal Judicial Commission* is involved in both the appointment processes of the state judges and of *Kadis*. So far, this commission has accepted all nominations that have been suggested by the religious institutions. The co-operation at regional level, in the *Harari People's National Regional State* (HPNRS), seems to follow similar pattern. According to one informant:

> The relationship between the regular courts and the Shariʿa courts is only an administrative relationship, not a legal relationship. [A]s long as we are Muslims we have some kind of knowledge about the Shariʿa law but we are not responsible for the application of the Shariʿa law.[56]

Representatives of the Ministry of Justice mentioned a few changes with regard to the cooperation. One informant stated that:

> Some years ago there was accusation of mismanagement of the filing of cases at the Shariʿa courts. And there was a decision to have the registrar of the Federal Supreme Court to administer the files of the Shariʿa courts in order to have the similar file system. In the past the Shariʿa courts used to have their own registrars.[57]

This demonstrates that the frame of cooperation is set by the respective proclamations, but is shaped and reshaped by the respective actors of the involved institutions. Regular dialogue and the establishment of consultative conflict resolution strategies support the exchange of knowledge of the governmental courts and the Shariʿa courts which may contribute to a better mutual understanding. Ethiopian governmental actors regulate the scope and extent of jurisdiction of Shariʿa courts de jure, even though some of the main features of Shariʿa court practice are highly contested, as will be shown in the following paragraphs.

---

55 See Art. 18 Proclamation 188/1999; Menberetsehai Tadesse, interview (23/ 24.03.2008).
56 Elias Yahya, interview (28.02.2008).
57 Abadir Mohamed, interview (05.01.2009).

4 Focal Features of the State Recognition

4.1 *The Mutual Consensus Requirement*

The consent of both parties to be adjudicated by the Shariʿa courts under Islamic law is one of the constitutionally enshrined requirements for the jurisdiction of Shariʿa courts in family matters.[58] The consent requirement is to safeguard the choice of legal forums. To promote the 'choice', the *Ethiopian Women's Lawyers Association* (EWLA), for instance, assists individuals who want to opt for the state judicial forums. A representative of the association explained:

> When they [Muslim women] are not going to be adjudicated by the Shariʿa law they come to us. [...] Most of them are not satisfied by the Shariʿa law, because they [the Kadis] are not going to support them, the women in Dire Dawa, but not only in Dire Dawa also in the surrounding rural area. [...]. We are going to prepare the case to the regular court [...].[59]

This shows that women seem to use the option of 'forum shopping' according to their individual hopes, expectations and demands, and not according to the expectations arising out of their religious affiliation.

However, the Shariʿa court practices seem to have implications for the choice of forums of individuals. The Kadis I interviewed in Addis Ababa, Dire Dawa and Harar criticised the consent requirement as a severe restriction of their authority and as contradictory to the perceived religious responsibility to settle private disputes according to local and religious dispute resolution mechanisms. Moreover the regulation is regarded as an unnecessary obstacle for Muslims.[60] This critical attitude materialises in the Kadis' practice of following an 'implicit' consent procedure where litigants must expressly state that they do *not* wish to be adjudicated by the Shariʿa courts. If the defendant is 'silent', or does not appear at the adjournment date, it is assumed that both parties accept to be adjudicated by the Shariʿa courts. The Proclamation 188/1999 stipulates, "in the absence of clear consent of the parties [...] the [Shariʿa] courts shall transfer the case to the regular federal court".[61] At the same time, it leaves space for an implied consent "where a party is properly

---

58 Art. 34(5) FDRE Constitution; Art. 4(2), 5 Proclamation 188/1999.

59 Afework Alemayehu, interview (28.11.2008).

60 Sheikh Adam Umar, interview (11.12.2008); Ustaz Abdullahi Duale, interview (28.11. 2008); Sheikh Eliyas Redman, interview (17.12.2008).

61 Art. 5(3) Proclamation 188/1999.

served with summons [...] does not confirm his objection or consent by appearing before the registrar, he shall be presumed not to have objected and the case shall be heard ex parte".[62] Moreover, the Shariʿa court practice shows that the consent requirement is sometimes completely ignored by the Kadis, as will be discussed below, which violates the constitutional requirement and the Proclamation 188/1999. The empirical data demonstrate that the Kadis are resistant to the idea that personal disputes are regulated by state judicial forums and they tend to articulate this unease in other religious forums such as at mosques.[63] Accordingly, the role of social pressure on individuals who might wish to take a decision contrary to group expectations should not be underestimated.[64]

4.2 *The Civil Procedure Code of Ethiopia (CPC-)Requirement*

4.2.1 Kadis' Knowledge of the CPC

As already mentioned above, the state-set legal frame stipulates: "[i]n conducting proceedings properly, the courts shall apply the civil procedure laws in force".[65] Despite this requirement, knowledge of the state procedure law is not (yet) a precondition for the appointment of a prospective Kadi. The judicial reality instead shows that Kadis of the Federal Shariʿa Courts, as for instance in Addis Ababa, apply the *Civil Procedure Code of Ethiopia* merely to the extent they became familiar with it in the course of their work. Sometimes they rely instead on Islamic procedural rules, in particular regarding the law of evidence, which follows a different internal logic regarding testimony. During my fieldwork in the course of 2008–09, the *Federal Supreme Court* was preparing a training programme for Kadis in order to avoid the negative consequences of the lack of procedural knowledge on the implementation of Proclamation 188/1999. It is interesting to note that the curriculum contained not only procedural code provisions and case-flow management, but also constitutional principles, cooperation with regular courts as well as day-to-day court administration.[66] Furthermore, since 2008, a ten days' training on the CPC and on constitutional principles was given to the Kadis as well as to all employees of the Federal Shariʿa Courts in Dire Dawa, which is be refreshed once a year. The training was prepared by the *Administrative Council Minister* of Dire Dawa and not by the regular federal courts. These efforts show that the governmental actors are aware of the fact that without profound legal knowledge of the

62 Art. 5(2) Proclamation 188/1999.
63 Adonawit Ayalew, interview (24.04.2009); Afework Alemayehu, interview (28.11.2008).
64 The impact of social pressure on the choice of judicial forums is beyond the scope of this analysis.
65 Art. 6(2) Proclamation 188/1999.
66 Menbereshai Tadesse, interview (23.03.2008).

procedural law that the Shariʿa courts are supposed to apply, one cannot expect that the proclamations are implemented. It can be only speculated whether Proclamation 188/1999 will be amended to the effect that procedural knowledge and loyalty to the Constitution become an explicit requirement for an appointment as Kadi. The state-organised courses have been positively received by the interviewed Kadis since the instruction facilitates the organisation and procedures of the courts, including the handling of the increasing case load.[67] However, a look at the regional level shows that, for example, in *Harari People's National Regional State* (HPNRS), the HPNRS Proclamation 3/1996 has been comprehensively implemented. Government training in CPC and on constitutional principles has been provided before the final appointment of Kadis.[68] In the HPNRS, all judges and Kadis are not only required to apply the CPC, but need to take an oath on the HPNRS Constitution before the Regional Council.[69] According to the president of the HPNRS *Supreme Court of Shariʿa*:

> We get training provided by the federal and regional government and some who come from abroad, from the United States, also trained us in civil procedure. We study, analyse and balance it with the Shariʿa also. Before I came into this position I was trained for three months.[70]

Moreover, the state and Islamic judiciary already cooperate during the appointment process. In the course of the selection procedure of candidates, the HPNRS-*Supreme Court* works closely together with the *Regional Council of Islamic Affairs*. A specific exam is prepared by a committee jointly with the HPNRS-*Council of Islamic Affairs* and the HPNRS-*Supreme Court of Shariʿa*. The *HPNRS Proclamation* 3/1996 does not require cooperation with the *Regional Council of Islamic Affairs* (RCIA), even though in practice the judicial actors view the involvement of RCIA-expertise as crucial at the stage of appointing appropriate Kadis. The exam is solely related to the proficiency in Islamic law since it has been impossible so far to find candidates who are versed in both, Islamic law and state procedural law. This regional example shows that the interpretation of the statutory law and the degree of its implementation rely severely on the political will, on the flexibility and creativity of the actors involved and on a fruitful cooperation of the Islamic and the state branches of the judiciary.[71]

67 Abdulahi Duale, interview (28.11.2008); Sheikh Jemal Adem, interview (25.11.2008); Sheikh Yusuf Mohammad, interview (23.11.2008); Sheikh Ezedin Abubeker, interview (27.11.2008).

68 Elias Yahya, interview (27.11.2008).

69 Art. 34 HPNRS-Proclamation 3/1996.

70 Ezedin Abubeker, interview (27.02.2008).

71 See comprehensively Seidel, Rechtspluralismus in Äthiopien, 146–8.

4.2.2 Law of Evidence and Testimony

Differences between the CPC and Islamic procedural law are particularly obvious regarding the law of evidence: Unlike the CPC, the Islamic law applied by the Shari'a courts has a strong gender bias. It follows, for instance, the principle that one male witness equates to two female witnesses. The Kadis have inferred from the Qur'anic stipulations in *sura* 2:282 a general rule even though this verse actually deals with financial obligations, transactions, and contracts. According to a systematic Quranic interpretation, seven further verses do not embed any gender disparity with regard to testimony in court.[72] The Shari'a courts are adhering by and large to one of the *fiqh* (Islamic jurisprudence) interpretations that women are endowed to responsibilities of child-care with the implication that 'mothering' develops inside them a state of emotion and feeling of pity for others.[73] Thus, "when one woman 'forgets' or is overwhelmed by her emotional state a second woman may 'remind' her."[74]

This interpretation has been criticised by many Muslim scholars[75] even though this argumentation seems to be based on a recognised *ḥadīṯ* compiled by al-Bukḫari.[76] Furthermore, it has been argued, the justification of the applied disparity is hardly tenable in times where women are literate, educated, and engaged in business matters.[77] The data I collected during my fieldwork indicate that the overall majority of the witnesses are male. On rare occasions, women are summoned to testify, especially in cases where no male witness is available or the issue is something where only a woman is able to testify. In these cases the Kadis generally follow the above-mentioned 2:1 principle.[78] However, the regional Shari'a court practice sometimes displays a rather flexible approach towards the Islamic testimony law. Thus, in HPNRS I observed that the testimony of an individual female was accepted as sufficient proof on a case-to-case basis. The following sample of a court hearing at the First-Instance Court of Shari'a in Harar[79] illustrates the flexible practice: A wife

72 Engineer, The Rights of Women, 63–5.

73 Muhammad 'Abduh, cit. in: Fadel, "Two Women, One Man," 187.

74 Tajudin Ahmed 2008, interview (20.02.2008), Ezedin Abubeker, interview (27.02.2008).

75 See comprehensively Shaham, "Women as Expert Witnesses," 41, 45; Kamali, Freedom, Equality and Justice in Islam, 68; Fadel, "Two Women, One Man," 187; Engineer, The Rights of Women, 63–4.

76 Al-Buḫari, Sahih al-Buhari, 281.

77 Abou El-Fadl, Speaking in God's Name, 157–8; Al-'Alwānī, „The Testimony of Women," 174.

78 Adonawit Ayalew, interview (28/29.11.2008, 24.04.2009); Temesgen Mergo 2009, interview (30.04.2009).

79 HNPRS-First-Instance Court of Shari'a, Court Hearing 28.11.2008.

claimed from her husband maintenance for herself, for the joint child as well as payment of her *mahr* (dowry). Both the plaintiff and the defendant appeared before the court. After about half an hour of negotiations the Kadi asked for a witness who could testify to the willingness of the defendant to pay the agreed amount of maintenance. On the request of the Kadi, the defendant named his mother as a witness, which was accepted by the Kadi. Moreover, the Kadi asked the plaintiff whether the mother was prepared to testify for a loan the defendant wished to take in order to pay the maintenance.[80] This case demonstrates that a female witness ('the mother') testifies for both the defendant (her son) and for the plaintiff (her daughter-in-law). Moreover, a situational and flexible handling of reasoning becomes visible. In addition, the testimony of the mother of the defendant reveals that the Kadi does not follow a gender-specific law of testimony. Moreover, the court hearing demonstrates the complex interaction of the disputing parties with the Kadi attempting to mediate the dispute by utilizing the wide scope of interpretation even regarding Islamic testimony law. How this space of independent reasoning or self-dependent legal decision (*ijtihād*[81]) is utilised relies very much on the respective legal perception and mind-set of a Kadi. Strong Egyptian and Somali influences in the HPNRS and their relatively flexible *Ḥanafīya* and *Šāfiʿīya* approaches, two of the Sunni *maḏāhib* (legal schools of thought), become visible as well.[82] It has to be mentioned that one can find all four Sunni legal schools of thought among Ethiopian Muslims, namely: Šāfiʿīya, *Malikīya, Ḥanafīya* and *Ḥanābila.*[83] The application of the legal schools of thoughts is handled rather flexibly as well. Shariʿa courts apply the respective legal school of the disputants, but also the school of the respective Kadi, which is in most of the cases the *Šāfiʿīya.* However other schools are also adhered to, particularly in circumstances where another legal school provides a more appropriate solution to specific contemporary problems. When it comes to testimony, the *Civil Procedure Code* does not distinguish regarding people's religious affiliation. In contrast to this, classical interpretations of *fiqh* agree on the principle that a non-Muslim is not acceptable as witness for Muslim litigants. The *Ḥanafīya* does accept the testimony of non-Muslims, but only in cases of emergency and if Muslim witnesses are not available. The Shariʿa court practice shows that the Kadis do not per se reject testimonies of Christians. The mutual testimony of Christians and Muslims is considered by the Kadis as an 'old rule', established through

80 Seidel, Rechtspluralismus in Äthiopien, 185–187.

81 For the debate on the scope and limits of *ʾiǧtihād*, see: Hallaq, "Was the gate of ijtihad Closed?," 3–41; Rohe, Das islamische Recht, 59–60; Abou El-Fadl, Speaking in God's Name, 38–9; Tucker, Women, Family and Gender," 13.

82 See comprehensively Seidel, Rechtspluralismus in Äthiopien.

83 Eliyas Redman, interview (17.12.2015).

the centuries-long coexistence of people of both religions.[84] A witness's religious affiliation is written down for the purpose of oath, i.e. a Christian is allowed to take an oath on the Bible or the Old Testament. However, even though Ethiopian Shariʿa courts do not reject the testimonies of Christians, regarding civil matters they by and large allow only Muslim witnesses.[85] The examples presented above illustrate that the praxis of the Shariʿa courts does not comply with the state-set frame since the CPC does not stipulate a gendered or faith based testimony law. These contradictions challenge the work of the Shariʿa courts as they leave them in a difficult situation regarding the application of procedural rules.[86] In order to navigate the different normativities in a flexible manner, Shariʿa court actors utilise well-established local practices. This becomes visible, for instance, in general clauses such as 'old rule'. However, they do not explicitly negotiate the normative conflict which arises out of the state-set legal frame.

4.3 *Islamic Family Law and the Revised Family Code* (RFC)

When comparing the applied Islamic family law with secular family law, some fundamental normative values are similar: Under both legal orders the family is considered the fundamental unit of society and is connected to a heterosexual marital bond. Before a marriage can be concluded in any form, certain procedural requirements have to be fulfilled. In order to reach a valid marriage status, the free and full consent of both spouses is the major element under both laws as well. However, there are also fundamental differences, regarding for instance age of marriage, interfaith marriages and polygyny.

4.3.1 Marriageable Age

Under Ethiopian state law, the minimum age of marriage for both spouses is eighteen years.[87] Under Islamic law the minimum age for marriage is flexible since biological factors such as puberty (*bulūgh*) and intellectual maturity (*rušd*) are taken into consideration.[88] However, despite the inherent conflicts between these norms resulting from the different gender specific constructions, mutual influences on both normative orders become visible within the state-recognised, legally plural arrangement: Some informants reported that some Kadis seem to treat the marriageable age requirement flexibly in

84 Sheikh Ezedin Abubeker, interview (27.02.2008).

85 Sheikh Tajudine Ahmed, interview (21.02.2008); Sheikh Ezedin Abubeker, interview (27.02.08).

86 Sheikh Jemal Adem 2008, interview (25.02.2008); Sheikh Tajudine Ahmed, interview (20.02.2008).

87 Art. 34(1) FDRE Constitution, Art. 215 RFC.

88 See comprehensively Rohe, Das islamische Recht, 79.

accordance with Islamic law.[89] Other Kadis and Muslim authorities plead for a standardised marriageable age and are in favour of the idea of attaining majority at the age of eighteen to protect the woman, and thus they instead apply the state law.[90] On the other hand, the *Ministry of Justice* is empowered to reduce the marriageable age on request by a maximum of two years due to the very diverse local social practices in Ethiopia.[91]

4.3.2 Inter-faith Marriages

The position of Islamic law toward interfaith marriages reveals a further gender bias. According to the sunni *fiqh*, Muslim men are allowed to marry female followers of other so-called 'book religions', while Muslim women may only marry Muslim men.[92] Thus, the Islamic concept is in total contradiction to the principles of the free choice of the spouses and of equality before the law, as guaranteed by the FDRE Constitution and by the RFC.[93] In Ethiopian Shariʿa court practice, both parties must be Muslim. This practice is contradictory to the general interpretations of the Sunni legal schools of thought, such as the Ḥanafīya.[94] According to Kadis of the federal Shariʿa courts, interreligious marriages are usually not certified before the Shariʿa courts, but instead before state courts. However, the presiding Kadi of the *Federal High Court of Shariʿa* in Dire Dawa emphasises that if a male Muslim and a female Christian ask for a marriage certificate, the Shariʿa courts are obliged to grant the request.[95] The temporary President of the *Federal Supreme Court of Shariʿa* Addis Ababa describes the judicial practice as follows:

> [S]ince this institution is a Muslim institution, we render a decision based on *nikāh* particularly for Muslims. This is our interest. But we do not close everything for Muslims because certain Muslim men conclude marriage with Christian females. We have some cases like this. We give a certificate for these marriages. But if it is vice versa, if a Christian man wants to marry a Muslim woman it is prohibited.[96]

89 Yusuf Mohammad 2009, interview (23.04.2009), Temesgen Mergo 2009, interview (30.04.2009).

90 Sheikh Adam Umar, Interview (11.12.2008), Sheikh Elyas Redman, Interview (17.12.2008).

91 Art. 7 I, II RFC.

92 Rohe, *Das islamische Recht*, 83. According to the legal schools of thoughts of most *Šia* Muslims, interreligious marriages are not permitted.

93 Art. 34(1), 25, 35 FDRE Constitution.

94 Hillina Tadesse „The Shari'a as Regards Women," 149.

95 Abdulahi Duale, interview (28.11.2008).

96 Adam Umar, interview (11.12.2008).

Regarding interfaith marriages, it has to be mentioned that a disparity exists between federal and regional legislation. The federal Proclamation 188/1999 does not exclude adjudication of inter-religious spouses, whether the marriage is concluded under Islamic law or not, as long as the mutual consent requirement is fulfilled. The regional *HPNRS Proclamation* 3/1996 declares that Shari'a court jurisdiction is restricted to Muslims, but irrespective of whether it is concluded under Islamic law or state law.[97] Accordingly, inter-religious marriages need to be certified at state courts since non-Muslims are categorically excluded.

4.3.3 Polygyny

Another contentious issue are polygynous marriages. Polygyny is a widespread social practice.[98] In contrast to this, the FDRE Constitution ensures equal rights in marriage. In accordance with the constitutional provisions, the *Criminal Code of Ethiopia* makes polygamy subject to penalty. However, it sets down an exception to the general rule: if a marriage is concluded according to the Islamic law that is generally recognised by the constitution, it is not punishable.[99] Ethiopian federal state family law is based on the concept of monogamy. It has to be mentioned that various regional states have already enacted their own family laws. There are some regions which have not done so yet. This is due to the draft commissions that have not been able to mediate and find a compromise between the various camps of opinion regarding the issue of polygamy.[100] Islamic law accepts polygyny under certain conditions such as the mental and financial capability to treat the wives properly, as well as restrictions, e.g. a maximum of four wives.[101] The enacted state laws that are based on the concept of monogamy are in conflict with the social reality of polygyny in Ethiopia. The examined Shari'a court practice shows that while polygyny is a widespread practice in the studied localities, the people usually do not come to the religious courts for legal recognition. One reason might be that the parties believe that they do not satisfy the Qur'anic requirements. It seems to them to be impossible to treat all wives equally in terms of attention, as well of supporting and providing adequate maintenance to each one.[102] Consequently, a huge gap between the Islamic law and social practices becomes visible. Nevertheless, the Shari'a court statistics in Addis Ababa and Dire Dawa show a significant percentage of registered polygynous marriages.

---

97 See Art. 26 HPNRS-Proclamation 3/1996.

98 Yusuf Mohammad, interview (23.04.2009); Jemal Adem, interview 2005.

99 See Art. 650–1 Criminal Code.

100 Husien Mama, interview (19.12.2008).

101 Quranic verse 4:4; 4:127.

102 Sheikh Adam Umar, interview (11.12.2008).

According to the Kadis, the consent of the first wife is not required for concluding additional marriages since the Qur'an clearly gives this right to men under certain conditions.[103] Furthermore, some argue that if the wife is not satisfied with her respective treatment in the polygynous constellation, she has a right to ask for divorce.[104] State law and Islamic law follow different normative logics and justifications. Secular law argues from the perspective of the right of equality for the spouses, whereas under the religious law, the tolerance of polygyny seems to rely on gendered ideas of an assumed status of males, often based on historical argumentation regarding the protection of widows and orphans, as well as of women in the case where the husband divorces her.[105] The question arises of whether historical and 'naturalised' arguments still fit the changing socioeconomic realities and an era in which polygyny is internationally criticised and condemned.

The above mentioned examples show that a number of procedural and substantive Islamic regulations and interpretations are different to the conception of the secular laws, especially with regard to gender equality. However, as the judicial realities in the Shari'a courts show, an adaption process towards state law can be observed, e.g. regarding the marriageable age. The state concept of the age of majority is perceived as a guideline by the Kadis. Especially in urban settings, Kadis feel more comfortable following this state concept of 18 years than applying the Islamic principle of puberty. On the other hand, regional state legislators grant space for *de facto* existing polygamous marriages as exceptions to the generally promoted concept of monogamy. These adaption processes are mutually dependent and locally shaped by the respective actors involved.

Despite *state* mechanisms of co-regulation such as financing of Shari'a courts, consensual jurisdiction and the imposition of the civil procedure code as procedural law, the state has only limited opportunities to regulate substantial decisions of Shari'a courts, as we will be shown in the following.

5 The Role of Cassation and Constitutional Interpretation

In order to navigate the nebulousness of state-recognised legal pluralism, i.e. to keep it as a framework in which the different normative concepts are defined in negotiation, the FDRE Constitution underwrites various institutional mechanisms to handle conflicts of interest arising within the interdependent

103 See Quranic Sura 4:3 and 4:127; 4:129.

104 Sheikh Yusuf Mohammad, interview (23.04.2009).

105 See Seidel, *Rechtspluralismus in Äthiopien*, 234–238.

spheres of state, groups and group members on a case-to-case basis. In this way, the constitution provides for mechanisms of judicial review which rest with state organs.

5.1 *The Cassation Benches of the Supreme Courts*

The power to review judicial decisions "[…] containing a basic error of law",[106] or [an error] of basic nature that may have the unfortunate consequence of shaking the constitutional or legal order,[107] rests with the cassation divisions of the state Supreme Courts at federal and regional levels. However, Proclamation 188/1999 states that, "[u]nder no circumstance shall a case brought before the courts of Shariʿa, the jurisdiction of which has been consented to, be transferred to a regular court".[108] One difficult issue is reviewing Shariʿa courts' decisions in light of internal pluralism of Islamic law visible in the four Sunni legal schools of thought applied across Ethiopia. Another problematic area is having a non-codified, or non-ascertained Islamic family law. A generally controversial question is whether a final decision of a *Supreme Court of Shariʿa* can be reviewed by any regular State court[109] since it challenges the autonomy of the established Shariʿa courts and their constitutional status. According to the Vice President of the *Federal Supreme Court*,

> […] if a party is not satisfied with the final judgement of the FSSC [Federal Shariʿa Supreme Court] they cannot come after exhausting the judiciary to the cassation division of the Federal Supreme Court challenging the decision of Shariʿa courts regarding their applied substantive law, but only regarding any basic error of procedural law.[110]

The presiding *Kadi* of the *Federal Shariʿa Supreme Court* Addis Ababa explains the cassation practice as follows:

> The cassation bench of the regular Supreme Court is only looking how the procedure is rendered based on the fundamental laws. They do not touch Shariʿa laws, because they do not have detailed knowledge on Shariʿa. However, we wish to be independent from the state courts in the sense that the cassation bench shall be established under the Shariʿa court in order to give free service for our Muslim society.[111]

---

106 Art. 80 III(a) FDRE Constitution.
107 Fasil Nahum, Constitution for a Nation of Nations, 102.
108 Art. 5 IV Proclamation188/1999.
109 Getachew Assefa "Federalism and Legal Pluralism," 24ff.
110 Menberetsehai Tadesse 2008, interview (23.03.2008).
111 Adam Umar, interview (11.12.2008).

Thus the cassation is limited to reviewing the application of the civil procedural law or whether fundamental principles of law have been violated. However, in most cases the parties claim a 'fundamental error of *Islamic* law',[112] a claim that is usually denied, since the judges of the regular Supreme Courts pronounce themselves unqualified due to their lack of knowledge of Islamic law. In addition to the power of cassation, the Ethiopian legal system has incorporated another control mechanism for guaranteeing the appropriate application of constitutional principles.

5.2 *The House of Federation (HoF) and the Council of Constitutional Inquiry (CCI)*

The power to interpret the FDRE Constitution has been given to the *House of Federation* in conjunction with the *Council of Constitutional Inquiry*.[113] The HoF is a political organ composed of elected representatives from the federal states of Ethiopia and is equivalent to a chamber of parliament in other countries. The CIC is composed of various members, the majority of whom are legal experts.[114] A reason for transferring the highest authority of constitutional interpretation to a rather political organ was the current governmental actors' unwillingness to allow certain conflicts between federal and regional governments to be settled by a judicial panel. The political organ is expected to safeguard the interests of the various regional states. This might indicate why the boundaries of legal concepts are negotiated on a case-to-case basis and why they are kept fluid on the general constitutional level. However, since constitutional interpretation also becomes relevant in individual complaints against the violation of basic rights, the question remains of whether this function should not instead be given to a judicial organ. In addition, the fact that decisions of the HoF/CIC are not publicised may prevent the development of a comprehensive debate among constitutional experts.[115]

When looking at the constitutional review of Shariʿa court decisions, the HoF/CIC seems to limit the scope of its review to procedural questions such as securing the constitutionally enshrined mutual consent requirement of parties, or to cases in which Shariʿa courts exceed their constitutionally granted mandate. The consensus requirement protects Muslims who do not wish to be adjudicated by Shariʿa courts. These contentious issues have led to the revision of some final decisions of the Shariʿa courts by the Cassation bench of the

112 Cassation bench Harari Regional Supreme Court, File No. 00924 / 10.04.1999 e.c.; 01022/ 26.11.2007; File No. 01007/ 05.05.2000 e.c.

113 Art. 62, 83 FDRE Constitution.

114 Art. 61, 82 FDRE Constitution; also Proclamation 251/2001; Proclamation 250/2001.

115 Scholler, *Recht und Politik in Äthiopien*, 204.

Federal Supreme Court and by the *House of Federation*. When reviewing, for instance, the landmark case 'Kedija',[116] the HoF emphasised that Article 34(5) FDRE Constitution enshrines the requirement that parties to a dispute consent to be adjudicated by Islamic law. Previously, the lower as well as the appeal Shari'a courts had passed similar decisions to the initial Shari'a court that were not compatible with the aforementioned constitutional provision. Moreover, the applicant had appealed to the *Federal Supreme Court*, which also decided against him.[117]

However, the question remains how it can be ensured that people do not surrender their fundamental constitutional rights by giving their consent to be adjudicated by Shari'a courts. How should a case be resolved if the 'right to equality' and 'women's rights' collide with the 'right to freedom of religion'? The Shari'a court practice reveals that even though the Kadis mostly decide in favour of the women and their offspring, some aspects of their rulings show a clear gender bias that can be attributed to a different understanding of women's rights. Furthermore, different concepts of gender equality are not only evident in secular and Islamic law, but also and especially in the various local practices. Does the voluntary character of Shari'a jurisdiction release the Ethiopian state from its responsibility to ensure the constitutionally enshrined individual rights of each group's members? Would such an exception mean the internal material logic of the Islamic normative order is not commensurable with the constitutionally guaranteed individual rights?

In an attempt at mutual recognition, conflict resolution approaches should not be categorised into strictly dichotomous notions of constitutionally guaranteed individual and collective rights. Accordingly, "[…] not all individual rights always trump all collective rights, for much depends on the relative importance of the rights in question and their context and consequences".[118] Any judgement about constitutionality must take into account that the individual actors are forming the groups, just as they are formed by the groups. Thus, subordination under religious normativities should not necessarily eliminate an individual's option to revoke his or her decision at a later time. Arguably, 'freedom of choice' is both a collective and an individual right. To curtail this right, and thus place the individual within a collective entity, would dissolve this individual right completely in favour of the collective freedom of religion. In taking an *a priori* decision in favour of local or religious rights,

116 The Kedija Case is comprehensively discussed in: Seidel, *Rechtspluralismus in Äthiopien*, 286–289.

117 HoF Protocol 2004: 57.

118 Parekh, *Rethinking Multiculturalism*, 216.

including regarding decisions of Shari'a courts as extra-constitutional, the individual rights enshrined in a constitution would ultimately be reduced to absurdity as well.

6 Concluding Remarks

The chapter has shown that Ethiopian governmental actors apply diverse strategies not to relinquish entirely authority for co-regulating the private sphere and to reserve for themselves a privileged negotiation position as 'guardians' of the constitutional state. Throughout history, governmental actors have utilised *divide et impera* strategies in various forms.

State recognition of local and religious legal orders may be described as challenging processes of conflict and accommodation between 'state identity' and the self-regulation claims of social groups. It has been demonstrated that the constitutional recognition of religious law opens up a space and forum for continuous negotiation processes between various actors. These negotiation spaces allow for a continuous (re-)structuring of power relations. The constitutional recognition of 'non-state' normative orders appears to be a legal tool for dealing with the fact that the *de facto* influence of state law is only marginal. By *de jure* recognizing Islamic law, governmental actors attempt to frame and limit the scope of recognised 'other' normative orders with a view to retaining a *de jure* 'final' say, striving to achieve their own hegemonic claims and to secure political and legal key areas. By taking into account the politically and demographically strengthened Muslim population, Ethiopia's political elites have realised that a state recognition of the legal perceptions of Muslim local communities may help to reduce, at least temporarily, conflicts of divergent normative values as well as to maintain the political status quo. Moreover, these state actors' efforts create the necessity to establish negotiation spaces due to the inevitable collisions of norms. Subsequent adaptations lead to innovative institutionalised conflict resolution mechanisms. The adaptation processes demonstrate the mutually constitutive heterogeneity of normative notions of order, which are always locally translated and moulded by an interplay of manifold actors.

As the example of the Shari'a courts has shown, the Kadis partly contest state demands and attempt to manoeuvre their claims by utilising their officially recognised status. However, the created normative spaces seem to be used to negotiate situational solutions to specific conflicts rather than to identify and formulate mutual values in light of and respect for the different moral beliefs. What seems to be needed is a continuous political dialogue and process of negotiation procedures regarding the legitimate enforcement of law as well as a functioning national legal mechanism to balance the powers of the various normative orders and to develop a set of conflict rules. A precondition for the smooth application of the existing procedural rules is mutual knowledge transfer. Without ensuring adequate training in state civil procedure as well as in the constitutional principles for the appointed Kadis across the country and without teaching Islamic legal principles and values to state judicial actors, it appears to be difficult to reach a successful implementation and openness of negotiations.

As mentioned above, the FDRE Constitution "shall not preclude the adjudication of disputes relating to personal and family matters in accordance with religious or customary laws"[119] so long as the parties consent. This regulation remains problematic.

Even though the FDRE Constitution has established various institutional mechanisms to balance diverging interests within the interdependent spheres of state, groups and group members, including certain mechanisms of judicial review, it does not provide a specific mechanism to deal with decisions of Shariʿa courts that are in conflict with constitutional principles. The federal constitution does not clearly state whether its 'supremacy clause' and enshrined provisions on human rights prevail over final decisions of Shariʿa courts when they conflict. As demonstrated, the FDRE Constitution and Shariʿa Courts Proclamation 188/1999 seem to have recognised the final substantive decisions delivered by Shariʿa courts instead as an exception to its 'supremacy clause'. This is because the FDRE Constitution recognises parallel personal and family laws based on ethno-religious frameworks. Such structure has to be maintained if the parties opt for one of the judicial systems. The issue of 'choice' of judicial forum seems to be crucial and is constitutionally guaranteed.

Moreover, gender issues might be more consistently addressed by systematically promoting 'gender equality' and its (pre-)conditions as well as by raising awareness of gender disparity so that women can make informed decisions as to which forum is to their best interest. Such pursuits coupled with the limited power of the state to encourage and facilitate reforms regarding the treatment of gender issues in Shariʿa courts can indeed gradually address the constitutional and human rights concerns.

Finally, one may conclude that Emperor Haile Selassie I's proclaimed idea to achieve 'unity' by solely formal recognition of 'diversity' seems to be

119 Art. 34(5) FDRE Constitution.

insufficient. Even though the constitutionally recognised legal pluralism creates certain negotiation processes, the actors involved utilise the created 'space' solely in the interest of their respective groups and make, if anything, situational concessions. As long as conflicts are not viewed as an opportunity to negotiate the apparent 'differences' with a view to identifying mutual values in light of and respect for the different moral beliefs, the project of 'unity in diversity' pursued by governmental actors remains unaddressed. Thus, quests for 'unity and diversity' by merely formal 'recognition' of legal plurality appear to be futile. However, state actors seem to be convinced that they must use the constitutionally granted 'space' to improve their co-regulatory position and thus to safeguard their own power resources.

Bibliography

Primary Sources

Interviews, Court Cases and Court Hearings

Abadir Mohamed Ibrahim, Member of the Research and Education Department of the Ministry of Justice. Interview by Katrin Seidel. Addis Ababa, 5 January, 2009.

Abdulahi Duale, Ustaz, *Presiding Kadi of the Federal High Court of Sharia Dire Dawa.* Interview by Katrin Seidel. Dire Dawa, 28 November, 2008.

Abdulahi Yusuph, *Lawyer in the HPNRS*. Interview by Katrin Seidel. Harar, 27 November, 2008.

Adam Umar, Sheikh, *Temporary President of the Federal Supreme Court of Sharia Addis Ababa.* Interview by Katrin Seidel. Addis Ababa, 11 December, 2008.

Adonawit Ayalew, *Registrar of the Federal Courts of Sharia Dire Dawa*, Interview by Katrin Seidel. Dire Dawa, 26 February, 2008; 28 November, 2008; 29 November, 2008; 24 April, 2009.

Afework Alemayehu, Vice-Coordinator and Councillor of Ethiopian Women Lawyers Association Dire Dawa. Interview by Katrin Seidel. Dire Dawa, 28 November, 2008.

Elias Yahya Abdulahi, *President of the Harari Regional State Supreme Court.* Interview by Katrin Seidel. Harar, 2 February, 2008; 27 November, 2008.

Eliyas Redman, Sheikh, *Vice-President of the Ethiopian Islamic Affairs Supreme Council.* Interview by Katrin Seidel. Addis Abeba, 17 December, 2008.

Ezedin Abubeker, Sheikh, *President of the Harari Regional State Supreme Court of Sharia.* Interview by Katrin Seidel. Harar, 2 February, 2008; 27 November, 2008.

Hashim Tewfik Mohammed, *Member of the Council of Constitutional Inquiry.* Interview by Katrin Seidel. Addis Ababa, 5 May, 2013.

Husien Mama, *Expert for Woman Rights and Benefit Respecting of the Ministry of Women Affairs.* Interview by Katrin Seidel. Addis Ababa, 19 December, 2008.

Jemal Adem Hassen, Sheikh, *Kadi of the Federal High Court of Sharia Dire Dawa*. Interview by Katrin Seidel. Dire Dawa, 25 February, 2008.

Menberetsehai Tadesse, *Vice-President of the Federal Supreme Court Addis Ababa*. Interview by Katrin Seidel. Addis Abeba, 23 March, 2008.

Tajudin Ahmed, Sheikh, *Former Presiding Kadi of the Federal Supreme Court of Sharia Addis Ababa*. Interview by Katrin Seidel. Addis Ababa, 20 and 21 February, 2008.

Temesgen Mergo Abu, Registrar of the Federal Courts of Sharia Addis Ababa. Interview by Katrin Seidel. Addis Ababa, 20 February, 2008, 11 December, 2008.

Yusuf Mohammad, Sheikh, *Kadi of the Federal First Instance Court of Sharia Dire Dawa*. Interview by Katrin Seidel. Dire Dawa, 23 April, 2009.

Cassation Bench of Harari Regional Supreme Court, Court Cases: File No. 00924/ 10.04.1999 e.c.; 01022/26.11.2007; 01007/05.05.2000 e.c.

House of Federation (HoF). 2004. *Protocol of the 2nd Regular Meeting of the 2nd House of Federation on 7 May, 1996 e.c.*, Addis Ababa.

Ethiopian Laws

Administration of Justice Proclamation No. 2/1942, Negarit Gazeta 1/2, Addis Ababa.

CC (Civil Code of the Empire of Ethiopia), Proclamation No. 165/ 1960, Negarit Gazeta 19/2, Addis Ababa.

Consolidation of the House of Federation and the Definition of its Powers and Responsibilities Proclamation No. 251/2001, Federal Negarit Gazeta 7/41, Addis Ababa.

Constitutional Amendment Proclamation No. 334/1974, Negarit Gazeta 33/22, Addis Ababa.

Constitution of the Fedaral Democratic Republic of Ethiopia, Proclamation No. 1/1995. Federal Negarit Gazeta 1/1, Addis Ababa.

Constitution of the People's Democratic Republic of Ethiopia Proclamation No. 1/1987. Negarit Gazeta 47/1, Addis Ababa.

Council of Constitutional Inquiry Proclamation No. 250/2001, Federal Negarit Gazeta 7/40, Addis Ababa.

CPC (Civil Procedure Code of Ethiopia), Proclamation No. 52/1965, Negarit Gazeta 25/3, Addis Ababa

Criminal Code of the Federal Democratic Republic of Ethiopia, Proclamation No. 214/ 2004, Federal Negarit Gazeta Extra Ordinary Issue 11/1, Addis Ababa.

Diredawa Administration Charter Proclamation No. 416/2004, Federal Negarit Gazeta 10/60, Dire Dawa.

Federal Court of Sharia Consolidation Proclamation, Proclamation No. 188/1999, Federal Negarit Gazeta 6/10, Addis Ababa.

Federal Courts Proclamation, Proclamation No. 25/1996, Federal Negarit Gazeta 2/13, Addis Ababa.

Federal Judicial Administration Commission Establishment Proclamation No. 24/1996, Federal Negarit Gazeta 2/12, Addis Ababa.

HPNRS Courts and Judicial Administration Commission Establishment Proclamation No. 3/1988 e.c. [Nr. 3/1996 g.c.], Harar Negari Gazeta of the HPNRS 1/3, Harar.

HPNRS Courts and Judicial Administration Commission Establishment Proclamation (amendment) Proclamtion No. 8/1991 e.c. [Nr. 8/1998 g.c.], Harar Negari Gazeta of the HPNRS 3/2, Harar.

HPNRS Courts and Judicial Administration Commission Establishment Proclamation (amendment) Proclamtion No. 17/1991 e.c. [Nr. 17/1998 g.c.], Harar Negari Gazeta HPNRS 4/11, Harar.

IRC Imperial Revised Constitution of Ethiopia 1955, Negarit Gazeta 15/2, Addis Ababa.

Proclamtion to Establish Kadis' Courts, No. 12/1942, Negarit Gazeta 1/2, Addis Ababa.

Proclamation to Provide for the Establishment of Naiba and Kadis Councils, No. 62/1944, Negarit Gazeta 3/9, Addis Ababa.

RFC (Revised Family Code), Proclamation No. 213/2000, Federal Negarit Gazeta Extra Ordinary Issue 6/1, Addis Ababa.

The Constitution of the Federal Democratic Republic of Ethiopia, 1995, Negarit Gazeta 1/1, Addis Ababa.

TPCE (Transitional Period Charter of Ethiopia), 1991, Negarit Gazeta 50/1, Addis Ababa.

National Statistics

CSA – *Central Statistical Agency*. 2008. Ethiopia. Statistical Abstract 2008. Addis Ababa.

PCCE – Population Census Commission of Ethiopia (Hg.). 2008. *Summary and Statistical Report 2007. Population and Housing Census of Ethiopia. Population Size by Age and Sex*. Addis Ababa: UNFPA.

Secondary Sources

Abbink, Jon. "A Historical-Anthropological Approach to Islam in Ethiopia: Issues of Identity and Politics." *Journal of African Cultural Studies* 11, no. 2 (1998): 109–124.

Abou El-Fadl, Khaled. "Legal Debate on Muslim Minorities. Between Rejection and Accommodation." *Journal of Religious Ethics* 22 (1994): 127–162.

Abou El-Fadl, Khaled. *Speaking in God's Name. Islamic Law, Authority and Women.* Oxford: Oneworld Publications, 2006.

Al-'Alwānī, Taha Jabir. "The Testimony of Women in Islamic Law." *The American Journal of Islamic Social Sciences* 13, no. 2 (1996): 173–196.

Al-Buḫārī, Muḥammad b. Ismā'īl. *Sahih al-Buhari: Nachrichten von Taten und Aussprüchen des Propheten Muhammad.* Translated and edited by Dieter Ferchl. Stuttgart: Reclam, 1991.

Alemayehu, Fentaw. "Legal Pluralism: Its Promises and Pitfalls for Ethiopia." *Jimma University Journal of Law* 1, no. 1 (2007): 35–66.

Al-Shafi'i, Muhammad b. Idris. *Al-Risāla Fī Usūl al-Fiqh. Treatise on the Foundation of Islamic Jurisprudence.* Translated and edited by Majid Kadduri. Islamic Text Society, 1987.

Ahmed, Amir. "Change and Continuity in Political Participation of Ethiopian Muslims", B.A. thesis, Addis Ababa University, 2006.

Amirpur, Katajun and Ludwig Ammann, eds. *Der Islam am Wendepunkt. Liberale und Konservative Reformer einer Weltreligion.* Freiburg i.B.: Herder, 2006.

Assefa, Fiseha. "Theory and Practice in Ethiopia's Ethnic Federalism." In *Ethnic Federalism. The Ethiopian Experience in Comparative Perspective*, edited by David Turton, 131–164. Addis Ababa: Addis Ababa University Press, 2006.

Assefa, Fiseha. *Federalism and the Accommodation of Diversity in Ethiopia. A Comparative Study.* Nijmegen: Wolf Legal, 2006.

Badr Ethiopia: Ethiopian Muslims' Federation 2007. "Questions and Dialogue forwarded to the Prime Minister Meles Zenawi". *Negashi*-OJ. Accessed 10 October, 2009. http://blog.ethiopianmuslims.net/negashi/wp-content/uploads/2007/05/public info_doc_muslimdelegation.pdf.

Bauberot, Jean. "Two Thresholds of Laïcization." In *Secularism and it's Critics*, edited by Rajeev Bhargava, 94–136. New Delhi: Oxford University Press, 2008.

Benda-Beckmann, Franz et al. "Rules of Law and Laws of Ruling: Law and Governance between Past and Future." In *Rules of Law and Laws of Ruling. On the Governance of Law*, edited by Franz Benda-Beckmann et al., 1–30. Farnham: Ashgate, 2009.

Benda-Beckmann, Franz. "Who is afraid of Legal Pluralism?" *Journal of Legal Pluralism and Unofficial Law*, 47 (2002): 37–82.

Benda-Beckmann, Franz und Keebet V. "The Dynamics, Chance and Continuity in Plural Legal Orders." *Journal of Legal Pluralism and Unofficial Law*, 53–54 (2006): 1–44.

Benda-Beckmann, Keebet. "Forum Shopping und Shopping Forums: Dispute Processing in a Minangkabau Village in West Sumatra." *Journal of Legal Pluralism*, 19 (1981): 117–159.

Bhargava, Rajeev ed. "What is Secularism for?" In *Secularism and its Critics*, 486–542. Delhi: Oxford University Press, 1998.

Clapham, Christopher. *Transformation and Continuity in Revolutionary Ethiopia.* Cambridge: Cambridge University Press, 1988.

David, René. "Sources of the Ethiopian Civil Code." *Journal of Ethiopian Law* 4, no. 2 (1967).

Dereje, Feyissa. "Muslims Struggling for Recognition in Contemporary Ethiopia." In *Muslim Ethiopia: The Christian Legacy, Identity Politics, and Islamic Reformism*, edited by Patrick Desplat and Terje Østebø, 25–46. New York: Palgrave Macmillan, 2013.

Desplat, Patrick und Terje Østebø eds. *Muslim Ethiopia: The Christian Legacy, Identity Politics, and Islamic Reformism*. New York: Palgrave Macmillan, 2013.

Desplat, Patrick. "Beyond the Politics of 'Othering': Shifting Representations of Christian-Muslim Relations in Ethiopia." *ORIENT, German Journal for Politics, Economics and Culture of the Middle East*, Special Issue 'Islam in Africa', (2012): 6–11.

Ehrlich, Eugen. *Grundlegung der Soziologie des Rechts*, Schriftreihe zur Rechtssoziologie und Rechtstatsachenforschung 4, no. 69, edited by Manfred Rehbinder. Berlin: Duncker & Humblot, 1989 [1913].

Ehrlich, Eugen. "Entgegnungen." In *Hans Kelsen und die Rechtssoziologie. Auseinandersetzungen mit Hermann U. Kantorowicz, Eugen Ehrlich und Max Weber*, edited by Stanley L. Paulson, 844–849. Aalen: Scientia, 1992 [1916].

Elliesie, Hatem. "Äthiopische Verfassungsentwicklung im rechtsvergleichenden und historischen Kontext (mit einigen zusätzlichen terminologischen Anmerkungen)." In *Aethiopica*, 12 (International Journal of Ethiopian and Eritrean Studies), edited by Siegbert Uhlig et al., 230–258. Wiesbaden: Harrassowitz Verlag, 2009.

Ende, Werner. "Ehe auf Zeit (*mut'a*) in der innerislamischen Diskussion der Gegenwart." *Die Welt des Islam* 20 (1980): 1–43.

Engineer, Asghar Ali. *The Rights of Women in Islam*. London: C. Hurst & Co, 1996.

Fadel, Mohammad "Two Women, One man: Knowledge power, and Gender in Medieval Sunni Legal Thought." *International Journal of Middle East Studies* 29, no. 2 (1997): 185–204.

Fasil Nahum. *Constitution for a Nation of Nations: The Ethiopian Prospect.* Lawrenceville: The Red Sea Press, 1997.

Getwachew, Alemu. "Ethiopia: Legal and Judicial Plurality and the Incorporation of Traditional Dispute Resolution Mechanisms within the State Justice System." In *Non-State Justice Institutions and the Law*, edited by Matthias Kötter Matthias et al., 80–99. Palgrave, 2015.

Getachew, Assefa. "Federalism and Legal Pluralism in Ethiopia: Reflections on their Impacts on the Protection of Human Rights." In *The Constitutional Protection of Human Rights in Ethiopia: Challenges and Prospects*, edited by Girmachew Alemu and Sisay Alemahu, 1–36. Addis Ababa: Addis Ababa University, 2008.

Griffiths, John. "What is Legal Pluralism?" *Journal of Legal Pluralism and Unofficial Law*, 24 (1986): 1–55.

Hallaq, Wael B. "Was the gate of ijtihad Closed?" *International Journal of Middle East Studies* 16, no. 1 (1984): 3–41.

Tadesse, Hillina. "The Shari'a as Regards Women." *Berchi. The Annual Journal of Ethiopian Lawyers Association* 1, no. 2 (2001): 117–157.

Hussein, Ahmed. "Islam and Islamic Discourse in Ethiopia (1973–1993)." In *New Trends in Ethiopian Studies*: Papers of the 12th International Conference of Ethiopian

Studies, 1: Humanities and Human Resources, edited by Herold G. Marcus, 775–801. Lawrenceville, NJ: Red Sea Press, 1994.

Idris, Ibrahim. "*Sheria: Its Development & Application with Special Emphasis in Ethiopia*", LL.B. thesis, Addis Ababa University, 1992.

Idris, Ibrahim. "Freedom of Religion and Secularization of State: The legal Status of Islamic Law and Sharia Courts in Ethiopia." In *New Trends in Ethiopian Studies: Papers of the 12th International Conference of Ethiopian Studies*, 2, edited by Harold Marcus, 151–156. Lawrenceville: Red Sea Press, 1994.

Idris, Ibrahim. "Constitutional Adjudication under the 1994 FDRE Constitution." *Ethiopian Law Review* 1, no. 1 (2002): 63–92.

Jembere, Aberra. "The Making of a Constitution in Ethiopia: The Centralization and Decentralisation of the Administration." In *New Trends in Ethiopian Studies: Papers of the 12th International Conference of Ethiopian Studies*, edited by Harold G. Marcus, 66–78. Lawrenceville, NJ: The Red Sea Press, 1994.

Jembere, Aberra. *Legal History of Ethiopia 1434–1974: Some Aspects of Substantive and Procedural Laws.* Leiden: Afrika-Studiecentrum, 1998.

Jembere, Aberra und Woldetensay Woldemelak. *An Introduction to the Legal History of Ethiopia 1974–2009*. Addis Ababa: Shama Books, 2011.

Kamali, Mohammad Hashim. *Freedom, Equality and Justice in Islam.* Cambridge: The Islamic Texts Society, 2002.

Kötter, Matthias and Gunnar Folke Schuppert eds. *Normative Pluralität ordnen. Rechtsbegriffe, Normenkollisionen und Rule of Law in Kontexten dies- und jenseits des Staates*. Baden-Baden: Nomos, 2009.

Legesse, Medhanit. *Major Changes by the Revised Family Law of 2000. Regarding Women's Rights and the Need to Enhance Awareness of the Society*. Addis Ababa: Addis Ababa University, 2008.

Merry, Sally E. "From Law and Colonialism to Law and Globalization." *Law and Social Inquiry* 28, no. 2 (2003): 569–590.

Moore, Sally Falk. "Law and Social Change: The Semi-Autonomous Social Fields as an Appropriate Subject of Study." *Law and Society Review* 7, no. 4 (1973): 719–746.

Moore, Sally Falk ed. "Certainties Undone: Fifty Years of Legal Anthropology 1949–1999." In *Law and Anthropology. A Reader*, 346–367. Malden: Blackwell Publishing, 2005.

Parekh, Bhikhu. *Rethinking Multiculturalism. Cultural Diversity and Political Theory.* Cambridge: Harvard University Press, 2000.

Perham, Dame Margery Freda. *The Government of Ethiopia.* London: Faber and Faber, 1969.

Ramstedt, Martin. "Anthropological Perspectives on the Normative and Institutional Recognition of religion by the Law of the State." In *Religious Rules, State Law, and Normative Pluralism – A Comparative Overview. Ius Comparatum – Global Studies in*

Comparative Law 18, edited by Rosella Bottoni, Rinaldo Cristofori and Silvio Ferrari, 45–59. Springer, 2016.

Rohe, Mathias. *Das Islamische Recht. Geschichte und Gegenwart.* München: C. H. Beck, 2009.

Santos, Boaventura de Sousa. "Law: A Map of Misreading. Toward a Post-Modern Conception of Law." *Journal of Law and Society* 14, no. 3 (1987): 279–302.

Santos, Boaventura de Sousa. *Toward a New Common Sense: Law, Science and Politics in the Paradigmatic Transition*. New York: Routledge, 1995.

Sbacchi, Alberto. *Ethiopia under Mussolini: Fascism and the Colonial Experience.* London: Zed Books, 1985.

Scholler, Heinrich. *Recht und Politik in Äthiopien. Von der traditionellen Monarchie zum modernen Staat.* Berlin: LIT, 2008.

Sedler, Robert Allen. *Ethiopian Civil Procedure.* Addis Ababa: Oxford University Press, 1968.

Seidel, Katrin. "State Recognised Legal Pluralism in Ethiopia: The Relationship between Islamic Family law and State Law." *Recht in Africa* 15, no. 1 (2012): 223–238.

Seidel, Katrin. *Rechtspluralismus in Äthiopien. Interdependenzen zwischen islamischem Recht und staatlichem Recht.* Koeln: Koeppe, 2013.

Shaham, Ron, ed. "Women as Expert Witnesses in Pre-Modern Islamic Courts." In *Law, Custom, and Statute in the Muslim World. Studies in Honor of Aharon Layish, Studies in Islamic Law and Society* 28. Leiden et al.: Brill, 2007.

Shukria, Mohammed. "*Sharia Courts of Ethiopia and their Status.*" LL.B. thesis, Addis Ababa University, 2001.

Sultan, Kassim. "*Protection of Religious Freedom in Ethiopian Institutions.*" LL.B. thesis, Addis Ababa University, 2004.

Trask, Robyn. "Challenges for Women and Law Reform in the Developing World." *BERCHI: The Annual Journal of Ethiopian Women Lawyers Association* 6 (2007): 81–87.

Trimingham, John Spencer. *Islam in Ethiopia.* London: Oxford University Press, 1952.

Tucker, Judith E. *Women, Family, and Gender in Islamic Law. Themes in Islamic Law* 3, Cambridge: Cambridge University Press, 2008.

Wagner, Ewald. "Harär History till 1875." In *Encyclopaedia Aethiopica* 2, edited by Siegbert Uhlig, 1015–1019. Wiesbaden: Harrassowitz, 2005.

Wasie, Yusuf Abdul. "Shari'a Courts in Ethiopia. Their Status, Organization and Functions." LL.B. thesis, Haile Selassie I. University Addis Ababa, 1971.

Zaki, Mustafa. "The Substantive Law Applied by Muslim Courts in Ethiopia. Possible Justifications for the Continued Application of the Sharia." *Journal of Ethiopian Law* 9, no. 1 (1973): 138–148.

Zewde, Bahru. *A History of Modern Ethiopia 1855–1991*. Addis Ababa: Addis Ababa University Press, 2005.

Legal Pluralism in the Southern West Bank: the Impact of Honour as a Factor on Developments towards an Increased Consideration of Rule-of-Law Principles in Clan-Based Justice

Ulrike Qubaja

1 Introduction

The chapter shall contribute to the understanding of the notion of *honour* in legal cases in Palestinian society. Cases that involve the concept of *honour* are often perceived as "different". They are not the typical type of case referred to in order to explain the functioning of legal pluralism by illustrating the rational reasoning of the agents. The general perception of the differentness of such cases is twofold: in several case studies agents of informal justice interviewed amicably described such cases as sensitive and highly difficult to solve. As an arbitrator of informal justice explained, relating specifically to cases of sexual assault:

> Cases of sexual assault are different. They are sensitive and very difficult, more difficult than blood [homicide]. And the compensation can reach a much higher level. Sometimes they ask for a million [Jordanian Dinar]. One has to use tricks regarding the facts.[1]

As the quote indicates, such cases mentioned above are difficult to solve, they involve high possible wins and losses and they legitimise means that would otherwise be conceived as illegitimate ("tricks"). This explanation points to a very pragmatic approach by clan-based justice to these cases. However, when I discussed such cases in several different forums in recent years – be it in a Palestinian or German-Arab, in academic or non-academic context – it was noticeable that the differentness was also perceived as stemming from the

1 Translation from a passage of an interview carried out in Hebron in 2015: *ḥālāt al-ʾiʿtidāʾ al-ğinsī ghayr. wa-hūwa ʿamr ḥassās wa-ṣaʿb ğiddan, aṣʿab min ad-damm. wa-yumkin yūṣal at-taʿwīḍ mablagh ʿaʿlā kthīr. aḥyānan byuṭlubū miliyōn. lāzim al-wāhid yitlāʿib bi-l-lī ṣār.* In this chapter a modification of the standard of the *Deutsche Morgenländische Gesellschaft* will be applied. While expressions, sentence structure and vowels of the spoken language are represented the spoken consonants are replaced by their pendants in Modern Standard Arabic. This shall ensure the comprehension by any person who understands Arabic.

 | DOI:10.1163/9789004398269_009

expectation of some kind of irrational moment. For cases of *honour* people often expected some rigid, culturally given mechanism that removed the case from rational comprehension. Discussants tended to choose a cultural approach in these cases more than they would for other cases, in which they would apply a rational-choice approach. As for my research an agent-centred rationalist approach proved explanatory for the functioning of legal pluralism and current developments, this raised the question, if strategical behaviour and pragmatism is as relevant for honour-centred cases.

Empirical data on informal justice in the Southern Palestinian West Bank which I collected between 2015 and 2016 suggest that while the outcomes of other types of cases reflect certain developments towards a growing consideration of certain principles of the rule of law, this cannot be observed for cases relating to the principle of female honour. For most types of cases such as homicide, accidents and battery, traditional instruments of informal justice that target the collective (e.g. exiling the family of the perpetrator) are applied less frequently and with a lesser magnitude than in the past; lethal revenge directed against other family members than the perpetrator has become rare; the question of actual guilt has become central as compared to the one of responsibility[2] derived from the conditions of the case. For cases relating to female honour no such development is evident: these cases are generally handled with a strong collective focus, official courts are avoided, the severity of instances of sexual assault is often downplayed or covered up, and marriage remains a frequent solution whenever an illegitimate relationship might be perceived, including cases of sexual assault.

This chapter shall shed light on the relation between the factor of female honour and the challenge of certain aspects of clan-based justice by norms attributable to principles of the rule of law. An agent based rationalist approach shall highlight the specific subjective rationalities of agents in cases relating to honour.

Following a conceptual introduction, different data shall be analysed and compared. The direction of procedure is from abstract to particular. To capture a rough picture of the relation of agents to clan-based justice on the one hand and to (quasi-)state-justice[3] on the other, survey-results of questions regarding the obligation to clan-based justice vs. state-justice as well as the recognition

2 According to clan-based justice a person has responsibility in a case if standing in some ownership relation or holding the obligation to protect a person, for example being the owner of the car that has been involved in a crime or in an accident or being the owner of the house where an assault has happened.

3 As the institutions oft he Palestinian Authority fulfil the functions of state institutions and are considered as such by respective people, in the following they will be referred to as state-institutions, e.g. *state-law*.

of vigilante justice are evaluated. Subsequently some results of questions regarding the opinion of the questioned people on proceedings and methods in two fictitious cases are analysed and compared to the conclusions above. In a third step, two cases relating to female honour are analysed and compared to the previous data.

The chapter seeks to find answers to the following questions:

- Do norms that can be attributed to rule-of-law principles have any impact on cases with *honour* as a central factor?
- How is the weight and stability of the norm that the honour of a female or family must be preserved or restored to be estimated?
- To what degree is the assumption of rational choice a sustainable concept for the explanation of the developments and outcomes in cases of honour in the field of legal pluralism?

1.1 *The Concept of Honour* (ʿirḍ/sharaf)

The term honour will be used for the two Arabic concepts of *sharaf* and *ʿirḍ*.[4] In Palestinian society both terms commonly bear the meaning *honour, good reputation, high rank* or *dignity*, whereby they are used for a status reflected by society more than for a personal perception of dignity or for the dignity of a human being as such.[5] Both terms refer to different aspects depending on whether they are used regarding males of females: applied to a female person, both terms primarily relate to her observance of the sexual-moral code of conduct, while for men they relate to their conduct regarding relationships of trust (*amāna*) as well as to their ability to ensure the safety and appropriate moral conduct of their closest female relatives. While the term *sharaf* is used in everyday language in a broader sense for the honour of groups, institutions or single persons, the term *ʿirḍ* is used in a more individual and legal sence: a man will spoil his *ʿirḍ* if he exploits a relationship of trust, but also if he proves incapable of protecting people under his protection. For a female, the term *ʿirḍ* is only used in a strictly legal sense, mainly in the context of sexual offenses.[6] In clan-based justice and reconciliation (*al-qaḍāʾ wa-ṣ-ṣulḥ al-ashāʾirī*) in the region of Hebron cases are only identified as honour-cases (*ḥālāt ʿirḍ aw sharaf*), if they bear a reference to the (potential) violation of a female's

4 Other concepts concepts that are sometimes translated with honour such as *wağh* (face, reputation) and *sumʿa* (reputation). Usually an offense againt the reputation (*sumʿa*) of a female is concidered as a potential affect on her honour, so there are no clear criteria for when a crime is an attack on a female's honour.

5 The term *karāma* rather refers to this concept of *dignity*.

6 Ḥuğğa, *Al-ʿurf al-ʿashāʾirī fi ʾl-ʾiṣlāh*, 189.

honour,[7] which automatically also constitutes a violation of the honour of her male relatives and of her family as a whole.[8] They include cases of sexual assault, cases of sexual relationships not legitimised by society, intruding into a family's home when females can be expected to be present, as well as slander and libel against a female by accusing her of contravening the moral code of conduct.

This chapter focuses on cases of offenses with a (potential) impact on a female's honour. The clarity of an offense as a setting is suited to demonstrating the impact of the concept of honour on options and choices in conflict and reconciliation. Such offences are considered as affecting the female's and her family's honour in multiple respects:

- The female's personal dignity (*karāma*) is violated,
- her honour (*ʿirḍ/sharaf*) is violated as an immediate effect of people knowing about the offense (even without her being suspected for having any responsibility for the crime),
- her honour may be violated by the suspicion and rumour that she bears some responsibility for the assault,
- the honour (*ʿirḍ/sharaf*) of her guardian and closest male relatives is violated as they have not been able to protect her,
- the honour of her family is violated if people suggest that they were not able to ensure her moral conduct.

Cases with a (potential) impact on a female's honour can result in the total loss of social status for the victim's close family, which in particular includes them being largely excluded from the marriage market: marriages generally depend on the consensus of the two spouses' close families. Well-respected families are careful not to "give"[9] their daughter to a family that has appeared not to be able to protect their female members, as this would be perceived as a neglect of their obligation to protect their daughter. Neither would they accept a daughter-in-law from a family whose honour has been violated as this might challenge their own honour, with them now being responsible for her protection. The sensitivity of these cases stems from the fact that the loss of honour is implemented by society, which presumes their knowledge of the incident. For clan-based justice this creates the paradox that on the one hand, cases of sexual assault demand a strong reaction, which somehow reflects the harm

7 Ibid., 190.

8 Abdelbaqi, *The administration of Criminal Justice in Palestine*, 250.

9 According to the patriarchal organization of society the girl is "given through marriage" to another family. This however does not cut existing family ties or responsibilities. On the contrary, a crime against the married woman will still be considered a crime against her family of origin.

caused, and on the other hand require a maximum of discretion to prevent the implementation of the loss of honour by society.

1.2 *An Agent-Based Approach*[10] *to Legal Pluralism*

For a concept of law and legal pluralism that is useful in a comparative context we first have to acknowlege that it is impossible to sharply differentiate between law on the one hand and mere social norms on the other. Any concept that equates law to state legislation appears artificial in settings of weak or failed states where non-state institutions fulfil the functions of state justice and non-state normative bodies are regarded as law. Concepts that define law by its function are not capable to distinguish law from other social norms: Concepts such as the one of the *living law* by Eugen Ehrlich, according to which law is "ordering and upholding every human association",[11] or the concept by John Griffiths who equates law with the "self-regulation of a 'semi-autonomous field'[12]" make the terms *law* and *social control* or *social norms* interchangeable. Applied to all kinds of social norms, the term law thus becomes detached from the respective concepts of law in society. Without an equivalent of the term in society there is no value added in the use of the term *legal* as opposed to *normative.* Baudouin Dupret argues for a concept of law and legal pluralism solely based on the perception of the respective people. He states: "law is what people consider as law [...] occurrences of legal pluralism are limited to these situations where people explicitly orient themselves to the fragmented spectrum of law".[13] So while we are not able to distinguish between law and other norms according to function, we may do this on the base of prevalent concepts in the respective societies. As most societies are strongly impacted by the concept of the modern nation state so are their concepts of law: Sets of norms are often considered as law, when they meet some degree of systematisation, enforceability or institutionalisation. Legal pluralism is perceived as such when other sets of norms challenge state legislation in certain fields and hence if agents are able to choose or combine between different legal orders.

---

10 Agent based approaches of legal pluralism focus on the behaviour of involved agents to choose and combine between the available legal systems and their normative collections, referred to as forum shopping. Keebet Benda-Beckmann, "Forum Shopping and Shopping Forums. Dispute Settlement in a Minangkabau Village in West Sumatra," Journal of Legal Pluralism (1981), 117–153.

11 Ehrlich, *Fundamental Principles of the Sociology of Law*, 24.

12 Griffiths, "What is Legal Pluralism," 38.

13 Dupret, Baudouin "Legal Pluralism, Plurality of Laws, and Legal Practices: Theories, Critiques, and Praxiological Re-Specification," 296.

In the Palestinian society of the West Bank and the Gaza Strip people differentiate between three main legal systems with respectively distinct foundations: the formal justice system of the Palestinian Authority, clan-based informal justice (*aṣ-ṣulḥ wa-'l-qaḍā' al-ashā'irī*) and religious justice, which is mainly *Sharīʿa*-justice. In addition, different Christian church-laws are applied in Christian communities and Israel applies Israeli military laws on Palestinians in the occupied territories. For the question of the constitution of legal pluralism in the West Bank, we take state law applied in the West Bank as a reference for what is law: State law is highly systematic and institutionalised. It has considerable means of implementation and it is clearly considered as law (*qānūn*) in Palestinian society. Other terms used in the formal legal field are *ḥaqq*,[14] referring to legally grounded rights or claims and *qaḍā'*,[15] meaning judiciary. Regarding the other legal systems, namely clan-based justice and religious-justice,[16] we can see that people refer to them as law for example by describing Islamic *Sharīʿa* as law of God (*qānūn allāh*) or referring to clan-based justice as customary law (*qānūn ʿurfī*). The legal terms *ḥaqq* and *qaḍā'* are also used in all legal systems.[17] There is no local Arabic term for *legal pluralism*. However, people do refer to this concept indirectly by for example explaining that besides official law, the Islamic *Sharīʿa* and clan-based justice (*al-qaḍā' al-ashā'irī*) are applied in Palestine, so they equate these systems in their role or function. All systems have considerable means of implementation with state authority in the case of state law, mechanisms of personal guarantee and a possible sanctions ranging from social exclusion to the exercise of violence in the case of clan-based justice, and a combination of the two by *Sharīʿa*-justice depending on its respective localisation. Moreover, all three meet a minimum degree of systematisation within their own institutions and the ability to subsume particular questions under superior norms. On this basis, we assume for our analysis of legal pluralism in the Palestinian West Bank the parallel existence of three different legal systems, each having its own fundamental principles and sources of legitimisation. Institutionally, these legal systems are partly integrated and interwoven: like in most Arab countries personal status law is regulated by denomination-specific legislation with separate *Sharīʿa*-courts in charge of the family affairs of Muslims; the oath is an important instrument of state justice that refers to religious law; the Islamic *Sharīʿa* is referred to as the

14 The term *ḥaqq* can be translated as *right, claim* or *entitlement.*

15 The term *qaḍā'* can be translated as *judgment, justice* or *judiciary*.

16 For the purpose of this chapter Israeli military law will be ignored, as it does not constitute an option for people seeking remedy.

17 In Egypt clan-based justice is also referred to as *ḥaqq al-ʿarab* in Palestine it is sometimes referred to as *ḥaqq ʿarab.*

main source of legislation by the Palestinian basic law of 2002[18] and *Sharīʿa* is frequently referred to as a source for legitimizing claims or rulings by all legal systems. People differentiate between these different justice systems, however, and mostly agree on the type of justice that is being used at any given moment. For our analysis we use an agent-based approach that focusses on the rationalities of the different agents involved. This is based on the assumption that in the legal field people tend to act strategically rather than according to a rigid set of norms or to mere habits. Reasons for this assumption are the potentially high gains and losses involved in this field, the existence of structures that promote rational reasoning (such as counselling and defence by legal experts), and the fact that the members of the conflicting parties usually find themselves in an exceptional situation which makes it impossible for them to act according to habits. Of course this strategic behaviour does not happen in a vacuum separate from social norms or values: choices need to be justified, so they are taken within a given normative framework, which is pluralistic and influenced by further factors. Agents choose according to their respective interests between socially acceptable options that are provided by different normative systems.

2 Principles of the Rule of Law, the Factor of Honour, and Pragmatism According to Data from Field Research

2.1 *Survey Data*

To understand in which respect cases relating to female honour are exempt from the general challenge to clan-based informal justice by norms attributable to rule-of-law principles, survey data targeting these norms are analysed here.[19] The questions analysed target the sense of obligation towards clan-based vs. state justice, the exclusion of women from an active role in clan-based justice, the acceptance of vigilante justice and the acceptance of forced marriage as a means of reconciliation. These issues do not stem from a merely theoretical rule-of-law perspective, but have been identified as central to contemporary discourses and developments of legal pluralism based on empirical findings.

18 Website "The Palestinian Basic Law," http://www.palestinianbasiclaw.org/basic-law/2002-basic-law, accessed 30 July, 2017.

19 The survey was carried out in 2015 in the Palestinian governorates of Hebron and Bethlehem. With a sample of 2173 questionnaires and a distribution of the regions and villages according to the sizes of their population, the survey can be considered as representative. The survey was carried out in Arabic with the assistance of a group of Palestinian law-students that were specially trained for the work.

2.1.1 Affiliation to Clan-Based Customary Justice

To give an impression of the feeling of obligation towards clan-based customary justice as opposed to the formal justice system we analyse the results of the following question:

According to your opinion, which of the following gives you a greater feeling of obligation?

a: A *ṣulḥ* agreement according to clan-based justice

b: The ruling of a formal court

A majority of 52.6% explained that they felt more obliged to a *ṣulḥ*-agreement as opposed to 40.2% who explained that they felt more obliged to a court ruling and a minority of 6.3% who explained that they felt obliged by both in the same way. The ratio a/b is with 57.7/35.2 for men significantly higher than the ratio for women with 48.2/44.7, which might be explained by their exclusion from any active role or participation in the system. Also, there are significant regional differences. In large areas the relation of people feeling more obliged by a *ṣulḥ* agreement to people feeling more obliged by a formal court ruling is more than 2/1. In the city of Dura, which has traditionally been the centre of clan-based justice, it 65.2/32.9, and it is as high as 70.4/23.5 in the villages of Yatta, a region with a significant Bedouin population. In contrast, in the city of Bethlehem the ratio is at 35.5/59.6; and in the predominantly Christian town of Beit Sahour it is 34.00/54.00.

The data suggest that clan-based justice has a strong implemental force in the whole southern West Bank, although there are significant variations with respect to region and gender.

2.1.2 Women in Informal Justice

Unlike in other sectors of society including the legal field,[20] women are still largely excluded from clan-based justice. They neither act as *ṣulḥ*-arbitrators nor do they even speak on their own behalf in official contexts of clan-based reconciliation. Only outside official gatherings may they be asked for their opinion or questioned as witnesses. The limitation of women to being only objects of clan-based justice rather than subjects within it may contribute to the specific perception and handling of cases relating to honour. While in other fields of society the presence of women has become the norm, which has led to a differentiated perception of women in different roles, in clan-based justice the concept of honor is given prerogative in the framing of the role of women.

20 For example in the formal justice sector in 2016 18.6% of judges in the West Bank were female. Palestinian Central Bureau of Statistics. http://pcbs.gov.ps/Downloads/book2237.pdf, p. 56, accessed 30 July, 2017.

Utmost effort is put into stressing the flawless conduct of the females involved in cases of conflict and even mentioning the name of a girl publicly among the men present can be considered as potentially affecting her honour. Assuming that a role of women as subjects of informal justice might change the handling of cases related to honour, we look at people's estimation of the importance of gender for the suitability of a person to act in re-conciliating people. For a better impression the importance of the factor *gender* is compared to the importance of the factor *high age*, which is traditionally regarded as a central quality of a *ṣulḥ*-arbitrator. As compared to the relevance of a high age, which 33.9% considered as "very important" and another 33.2% considered as "important", the factor gender was considered as "very important" by a large majority of 61.8% and as "important" by another 15.0%. On the other hand it was considered as not important by 10.8% and as not important at all by only 7.8%. Regarding the consideration of the factor gender the discrepancy from region to region is high. While in all the cities and villages of the Hebron governorate at least, over all 70.0% considered this factor as important[21] with a maximum of 81.0% in the city of *Dūra*, but in the area of Bethlehem we see extreme variations, with 93.3% in the village of *Zaʿtara* and only 36.0% of the mostly Christian city of Beit Sahour considering gender as important. Also there is also a noticeable discrepancy in the estimation of the factor gender between men and women. While 71.3% of women consider this factor as important, even 83.1% of men do so.

This data shows that except for a few Christian-influenced towns, the exclusion of women from an active role in clan-based justice remains unchallenged. Since the remaining exclusion of women prevents a challenge to the perception of women by the reality of their involvement, the lack of challenge to the exclusion of women may also indicate that honour remains a consistently weighty factor in cases referring to women.

2.1.3 Acceptance of Methods That Contradict Rule-of-Law Principles, as Seen in Exemplary Cases

In order to judge whether cases relating to honour are exempt from the challenge which rule-of-law principles make to methods of clan-based justice, we must first look at data that reveal this challenge. It affects some widely applied principles and mechanisms, such as the right to violent retaliation in the form of attacks on family members and their property in cases of manslaughter and sexual offences, as well as the method of exiling the family of

21 Here *important* includes the options "important" and "very important".

the perpetrator. Subsequently we will examine the survey data on a fictitious case of sexual assault.

Reconciliation for an offense is generally based on the idea that the offense generates a right of retaliation. Reconciliation lets people waive this right in return for compensation, for other conditions they demand or for an apology. In cases of severe crimes such as homicide, the families of the victims usually openly declare their willingness to retaliate, the declaration often being supported by the gathering of young men from the family and their parading with weapons. The following question shall enable an estimation of to what extent this principle is put into question:

According to your opinion, when does the family have the right to use violence?

- Always when their rights or dignity are attacked
- Only in cases where a family member was killed or wounded
- Always when the state is not able to punish the perpetrator appropriately
- They do not have this right at all – except in immediate self-defence – as only the state has the right to use force
- other: [space for individual answer][22]

With a total of 22.7%, a minority held the opinion that families do not have the right to use violence at all, while another minority of 19.5% thought that they always had the right when their rights or dignity were attacked. 17.2% limited the right to cases involving the killing or wounding of family members, while a relative majority of 35.6% held that they had the right when the state was not capable of appropriate punishment. A small minority of less than 5% gave alternative answers or combined different points. Accordingly, in total an absolute majority of 58.3% supported in principle the primary responsibility of the state to prosecute (groups c and d). The large size of the group that makes the state's monopoly of violence conditional on its ability to impose an appropriate punishment reflects the existing dilemma between the theoretical approval of rule-of law principles and the perception of a conflicting reality of weak state structures.[23] It also indicates the pragmatism that guides people in dealing with the existence of parallel justice systems in Palestinian society. Although agreeing in principle with a norm that excludes an alternative, they turn to another concept because they perceive one system as insufficient. A greater feeling of obligation towards clan-based justice correlates with approval of a right to use violence: 23.5% of the group that explained that they felt

22 It was possible to combine the above answers or give an alternative. However, only a small minority of people did so.

23 Abdelbaqi, *The administration of Criminal Justice in Palestine*, 235.

more strongly obliged by a *ṣulḥ*-contract than by the ruling of a formal court opted for the family always having the right to use violence when their rights or dignity are attacked, while only 15.4% of the group that explained that they felt more obliged by the ruling of a formal court recognised this right. However in both groups there was still a total majority in support of the primary responsibility of the state to prosecute, with a large relative majority of over 35% (35.5% and respectively 36.1%) opting for the "pragmatic" answer that families had this right when the state was not able to punish the perpetrator appropriately. The results suggest that the right to retaliate by using violence is clearly challenged by the principle state persecution. However, this principle is handled in a pragmatic way by tying its applicability to the perceived capability of the state. Both the challenge and the pragmatic approach are prevalent in all parts of society, including the group with a stronger feeling of obligation towards clan-based justice.

To reconstruct the considerations of people in actual cases, people were asked about their position on typical aspects of clan-based justice in hypothetical cases (which are simplified and adapted versions of real, previously studied cases). In the following we analyse answers relating to a case of manslaughter and set them in relation to those to a case of sexual assault.

The case of manslaughter was described as follows:

Between two neighbouring families there occurred a fight in which a young man of one family stabbed a young man of the other with a knife. The latter was severely hurt and later died in the hospital. The police arrested all the involved persons. During the term of the *fawrat ad-damm*,[24] the family of the victim started to burn houses of the family of the perpetrator. Arbitrators intervened and reached a truce for the first three days and a third, after which the family of the perpetrator sent a delegation to the other family [...]. The

24 In severe cases such as homicide and honour cases, there is considered to be a period of three and a third days in which the victim's family has the right to burn property of the family of the perpetrator or destroy it by other means and to attack male adult relatives of the other family. This period is called *fawrat ad-damm*, which can be translated as *surge of the blood*: Birzeit University, *Al-qaḍā'- ghayr an-niẓāmī. siyādatu 'l-qānūn wa-ḥall an-nizā'āt fī filasṭīn, In: silsilatu 'l-qānūn wa-'l-muğtama'* (*Birzeit 2006*): 217. Damages caused in this time are usually not counted towards the final reconciliation. Traditionally, a large value in property is destroyed during these days. However in recent years this practice has declined. Crimes committed during this time are often either not persecuted by formal justice or the cases are dropped once the *'aṭwa*-agreement is signed.

conditions of the *ʿaṭwa*[25] included the payment of 1000 Jordanian Dinar (JD)[26] as *frāsh al-ʿaṭwa,*[27] the refund of expenses of 30,000 JD and the payment of 40,000 JD as part of the *dīyya*[28] as well as exiling the closest family members of the perpetrator and the participants in the crime. The blood of the perpetrator would remain wanted [the family of the victim would not waive their right of lethal revenge against the perpetrator himself]. The participants in the crime were released based on the contract of the *ʿaṭwa.*

The following questions were asked about debatable methods or options in this case:

- Is it acceptable that the family of the victim burns the houses of the family of the perpetrator?
- Is it right to exile the family of the perpetrator?
- What is your opinion about the fact that the *dīyya* is paid by the perpetrator's family (and not by himself)?
- Is it the right of the family of the victim to kill the young man?
- Should the damages that occurred during *fawrat ad-damm* be counted and offset?

To the question of whether it was acceptable that the family of the victim burned the houses of the family of the perpetrator, a minority of 11.7% considered it as "their right during the first three and a third days", as traditionally considered so in clan-based justice, while 51.7% voted for the option that they had no right to do so. A large minority of 36.4% voted for the option that it was not their right, but a natural reaction in the face of the death of a family member. These numbers confirm the normative change with a large majority rejecting an instrument of collective punishment that has traditionally clearly been considered as part of the rights of the victim's family. This is confirmed by the answers to the question if these damages should be offset in the final

25 The *ʿaṭwa* is the most prominent instrument of clan-based reconciliation. Any crime generates a rightful claim (*ḥaqq*) for the family of the victim. The *ʿaṭwa* includes the acceptance by the relevant family or families of their responsibility, the declaration of their willingness to reconcile and the request for a truce or final reconciliation. In cases of unclear facts they may ask for an *ʿaṭwat taftīsh*, a period of truce that allows them to carry out investigations. However most cases involve an *ʿaṭwat ʾiʿtirāf*, an *ʿaṭwa* based on confession. In severe cases the conditions agreed upon are written down in a contract. They usually involve a truce period of one year, after which the *ʿaṭwa* has to be renewed or a final reconciliation is reached.

26 At the time one JD was worth 1.3 Euro.

27 *The frāsh al-ʿaṭwa* can be translated as 'mattress *ʿaṭwa*.' As a symbol for the willingness to pay compensation, it is perceived as the foundation on which reconciliation takes place. The payment is offset by the final amount of compensation.

28 The *dīyya* is the blood money regulated by Islamic law.

reconciliation, which is often discussed, but in fact not done in clan-based justice. Here a large majority of 70.6 % opted for them to be offset. A closer look at the groups that generally represent positions that are in tension with rule-of-law principles, namely the group that feels more obliged by a *ṣulḥ*-agreement than by a court ruling and the group that opted for the answer that families always had the right to use violence when their rights or their dignity were attacked, reveals that this normative development is inherent to all sectors of society not just people closely affiliated to state-justice: A clear majority of 65.6% of the group feeling more strongly obliged to clan-based justice opted for the offset of damages while a majority of 50.7% did so from the group that believed families always had the right to use violence when their rights or dignity were attacked.

The question of whether the close family of the perpetrator should be exiled, a common method in cases of manslaughter still today, also reveals the normative challenge by rule-of-law principles, as well as the pragmatic approach of people to such issues: while a minority of 29.9% opted for the version that the family should be exiled as they bore responsibility for their son, a slightly bigger group of 30.2% opted for the answer that they should not be exiled as they were not responsible for the mistake of their son and a relative majority of 39.6% opted for the rather pragmatic answer that, although they were not responsible, they should be exiled for the protection of civil peace.

Regarding the question of whether the family has the right to kill the perpetrator, a relative minority of 44.5% opted for the answer that this was (generally) their right, while a relative majority of 48.4% opted for the answer that it was not their right as revenge was unacceptable and only the state had the right and responsibility to punish, while minorities of 4.8% and 2.0% respectively opted for the answers that it is their right, if the state's punishment is less then death penalty or lower than a certain number of years in prison specified by the interviewees. In the light of the fact that in clan-based justice in cases of killing it is clearly considered the right of the family of the victim to kill the perpetrator in revenge, often backed by the local interpretation of Islamic law according to which a perpetrator of a deliberate killing should be killed, the fact that almost half of the people asked rejected this norm, may further indicate the change towards an increasing consideration of rule-of-law principles. Even from the group that opted for the answer that families always had the right to use violence when their rights or dignity were attacked, a large minority of 38.0% opted for the answer that it was not their right to kill the perpetrator, which again indicates that the growing rejection of revenge is not limited to certain groups affiliated to state law. In contrast to the questions regarding burning houses and exile, a far smaller group indicated that they were willing to choose lethal vengeance against the perpetrator over the other normative system if the preferred one failed.

Unlike in the case of collective punishment and, to a lesser degree, revenge, implementing the principle of collective responsibility by distributing the burden of paying the *dīyya* on the whole family is not questioned in a similar way. Asked about their opinion on the fact that the whole family of the perpetrator shared in paying the *dīyya*, only 7.1% voted for the option that this was unjust as the family was not responsible for the wrongs of their son, while 77.4% explained that it was just as they had a share in the responsibility because they raised their son and 15.1% opted for the answer that it was unjust but an effective means to prevent such crimes in the future. These numbers suggest that the increasing consideration of rule-of-law principles does not stem from a vanishing affiliation to the clans or from the renunciation of collective responsibility.

We can conclude that central norms of clan-based justice such as exiling the family of a perpetrator, revenge against the perpetrator of a deliberate killing and the right of the family to attack in the context of *fawrat ad-damm*, which contradict to principles of the rule of law, are strongly challenged in Palestinian society. This challenge comes from all parts of society including the ones affiliated to informal justice and the ones generally in favour of the right to use violence as means of retaliation. However pragmatic approaches resist this challenge, as indicated by the relatively large groups that agree to the respective methods for practical reasons, although in principle opposing them. Meanwhile neither recourse to clan-based justice as such, nor the clan-system itself and the principle of collective responsibility by clans and families seems to be similarly challenged.

To find out whether the challenge to certain methods of clan-based justice by rule-of-law principles is weaker or even absent in cases relating to honour, we examine the results of the relevant questions about methods in a case of rape.

The case was described as follows:

A young girl informed her family that she was raped by the driver of a public taxi. The driver admitted that there had been a sexual relationship between them but claimed that it was consensual. The family of the girl hesitated to go to the police out of fear that everyone would talk about the case; they considered killing them both. Based on this the family of the young man approached *ṣulḥ*-arbitrators to solve the problem confidentially. The latter pressured the family of the young man to ask for the hand of the girl in marriage under conditions that appeased the family of the girl, such as a high amount of gold and a high dowry.

The following questions were asked regarding controversial methods or options in cases relating to honour:

- Is it right to kill the perpetrator [that the family of the victim kills the perpetrator]?
- Is it right that the family of the girl considers killing her?
- Is it right that the girl is made to marry the young man?

According to several interviews with *ṣulḥ*-arbitrators the three options above are the common choices in the case of severe sexual offenses. While until about 20 years ago, families tended to kill both the perpetrator and the victim when such cases became public, today it is more likely that only the perpetrator is killed. The most common method, however, is to disguise the crime by having the perpetrator marry the victim.[29] To seek remedy from formal justice is however not seen as an option as this would expose the case to the public while not providing the restoration of honour.[30]

In answer to the question about whether it was right to kill the perpetrator, 19.2% opted for the answer that this was the right of the family, while a large majority of 74.7% argued that this was not their right and 5.3% opted for the answer that it was not their right but that there was no alternative choice. The answers may be influenced by the setting of the case in which the marriage solution was described as an alternative. However the strong rejection of a common method also indicates an impact of rule-of law norms on its acceptance. The even stronger rejection of the option to kill the girl by 85.9% of the people, in spite of the concept of clan-based justice, according to which killing the girl would cleanse the honour of the family, indicates a normative change towards the consideration of an individual responsibility.

The answers to the question on whether it was right to let the young girl marry the young man reflects the existing normative challenge while explaining why this challenge is not translated into outcomes that more strongly consider rule-of law-norms. 43.1% voted for the option that it was right to let them marry, while 24.1% explained that it was not and a large minority of 32.0%

29 Abdelbaqi, *The administration of Criminal Justice in Palestine – development, reform and challenges*, 235.

30 Some people interviewed held the opinion that the recourse to formal justice was even interpreted as a sign of weakness, since it would reveal that the family was not able to defend their females on their own. However many others considered this perception as outdated.

explained that it was another injustice/abuse[31] against the girl but there was no alternative solution. So while a 56.1% majority either considered the marriage solution not to be right or as an injustice/abuse against the girl, at the same time a large majority of a total of 75.1% still agreed to the marriage option.[32] Compared to other methods that contradict rule-of-law principles, such as exiling the family of the perpetrator and burning houses, the group that either supports this method without reservation or for pragmatic reasons is even larger. This suggests that cases that relate to honour are affected by the impact of rule-of-law norms, but less so than other cases and are even more subject to pragmatic considerations that might lead to these norms not being reflected in the outcome of the case.

2.2 *Reconstruction and Analysis of Two Cases Concerning Honour as a Central Concern*

For a closer understanding of the weight of the factor honour on the one hand and the impact of normative change towards an increasing recognition of rule-of-law principles on the other, two cases with honour as a central concern are briefly analysed here. The first is a case of sexual assault against a young girl, which after a failed trial according to clan-based justice ended in a lethal act of revenge and a subsequent reconciliation agreement. The second is the case of a takeover of the Facebook account of a young girl by a young man resulting in an ersatz trial, the concealment of the crime and eventual formal forgiveness. While in both cases the impact of rule-of-law principles can clearly be detected, in both cases the outcome does not reflect these norms.

2.2.1 A Case of Sexual Assault and Attempted Rape

In autumn 2015 a young girl was abducted and sexually assaulted[33] by a young man as she was on her way back from a village in the region of Hebron to an Arab town in Israel. When she entered a public taxi the driver and another young man opened a conversation by commenting that she seemed not to be

31 Translation for the Arabic word *ẓulm*.

32 For these questions there are only small variations according to gender. 20.4% of women opted for that it was the right of the family to kill the perpetrator as compared to 18.0% of men, while 8.8% of women opted that it was right to kill the girl as opposed to 8.1% of men and only 42.1% of women opted that it was right to let them marry as opposed to 44.2% of men.

33 The case study is based on in depth interviews with close family members of all conflicting parties, the mayor of the village and with several re-conciliators. Additionally a larger number of short interviews were carried out with people of the village to assess the public opinion regarding the developments and outcome of the case. The researchers also attended and videotaped all the official gatherings.

from the area. When she explained that her father was the *Shaykh*-X[34] from the same village and that she was on her way to her mother's family, the driver[35] tried to build up trust by revealing their family ties, with him being a close relative of her father. As the young men kept talking to her the girl felt increasingly uncomfortable and demanded to return to her family. The driver however picked up a brother of the accomplice on the way and drove to a tent in a remote area where he asked her to come in for coffee. The girl initially refused to enter but then obeyed out of fear. Later, in the presence of the other two men and the owner of the tent, the taxi driver attacked the young girl, stripped her, touched her in a sexual way and tried to rape her. However she was able to make him stop the assault and drive her to the checkpoint.[36] When she arrived home she called her father to tell him about the assault.

The family of the victim complained to some *ṣulḥ*-arbitrators of the village. Convinced by the credibility of the report, their initial suggestion was to pressure the family of the main perpetrator to ask for the hand of the girl in marriage, for which his family was to offer favourable conditions. The girl's father, a pious man and *daʿwa*-missionary,[37] strongly rejected this proposal as un-Islamic and a form of blatant injustice against his daughter. He demanded "the right of the girl" (*ḥaqq al-bint*) by all legal means, in which he was supported by members of his close family.[38] The girl's family officially made their claim to the clan-based authorities as well as to local officials. The police arrested the perpetrator and the accomplices in the crime[39] and stationed security forces at the homes of the people involved. During the following days the family of the girl attacked individuals and property of the family of the perpetrator. Meanwhile *ṣulḥ*-arbitrators, clan-elders and representatives of the town hall

34 The term sh*aykh* refers either to society elders or to men who are known as very religious.

35 For ease of understanding and as there is a consensus about their roles, in the following the taxi driver will be referred to as the perpetrator and the other young men will be referred to as the accomplices in the crime.

36 Here the reconstruction of the case has to rely on the official version that was publicly told. It should be mentioned that even if a woman was raped, this would usually not enter the official version of the case if no pregnancy occurred and she was not killed, as an actual rape would diminish her chances of marrying. Similarly, details of the crime are omitted.

37 The term *daʿwa* can be translated as *call* or *invitation.* It refers to the Islamic concept of mission.

38 Family is organized partrilineally. The close family includes paternal uncles and their descendants.

39 Such arrests frequently precede the existence of reasonable grounds to suspect the involvement into a crime and can be considered as a preemptive measure to protect the suspects from revenge and to prevent clashes. Often arrests are used to pressure the involved families into a reconciliation process.

made efforts to impose a truce and initiate a reconciliation process.[40] At this juncture the city hall prevented the police from interfering since the arrest of members of the girl's family might have hindered the reconciliation process.

After some days of riots a large delegation of *ṣulḥ*-arbitrators and notables of the village paid the girl's family a visit at their home to ask for an *ʿaṭwa*, which included the acknowledgement of responsibility for the crime by the perpetrator's family and the willingness to pay compensation. The conditions of the *ʿaṭwa* were negotiated between the closest male relatives of the girl, the representatives of the family of the perpetrator, and the arbitrators present. The terms agreed upon included a truce of one month and the subsequent holding of a *manshad*, a clan-based tribunal presided over by an informal judge who would pass judgement over the young men and publicly declare the innocence and the undamaged honour of the girl. It was further agreed that the perpetrator and accomplices in the crime would be banned from the neighbourhood the family of the girl lived in. During the truce both sides would abstain from any aggressions including slander.

Clashes did not cease and both sides accused each other of breaking the truce. The perpetrator's family, a wealthy and rather educated family with excellent relations to the judiciary and to the security sector, meanwhile unofficially withdrew their confession and started vilifying the family of the girl in different forums by accusing the father of trading with honour (*tiǧārat sharaf*[41]), among other accusations. Although according to clan-based justice, breaking the terms of an *ʿaṭwa* is considered a severe crime against the respective guarantor, called *taqṭīʿ al-wiǧh*,[42] no new conflict between either of the two sides and the respective guarantors evolved and they continued with the reconciliation process. The families agreed on a well-respected and wealthy person from a nearby town as *manshad*[43] and that the tribunal would take place in a neighbouring village. Over 1000 men attended the tribunal, most of them

---

40 It is characteristic of clan-based justice that the *ṣulḥ*-arbitrators interfere and initiate a reconciliation process even if neither side of the conflict requests their interference.

41 In other words, he had sold the honour of his daughter for the expected amount of compensation, an action considered especially shameful.

42 The term *taqṭīʿ al-wiǧh* can be translated as *chopping of the face*. The term *ʿiṭṭiyāḥ al-wiǧh* is used synonymously, meaning *making (someone) lose his face*. Birzeit University, *Al-qaḍāʾ- ghayr an-niẓāmī. siyādatu ʾl-qānūn wa-ḥall an-nizāʿāt fī filasṭīn*, In: *silsilatu ʾl-qānūn wa-ʾl-muǧtamaʿ*, 210.

43 A *manshad* is a judge of clan-based justice specialized on cases of honour and *taqṭīʿ al-wiǧh*. The term *manshad* is used for both, the judge and the tribunal he presides. Ghayth, Muḥammad Ḥasan Abū Ḥammād, *Qaḍāʾ al-ʿashā-ir fī ḍaū al-shariʿ al-ʾislāmī* (Jerusalem: Modern Arab Press, 1990), 17.

elder men representing the families of the area.[44] After a formal greeting and reference to Islamic traditions that endorse the reconciliation between people, the *manshad* asked for the guarantors. The *mukhtār*[45] of the clan, which both families belonged to, explained he would be warrant for both sides. The *manshad* asked for a description of the case explaining that he would judge based on what he heard. The girl's paternal uncle spoke for the side of the victim's family describing the events, stressing the personal suffering of the girl and the special relationship of trust created by the fact that the perpetrator was driving a public taxi and that he was a relative of the girl's father. Subsequently the *mukhtār*, who had the right to defend the accomplices in the crime, explained that he would not defend them but leave the ruling in the hands of the *manshad*. However he suggested taking into account later attacks against his family that happened during the clashes. The *manshad* rejected this claim and proceeded by announcing and explaining his ruling: The sentence included a compensation the perpetrator and his accomplices were to pay to the family the girl, their banning from the area the girl's family lived in and the cleansing of the girl's honour. Resorting to clan-based law and *sharīʿa*-law the *manshad* specified an amount of compensation for each of the single aspects of the crime. He sentenced the families of the perpetrator and the accomplices to pay the following:

- 200,000 (JD) for the betrayal of a relationship of trust (*amāna*) created by the fact that the perpetrator was driving a public taxi.
- 50,000 for letting her enter a disrespectable place.
- 180,000 JD for the distance he abducted her, 6 JD[46] for each meter with an overall distance of about 30 km.
- 67,500 JD to buy his hand back: according to the *manshad*, the hand that touched the girl should be cut off. However according to *sharīʿa*-law, a hand was attributed to half of the *dīyya* that was set for murder.
- 150,000 JD for the crime of attacking the girl and trying to rape her.
- 200,000 for aggravating circumstances as the girl belonged to his paternal relatives, whom he was obliged to protect.

44 Reconciliation gatherings are in principle not attended by women. The author and her female research assistant where the only women present after acquiring the approval from the *manshad* and from the family of the girl.

45 The *mukhtār* is one of the family elders usually chosen for a life-time, who represents the family or clan.

46 The *manshad* explained that according to *ʿurf*, the distance and amount of compensation were calculated in camels. However this was not compatible with today's times since camels were not used anymore.

- For the crimes of the accomplices, who were also relatives of the girl, he calculated 150,000 as their crimes were considered less grave and they did not touch the girl.

Additionally the *manshad* announced that the girl had maintained her honour as she had behaved honourably in every respect and the crime had happened against her will. He sentenced the families of the accused to symbolically cleanse the girl's honour (*bayāḍ ʿirḍ al-bint*) by fully covering her father's home with white cloth. He ruled that the family of the perpetrator would pay a rounded 850.000 JD and the family of the accomplices would pay 150.000 JD to the family of the girl within the following days, stressing that considering the infamy of the crime the amount was not too high. The tribunal was closed by the *manshad* declaring that he would not take the allowance agreed upon[47] and by another speaker thanking him for his generosity and thanking the people for their attendance.

The attendants of the tribunal reacted positively. People explained that the amount was high but justified and important for the deterrence and the prevention of similar crimes in the future. Some people explained that finally clan-based justice had given priority to the rights of women and girls and demonstrated that no one could harass a female without consequence. In spite of this initial support, the public perception of the case changed, when the family of the perpetrator refused to pay. Although considered as a gesture of disrespect against the guarantors and against the *manshad* by clan-based justice, the family's refusal to pay was also perceived as a sign of the family's strength. As clashes continued and the police took strong actions against the girl's family,[48] people realised the family's vulnerability and started criticizing their choice of a public tribunal, arguing that they had now ruined their daughter's future, despite having had the chance to solve the case quietly. Some people started questioning the honourable intention of the father, suggesting that he sacrificed his daughter's honour in order to become rich. A few months later close family members of the girl expressed regret for their choice. They explained that, whatever they decided to do would be used against them: if they asked for the money, people would accuse them for trading with honour; if they took revenge, people would say they killed for money; and if they forgave, people would consider them weak. Most family members who had initially supported

47 Traditionally a *manshad* receives an allowance for his time and his expenses. However not to accept the allowance is considered as a generous and honourable act.

48 Some *ṣulḥ*-conciliators interviewed were of the opinion that the police action against the family of the girl was to be explained by the influence of the father of the perpetrator on members of the police. This cannot be proven. However it clearly weakened the position of the family of the girl.

the approach of seeking remedy for the girl by a public tribunal explained they would have opted for a quiet solution or even waived their rights if they had foreseen the social consequences.

The official court considered the ruling of the *manshad* as a final reconciliation that included the forgiveness from the side of the victim. In the Jordanian penal law of 1960, applied in the Palestinian territories until today, there is no formal reference to clan-based justice. However the *forgiving* (*tasāmuḥ*) by the injured party allows the dropping of the charges, the release on bail or the substantial reduction of the sentence depending on the crime.[49] Accordingly, the accomplices were released without charge, while the perpetrator was released on bail after some months. When released, he allegedly entered the area the family of the girl lived in. In response, three of her paternal cousins attacked him and beat him to death.[50] His family reacted in a calmly, as the killing was perceived as an act of revenge rather than murder and as the young man was considered to have brought shame on the family. The families of the young men who killed the perpetrator sent a delegation of *ṣulḥ*-conciliators to his family to negotiate the terms of an *ʿaṭwa*. They explained that it was never their intention to kill, but that they only wanted to beat him since he had come close to the girl's father's home, which he was banned from by the agreement. It was agreed on a payment of 70.000 JD retribution to the family of the young man, the usual amount in cases of intentional killing, and to an immediate reconciliation.

Society's reaction to the final outcome was highly affirmative: All people of the village that were interviewed randomly hold the opinion that the killing of the perpetrator was the right of the girl's family. They argued that the family needed to react to the shame, especially since the perpetrator was released and the other family did not respect the judgment of the *manshad*. Most people were of the opinion that the girl's family had eventually restored their honour by taking revenge. Some of the interviewees found the family of the perpetrator responsible for his death as they had refused to pay and exposed him to a very probable revenge. Meanwhile people declared their respect for the perpetrator's family as they accepted the *dīya* and allowed the case to be closed. Several of the interviewees even interpreted the approach of the family of the perpetrator not to pay but to escalate the conflict and to obtain his release as

49 Penal Code No. 16 (1960) Art. 52, 53 and 99. Birzeit University, *Al-qaḍāʾ- ghayr an-niẓāmī. siyādatu ʾl-qānūn wa-ḥall an-nizāʿāt fī filasṭīn*, In: *silsilatu ʾl-qānūn wa-ʾl-muǧtamaʿ*: 217.

50 The young men were arrested but probably won't face a high sentence, as they framed the killing as not intended and as the other family forgave them. Even in cases of murder prison scentence is often reduced to a few years in case of pardon by the family of the victim. (Interviews with two different judges in the region of Hebron, 2016.).

an act of sacrificing their son by exposing him to revenge in order to diminish the claim of the family of the girl and to restore their reputation. They expressed their support for this proceeding, arguing that if a person repeatedly dishonoured the family, one should refuse to pay and leave him to the revenge of the other side.

2.2.2 A Takeover of the Facebook Account of a Young Girl

The second case described here occurred in summer 2015. The owner of an educational centre who belonged to an influential family clan in Hebron discovered libelous comments against him and his centre posted via a Facebook account of a young girl. He searched for the family of the girl by the way of her school principal, who cooperated to avoid police involvement that would publicly reveal the girl's name. The owner of the centre approached the family with the issue. The girl explained that she had no control over her account as it had been hacked and that the posts had not been hers. Subsequently the family of the girl tried to solve the problem, because according to informal justice the case of libel fell into their responsibility and because the takeover of the account of a girl by a young man and the posting in her name was an attack on its own. Since the latter had the potential to affect her reputation regarding her moral conduct, it was considered an attack on her honour and on the honour of her family, besides being an attack on her privacy. The family did not make her responsible in any respect but included her and her interest and opinion in their efforts. Although they thought that such an attack should be prosecuted by formal justice, they did not approach the police as they were afraid that people would talk about the case, which might affect the girl's reputation. Hence the family researched on their own: Assisted by family members the girl contacted the perpetrator by the way of her old Facebook account and started a conversation that eventually led him to want to meet her personally. Having identified the young man, the girl's brother spotted him out in a supermarket, where he attacked him, dragged him to a separate room, beat him so seriously that the young man needed treatment in a hospital, and took his phone as proof. Subsequently the family of the girl confronted the family of the young man with the case and with the fact that many private pictures of other girls from Hebron were saved on the phone, a matter considered to be an attack on their honour. The accused's family immediately apologised and explained that their son had disgraced them and that his actions were against their values. In doing so, they did not mention the attack on their son in any way. However they asked for the memory card arguing that the data was too sensitive to be kept by anyone. The girl's father at first refused, as he intended to keep the memory card as proof. However as he did not want to be accused of owning inappropriate pictures of girls of other families or even of contributing to their disclosure, he later destroyed the card in front of their eyes. Although the crime against the girl was clearly considered a greater crime than the libel against the owner of the centre, in order not to disclose anything connected to the reputation of the girl, it was decided to only hold a formal *aṭwa* relating to the case of libel against the owner of the centre. For this the family of the perpetrator sent a delegation of well-respected elder men, including well known *ṣulḥ*-arbitrators, to the family of the owner of the educational centre. The gathering was held in a ritualised way and included some religious elements and frequent mutual expressions of respect and connectedness. After the father of the owner of the centre described the case with some indirect references to the case of the family of the girl – for example by explaining that the reputation of a young man is not less sensitive than the reputation of a girl – the speaker of the family of the young man stressed the despicableness of the crime and explained that they were ready to pay whatever (compensation) the family of the affected asked. Following long negotiations the families agreed on a payment of 10,000 JD,[51] but when the money was formally handed over the family of the owner of the centre explained that they forgave them and that they would not take any compensation. However they threatened the family that if the young man ever repeated such crimes, he would be killed. While the family of the owner of the centre explained that they were content with the outcome, the family of the girl explained that on one hand they were glad that the family of the young man was made responsible, as this might make him think twice before committing such a crime in the future; on the other hand, they complained that the way the systems worked precluded any form of punishment, be it financial or in the form of a prison sentence, and hence stripped them and their daughter of their rights. The girl herself explained that she would have preferred a formal prosecution, however she was glad to experience the support of her family as another family would have blamed their daughter in such a case.

2.2.3 Analyses

In both cases described here agents' choices at certain times have been influenced by their explicit commitment to some norms that can be attributed to principles of the rule of law. In the case of sexual assault, the rejection of the suggested marriage-solution by the family of the girl with reference to her individual rights, the initial rejection of killing the perpetrator in revenge and the option for a public trial that included state-persecution can be seen to reflect

51 At the time of this case one JD was about 1.3 Euro.

rule-of-law principles. In the case of the takeover of the Facebook account the girl's family's statement of their principle preference for official prosecution, their refusal to consider the option of a forced marriage as a solution and their choice of granting their daughter an active role in the process by contacting the perpetrator via Facebook to find out his identity reflects an affiliation to rule-of-law principles.

However in both cases, methods and mechanisms attributable to the paramount objective of preserving or restoring the honour of the girl more or less directly prevented these principles being reflected in the outcomes of the cases. In general, agents acted rationally in line with their objectives. This was confirmed by different agents in the interviews, except in the case of the violence during the *fawrat ad-damm* in the case of sexual assault, which was partly framed as an emotional reaction, and in that of the violence against the perpetrator in the Facebook case, which was framed as the personal reaction of an angry young brother. However, these actions served to demonstrate strength and the willingness to retaliate and were not condemned by any family members. Also the the allocation of roles with young men being responsible for the use of force and the demonstration of the willingness to do so and elder men being responsible for diplomacy is a typical scheme that allows the exertion of pressure during negotiations. So we can assume these actions to be strategical. Meanwhile key choices, namely the suggestion of a marriage solution, the choice in favour of the holding of a *manshad* and the attack against the perpetrator that resulted in his death in the case of sexual assault, as well as the autonomous persecution of the Facebook perpetrator by the family of the girl and the confiscation of his telephone, were made to achieve the paramount objective of preserving or restoring the honour of the respective girls. Aspects contradicting rule-of-law principles that can be attributed to the respective instruments of informal justice or structures between the legal systems were accepted in consequence, such as the effective denial of defence for the accused in the *manshad*, the release of the perpetrators based on the ruling of the *manshad*, the extremely high compensation that would have ruined the family of the perpetrator in the case of sexual assault, as well as, in the Facebook case, ignoring the violence done against the young man by the parties of the *aṭwa* and the threat of killing him if he repeated such actions.

While the objective of preserving or restoring the honour of the respective girls and consequently their families' honour proved decisive in the choice of methods, reference to the centrality of the principle of honour in these cases and to their consequent sensitiveness served to justify methods that contradicted rule-of-law principles, such as the city hall pressuring the police to refrain from arresting members of the family of the girl during *fawrat ad-damm* (a clear breach of state law by an institution of the state system), the general approval of the deadly revenge against the perpetrator in the case of sexual assault, and the search for the girl by way of her school.

We can see that the main objectives in these cases that led to or justified methods contradictory to the rule of law are related to the principle of honour, namely the preservation or restoration of honour and the preservation or restoration of civil peace threatened by the principle of honour. Regarding the effectiveness of the respective choices, we can say that in both cases the different agents achieved their main objectives and a satisfactory situation. In both cases *ṣulḥ*-arbitrators were able to re-conciliate and hence restore or preserve civil peace, which we can assume to be their main objective. They were also able to present themselves as successful in their role as experts applying clan-based customary justice, as they determined the rituals and the methods. Achieving agreements within the standards of clan-based customary justice regarding the high level of compensation and forgiveness, they were able to demonstrate the effectiveness of the system. In the case of sexual assault, a stable outcome was reached with the family of the girl having been able to restore their honour, while the family of the young man prevented a loss in reputation, proved themselves to be a strong family and profited financially. In the Facebook case, the family of the girl managed to cleanse themselves of the accusation that their daughter had committed an offense, demonstrated that an attack against their daughter would not remain without a reaction and achieved a formal process against the perpetrator within the frame of an *aṭwa*. The family of the owner of the centre was also able to demonstrate, that they would not tolerate an offense against them, demonstrated their strength by enforcing a high amount of compensation and increased their status through forgiveness. Meanwhile the family of the young man was able to avoid negative consequences such as formal prosecution and being forced to pay compensation. Hence in both cases informal justice was effective in realizing the main objectives of the involved parties while reaching a stable outcome.

For both cases we can conclude that process and outcome can be explained by objectives of the respective agents and their mostly pragmatic approaches. In this context, the preservation or restoration of honour can be seen as the paramount objective. The approval of methods which contradict rule of-law-principles can largely be attributed to the paramount norm of protecting family honour and civil peace in the context of honour. The principle of honour has been shown to be so influential that an impact of rule of law norms cannot be perceived in the final outcome of either case. On the contrary, the deadly revenge that is widely approved by the population in the case of sexual assault and the vigilante justice that is not even questioned, in combination with the absence of punishment and formal persecution in the Facebook case, mean that the outcomes of both cases strikingly contradict rule of law principals.

3 Conclusion

Both the survey and the case studies show that rule-of-law principles, such as the principle of the state's responsibility for the prosecution of crimes, the rejection of vigilante justice and the rejection of collective punishment do have an impact on cases with and without the factor of female honour. Regarding the quantitative data for all cases we can identify a challenge to traditional norms of clan-based justice by rule-of-law principles, as well as a pragmatic approach with openness to accepting otherwise unacceptable methods out of necessity. Regarding the case studies, the initial approaches of the families in both cases suggest the consideration of rule – of-law norms, such as the rejection of a marriage solution, the refusal to allow any negative impact on the respective girls and the rejection of lethal revenge. This development cannot be attributed to a general challenge to the system of clan-based justice or clan structures in general, as the strong feeling of obligation towards clan-based justice and the strong approval of the responsibility to share in paying the *dīyya* show.

Meanwhile both sets of data, but in particular the case studies, suggest the objective of preserving or restoring family honour as well as the connected objective of preserving civil peace, play a paramount role. This can be seen in the large majority of 75.1% approving a marriage solution in the case of rape while at the same time a large group of this majority considered the solution a form of oppression against the girl, and becomes even more obvious in both case studies, notably with the strong approval of lethal revenge in the one case and the avoidance of any formal process and the unquestioned acceptance of severe violence in revenge in the other. The fact that the paramount necessity to preserve or restore honour was not questioned by either agent but also the absence of any challenge to informal justice by the participation of women suggests that the impact of the honour as a factor is stable.

Finally, regarding the question of the explanatory power of a rationalist approach, the case studies have shown that developments and outcomes in both cases can convincingly be explained by the objectives of the different agents, whereby the factor of honour was the basis of key objectives. The quantitative data showing relatively large groups that accept, for pragmatic reasons, methods contradictory to their own moral viewpoint, also verify that legal pluralism is handled in a very pragmatic way, rather than in one based on ideology or habitus.

Bibliography

Abdelbaqi, Mustafa. *The Administration of Criminal Justice in Palestine. Development, Reform and Challenges.* Berlin: Duncker & Humbold, 2010.

Abd-Elsalam, Ahmed. *Das Beduinische Rechtssystem. Konzepte – Modelle – Transformation.* Beirut/Würzburg: Orient-Institut/Ergon-Verlag, 2015.

Benda-Beckmann, Keebet. "Forum Shopping and Shopping Forums. Dispute Settlement in a Minangkabau Village in West Sumatra." *Journal of Legal Pluralism* 13, no. 19 (1981): 117–159.

Birzeit University, Institute of Law. "Al-qaḍā'- ghayr an-niẓāmī. siyādatu 'l-qānūn wa-ḥall an-nizāʿāt fī filasṭīn." In: *silsilatu 'l-qānūn wa-'l-muǧtamaʿ*. Birzeit University, Department of Law, 2006.

Dupret, Baudouin. "Legal Pluralism, Plurality of Laws, and Legal Practices: Theories, Critiques, and Praxiological Re-Specification." *European Journal of Legal Studies* 1, no. 1 (2007 a): 296–318.

Ghayth, Muḥammad Ḥasan Abū Ḥammād. *Qaḍā' al-ʿashā'ir fī ḍaū al-shariʿ al-'islāmī.* Jerusalem: Modern Arab Press, 1990.

Ginat, Joseph. *Blood Disputes among Bedouin and Rural Arabs in Israel.* Pittsburgh: University of Pittsburgh Press, 1987.

Griffiths, John. "What is Legal Pluralism?" *Legal Pluralism & Unofficial Law* 18, no. 24 (1986): 1–55.

Ḥuǧǧa, ʿĀdil Muḥammad. *Al-ʿurf al-ʿashā'irī fī l-iṣlāḥ*. Dura: Published by author, 2002.

Shahar, Ido. "State, Society and the Relations Between Them. Implications for the Study of Legal Pluralism" *Theoretical Inquiries in Law* 9, no. 2 (2008): 417–441.

Steward, Frank Henderson. *Honour.* London/Chicago: The University of Chicago Press, 1994.

Terris, Robert, and Vera Inoue-Terris. "A Case Study of Third World Jurisprudence. Palestine. Conflict Resolution and Customary Law in a Neopatrimonial Society." *Berkley Journal of International Law* 20, no.2 (2002): 462–492.

Woodman, Gordon R. "The Idea of Legal Pluralism." In *Legal Pluralism in the Arab World*, edited by Baudouin Dupret, Maurits Berger, and Laila al-Zwaini, 4–20. Hague/London/Boston: Kluwer Law International, 1999.

Legal Pluralism in Indonesia: the Case of Interfaith Marriages Involving Muslims

Judith Koschorke

1 Introduction

> Is it really impossible in the Indonesian state that two people who are in love can freely marry without one of them having to convert?
>
> E. SUNDARI and E. SUMIARNI[1]

Indonesia is a pluralistic country that acknowledges cultural and religious diversity in its state motto *Bhinneka Tunggal Ika* (Unity in Diversity). It is also the country with the largest Muslim population worldwide. In contrast to Middle Eastern states with a majority Muslim population, however, Islam is not the official state religion in Indonesia. Furthermore, the constitution does not mention Islam or Shariʿa, let alone grant them a superior status.[2] Nevertheless, Indonesia is not a secular state either. This is because the 'Belief in One Supreme God' or *Ketuhanan Yang Maha Esa* (whether Muslim, Catholic, Protestant, Hindu, Buddhist or Confucian) is the first of the five basic principles of the constitutionally sanctioned Indonesian state philosophy called *Pancasila*.[3] According to this principle, every citizen has to profess one of the aforementioned state-recognised religions and the state in turn recognises these religions and their values as valuable sources of family law.

In this quite unique setting of the Indonesian state as being neither religious nor secular,[4] interfaith marriages are constantly and controversially

1 "Tidak mungkinkah di negara Indonesia bagi 2 (dua) orang yang sudah saling jatuh cinta bebas menikah tanpa masing-masing harus berpindah agama?" Quoted from the petition of the Constitutional Court proceeding on the judicial review of Art. 2 (1) Marriage Law on marriage validity, Mahkamah Konstitusi No 68/Puu-XII/2014 (decided 18 June, 2015), 51.

2 Otto, "Sharia and National Law in Indonesia," 456–7.

3 The other four principles are Just and Civilized Humanism (*Kemanusiaan Yang Adil dan Beradab*), Indonesian National Unity (*Persatuan Indonesia*), Democracy (*Kerakyatan Yang Dipimpin oleh Hikmat Kebijaksanaan dalam Permusyawaratan Perwakilan*) and Social Justice for All People of Indonesia (*Keadilan Sosial bagi Seluruh Rakyat Indonesia*). They are contained in the preamble of the 1945 Constitution; Undang-Undang Dasar Negara Republik Indonesia Tahun 1945, most recently revised in the fourth amendment in 2002.

4 At several occasions, different groups attempted to make Indonesia an Islamic state. On the dropped *Jakarta Charta* that would have made Islamic law applicable for Muslims via the constitution, see Lindsey, *Islam, Law and the State*, 38–40.

 | DOI:10.1163/9789004398269_010

debated. According to Otto, they, "remain one of the most problematic areas" in the Indonesian Marriage Law (Undang-Undang No. 1 Tahun 1974 Tentang Perkawinan), enacted in 1974 to substitute the colonial plural system of marriage laws.[5] As a result of political and social struggles over the integration of religious law – and Islamic law in particular – into a unified national statute in the early-1970s, the Marriage Law does not contain any regulation explicitly allowing or prohibiting marriage across religious lines.[6] Instead, it only declares that a marriage is valid "if performed in accordance with the respective religious law(s) and belief(s) of the couple concerned" (Art. 2 (1) Marriage Law).[7] The explanatory part of the law reads that with Art. 2 (1) Marriage Law, "there is no marriage beyond the law of the respective religion(s) and belief(s) in accordance with the 1945 Constitution".[8] However, the exact stance of the state-recognised religions concerning the validity of interfaith marriages has not been defined by statute law. Furthermore, the Indonesian system of marriage administration precludes marriages between Muslims and non-Muslims "as a bureaucratic possibility".[9] The Application Act of the Marriage Law determines two distinct bodies whose authority over citizens is defined by religious affiliation: an Islamic branch responsible for Muslims and a civil branch with authority over non-Muslims.[10] Registration does not constitute a formal

5 Otto, "Sharia and National Law in Indonesia," 464. Ethnicity and religious affiliation regulated the colonial system of marriage laws in force until the promulgation of the 1974 Marriage Law. For Europeans and Chinese, Dutch civil law applied. Native Christians in Java, Minahasa and Ambon were governed by the Huwelijks Ordonnantie Christen Indonesiers ((HOCI), Stb. 1933 No. 74) enacted in 1933. Uncodified Shafi'i law applied for Indigenous Muslims and indigenous non-Muslims fell under uncodified customary laws; Azra, "The Indonesian Marriage Law of 1974," 79–80.

6 For information on the struggles and the law-making process itself see for example Katz and Katz, "The New Indonesian Marriage Law," 660–64.

7 "Perkawinan adalah sah, apabila dilakukan menurut hukum masing-masing agamanya dan kepercayaannya itu," Art. 2 (1) Marriage Law. The plural in the translation is set in brackets because grammatically it is possible to understand the article as stipulating that both spouses must have the same religion as well as that they can adhere to different religions.

8 "[T]idak ada perkawinan di luar hukum masing-masing agamanya dan kepercayaannya itu, sesuai dengan Undang-Undang Dasar 1945." Official Explanation of Art. 2 (1) Marriage Law.

9 Lukito, "Trapped between Legal Unification and Pluralism," 42.

10 Art. 2 of 1975 Application Act of 1974 Marriage Law (Peraturan Pemerintah Nomor 9 Tahun 1975 Tentang Pelaksanaan Undang-Undang Nomor 1 Tahun 1974 Tentang Perkawinan). In the following, the institutions will be termed Islamic registry and civil registry based on their Indonesian names (Kantor Urusan Agama and Kantor Catatan Sipil). In this context, the term 'civil' does not mean 'non-religious', but simply 'non-Islamic'. This applies also for the judiciary in civil law matters, with Islamic courts responsible for Muslims and civil

condition to marriage validity, but it is obligatory and the requirement for the marriage to be acknowledged by the state and have its legal effects (Art. 2 (2) Marriage Law).

The dependency of marriage validity on religious law and the dualism of marriage administration have led to considerable difficulties for interfaith couples intending to marry. Particularly when a Muslim party is involved, marriage registrars of both branches have tended to refuse their services, invoking their own lack of authority and religious law. In classical Islamic jurisprudence (*fiqh*), the view is generally held, based on several Quranic verses, that Muslims are prohibited from marrying non-Muslims. As an exception to this rule, based on Quran 5:5 and early Islamic practice, Muslim men are allowed to marry women of *ahl al-kitāb* (Christians and Jews), as according to the majority opinion in classical Sunni *fiqh* including the Shafiʿi school of law predominant in Indonesia.[11] In contrast to this, the dominant interpretation of Indonesian Islam as mirrored by the legally non-binding Kompilasi Hukum Islam (Compilation of Islamic Law) of 1991 and by major Indonesian *fatwā* organs has come to prohibit marriage with non-Muslims altogether.

Although it is "generally regarded as common knowledge in Indonesia that marriage between persons of different religions is not allowed" unless religious difference is eliminated by conversion, the dependency of marriage validity on religion as laid down in Art. 2 (1) Marriage Law has never been authoritatively interpreted to contain an outright ban on interfaith marriages.[12] Consequently, legal scholars and practitioners are at odds over differing interpretations of the provision itself and the Marriage Law in general, depending on whether they attach greater importance either to religious law or to constitutional and human rights. Despite the legal confusion on the validity of interfaith marriages, the conclusion of such marriages has never ceased. According to the Indonesian civil law scholar Wahyono Darmabrata, there are four principal means to circumvent the national Marriage Law; one of them being (temporary) conversion practiced by one of the partners to eliminate the difference

courts having jurisdiction over adherents of the other state-recognised religions. Both branches apply the national Marriage Law and the Supreme Court supervises their judgements. As will be shown in part two of this chapter, there are civil courts that ignore this division of authority and hear cases of interfaith couples with a Muslim party that have been denied marriage permission or registration at the registries.

11 Leeman, "Interfaith Marriage in Islam," 755 f. However, the exact definition of who belongs to *ahl al-kitāb* differs between and within the schools. For a classical discussion, see Maṭraǧī, *al-Ḥāwī l-Kabīr lil-Imām Abī l-Ḥasan ʿAlī b. Muḥammad b. Ḥabīb al-Māwardī*, 305–312.

12 Cammack, "Legal Aspects," 129.

in religious affiliation (at least for the wedding ceremony).[13] In fact, following Seo, "inter-religious marriage has been principal in generating conversion in contemporary Indonesia", making conversion less focused on spirituality and "more a matter of state administration".[14] As an alternative, interfaith couples marry in two religious ceremonies and register their marriage as a non-Islamic one in the civil registry.[15] A third option is to file a suit: As will be shown, civil courts order civil registries to perform and register marriages concluded in a ceremony in accordance with the non-Muslim partner's religion or marriages concluded in a non-religious civil ceremony.[16] Wealthier couples simply go abroad (mostly to Singapore or Australia) for marriage and have it acknowledged by the Indonesian state subsequently.[17] Couples can also marry in an unofficial religious ceremony (*nikah sirri*) and refrain from registration with the consequence of the marriage being non-existent in the eyes of the state.

This chapter discusses how the Indonesian state tries to find a balance between, on the one hand, the principle *Ketuhanan Yang Maha Esa* (Belief in One Supreme God) and the dominant Islamic legal discourse which proscribes interfaith marriage, and, on the other, implementing constitutional and human rights. The dilemma between provoking outright opposition by Muslim groups and sacrificing basic rights becomes especially obvious regarding constitutional guaranties such as equality before the law and religious freedom (Art. 28 D (1) and Articles 28 E and 29 (2) Constitution) as well as international law obligations.[18] Accordingly, state bodies such as Komnas HAM (National Commission on Human Rights) push for change that explicitly offers a legal solution for interfaith couples wishing to marry.[19] The first part of the chapter portrays the dominant Indonesian interpretation of Islamic law proscribing interfaith marriages as reflected by the Compilation of Islamic

---

13 Hukum Online, "Empat Cara Penyelundupan Hukum Bagi Pasangan Beda Agama."

14 Seo, "Falling in Love," 67–68.

15 For example, in 2011 the humanitarian organisation *Pondok Kasih Foundation* staged an interfaith mass wedding in cooperation with private sponsors and the Jakarta government. 4,541 couples were married that day in Islamic, Protestant, Catholic, Buddhist and Hindu ceremonies; Quiano, "4,500 Couples Participate in Indonesian Interfaith Marriage Ceremony."

16 Wasman and Nuroniyah, *Hukum Perkawinan Islam di Indonesia*, 301–2. See the discussion in the second part of this chapter.

17 Wahyuni, *Nikah Beda Agama*, 6–7.

18 Indonesia is a member of the Universal Declaration of Human Rights (UDHR) and has more recently ratified the United Nation treaties on civil and political as well as economic, social and cultural rights.

19 Ihsanuddin, "Komnas HAM Dukung Perkawinan Beda Agama Dilegalkan."

Law and the *fatāwā* of the two Muslim mass organisations Nahdlatul Ulama (Ulama Awakening, NU) and Muhammadiyah, as well as the Indonesian state-endorsed national *fatwā* council Majelis Ulama Indonesia (Indonesian Ulama Council, MUI).[20] Nevertheless, several Indonesian Muslim organisations and scholars such as Ulil Abshar Abdalla of Jaringan Islam Liberal (Network of Liberal Islam) challenge this restrictive interpretation of Islamic law.[21] In the second part, differences and major developments in the practice of the dual system of Islamic and civil courts will be outlined, paying special attention to the new Administration Law of 2006 (Undang-Undang No. 23 Tahun 2006 Tentang Administrasi Kependudukan). Containing a "veiled invitation" to legalise interfaith unions, the law and its application in civil courts will be analysed as a, "stealth strategy for legal change" adopted by the Indonesian state.[22] The final part discusses the Constitutional Court's treatment of the appeal lodged against Art. 2 (1) Marriage Law that the court rejected in June 2015. The petitioners argued that the state was violating several constitutional rights as well as international human rights obligations through the registries' refusal of interfaith marriages.

Whereas the issue of interfaith marriages in Indonesia has already received scholarly attention,[23] the new Administration Law and its application in civil courts as well as the judicial review of Art. 2 (1) Marriage Law still constitute a gap in research not only in Indonesian but also in international academia. By analysing these recent developments, this chapter sheds some light on the state's management of legal pluralism between statute law and religious laws. It argues that, given the sensitivity of the subject and the inseparability of marriage and religion especially in the dominant Islamic discourse, legal change regarding interfaith marriages is most likely to occur through the backdoor.

---

20 Founded in 1926, Nahdlatul Ulama (NU) is the largest Muslim mass organisation in Indonesia with an estimated membership of 30 million. The organisation represents traditionalist Islam. Muhammadiyah is the second largest Muslim mass organisation in Indonesia after the NU. Founded in 1926, it has an estimated 29 million members. The organisation claims to represent a moderate Islam. Majelis Ulama Indonesia (MUI) was established with support from the Indonesian government in 1975 in order to unify the Muslim community and to represent Islam towards the government. It comprises members of all Indonesian Muslim organisations and groups including NU and Muhammadiyah.

21 Ali, "Fatwas on Interfaith Marriage in Indonesia," 24. For information on the network itself, see Ali, "The Rise of the Liberal Islam Network (JIL) in Contemporary Indonesia," 1–16.

22 Cammack, "Legal Aspects," 126–27.

23 See the literature used in this chapter.

2 The Indonesian Islamic Discourse on Interfaith Marriages

Up to 1991, no unified interpretation of Islamic family law in general and particularly on the issue of interfaith marriages existed in Indonesia, the consequence being that Islamic courts derived their rulings directly from the various *fiqh* books when applying the national Marriage Law. This changed with the Compilation of Islamic Law (KHI) promulgated in order to ensure legal certainty and unify the diverse practices of the Islamic courts.[24] Indonesian Islamic scholars from various orientations were involved in its compilation process.[25] The Compilation prohibits interfaith marriages altogether, in that it declares non-adherence to Islam as a marriage obstacle regardless of gender.[26] This prohibition of marriage with non-Muslims marks the culmination of a process of what Cholil describes as a "hardening of Islamic law" on the issue.[27] Against the background of the KHI's self-understanding to reflect a specifically Indonesian school of Islamic law in the areas of marriage, inheritance and religious endowments (ind. *wakaf*),[28] the complete ban on interfaith marriages has to be understood as reflecting the idea of a distinctly Indonesian Islam. Notably, an earlier draft of the Compilation adopted the more permissive interpretation of Islamic law to allow marriages between Muslim men and women of *ahl al-kitāb*, thus indicating the disagreement of Indonesian Islamic scholars on the issue.[29]

Issued only by presidential decree, the Compilation is not statute law and thus not legally binding to judges.[30] However, despite being a "bureaucratic handbook", it has "operated in practice almost as if it were binding law for the Islamic courts and most other state bureaucratic institutions in Indonesia that deal with the Islamic legal issues it covers".[31] The Compilation plays an important role in the public understanding of Indonesian Islamic law as prohibiting

---

24 To homogenise Islamic court practices, the state determined thirteen classical *fiqh* books as a basis of decision-making already in 1958. See Wahid, *Fiqh Indonesia*, 110–11, 120.

25 For details on the process, see ibid., 113–38.

26 Art. 40 and 44 Compilation of Islamic Law.

27 Cholil, "The Politico-Religious Contestation," 139.

28 Mawardi, "The Political Backdrop of the Enactment of the Compilation of Islamic Laws in Indonesia," 127–28.

29 Cammack, "Legal Aspects," 122.

30 Wahid, *Fiqh Indonesia*, 131–36. The preamble of the official explanation declares the Compilation to be a guideline (*pedoman*) for the judges in the Islamic judiciary; see Official Explanation of Compilation of Islamic Law, paragraph 5; and Presidential Instruction No. 1 Year 1991, point B.

31 Lindsey, *Islam, Law and the State*, 69.

interfaith marriages altogether and since the vast majority of Indonesian citizens are Muslim, it catalyses the understanding of the Indonesian Marriage Law as prohibiting interfaith marriages.[32]

By outlawing interfaith marriages, the Compilation adopts the position taken in the Indonesian *fatāwā* of the two Muslim mass organisations Nahdlatul Ulama (NU) and Muhammadiyah, as well as the Indonesian state-endorsed national *fatwā* council MUI (Indonesian Ulama Council). Whereas the *fatāwā* are unequivocal in the cases of interfaith marriages that are unanimously considered forbidden in classical *fiqh*, they differ in their reasoning why marriages between Muslim men and women of *ahl al-kitāb* are proscribed. The NU explains the restrictive interpretation by quoting from different Shafiʿi *fiqh* texts elaborating that a marriage between a Muslim man and a *kitābiyya* is essentially allowed but the concept of *kitābī* people is restricted to the time of the Prophet due to corruption of belief.[33] In contrast to this *taqlīdī* approach (adoption of a verdict reasoned by previous scholars), the MUI and Muhammadiyah *fatāwā* argue from the perspective of Islamic legal theory, namely *maqāṣid al-sharīʿa* (foundational objectives of Islamic law). They reason that the harm (*mafsada*) resulting from marriages between Muslim men and women of *ahl al-kitāb* is greater than its benefits (*maṣlaḥa*). They thus cast the prohibition of such marriages as the prevention of harm (*sadd al-dharīʿa*).[34]

The 'hardening of Islamic law' on interfaith marriages as mirrored by the Compilation and Indonesian *fatāwā* has its origins in the specific sociopolitical background of tensions between Muslims and Christians in modern Indonesia. In an atmosphere of Christianophobia, marriages between Muslims

32 Cammack, "Legal Aspects," 130.

33 The NU issued the first Indonesian *fatwā* on interfaith marriages in 1962 and reissued it in 1968 and 1989 to readdress and confirm the NU's stance in view of dissenting opinions among Indonesian Muslims and particularly the NU members. The *fatwā* quotes extensively from works of Ibrāhīm al-Sharqāwī and Abū Isḥāq al-Shīrāzī in Arabic followed by an Indonesian translation; Lajnah Ta'lif Wan Nasyr, *Ahkamul Fuqaha, Solusi Problematika Aktual Hukum Islam*, 434–38.

34 The MUI issued its first *fatwā* on interfaith marriages in 1980 and an elaborated version thereof in 2005; Majelis Ulama Indonesia, Perkawinan Campuran: Putusan Musyawarah Nasional II tanggal 11–17 Rajab 1400 H, bertepatan dengan tanggal 26 Mei-1 Juni 1980 M; and Majelis Ulama Indonesia, Fatwa Nomor: 4/MUNAS VII/MUI/8/2005. It is important to note that the local Jakarta MUI issued an evidently contradicting *fatwā* in 1986. It explicitly allowed interfaith marriages regardless of gender, invoking Islamic reformers such as Muhammad ʿAbduh and Rashid Ridha; Mulia, "Promoting Gender Equity," 271. The Muhammadiyah issued its *fatwā* proscribing marriage with non-Muslims in 1989; Majelis Tarjih dan Tajdid, Salinan Keputusan Muktamar Tarjih Muhammadiyah XXII [6 s.d. 10 Rajab 1409 H / 12 s.d. 16 Februari 1989, di Malang, Jawa Timur] Tentang Nikah Beda Agama.

and Christians have been understood as a means of Christianisation.[35] Since the liberalisation of civil society after the fall of the New Order regime in 1998, the debate on marriages between Muslims and non-Muslims has been shifting from a mainly interreligious debate towards a debate within Indonesian Islamic society, namely between conservative and liberal Islamic groups.[36] With its second *fatwā* on interfaith marriages issued in 2005, the MUI reacted to those liberal trends that in the eyes of the council wrongly allow marriage with non-Muslims "under the pretence of human rights and benefits" (*dengan dalih hak asasi manusia dan kemaslahatan*).[37] As stated in the introduction of the *fatwā*, interfaith marriages had not only been provoking debates within the Islamic community itself, but had also caused unrest within society as a whole.[38] In fact, many Indonesians argue that the restrictive interpretation of Islamic law as reflected in the Indonesian *fatāwā* and the Compilation should be abandoned in favour of the majority opinion of classical *fiqh* or even an outright legalisation of marriage with non-Muslims. Aside from individuals who argue against an Islamic prohibition of interfaith marriages, there are services facilitating the process by providing private Islamic authorities that are willing to perform marriage ceremonies involving a non-Muslim party. One of these organisation is Pusat Studi Agama dan Perdamaian (Study Centre on Religion and Peace) led by Ahmad Nurcholish, who himself as a Muslim is legally married to a Confucian woman.[39]

---

35 Cholil, "The Politico-Religious Contestation," 148–54, Ali, "Fatwas on Interfaith Marriage in Indonesia," 22. The tension between Muslims and Christians is also reflected in the 1981 MUI *fatwā*, which prohibited Muslims from participating in Christian Christmas celebrations; ibid., 18. Among others, Seo points to the fact that in the first place economic considerations determine which partner converts. Accordingly, interfaith marriages do not necessarily lead to conversions to Christianity as feared by Muslim groups; Seo, "Falling in Love" 89–93.

36 Cholil, "The Politico-Religious Contestation," 155–56.

37 Majelis Ulama Indonesia, Fatwa Nomor: 4/MUNAS VII/MUI/8/2005, 472. The MUI issued further *fatāwā* against liberal views among Indonesian Muslims in the same year. One of them is the *fatwā* on religious pluralism, interpretations of Islamic law based on liberal thought and Islamic secularism. As declared in the introduction of the *fatwā*, the MUI felt the need to readdress the issues because, interpretations contradicting the teachings of Islam, such as regarding the equality of religions, liberal interpretations of Quran and Sunna and the perception that religion was only to be used in one's private relationship with God, would have gained a foothold in society; Majelis Ulama Indonesia, Fatwa Nomor: 7/MUNAS VII/MUI/11/2005 tentang Pluralisme, Liberalisme dan Sekularisme Agama.

38 Majelis Ulama Indonesia, Fatwa Nomor: 4/MUNAS VII/MUI/8/2005, 472.

39 According to Ahmad Nurcholish, Pusat Studi Agama dan Perdamaian had concluded 638 interfaith marriages in all over Indonesia by June 2015; Affan and Franciska, "Ahmad

The Indonesian Islamic proscription of marriages with non-Muslims is also called into question by state institutions. In 2004, the Ministry of Religious Affairs installed a committee of Islamic legal experts with the task to compile a draft Islamic family law in conformity with international human rights law. The draft – known as *Counter Legal Draft Kompilasi Hukum Islam* (Counter Legal Draft to the Compilation of Islamic Law, CLD-KHI) – was supposed to become statute law and substitute the Compilation. It was compiled using interpretations of Quran and Sunna in accordance with local Indonesian wisdom, *maṣlaḥa*, and *maqāṣid al-sharīʿa*.[40] By using this methodological framework, the CLD-KHI "was both a radical attack on the influence of traditional *fiqh* in Indonesian private law for Muslims and a defence against resurgent Islamist moral conservatism," as argued by Lindsey.[41] The committee, headed by the prominent feminist scholar Siti Musdah Mulia, pointed out nineteen crucial issues within the Compilation, including the regulation of interfaith marriages.[42]

The CLD-KHI contradicts the Compilation and the aforementioned *fatāwā* by allowing not only marriages between Muslim men and women of *ahl al-kitāb*, but marriages across religious lines in general.[43] According to Mulia, there is no Quranic verse that clearly forbids or allows marriage with non-Muslims given the diverse possible interpretations of the core categories *kāfir*, *mushrik* and *ahl al-kitāb* in the relevant passages and the different opinions on abrogation. She considers the existing opinions on the legal status of such marriages, whether prohibiting or allowing them, "merely a matter of ijtihad (process of critical reasoning)".[44] In contrast to the *fatāwā*, Mulia regards marriage as belonging to the area of Islamic law that deals with interpersonal relationships (*muʿāmalāt*) and not as an act of worship belonging to the unchangeable area regulating the relationship between humans and God (*ʿibādāt*). She thus applies the legal rule in Islamic *fiqh* to allow matters that the authoritative texts neither clearly allow nor forbid (*al-aṣl fī l-ashyāʾ al-ibāḥa*).[45] Some Muslim groups celebrated the CLD-KHI. However, criticism from others was so strong that the government withdrew it from consideration in parliament.

Nurcholish dan Pernikahan Beda Agama." The famous Paramadina organisation stopped its services in 2005; Cammack, "Legal Aspects," 124.

40 Wahid, *Fiqh Indonesia*, 209–14.

41 Lindsey, *Islam, Law and the State*, 80.

42 Mulia, "Promoting Gender Equity," 256.

43 Art. 49 CLD-KHI allows marriage between Muslims and non-Muslims on condition that both parties are aware of the distinct features that a marriage between a Muslim and a non-Muslim party might have and that they mutually respect the right to perform their respective religious beliefs.

44 Mulia, "Promoting Gender Equity," 275.

45 Ibid.

Thus far, the parliament has not passed any draft of decisively Islamic family law so that the Compilation still represents the state-endorsed Indonesian version of Islamic family law.

3 The (Non-)Regulation of Interfaith Marriages in the Marriage Law of 1974 and the Dual System of Islamic and Civil Courts

Whereas the general public holds that Art. 2 (1) Marriage Law rules out interfaith marriages, legal scholars and practitioners are divided on the issue. Within Indonesian legal discourse, three main lines of reasoning regarding the legal status of marriage across religious lines can be identified. In line with the public opinion, some interpret Art. 2 (1) Marriage Law as covering interfaith marriages and regard their validity as being dependent on the respective religious doctrines of both parties.[46] Others regard the article as covering only individuals with the same religious affiliation. They either hold that interfaith marriages are thus unlawful in Indonesia or they assume a legal vacuum and regard them as valid based on the Dutch Mixed Marriage Act from 1898 (Regeling op de Gemengde Huwelijken (RGH) Stb. 1898 No. 158). They refer to Art. 66 Marriage Law, which repeals relevant colonial statutes only to the extent that they were inconsistent with or regulated otherwise in the Marriage Law.[47] The colonial Mixed Marriage Act regulated marriages between citizens that belong to two different legal groups stating that differences in religions are not a marriage obstacle (Art. 7 (2) Mixed Marriage Act). It ruled that marriage between legal groups was to be concluded according to the law of the husband (Art. 6 Mixed Marriage Act).[48] Since the act disregarded Islamic marriage prescripts by allowing marriages between Muslim women and non-Muslim men,

46 Butt, "Polygamy and Mixed Marriage in Indonesia," 277. According to Lukito, this group predominantly consists of religious scholars who regard interfaith marriages as contradicting religious law; Lukito, "Trapped between Legal Unification and Pluralism," 37.

47 Cammack, "Legal Aspects," 114.

48 The Muslim woman was not required to convert to her husband's religion, but had to follow her husband's religious laws in the realms of marriage; Butt, "Polygamy and Mixed Marriages in Indonesia," 276. She had to obtain the local Islamic authority's approval to prove that the law to which she adhered did not prohibit the intended marriage (Art. 7 Mixed Marriage Act). Given the consensual prohibition of marriages between Muslim women and non-Muslim men, local authorities usually denied this approval. Nevertheless, the marriage was usually granted if taken to civil court (Art. 8 Mixed Marriage Act); Syahuri, *Legislasi Hukum Perkawinan di Indonesia*, 81.

it provoked considerable protest among Muslims.[49] A third group of more current scholars argues that interfaith marriages are allowed considering them to be a matter of human rights. They either hold that Art. 2 (1) Marriage Law covers interfaith marriages and apply liberal interpretations of religious law or argue that the article does not cover them and base their decision on constitutional and human rights.[50]

Against the background of various possible interpretations of Art. 2 (1) Marriage Law and the Marriage Law as a whole, it is feasible to state that despite the goals of legal unification, a certain degree of pluralism regarding religious and colonial law has been maintained. In fact, rather than overcoming the consequences of the colonial plural legal order, the Marriage Law divides citizens into different legal groups by making the very definition of marriage validity dependent on the religious laws of the six state-recognised religions. This lack of clarity regarding the validity of marriages has led Katz and Katz to describe it as "law without law".[51]

Since the enactment of the unified Marriage Law in 1974, two major developments in the practice of Islamic and civil judiciary and administration are discernible. In the period after the promulgation of the national Marriage Law, the branches continued their respective established pre-Marriage Law practice by using distinct interpretations of the scope of Art. 2 (1) Marriage Law. Islamic courts began to hold that the provision applied for interfaith marriages and that they were valid as long as they were concluded between Muslim men and women of *ahl al-kitāb*.[52] In contrast to this, civil courts reasoned that there was a legal vacuum on interfaith marriages in the law and continued to apply the colonial Mixed Marriage Act.[53] Accordingly, interfaith marriages involving Muslims – especially those who were turned away at the Islamic registry when it invoked Islamic law – were registered in the civil registry.[54] At least

49 On 14 September, 1952, for example, there was a mass demonstration in front of the Jakarta Tanah Abang mosque as a reaction to a marriage between a Muslim woman and a Protestant man that had been legalised by the court after the local Islamic authority evaluated the marriage as violating Islamic law; ibid., 81.

50 Lukito, "Trapped between Legal Unification and Pluralism," 38. Another group of legal scholars – which is relatively small – holds that interfaith marriages are regulated by the Marriage Law, namely within Art. 57 on mixed marriages; see Wasman and Nuroniyah, *Hukum Perkawinan Islam di Indonesia*, 298.

51 Katz and Katz, "The New Indonesian Marriage Law," 667.

52 Cammack, "Legal Aspects," 115–16. Since Judaism does not belong to the state-recognised religions, a Jewish wedding ceremony cannot establish legal marriage in the Indonesian context.

53 Butt, "Polygamy and Mixed Marriage in Indonesia," 277–8.

54 Pompe, "A Short Note on Some Recent Developments," 262.

from the 1980s onwards, however, this permissive approach towards interfaith marriages involving Muslims in both the civil and Islamic branch has changed. This policy change has been due to two developments, one of them being the 'hardening of Islamic law'[55] as promoted in the *fatāwā* and the Compilation of Islamic Law outlined in the previous chapter. At least since the enactment of the Compilation, Islamic courts and marriage administration have tended to judge based on the general prohibition of interfaith marriages.[56] The other development has been Muslim criticism of the civil registries' role in performing marriages that involve Muslims despite lacking legal authorisation. This criticism led to civil registries turning away interfaith couples which included a Muslim party.[57]

Up to the late 1980s, the Indonesian Supreme Court endorsed the application of the Dutch Mixed Marriage Act to fill the acknowledged legal vacuum on interfaith marriages.[58] This changed in 1989 with the influential and controversial decision in the so-called Andi Vony case, which is still the most recent Supreme Court ruling and the "most authoritative statement on the permissibly of interreligious marriage"[59] under the Marriage Law. The case involved Andi Vony, a Muslim woman, and a Protestant man who wanted to marry although prohibited by prevailing opinion under Islamic law.[60] Instead of applying the Mixed Marriage Act via Art. 66 Marriage Law, the Supreme Court based its decision to allow matrimony on the constitutional right to equality before the law (Art. 27 of the Constitution). The court reasoned that this right

55 Cholil, "The Politico-Religious Contestation," 139.

56 Ibid., 146.

57 For details on the struggle over the competencies of the civil registries regarding marriages involving Muslims see Bowen, *Islam, Law and Equality*, 241; Butt, "Polygamy and Mixed Marriage in Indonesia," 278; Cammack, "Legal Aspects," 121. Measures taken to prevent the conclusion of marriages involving Muslims in the civil registries did not have the desired effect: Notwithstanding Muslim pressures and a corresponding presidential instruction, the Jakarta Civil Registry, for example, performed 239 marriages involving a Muslim party between April 1985 and July 1986. Of these cases, 127 were marriages between Muslim women and non-Muslim men. The Jakarta Civil Registry even issued special regulations for the conclusion of marriages involving Muslims in its regency; Wasman and Nuroniyah, *Hukum Perkawinan Islam di Indonesia*, 301–2.

58 See for example Putusan Mahkamah Agung No 1650k/Sip/1974, decided 13 November, 1979.

59 Cammack, "Legal Aspects," 118.

60 Andi Vony filed the suit after the Jakarta Civil Court had confirmed the Islamic and civil registries' denial to perform marriage with reference to Quran 2:221, the New Testament and the lack of authority to marry Muslims. Dissatisfied with the decision, Andi Vony turned to the Supreme Court; Putusan Mahkamah Agung Nomor 1400K/PDT/1986, printed in Sairin and Pattiasina, *Pelaksanaan Undang-Undang Perkawinan*, 363–75.

included the "basic right to marriage with fellow citizens even if there is a difference in religion"[61] and declared the Mixed Marriage Act invalid due to its normative origins divergent from those of the Marriage Law.[62] To overcome the problem of marriage registration in the case involving a Muslim party, the court argued that Andi Vony could not have wanted to conclude her marriage in accordance with Islamic religious prescriptions because she – as a Muslim woman – had turned to the civil registry. This supposed intention to marry not following Islam led the court to the conclusion that Andi Vony no longer "paid attention to her religious status" (*tidak lagi menghiraukan status agamanya*). Consequently, the civil registry as "the only agency that has the authority to perform or help perform marriages between prospective husband and wife *who are both non-Muslims* (emphasis mine)" had to accept the marriage.[63] Thus, the court justified the civil registry's authority to perform the marriage by implicitly suggesting that Andi Vony was no longer a Muslim, even though in general it considered the case as an interfaith marriage.

Following Lukito, the Supreme Court's acceptance of interfaith marriage "based on general principles enshrined in the Constitution, was ample proof that the teachings of Islamic law would have to make way when these conflicted with state law".[64] The court's tacit assumption that Andi Vony abandoned Islam is nevertheless not only questionable regarding her diametrically opposite testimony in court and the constitutional right to religious freedom.[65] It is also problematic regarding Islamic law itself because the latter harshly and unanimously prohibits apostasy.[66] Accordingly, the judgement might have

61 "[H]ak asasi untuk kawin dengan sesama warganegara sekalipun berlainan agama"; Sairin and Pattiasina, *Pelaksanaan Undang-Undang Perkawinan*, 371.

62 As a colonial law originating from the civil law tradition, the act followed a "very different principle and philosophy" (*perbedaan prinsip maupun falsafah yang amat lebar*) that was incompatible with the religious concept of marriage under the national Marriage Law, the court reasoned; ibid., 371.

63 "[S]ebagai satu-satunya instansi yang berwenang melangsungkan atau membantu melangsungkan perkawinan *yang kedua calon suami istri tidak beragama Islam* (emphasis mine)"; ibid., 373–4.

64 Lukito, "Trapped between Legal Unification and Pluralism," 53.

65 Several scholars interpret the decision to entail apostasy, see for example Bowen, *Islam, Law and Equality*, 242; Butt, "Polygamy and Mixed Marriage in Indonesia," 279; Cammack, "Legal Aspects," 118. On the other hand, Lukito does not speak of apostasy; see Lukito, "Trapped between Legal Unification and Pluralism," 48. During the hearings, Andi Vony described herself as a Muslim; Sairin and Pattiasina, *Pelaksanaan Undang-Undang Perkawinan*, 369.

66 According to most schools of law, apostasy is a *ḥadd*-crime (offence with fixed mandatory punishments that violates a claim of God based on Quran) to be punished with death, see Peters, *Crime and Punishment in Islamic Law*, 65.

paid respect to Islamic marriage law in that it circumvented the prohibited union between a Muslim woman and a Christian man, but then it clearly violated Islamic penal law in a severe manner.[67] In addition, it seems questionable to speak of a right to marriage across religious lines if the court effectively regarded Andi Vony as an apostate. Indonesian legal circles, including civil court judges, have interpreted the judgement to mean that Andi Vony followed her partner's religion – Protestantism – in the realms of marriage.[68] The similarity to the Dutch Mixed Marriage Act declared invalid in the very same judgement is therefore undeniable. The Supreme Court decision thus confirmed the fear of Muslim critics that interfaith marriages lead to conversions to Christianity. Since the mid-1990s then, "it has been extremely difficult, if not impossible, to register inter-religious marriages ... without one partner changing his or her religion".[69]

The unclear legal status of interfaith marriages in the national 1974 Marriage Law and the difficulties of interfaith couples in obtaining legal marriage have been criticised repeatedly. For example, in 1992, the then Minister of Religious Affairs Munawir Sjadzili argued for a new bill expressly allowing interfaith marriages. Because of strong opposition, efforts like this have so far been without any result.[70] However, the Administration Law passed in 2006 marks a new development in the issue of interfaith marriages. The law substitutes the plural colonial administrative regulations still in force, particularly in the realm of civil administration, and it originates from a human rights framework.[71] Being primarily procedural in nature, it was passed "almost unnoticed and hardly debated in public".[72]

---

67 Except for Aceh, there is no Islamic penal law applied in Indonesia. Apostasy is not punishable by state law but might entail negative social consequences; see Butt, "Polygamy and Mixed Marriage," 279–80.

68 Baidi, "Fenomena Nikah Beda Agama di Indonesia," 685; Hukum Online, "Kawin Beda Agama Menurut Hukum Indonesia."

69 Bowen, *Islam, Law and Equality*, 242.

70 For example, Sjadzili's proposal gained some support from other high-ranking government officials such as the then Minister of Home Affairs, the Chairman of the Supreme Court as well as the Minister of Justice but was severely criticised by some Muslim scholars such as Hasan Basri, the then Chairman of MUI; Ali, "Fatwas on Interfaith Marriages," 19.

71 In its preamble, constitutional and human rights play a prominent role and its official explanation refers to the fact that various United Nations conventions "clearly guarantee every citizen the right to establish a family and to have progeny through valid marriage [...] and guarantee the freedom to possess a religion." ([*D*]*dengan tegas menjamin hak setiap Penduduk untuk membentuk keluarga dan melanjutkan keturunan melalui perkawinan yang sah* [...], *menjamin kebebasan memeluk agama*); Official Explanation of the Administration Law.

72 Bedner and van Huis, "Plurality of Marriage Law," 181.

As a reaction to the civil registrars' reluctance to perform and register interfaith marriages by referring to religious law, the Administration Law not only stresses that registrars have no authority whatsoever to evaluate religious marriage obstacles.[73] With Art. 35 Administration Law, it also contains a 'veiled invitation'[74] for civil courts to formalise interfaith marriages. The article provides that registration in the civil registry is also mandatory for marriages "that have been decreed by court" (*yang ditetapkan oleh Pengadilan*). It is only in the explanatory part of the law that the provision is specified to apply for interfaith marriages. The explanation explicitly states that the expression "a marriage that has been decreed by court" refers to "a marriage that is concluded between two persons of different religious affiliation".[75] The fact that interfaith marriages are mentioned in an obscure manner and only in the official explanation of the code once again shows the "sensitivity of the subject" and "how difficult it is to address the question directly."[76] Even though the provision and its explanation do not grant a formal right to marry across religious boundaries in their wording, they are nevertheless to be considered as a "stealth strategy for legal change"[77] in the state's dilemma between granting basic rights in the issue of interfaith marriages and preventing opposition from Muslim groups.

A survey of civil court decisions on the validity of interfaith marriages involving Muslims that are accessible in the official Supreme Court database indicates that civil judges do not interpret Art. 35 Administration Law in itself as a sufficient ground to grant the petitions.[78] Nonetheless, the general trend seems to be that courts grant such claims, regardless of the specific constellation of

---

73 Ibid. As Bedner and van Huis put it, "registration offices only register and have to defer to the judgement of religious authorities and courts." See Art. 34 Administration Law.

74 Cammack, "Legal Aspects," 126.

75 "Yang dimaksud dengan 'Perkawinan yang ditetapkan oleh Pengadilan' adalah perkawinan yang dilakukan antar-umat yang berbeda agama," Official Explanation of Administration Law, Art. 35 a. In fact, the Marriage Law had already provided the possibility for interfaith couples to go to court after the (civil) registry's refusal of matrimony (Art. 21 Marriage Law). However, the regulation in the Administration Law explicitly refers to interfaith couples and gives formal authority to civil courts to legalise interfaith marriages.

76 Cammack, "Legal Aspects," 126.

77 Ibid.

78 The official Supreme Court database (Direktori Putusan Mahkamah Agung Republik Indonesia, http://putusan.mahkamahagung.go.id) covers judgements of the different branches of judiciary. It is striking that the vast majority of uploaded judgments on the validity of interfaith marriages are from the Surakarta Civil Court. However, it is unclear whether this reflects the proportions of cases brought to the courts or rather originates from the keyword search conducted or the upload performance of Indonesian courts in general. Only in one of the 20 analysed judgements is the claim granted solely based on Art. 35 Administration Law; Pengadilan Negeri Surakarta No. 73/Pdt.P72007/PN.Ska.

gender and religious affiliation. They base their decisions on constitutional and (inter-)national human rights laws.[79] It is striking that the only two negative decisions are based on the interpretation of Art. 2 (1) Marriage Law as covering and permitting interfaith marriages if the parties' religions do so.[80] In contrast to this approach, the vast majority of judgements allowing the conclusion of marriage are based on the assumption that the Marriage Law does not regulate interfaith marriages and that difference in religion does not count as an impediment to marriage.[81] In all of the adjudications, the judgements – whether directly or indirectly and to different degrees – quote from or refer to the Supreme Court's decision in the Andi Vony case.[82] The argument of mutual love and the parties' desire to marry notwithstanding different religious affiliations play a major role and the adjudications draw heavily on the constitutional rights of equality before the law (Art. 28 D (1)), religious freedom (Art. 28 E and Art. 29 (2)) and the right to establish a family through valid marriage (Art. 28 B (1)).[83]

With regard to the line of reasoning followed by the courts, the decisions applying Art. 35 Marriage Law can be classified into three main groups. Within the first group, the main legal basis for allowing interfaith marriages and their inclusion in the civil registry is the Dutch Mixed Marriage Act, even though

79 Out of the 20 decisions, the courts refused the petitions in two cases. See Pengadilan Negeri Ungaran No. 08/Pdt.P./2013/PN.Ung and Pengadilan Negeri Blora No. 71/Pdt.P/2017/PN.Bla.

80 The Blora Civil Court in Central Java based its rejection of a marriage between a Muslim woman and a Protestant man on both Quran 2:221 and Art. 44 Compilation of Islamic Law as well as a Protestant cleric; Pengadilan Negeri Blora No. 71/Pdt.P/2017/PN.Bla, 10. The Civil Court of Ungaran on the other hand was willing to accept a marriage between a Muslim man and a Protestant woman on condition that a somewhat religiously sanctioned ceremony took place. Rather than referring to authoritative texts, the court reasoned that some religious authorities allowed and practiced interfaith marriage ceremonies as a realisation of *Pancasila* and the constitution. The couple wanted to marry in a non-religious ceremony; Pengadilan Negeri Ungaran No. 08/Pdt.P./2013/PN.Ung, 31–22.

81 Only in one of the uploaded decisions does a court follow the assumption that the Marriage Law regulates interfaith marriages, namely within Art. 57 on mixed marriages. Interestingly, in its adjudication, the court substitutes the phrase "because of difference in nationality and one party is Indonesian citizen" by "because of difference in religion". Adhering to the pre-Marriage Law concept of 'mixed marriage' as defined in the colonial Mixed Marriage Act, the judge overlooks the wording of the provision; Pengadilan Negeri Lumajang No. 198/P/2013/PN.Lmj, 6.

82 See for example Pengadilan Negeri Surakarta No. 118/Pdt.P/2016/Pn.Skt.,12.

83 See for example Pengadilan Negeri Surakarta No. 92/Pdt.P/2010/PN.Ska., 11–12; Pengadilan Negeri Wonosobo No. 27/Pdt.P/2014/PN.Wsb., 8.

the Supreme Court declared this act invalid in the Andi Vony case.[84] In the second group, the courts invoke the 1970 Law on Judicial Power (most recently revised in 2009), regarding the principles of legal reasoning by judges.[85] The law covers the basic features of the Indonesian legal system such as the different judicial bodies, the appeals process and basic procedural principles.[86] In the third group, the decisions draw exclusively on rights of liberty as enshrined in the constitution and/or ratified international human rights law.[87] Two of the analysed judgements stand outside of this categorisation: In addition to the abovementioned judgement based on Art. 57 Marriage Law on mixed marriages, there is a Surakarta Civil Court decision that uses a circular letter from the Ministry of Home Affairs issued in 1990 as a legal basis in order to comply with the couple's wish for civil marriage. Technically, the letter is not intended for adherents of the state-recognised religions, as it deals with the registration of marriages between adherents of indigenous religious beliefs.[88]

Civil courts thus do not always order the civil registries to perform and register wedding ceremonies in line with the non-Muslim partner's religion. Given the absence of further procedural regulations like that announced by Art. 38 Administration Law, and notwithstanding the exclusion of non-religious marriages in the Marriage Law, they sometimes decree the conclusion

84 Pengadilan Negeri Surakarta No.112/Pdt.P/2008/PN.Ska.; Pengadilan Negeri Surakarta No. 115/Pdt.P/2008/PN.Ska.; Pengadilan Negeri Surakarta No. 79/Pdt.P/2009/PN.Ska.; Pengadilan Negeri Surakarta No. 92/Pdt.P/2010/PN.Ska.; Pengadilan Negeri Surakarta No. 156/Pdt.P/2010/PN.Ska.; Pengadilan Negeri Surakarta No. 90/Pdt.P/2011/PN.Ska.; Pengadilan Negeri Surakarta No. 111/Pdt.P/2011/PN.Ska. Belonging to the civil law tradition, Supreme Court decisions are not binding to lower courts; Butt, "Polygamy and Mixed Marriage," 279.

85 Pengadilan Negeri Surakarta No. 124/Pdt.P/2016/PN.Skt.; Pengadilan Negeri Surakarta No. 46/Pdt.P/20167PN.Skt.; Pengadilan Negeri Surakarta No. 118/Pdt.P/2016/PN.Skt.; Pengadilan Negeri Surakarta No. 153/Pdt.P/2011/PN.Skt.; Putusan Pengadilan Negeri Probolinggo No. 17/Pdt.P./2014/PN.Prob.; Pengadilan Negeri Pati No. 85/Pdt.P/2014/PN.Pti.

86 Undang-Undang No. 14 Tahun 1970 Tentang Ketentuan-Ketentuan Pokok Kekuasaan Kehakiman.

87 Pengadilan Negeri Magelang No. 04/Pdt.P/2012/PN.MGL.; Pengadilan Negeri Wonosobo No. 27/Pdt.P72014/PN.Wsb.

88 Pengadilan Negeri Surakarta No. 32/Pdt.P/2014/PN.Ska. The Circular Letter No.477/2535/POUD stipulates that marriages between persons who claim not to follow any of the six state-recognised religions cannot be registered in accordance with the Marriage Law and its respective implementation regulations. The letter continues that in order to meet society's needs, such marriages are to be decreed by court and registered in the civil registry after a non-religious ceremony; see Sidharta, "Undang-Undang Perkawinan Ditinjau dari Segi Hukum Antar Tata Hukum pada Dewasa Ini," 344–45.

of civil marriages.[89] In a case decided in 2014, the Probolinggo Civil Court explicitly directed the civil registry to marry an interfaith couple in a non-religious ceremony based on the Law on Judicial Power after having discussed the permissibility of civil marriage in the International Bill of Human Rights and the absence of its regulation in the Marriage Law.[90] In general, the positive judgements barely mention religious law while they essentially order the conclusion of marriages that are non-existent in the eyes of at least one party's religion.[91] This dual nature of the concepts regarding the validity of marriages in state law and religious law is best exemplified by the disclaimer contained in several Surakarta Civil Court decisions based on the application of the Mixed Marriage Act, stating that:

> [A]lthough the Petitioners' claim has been granted, it is inevitable that the Petitioners' marriage is invalid [*tidak sah*] in the eyes of religion (whether Islam or Protestantism) corresponding to the condition of Art. 2 (1) Marriage Law. As it is judged as invalid from the viewpoint of religion, the sin [*dosa*] of the relationship between Petitioner I and Petitioner II as husband and wife is the Petitioners' responsibility to God. The state only gives a solution via national statute law for a marriage between two persons willing to marry who both want to keep their religious affiliation [i.e. without conversion of one party to eliminate religious difference.][92]

---

89 According to Art. 38 Administration Law, further regulations regarding the exact conditions and procedures of marriage registration decreed by court will be issued by Presidential Regulation.

90 Pengadilan Negeri Probolinggo No. 17/Pdt.P./2014/PN.Prob. Interestingly, the court does not speak of 'marriage' (*perkawinan*), but of "agreement to a household bond like husband and wife with all respective legal effects" (*kesepakatan ikatan membentuk rumah tangga layaknya suami istri dengan segala akibat hukumnya*). This clearly shows the distinct concept of the marriage at hand compared to the religious concept of marriage in the Marriage Law; Pengadilan Negeri Probolinggo No. 17/Pdt.P./2014/PN.Prob, 13. See also in this regard Pengadilan Negeri Surakarta No. 32/Pdt.P/2014/PN.Ska.

91 In most of the cases, the judges only mention religion or religious law as the reason why the marriage at hand cannot be concluded according to Art. 2 (1) Marriage Law; see for example Pengadilan Negeri Wonosobo No. 27/Pdt.P/2014/PN.Wsb.

92 "[M]eski permohonan Para Pemohon dikabulkan adalah hal yang tidak dapat dihindarkan perkawinan Para Pemohon adalah tidak sah menurut Agama (baik Islam atau Kristen) sesuai ketentuan pasal 2 ayat (1) Undang-Undang No. 1 Tahun 1974 tentang Perkawinan, maka oleh karena dari sudut agama dinilai tidak sah, tentang dosa hubungan antara Pemohon I dan Pemohon II sebagai calon suami istri adalah merupakan tanggung jawab Para Pemohon kepada Tuhan, Negara melalui Peraturan Perundang-undangan Nasional yang hanya memberi solusi bagi perkawinan antara kedua calon mempelai yang masing-masing tetap mempertahankan tentang keyakinan agamanya," Pengadilan Negeri Surakarta No. 92/Pdt.P/2010/PN.Ska, 12. Other Surakarta Civil Court judgements based

In respect of Art. 35 Administration Law as a 'stealth strategy for legal change',[93] the general trend thus seems to be that civil courts follow the 'veiled invitation' to allow interfaith marriages. With all due caution given the sample size of the survey and the assumed incompleteness of the Supreme Court database, Lukito's conclusion regarding the Supreme Court's judgement in the Andi Vony case can therefore also be drawn regarding the application of Art. 35 Administration Law: "[t]he teachings of Islamic law would have to make way when these conflicted with state law".[94] It is striking in this regard that almost all positive judgements draw on the Supreme Court's reasoning in the Andi Vony case, except for the part indicating the abandonment of religion or the invalidation of the Mixed Marriage Act. Thus, the courts deviate from this part of the Supreme Court's reasoning and instead use different legal bases to decide their cases in a way they consider to be more fitting and accurate. In doing so, the civil courts also find legal bases for meeting the parties' wish for civil marriage at the expense not only of the concept of marriage as enshrined in the Marriage Law but also of religion itself. However, Art. 35 Administration Law is not always interpreted to allow interfaith marriages, as the two negative judgements show. The regulation might also make interfaith marriage registration more difficult if civil registries understand the court decision as a condition for marriage permission and registration.[95]

4 Who Is to Define Religious Law? The Judicial Review of Art. 2 (1) Marriage Law in the Indonesian Constitutional Court

The discussion on interfaith marriages reached its most recent peak after four legal consultants and one law student brought the debate to the Constitutional Court in September 2014. The case attracted much attention from the media. The petitioners claimed that Art. 2 (1) Marriage Law was materially and formally

on the Mixed Marriage Act contain a passage parallel to the Supreme Court's reasoning in the Andi Vony case. The court "regards the Petitioners as having given up their religious beliefs which prohibit the existence of interfaith marriages" (*menganggap Para Pemohon melepaskan keyakinan agamanya yang melarang adanya perkawinan beda agama*) in order to grant the claim; see for example Pengadilan Negeri Surakarta No. 156/Pdt.P/2010/PN.Ska., 14. In one case, the judgement contains both, the disclaimer and the assumption of apostasy; see Pengadilan Negeri Surakarta No. 79/Pdt.P/2009/PN.Ska., 8.

93 Cammack, "Legal Aspects," 126.

94 Lukito, "Trapped between Legal Unification and Pluralism," 53.

95 In one of the cases, a civil registry made a court judgement a condition for the registration of a marriage that had already been concluded in a Catholic ceremony; Pengadilan Negeri Magelang No. 04/Pdt.P/2012/PN.MGL.

unconstitutional and in conflict with *Pancasila* state philosophy as well as with ratified international human rights law, as it had been used by the registries to refer to religious law to dismiss interfaith marriages. They argued that the non-accommodation of inner-religious pluralism on the validity of interfaith marriages in favour of interpretations of religious laws as prohibiting them violated the rights to freedom of religion and marriage.[96] Furthermore, they claimed that without even considering the different interpretations between and within the respective religions, Art. 2 (1) Marriage Law did not establish legal certainty by leaving space for multiple interpretations on the validity of interfaith marriages, leading to unequal and discriminative treatment of citizens in the registries.[97] They also referred to the hidden remedy offered by Art. 35 Administration Law and argued that this "legal channel" (*jalur hukum*) constituted no real solution since judges could still decide to refuse the claims brought before them.[98] In order to harmonise Art. 2 (1) Marriage Law with the constitution and international human rights treaties, the petitioners suggested changing it. According to them, the article should read: "A marriage is legitimate if it has been performed according to the laws of the religions and beliefs of the parties concerned, *as long as the interpretation of the religious laws and beliefs is placed in the hands of the couple willing to marry* (emphasis mine)."[99] Accordingly, the petitioners upheld the dependency of marriage validity on religious law, but rather than delegating the authority to determine the exact stance of religion in the matter to the state via the registries, they suggested handing it to the couple wishing to marry.[100]

---

96 The petitioners argued that the registrars were becoming the "last instance" (*penentu akhir*) in the interpretation of religious laws. In doing so, the state was determining the 'right' interpretation of religious laws and imposing them on its citizens via its apparatus, despite Indonesia not being a religious state; Mahkamah Konstitusi No 68/Puu-XII/2014, 21. Referring to the right to marry, the petitioners claimed that as long as registrars used difference of religion as a marriage obstacle, not only the constitutional right to marriage but also the ratified International Bill Of Rights were violated since the latter prohibited treating religion as a marriage obstacle; ibid., 24.

97 Ibid., 27–35; 37. In addition, they reasoned that the provision failed to fulfil its own purpose because, rather than ensuring that every marriage was concluded by applying religious laws, citizens were being forced to follow their partner's religious law to obtain legal marriage or – even worse – to commit apostasy, an act unacceptable in every religion; ibid., 46, 51–53.

98 Ibid., 29–30.

99 "Perkawinan adalah sah apabila dilakukan menurut hukum masing-masing agamanya dan kepercayaannya itu, sepanjang penafsiran mengenai hukum agama dan kepercayaannya itu diserahkan kepada masing-masing calon mempelai," ibid., 5.

100 Ibid., 6.

The Constitutional Court perceived the case as a highly sensitive issue that touched the very self-understanding of the Indonesian state. Therefore, it invited the president and official representatives of all state-recognised religions as well as a coalition of NGOs concerned with problems related to human rights, tolerance and peace to give their opinion as interested parties (*pihak terkait*).[101] MUI, Muhammadiyah, NU, and the fundamentalist organisation Front Pembela Islam (Islamic Defenders Front, FPI)[102] represented Islam. After a lawsuit lasting more than one year, the court rejected the judicial review as "having no legal basis" (*tidak beralasan hukum*).[103] In its relatively short statement, the court explained that "in the life of nation and state based on *Pancasila* and the Constitution, religion becomes the foundation and the state has an interest in matters of marriage."[104] It emphasised the social relevance of religion in Indonesia as well as the religious aspect of marriage and reaffirmed that the state-recognised religions were to decide on marriage validity, whereas the state only intervened in administrative matters.[105] In an implicit manner, the court thus argued that the state did not intervene in religious matters when refusing marriage, as the petitioners had claimed, but only accommodated religious laws. Referring to Art. 28J (2) Constitution on the limitation

101 The president was represented by the then-Minister of Justice and Human Rights. As representatives of the state-recognised religions the following were invited: four representatives of Islam (MUI, Muhammadiyah, NU, FPI), and the official representatives of the other state-recognised religions from Persekutuan Gereja-Gereja di Indonesia (Protestantism), Perwakilan Umat Buddha Indonesia (Buddhism), Konferensi Waligereja Indonesia (Catholicism) and Parisada Hindu Dharma Indonesia (Hinduism), Majelis Tinggi Agama Khonghucu Indonesia (Confucianism).

102 Founded in the late-1990s, Front Pembela Islam (FPI) is a fundamentalist organisation with similarities to a paramilitary group. It aims at stipulating a fundamentalist interpretation of Islamic law for Muslims in Indonesia; Jahroni, "Defending the Majesty of Islam."

103 Note, however, that Constitutional Court judge Maria Farida Indranti wrote a concurring opinion: She agreed with the decision to reject the judicial review but not with the reasoning forwarded by the other judges. She argued that the petitioners were right in claiming that Art. 2 (1) Marriage Law is problematic regarding constitutional guaranties and international human rights obligations, particularly regarding the validity of interfaith marriages. According to her, the Marriage Law should indeed contain a regulation that provides a solution for interfaith couples wishing to marry. She argued, however, that the petitioners' proposal would equally well incur legal uncertainty and multiple possible interpretations. For this reason the judicial review was to be rejected; ibid., 160–62. Notably, Judge Indranti was the only female judge and also most probably the only non-Muslim member in the panel of nine judges.

104 "[D]alam kehidupan berbangsa dan bernegara berdasarkan Pancasila dan UUD 1945, agama menjadi landasan dan negara mempunyai kepentingan dalam hal perkawinan." Ibid., 153.

105 Ibid.

of constitutional rights, the court elaborated that in order to prevent conflicts while putting into practice the constitutional right to marriage, the state had to issue regulations, "in accordance with moral considerations, religious values, security, and public order in a democratic society."[106]

The court's rejection of the judicial review mainly reflects the arguments forwarded by the government, MUI, and FPI, who explicitly called on the court to reject the petition since in their eyes, Art. 2 (1) Marriage Law did not violate any constitutional rights but in fact was ensuring them.[107] MUI and FPI took up the petitioners' constitutional and human rights law rationale and referred to the role of religion in the *Pancasila* state, instead of focussing on Islam. In their statements, the three interested parties defined marriage as "sacred" (*sakral*) and an act of "worship" (*ibadah*), with the result that it could not be treated only as a civil law action.[108] They argued that to realise *Pancasila*, the state was obliged to secure the ideals of every religion based on *Ketuhanan Yang Maha Esa*.[109] The state performed this duty by accommodating religious law in the exact same manner as interpreted by religious authorities in applying Art. 2 (1) Marriage Law. In doing so, the dependency of marriage validity on religious law as stipulated by the article was the exact realisation of the right to worship in accordance with religion as guaranteed under Art. 29 (2) Constitution.[110] By implicitly defining religious freedom as the duty to profess religion in accordance with authoritative interpretations of religious law and neglecting the aspect of negative freedom of religion, the interested parties thus promoted an understanding of the concept distinct from the one prevalent in international human rights treaties. The government and FPI also pointed to the fact that it was impossible to guarantee the rights of both parties in a marriage if they did not adhere to the same religion, given the distinct and contradictory rules and procedures in the respective religious laws.[111] As done by the Constitutional Court judges, the government and MUI placed Art. 2 (1) Marriage Law in the

106 "[S]esuai dengan pertimbangan moral, nilai-nilai agama, keamanan, dan ketertiban umum dalam suatu masyarakat demokratis." Ibid., 151.

107 Ibid., 78, 98, 122.

108 Ibid., 79, 81, 98.

109 According to FPI, legalising interfaith marriage as proposed by the petitioners would be "the gateway to a liberty that destroys the values and purity of a religion" (*pintu masuk kebebasan yang menghancurkan nilai-nilai dan kemurnian suatu agama*), possibly one day leading to the legalisation of same sex-marriage; ibid., 95.

110 In this context, the MUI argued that the state regulated its citizens to respect their respective religious laws because the Indonesian state was obliged to acknowledge and protect them. Since the state was based on *Ketuhanan Yang Maha Esa*, this included religious laws pertaining to marriage; ibid., 117.

111 Ibid., 98.

context of the constitutional regulation on limitations of individual rights and freedoms (Art. 28 J (2) Constitution).[112]

In the eyes of the government, MUI and FPI, the petitioners' proposal was an attempt to install foreign, secular values into the Marriage Law, which would not only lead to social disorder, but was also incompatible with the state being based on *Ketuhanan Yang Maha Esa* and the right to worship in accordance with religion.[113] According to FPI, the proposal was "not only a strike against religious norms but [it would] also render the customary marriage procedures of every single ethnic group in Indonesia meaningless."[114] Assuming that every citizen was a religious being wishing to conclude marriage in accordance with religious law and considering marriage as an act of worship, the issue of interfaith marriages becomes a question of belief in the parties' line of reasoning. As the MUI put it, the different legal circumvention practices used by society to get married despite difference of religion constituted an act of disobedience against religious law rather than raising doubts about the constitutionality of the norm.[115] Reacting to the petitioner's human rights law argument, the MUI claimed that owing to the distinct "social-religious cultural reality of Indonesia" (*realitas sosio-religio-kultur Indonesia*) human rights could not be implemented as freely as in other states.[116] Limiting marriage only by age and the consent of both parties and not by religion – as regulated in international human rights law – would certainly lead to legal disorder with consequences beyond description. Furthermore, the acknowledgment of the UDHR did not affect the state's right to issue regulations to maintain social order, equally being a collective right honoured by the universal values of international human rights.[117]

In contrast to the line of reasoning forwarded by the government, MUI and FPI, the NGO Tim Advokasi Untuk Kebhinekaan and the representatives of the Catholic and Protestant Church largely supported the petitioners' criticism on

112 Ibid., 79, 118.

113 Ibid., 80. The MUI declared that the petitioners' proposal would be a step back to colonial law, legalising interfaith marriages even though they were invalid in the eyes of religion; ibid. 120. In a similar manner, the FPI argued that the concept of marriage envisioned by the petitioners was based on a civil law promise only and thus simply "cohabitation" (*kumpul kebo*); ibid., 97.

114 "[B]ukan hanya norma agama yang ditabrak melainkan tata cara atau adat-istiadat pernikahan setiap suku-suku di Indonesia menjadi tidak berarti." Ibid., 97.

115 Ibid., 119.

116 Ibid., 121.

117 "[T]idak mengurangi hak negara Indonesia untuk mengatur lebih lanjut agar tercapai tertib sosial yang juga sama-sama merupakan hak kolektif yang dijunjung tinggi oleh nilai-nilai universal hak asasi manusia." Ibid., 121.

the application of Art. 2 (1) Marriage Law.[118] The statements of the other related parties neither included any explicit statement on the constitutionality of Art. 2 (1) Marriage Law, nor a plea to reject or accept the petition. They instead contained a discussion on both the concept of marriage and the validity of interfaith marriage in their respective religions with Hinduism proscribing matrimony with non-Hindus and Confucianism only allowing for a blessing as a recognition and notification that marriage has been concluded.[119] The two Muslim mass organisations Muhammadiyah and NU declared their positions from the perspective of Islamic law, Muhammadiyah referring to its *fatwā* and NU listing the different stances in classical Islamic law arguing for an Islamic proscription of interfaith marriages.[120] The representative of Buddhism refrained from presenting legal opinions.[121]

In summary, the Constitutional Court's decision and the rejection of the judicial review of Art. 2 (1) Marriage Law show the central importance of religion and religious law within the Indonesian legal discourse on marriage to the detriment of religious freedom and the right to marriage as understood in international human rights law. During the process, all involved parties argued with distinct interpretations of both the *Pancasila*-state philosophy and *Ketuhanan Yang Maha Esa*. At the same time, the decision to reject the judicial review is a further example of the Constitutional Court's, "critical position as an arbiter between the central government and Islam, because the Constitution contains both Pancasila – Indonesia's state ideology, which requires a role for religion within the state – and provisions guaranteeing freedom of religion for

118 Tim Advokasi Untuk Kebhinekaan framed the issue of interfaith marriages as one of human rights, pointing out the negative consequences of non-registration for women and children; ibid., 102–5. The Protestant Church argued that the article ignored the Indonesian plural reality and – if interpreted narrowly – violated the human right to conclude marriage with a fellow citizen. The state's denial of legal marriage was leading to moral and spiritual decay. They campaigned for a regulation facilitating the conclusion of interfaith marriages; ibid., 130–32. The Catholic Church reasoned that the state's main goal was ensuring human rights and therefore the article had to be interpreted to realise freedom of religion and the right to marriage. Both rights were often being denied by the civil registries' refusal of interfaith marriages that had already been concluded in a religious ceremony; ibid. 134–35.

119 Ibid., 143–44; 135–43.

120 Ibid., 100–102; 123–26. Muhammadiyah only briefly pointed to the constitutional relevance of the Islamic prohibition of interfaith marriages by arguing that the Islamic registries' refusal to perform and register marriages between Muslims and non-Muslims did not constitute a violation of the constitution because the marriage could be registered in the civil registry; ibid. 101.

121 Ibid., 132.

citizens."[122] This is because, as argued by Tobroni, the decision places the state in an intermediate position, since it neither supports nor rejects interfaith marriages. In addition, it neither supports those parts of society who plea for legal change, nor those groups – above all Islamic ones – that consider interfaith marriages a violation of religious law. As Tobroni puts it: "The decision of the Constitutional Court is simply a confirmation that the state is obliged to carry through the implementation [i.e. registration] in accordance with the religious organisation's interpretation of its religious doctrines."[123] By maintaining the status quo, the court leaves open the possibility for interfaith couples to get married, albeit facing difficulties in having their marriage registered. It also leaves it up to the administration at local levels to define their policy towards interfaith marriages and to diverge from the dominant interpretation of religious laws. Against this background, the decision can be seen as the continuation of the "wait-and-see attitude" that the state has adopted in approaching interfaith marriages with the promulgation of the national Marriage Law in 1974.[124]

5 Conclusion

Notwithstanding the Constitutional Court's rejection of the judicial review on Art. 2 (1) Marriage Law in 2015, the validity of interfaith marriages remains one of the most controversial issues both in Indonesian Islamic discourse and the national discourse on the Marriage Law. Openly challenging the status quo, the petition for the judicial review of Art. 2 (1) Marriage Law on marriage validity has been perceived as a threat to Islam, with marriage being understood not as a private matter but as a central aspect of belief and worship. It has also been perceived as questioning the state's very foundation of *Ketuhanan Yang Maha Esa*. In this setting of inseparability between marriage and religion, the issue of interfaith marriage is also highly political because it touches the state's position vis-à-vis Islam. The Constitutional Court's invitation to the hardliner organisation FPI – known for its radical handling of perceived deviants –[125] rather than some moderate or liberal organisation to become an interested

122 Butt, "Islam, Family Law and Constitutional Context in Indonesia," 280.

123 "Apa yang diputuskan MK hanyalah menegaskan kewajiban negara untuk membantu pelaksanaan negara sesuai dengan tafsir organisasi keagamaan atas ajaran agamanya." Tobroni, "Kebebasan Hak Ijtihad Nikah Beda Agama pasca Putusan Mahkamah Konstitusi," 618.

124 Pompe, *The Indonesian Supreme Court*, 464.

125 Lindsey, *Islam, Law and the State*, 408–9, 424.

party in the proceedings also has to be seen against this background of political considerations. The involvement of groups promoting interpretations of Islam more favourable to interfaith marriages would have reflected the ongoing controversial debate on the issue within the plural Muslim Indonesian society as well as the aspect of pluralism equally covered by *Pancasila*. Due to the high sensitivity of the issue and its potential to cause considerable social and political unrest, it is likely that the reason for the inclusion of a group that openly challenges the state's legitimacy and demands the installation of an Islamic state is to be found in an attempt to prevent an escalation of the conflict. Given the symbolic relevance of Art. 2 (1) Marriage Law, which seems to make the provision untouchable in a state based on *Ketuhanan Yang Maha Esa*, the Constitutional Court had no choice other than to reject the judicial review. This is especially true since the stipulation of marriage validity had almost led to social disruption in the 1970s during the national family law-making process. Against this background, it seems unlikely that legal change will occur by reforms of the Marriage Law itself but rather through the backdoor via procedural reforms, as with the promulgation of the Administration Law and court practice in general.

The protection of the majority opinion within Indonesian society regarding religious matters – or at least the one dominating the discourse – at the expense of individual reasoning and individual religious freedom has also been a Constitutional Court practice in other matters of freedom of religion with the purpose of avoiding social unrest. Thus, the decision on the constitutionality of Art. 2 (1) Marriage Law shows similarities to the rejected judicial review on the so-called Blasphemy Law in 2001, which prohibits dishonouring religion, where the court reasoned that "the religion of the individual cannot be separated from the religion of the community".[126] In this respect, the Constitutional Court decision stands in contrast to the state approach to the legal pluralism of religious laws and constitutional and human rights laws as adopted in the Supreme Court decision in the Andi Vony case and the 'veiled invitation' in the Administration Law that explicitly attach higher importance to individual rights. With regard to the solution offered by Art. 35 Administration Law it is important to note that its legal force remains unaffected by the rejection of the judicial review. Although the legal situation has not changed, it is nevertheless to be expected that in the future, civil courts will show a stronger tendency to reject the conclusion of at least civil marriages, given the continued emphasis on the religious nature of marriage.

126 Lindsey, *Islam, Law and the State*, 53.

Finally, it needs to be stressed that the outright prohibition of interfaith marriages as promoted in the Indonesian *fatāwā* and the Compilation of Islamic Law remains far from being undisputed. Most notably, it has been the Ministry of Religious Affairs who has given impetus for an Islamic draft law meeting international human rights standards and allowing interfaith marriages to replace the Compilation of Islamic Law. At present, the planned enactment of an Islamic family law statute that is legally binding for Indonesian Muslims is still in the making. However, given the sensitivity of interfaith marriages, it seems unlikely that an outright and explicit legalisation would pass parliament anytime soon.

Bibliography

Affan, Heyder and Christine Franciska. "Ahmad Nurcholish dan Pernikahan Beda Agama." Detik News, 1 July, 2015. Accessed 22 June, 2017. https://news.detik.com/bbc-world/2957268/ahmad-nurcholish-dan-pernikahan-beda-agama.

Ali, Muhamad. "Fatwas on Interfaith Marriage in Indonesia." *Studia Islamika. Indonesian Journal for Islamic Studies* 9 (2003): 1–33.

Ali, Muhamad. "The Rise of the Liberal Islam Network (JIL) in Contemporary Indonesia," *The American Journal of Islamic Social Sciences* 22 (2005): 1–16.

Azra, Azyumardi. "The Indonesian Marriage Law of 1974. An Institutionalisation of the Shariʿa for Social Changes." In *Shariʿa and Politics in Modern Indonesia*, edited by Arskal Salim and Azyumardi Azra, 76–95. Singapore: Institute of Southeast Asian Studies, 2003.

Baidi, Yasin. "Fenomena Nikah Beda Agama di Indonesia: Telaah terhadap Putusan Mahkamah Agung Republik Indonesia No. 1400 K/Pdt/1996." *Sosio-Religia* 9 (2010): 671–89.

Bedner, Adrian, and Stijn van Huis, "Plurality of Marriage Law and Marriage Registration for Muslims in Indonesia: a Plea for Pragmatism." *Utrecht Law Review* 6 (2010): 175–91.

Bowen, John R. *Islam, Law and Equality in Indonesia. An Anthropology of Public Reasoning*. Cambridge: Cambridge University Press, 2003.

Butt, Simon. "Polygamy and Mixed Marriage in Indonesia: Islam and the Marriage Law in the Courts." In *Indonesia: Law and Society*, edited by Tim Lindsey, 266–87. Annandale: The Federation Press, 2008.

Butt, Simon. "Islam, Family Law and Constitutional Context in Indonesia." *Pacific Rim Law & Policy Journal* 19 (2010): 279–301.

Cammack, Mark. "Legal Aspects of Muslim-non-Muslim Marriage in Indonesia." In *Muslim-non-Muslim Marriage. Political and Cultural Contestations in South East*

Asia, edited by Gavin W. Jones, Chee Heng Leng, and Maznah Mohamad, 103–38. Singapore: Institute of Southeast Asian Studies, 2009.

Cholil, Suhadi. "The Politico-Religious Contestation. Hardening of the Islamic Law on Muslim-non-Muslim Marriage in Indonesia." In *Muslim-non-Muslim Marriage. Political and Cultural Contestations in South East Asia*, edited by Gavin W. Jones, Chee Heng Leng, and Maznah Mohamad, 139–58. Singapore: Institute of Southeast Asian Studies, 2009.

Hukum Online. "Empat Cara Penyelundupan Hukum Bagi Pasangan Beda Agama. Meskipun Sudah Dilarang, Perkawinan Beda Agama Masih Terus Dilakukan. Berbagai Cara Ditempuh, demi Mendapatkan Pengakuan dari Negara." *Hukum Online*, 1 November, 2006. Accessed 27 June, 2016. https://www.hukumonline.com/berita/baca/hol15655/empat-cara-penyelundupan-hukum-bagi-pasangan-beda-agama.

Hukum Online. "Kawin Beda Agama Menurut Hukum Indonesia." *Hukum Online*, 4 March, 2011. Accessed 22 June, 2017. https://www.hukumonline.com/klinik/detail/cl290/gimana-caranya.

Ihsanuddin. "Komnas HAM Dukung Perkawinan Beda Agama Dilegalkan." Kompas, 5 September, 2014. Accessed 8 July, 2017. https://nasional.kompas.com/read/2014/09/05/08424991/Komnas.HAM.Dukung.Perkawinan.Beda.Agama.Dilegalkan.

Katz, June S. and Ronald S. Katz. "The New Indonesian Marriage Law: A Mirror of Indonesia's Political, Cultural, and Legal Systems." *The American Journal of Comparative Law* 23 (1975): 653–81.

Leeman, Alex B. "Interfaith Marriage in Islam: An Examination of the Legal Theory Behind the Traditional and Reformist Positions." *Indiana Law Journal* 84 (2009): 121–57.

Lindsey, Tim. *Islam, Law and the State in Southeast Asia. Volume I: Indonesia*. London: I.B. Tauris, 2012.

Lukito, Ratno. "Trapped between Legal Unification and Pluralism. The Indonesian Supreme Court's Decision on Interfaith Marriage." In *Muslim-non-Muslim Marriage. Political and Cultural Contestations in South East Asia*, edited by Gavin W. Jones, Chee Heng Leng, and Maznah Mohamad, 33–57. Singapore: Institute of Southeast Asian Studies, 2009.

Maṭraǧī, Mahmud, ed. *Al-Ḥāwī l-Kabīr lil-Imām Abī l-Ḥasan ʿAlī b. Muḥammad b. Ḥabīb al-Māwardī*, 23 vols. Beirut: Dār al-Fikr, 1994.

Mawardi, Ahmad Imam. "The Political Backdrop of the Enactment of the Compilation of Islamic Laws in Indonesia." In *Shariʿa and Politics in Modern Indonesia*, edited by Arskal Salim und Azyumardi Azra, 125–147. Singapore: Institute of Southeast Asian Studies, 2003.

Mulia, Siti Musdah. "Promoting Gender Equity through Interreligious Marriage. Empowering Indonesian Women." In *Muslim-non-Muslim Marriage. Political and*

Cultural Contestations in South East Asia, edited by Gavin W. Jones, Chee Heng Leng, and Maznah Mohamad, 255–82. Singapore: Institute of Southeast Asian Studies, 2009.

Jahroni, Jajang J. "Defending the Majesty of Islam: Indonesia's Front Pembela Islam (FPI) 1998–2003." *Studia Islamika. Indonesian Journal for Islamic Studies* 11 (2014): 197–256.

Otto, Jan Michiel. "Sharia and National law in Indonesia." In *Sharia Incorporated: A Comparative Overview of the Legal Systems of Twelve Muslim Countries in Past and Present*, edited by Jan Michiel Otto, 433–90. Leiden: Leiden University Press, 2010.

Peters, Rudolph. *Crime and Punishment in Islamic Law. Theory and Practice from the Sixteenth to the Twenty-first Century*. Cambridge: Cambridge University Press, 2005.

Pompe, Sebastiaan. "A Short Note on Some Recent Developments with Regard to Mixed Marriages in Indonesia." *Bijdragen tot de Taal-, Land- en Volkenkunde* 147 (1991): 261–272.

Pompe, Sebastiaan. *The Indonesian Supreme Court: A Study of Institutional Collapse*. Ithaca: Cornell Southeast Asia Program Publications, 2005.

Quiano, Kathy. "4,500 Couples Participate in Indonesian Interfaith Marriage Ceremony." CNN Belief Blog, 20 July, 2011. Accessed 2 June, 2017. http://religion.blogs.cnn.com/2011/07/20/4500-couples-participate-in-indonesian-interfaith-marriage-ceremony/.

Sairin, Weineta, and Joseph Marcus Pattiasina. *Pelaksanaan Undang-Undang Perkawinan dalam Perspektif Kristen: Himpunan Telaah tentang Perkawinan di Lingkungan Persekutuan Gereja-Gereja di Indonesia*. Jakarta: Gunung Mulia, 1996.

Sidharta, P.H. "Undang-Undang Perkawinan Ditinjau dari Segi Hukum Antar Tata Hukum pada Dewasa Ini." *Jurnal Hukum dan Pembangunan* 22 (1992): 344–53.

Seo, Myengkyo. "Falling in Love and Changing Gods: Inter-religious Marriage and Religious Conversion in Java, Indonesia." *Indonesia and the Malay World* 41 (2013): 67–96.

Syahuri, Taufiqurrohman. *Legislasi Hukum Perkawinan di Indonesia. Pro-Kontra Pembentukannya hingga Putusan Mahkamah Konstitusi*. Jakarta: Kencana, 2013.

Tobroni, Faiq. "Kebebasan Hak Ijtihad Nikah Beda Agama pasca Putusan Mahkamah Konstitusi. Freedom of Ijtihad on Interfaith Marriage after Constitutional Court's Decision." *Jurnal Konstitusi* 12 (2015): 604–30.

Wahid, Marzuki. *Fiqh Indonesia: Kompilasi Hukum Islam dan Counter Legal Draft Kompilasi Hukum Islam dalam Bingkai Politik Hukum Indonesia*. Bandung: Penerbit Marja, 2014.

Wahyuni, Sri. *Nikah Beda Agama: Kenapa ke Luar Negeri?* Cetakan: PT Pustaka Alvabet, 2016.

Wasman, H., and Wardah Nuroniyah. *Hukum Perkawinan Islam di Indonesia: Perbandingan Fiqih dan Hukum Positif*. Yogyakarta: Teras, 2011.

Fatāwā

Majelis Tarjih dan Tajdid. Salinan Keputusan Muktamar Tarjih Muhammadiyah XXII [6 s.d. 10 Rajab 1409 H / 12 s.d. 16 Februari 1989, di Malang, Jawa Timur] Tentang Nikah Beda Agama. Majelis Tarjih dan Tajdid. Pimpinan Pusat Muhammadiyah. Accessed 4 June, 2016. http://tarjih.muhammadiyah.or.id/download-makalah-seminar-perkawinan-beda-agama-714.html.

Lajnah Ta'lif Wan Nasyr. *Ahkamul Fuqaha, Solusi Problematika Aktual Hukum Islam: Solusi Problematika Aktual Hukum Islam. Keputusan Muktamar, Munas, dan Konbes Nahdlatul Ulama (1926–2010 M)*. Surabaya: Khalista, 2011.

Majelis Ulama Indonesia. Perkawinan Campuran: Putusan Musyawarah Nasional II tanggal 11–17 Rajab 1400 H, bertepatan dengan tanggal 26 Mei–1 Juni 1980 M. *Majelis Ulama Indonesia*. Accessed 25 June, 2017. http://mui.or.id/wp-content/uploads/2017/02/05.-Perkawinan-Campuran.pdf.

Majelis Ulama Indonesia. Fatwa Nomor: 4/MUNAS VII/MUI/8/2005 tentang Perkawinan Beda Agama. *Majelis Ulama Indonesia*. Accessed 25 June, 2017. mui.or.id/wp-content/uploads/2017/02/38.-Perkawinan-Beda-Agama.pdf.

Majelis Ulama Indonesia. Fatwa Nomor: 7/MUNAS VII/MUI/11/2005 tentang Pluralisme, Liberalisme dan Sekularisme Agama. Majelis Ulama Indonesia. Accessed 29 June, 2017. http://mui.or.id/wp-content/uploads/2017/02/12.-Pluralisme-Libera lisme-dan-Sekularisme-Agama.pdf.

Laws and the Like

1889 Mixed Marriage Act [Regeling op de Gemengde Huwelijken (RGH) Staatsblad 1898 Nomor 158].

1945 Constitution [Undang-Undang Dasar Negara Republik Indonesia Tahun 1945].

1970 Law on Judicial Power [Undang-Undang No. 14 Tahun 1970 Tentang Ketentuan-Ketentuan Pokok Kekuasaan Kehakiman].

1974 Marriage Law [Undang-Undang Perkawinan No. 1 Tahun 1974 Tentang Perkawinan].

1975 Application Act of 1974 Marriage Law [Peraturan Pemerintah Nomor 9 Tahun 1975 Tentang Pelaksanaan Undang-Undang Nomor 1 Tahun 1974 Tentang Perkawinan].

1991 Compilation of Islamic Law [Kompilasi Hukum Islam].

2006 Administration Law [Undang-Undang No. 23 Tahun 2006 Tentang Administrasi Kependudukan].

Court Decisions (http://putusan.mahkamahagung.go.id)

Mahkamah Konstitusi No. 68/Puu-XII/2014. Decided 18 June, 2015.

Mahkamah Agung No. 1400K/PDT/1986. Decided 1 January, 1989.

Mahkamah Agung No. 1650k/Sip/1974. Decided 13 November, 1979.

Pengadilan Negeri Surakarta No. 73/Pdt.P72007/PN.Ska. Decided 27 June, 2007.

Pengadilan Negeri Surakarta No. 112/Pdt.P/2008/PN.Ska. Decided 9 September, 2008.

Pengadilan Negeri Surakarta No. 115/Pdt.P/2008/PN.Ska. Decided 17 September, 2008.
Pengadilan Negeri Surakarta No. 79/Pdt.P/2009/PN.Ska. Decided 30 April, 2009.
Pengadilan Negeri Surakarta No. 92/Pdt.P/2010/PN.Ska Decided 28 June, 2010.
Pengadilan Negeri Surakarta No. 156/Pdt.P/2010/PN.Ska. Decided 5 July, 2011.
Pengadilan Negeri Surakarta No. 153/Pdt.P/2011/PN.Skt. Decided 30 June, 2016.
Pengadilan Negeri Surakarta No. 90/Pdt.P/2011/PN.Ska. Decided 5 July, 2011.
Pengadilan Negeri Surakarta No. 111/Pdt.P/2011/PN.Ska. Decided 22 August, 2011.
Pengadilan Negeri Magelang No. 04/Pdt.P/2012/PN.MGL. Decided 7 February, 2012.
Pengadilan Negeri Ungaran No. 08/Pdt.P./2013/PN.Ung. Decided 5 February, 2013.
Pengadilan Negeri Lumajang No. 198/P/2013/PN.Lmj. Decided on 23 February, 2013.
Pengadilan Negeri Probolinggo No. 17/Pdt.P./2014/PN.Prob. Decided 8 April, 2014
Pengadilan Negeri Surakarta No. 32./Pdt.P/2014/PN.Ska. Decided 12 March, 2014.
Pengadilan Negeri Wonosobo No. 27/Pdt.P/2014/PN.Wsb. Decided 21 May, 2014.
Pengadilan Negeri Pati No. 85/Pdt.P/2014/PN.Pti. Decided 11 December, 2014.
Pengadilan Negeri Surakarta No. 46/Pdt.P/2016/PN.Skt. Decided 7 March, 2016.
Pengadilan Negeri Surakarta No. 118/Pdt.P/2016/PN.Skt. Decided 30 May, 2016.
Pengadilan Negeri Surakarta No. 124/Pdt.P/2016/PN.Skt. Decided 31 May, 2016.
Pengadilan Negeri Blora No. 71/Pdt.P/2017/PN.Bla. Decided 8 April, 2017.

Contextualising Malaysia's Islamic Law: a Nuanced Perspective

Karen Meerschaut and Werner de Saeger

1 Introduction

With a continuous stream of news about various barbaric actions committed by the "Islamic State", and the recent wave of jihadist attacks in our own backyard all across Europe, Islam and Islamic law, and its potential tensions with basic human rights norms, are once more at the forefront of public consciousness. There seems no escape from the antagonistic notion that Islamic Law and international standards of Human Rights are diametrically opposed and irreconcilable.[1] A respected institution such as the ECHR declared in a ruling of 13 February 2003 in the case of the Refah party versus the Turkish state that

> syariah is incompatible with the fundamental principles of democracy as set forth in the ECHR (…) It is difficult to declare one's respect for democracy and human rights while at the same time supporting a regime based on Syariah, which clearly diverges from Convention values, particularly with regard to its criminal law and criminal procedure, its rules on the legal status of women and the way it intervenes in all spheres of private and public life in accordance with religious precepts.[2]

Answering questions and assertions about the compatibility of Islamic law with liberal democracies with a plain 'no' misses out on a vital part of the real issue, overlooking the complexity and diversity of Islamic religion and Islamic legal practices.

1 Lepard, Emon, Ellis, and Glahn, "Book Review *Islamic Law and International Human Rights Law: Searching for Common Ground*," 379–83.

2 ECHR 13 February, 2003, Refah Partisi (the Welfare Party) and Others v. Turkey, par.123. In another article, I have already examined how the ECtHR approaches the issue of legal pluralism and Islam and contrasted it with the Malaysian approach: Meerschaut and Gutwirth, "Legal Pluralism and Islam in the Scales of the European Court of Human Rights." In the Dahlab case the Court upheld a similar line of reasoning with regard to the wearing of the Islamic headscarf: 'It (…) appears difficult to reconcile the wearing of an Islamic headscarf with the message of tolerance, respect for others and above all, equality and non-discrimination (…)': ECHR 15 February, 2001, Dahlab v. Switzerland, par. 111, p. 13 (decision of inadmissibility).

 | DOI:10.1163/9789004398269_011

In this chapter we will discuss the issue of the accommodation, application and reform of Islamic law in Malaysia. This country provides an important opportunity to rethink and discuss the relationship between the state and religious practices, including the accommodation of Islamic Law, in multi-faith democratic constitutional states. Malaysia already long serves as a major point of reference in international and academic research and in literature on multiculturalism, plural states and modern Islamic societies.[3] Malaysia is famously known for its vibrant multi-ethnic and multi-religious Muslim-majority society. Like many British ex-colonies, it is also well known for its legal pluralism: the national law accommodates civil, Islamic, and indigenous 'native' laws. Malaysia is often quoted in literature as a moderate or modern Islamic country, different from Muslim countries in the Middle East and North Africa. As Siti Zubaidah Ismail points out: "Malaysia enjoys positive global attention for being a reputable non-Arab moderate Islamic country. Islam in Malaysia is deemed to be moderate, progressive, and fast developed".[4] He also refers to anthropologists like Peletz who asserts that the Islamisation process in Malaysia cannot be compared with,

> the conventional areal foci of Islamic studies – that is the Middle East and North Africa, as Malaysia, a religiously and ethnically diverse Muslim-majority country, in recent decades, has experienced stunning economic transformation and patterns of sustained growth that are probably second to none in the Muslim world.[5]

Peletz even refers to Shamsul's description of the Malaysian case as "*the shining light of moderate Islam*".[6] Its political leaders of the dominant party UMNO are also eager to underscore this and even label Malaysia as a model for other Islamic countries. In 1994,[7] Horowitz extensively described the Malaysian Islamic family law reforms of the 1980s. He perceived the resulting system of Islamic courts and legislation in Malaysia as very "Western", "modern",

3 See for example: Hooker, *Islamic Law in South-East Asia*; Peletz, *Religious Courts and Cultural Politics in Malaysia*; Hefner, *Pluralism and Citizenship in Malaysia*; Hooker en Othman, *Malaysia. Islam, Society and Politics*.

4 Ismail, "At the Foot of the Sultan: The Dynamic Application of Shariah in Malaysia," 69–81.

5 Peletz, "Malaysia's Syariah Judiciary as Global Assemblage," 605.

6 See also Peletz, Malaysia's Syariah Judiciary as Global Assemblage, 605: "The Malaysian case is of further significance in that the nation's political and religious elites enjoy a reputation in many parts of the World for representing the best of Islam and modernity, if not the shining light of moderate Islam (Shamsul A.B. 2001: 4709)."

7 Horowitz, "The Qur'an and the Common Law: Islamic Law Reform and The Theory of Legal Chance," 233–93 (part I); 543–80 (part II).

"rational" and – at the same time – "Islamic".[8] Horowitz's analysis drew our attention to Malaysia being an interesting and relevant case, which could eventually also relativise the widely shared perception that *Syariah* is fundamentally incompatible with the principles of a democratic constitutional state and human rights. The Malaysian approach we explored showed, at least in its initial phase, that accommodation and a strong form of legal pluralism does not *per se* defeat [and annihilate] or erode the democratic constitutional state or fundamental notions of liberal democracy.[9] On the contrary, as Horowitz observed, in the eighties of the previous century, academics, lawyers and other parties involved in the abovementioned Islamic family law reforms in Malaysia, argued that 'Islamic law, properly understood, is a regime of rights'. The reformers wished to put an end to the *qāḍīs'* tendency of prioritising conciliation, family obligations, and values[10] at the expense of rights and rules of evidence and procedure.[11] Anthropologists, like Peletz in 2015, confirmed that Horowitz's observations of 1994 are still relevant today: "compared to their predecessors in the late 1980s the discourses and the practices of the syariah court are far more overtly Islamic and simultaneously far more consistently and explicitly informed by procedures and other phenomena drawn directly from the secular common-law judiciary".[12] However Peletz's observation does not mean that the Islamic law as applied in Malaysia is indeed so favourable or even respectful of women's rights. Indeed, as we will see, the legal changes in the application of Islamic law since the eighties in Malaysia, although very hopeful in the beginning, currently paint a less rosy picture for women's rights and the

8 As Horowitz brilliantly described, this process of change has produced paradoxical and hybrid results: it has turned out to be more Islamic and more Western at the same time. While the desire for Islamic authenticity was very strong, the secular legal system remained an object of respect for the reformers: Horowitz, "The Qur'an and the Common Law," 233–93.

9 It was thought, amongst others by the authors of this chapter, that Malaysia might offer a valuable opportunity to let the western world see that "third" paths are possible between the extremes of modern secularism and Islamic theocracy. In the west it is generally feared that judicial accommodation of Muslim religious practices will erode the secular rule of law. This raises a question (covered in Karen Meerschaut's doctoral research) crucial to the nature of our constitutional democracy: can we legally accommodate a diversity of religious legal practices among our citizens and, if so, within which limits?

10 Instead of the previously mediating and moralising style of the local *qāḍī*, judges had become more inquisitorial in their adjudicating (or more passive when lawyers were involved in the case), and greater emphasis was put on evidence, especially in written form. Peletz, *Islamic Modern*, 297, fn. 16.

11 Peletz, *Islamic Modern*, 109, fn. 13, 110, 118, fn. 16 and 125.

12 Peletz, "A tale of two courts," 154.

religious liberties of Muslims.[13] In a few recent articles, Tamir Moustafa underscores some remarkable points:

1) The state approbation and interpretation of Islamic law is subverting constitutional principles of liberal democracy that are enshrined in the 1957 constitution but also the basic legal principles of Islamic legal theory (*usul al-fiqh*) themselves.[14]
2) The codification of Islamic family law has narrowed the scope of rights that women could claim in classical Islamic jurisprudence.[15]

The question of whether Malaysia is a secular or an Islamic state is today much debated, both within Malaysia and in academic literature about the country. None of us would provide a satisfactory answer by merely choosing one of the two stated options. We would have to answer, "It's complicated", and give a more detailed explanation of the Malaysian Constitution, politics, history, the expanded and powerful state religious bureaucracies, and various other socio-anthropological elements.

2 Superdiversity and Legal Pluralism in Malaysia: Brief Background

The long-existing diversity of the people, religion and law (customs) has marked Malaysia's legal system: according to constitutionalist Harding, this diversity,

> has extended into the legal world; just as a street in Malacca houses a Buddhist temple, a Hindu Temple, a mosque and a Catholic church,

13 Our research, and other research about other Muslim countries, shows that legal reforms in Islamic law will either build towards more gender equality or towards a stricter, more orthodox interpretation of religiously inspired rules, depending on a wide range of political and legal factors, such as power-sharing configurations between state institutions (bureaucratic power struggles), religious leadership and strategic players such as feminist organisations, human rights lawyers, intellectuals and radical Islamic groups. Otto, "The compatibility of syariah with the rule of law," 149. See also Horowitz (part 1): footnote 9. See also Mahmood, "The politics of Shari'ah Reform," 1–2.

14 According to Moustafa, Malaysia appears to be a religious state and he emphasises the remarkable state monopoly on religious interpretation, at least for the Malaysian Muslims who are subject to such rules and regulations (60% of the population). Moreover he argues that Malaysia provides a textbook example of how core principles in *usul al-fiqh* (Islamic legal theory) are subverted as a result of state appropriation. Moustafa, "Judging in God's Name," 152–67.

15 Moustafa, "Islamic Law, Women's Rights, and Popular Legal Consciousness in Malaysia," 178.

> so the Malaysian legal system caters very adequately, in a way which European legal systems clearly do not, for several varieties of law, even providing Special Courts in Sabah and Sarawak to administer 'native' law to the indigenous population.[16]

Muslims make up the majority of the Malaysian population (composed of four major categories: Malays, all of whom are by constitutional definition Muslims,[17] Chinese, Indians, and others). All Malays speak the Malay language and the majority identify themselves as Sunni Muslims belonging to the *Shafi'i* legal school of Islam. Malaysia is characterised by a very prominent expression of the Islamic identity in the public sphere: the headscarf is omnipresent – but *purdah* (the term used in Malaysia for a veil that conceals the face) and *serban* (Muslim headgear for men) are forbidden in public institutions – foods and goods for the Muslim market need to comply with specific requirements before they can be labelled as halal food.[18] Islamic (law) schools play an important role in the education system and there exist Islamic bank and insurance companies, Islamic hospitals, radio channels, and so on.[19] During the last decades we have been able to observe considerable government efforts to introduce new Islamic legislation, including the upgrading and reorganising of the Syariah courts,[20] Islamic (law) schools and universities, and in general an

16 Harding, "Comparative law and legal transplantation in South East Asia," 242. According to Harding this system is very efficient: Harding, *Law, Government and the Constitution in Malaysia*, 216.

17 Article 160 of the FC defines a Malay as a person who professes the Muslim religion, habitually speaks the Malay language and conforms to Malay customs. While this article 160(2) used to be merely interpreted as an interpretative clause, discussion about it remains. The Malaysian courts have interpreted this clause as meaning that 'as Malay', a person 'remains in the Islamic faith until her dying days'. See cases *Daud bin Mamat* (2001) and *Lina Joy* (2001 and 2007). See Chevallier-Govers, "The rule of law and legal pluralism in Malaysia," 101. She writes that the question remains whether a Malay apostate would lose his identity and the status of being a 'Malay'.

18 In Malaysia; the use of this/such and other similar labelling is controlled under the 'Trade Description Act (Usage of HALAL/Permissible' statement) 1975.

19 Ismail, "The Dynamic Application of Shariah in Malaysia," 70: "In the area of Islamic banking and finance, education, business and social matters, Malaysia is ahead of her counterparts and has become the flag bearer for incorporating Islam into mainstream society by having services and facilities compliant with Shari'ah or Islamic law. Lately dubbed as a 'hub' for the Islamic finance industry and halal businesses […]."

20 The reforms involved a significant upgrading and expansion of the Islamic judiciary, improving the infrastructure (adequate buildings and facilities) increasing the number of better-trained staff and Syariah judges, enhancing their pay and recognition, a commitment towards making "Malaysia a hub for 'Sharia compliant' products and institutions," the establishment of the International Islamic University, the Institute of Islamic

increasingly prominent place of Islam in the public, political and legal arena. Simultaneously, Malaysia has developed itself into one of the most economically prosperous Muslim-majority countries, one of the so-called Asian tigers: Malaysia has evolved in the course of a single generation into a country with important middle classes and growing civil societies.[21] In the remainder of this chapter we will dig deeper into two issues, namely the constitutional relation between religions, especially Islam, and the state and how this relation is challenged by the Islamic resurgence movement since the 70s and the currently stronger Islamist demands.

Against that backdrop, we will also very briefly discuss the reforms that have taken place in Islamic law since the 80s of the twentieth century in family and penal matters. Especially in the 80s and 90s, "a plethora of new legislation was issued at the state and federal levels that formalized substantive and procedural aspects of 'Islamic law'".[22] These changes were carried out in a legal and technical manner recognisable to the West: as it happens, by means of a formal and systematic elaboration of legislation by parliaments and through jurisprudence by courts.[23] To what extent contemporary legislative and jurisprudential evolutions are challenging the rule of law and the supremacy of the constitution and basic principles of Islamic uṣūl-al-fiqh (see Moustafa, Asifah Quraishi-Landes etc.) is the nexus of our legal analysis. Finally, some reflections on the challenges and issues of developing Islamic law in Malaysia will be given.

Understanding (IKIM), and the Islamic Missionary Foundation of Malaysia (YADIM), and the founding of Islamic banks, Islamic pawnshops as well as other financial institutions. "So methodical and thorough was this programme of Islamization that Malaysia was touted by many Muslim countries as a model by which the demands of the Sharia could be harmonized with those of modernity." See Aljunied, "Demarginalizing the sharia," 135.

21 Peletz *Islamic Modern*, 5; Peletz, "The cultural politics of legitimacy," 240–273; Peletz, "Malaysia's Syariah Judiciary as Global Assemblage," 605 and Peletz, "A tale of two courts": "Malaysia, probably the most successful Muslim-majority country in the world in terms of its burgeoning middle classes and the stunning rates of urbanization, economic growth, and educational attainment it has sustained over the past few decades." He refers also to "robust civil-society activism that manages to ameliorate, subvert, or elude the dominant trend." See for more on Islamisation policies of UMNO and civil society groups, articles from the political scientist Francis Kok Wah Loh.

22 Moustafa, "Judging in God's name?," 161.

23 The British and after independence the Malaysians systematised and institutionalised Syariah Law through legislation and secular jurisprudence. The development of Islamic law was primarily left to secular jurists and judges. It is unsurprising, therefore, that Horowitz refers to an 'Islamicisation of the law', rather than a 'juridicisation of Islam', and claims that this phenomenon continued to run its course after independence.

3 The Position of Islam and Islamic Law within the Constitutional Framework

The Federation of Malaysia – comprising 13 states and 3 federal territories – formally endorses the principles of a democratic constitutional state, namely democracy, checks and balances, fundamental rights and liberties and the *rule of law*. But the Malaysian constitution also departs in several regards from the current constitutional models of Western liberalism, in particular with its specific integration of religious (Islamic) law.

Although the Constitution drawn up at independence in 1957 was inspired by the Western (British) liberal constitutional model, it also opts for what some authors have, for the Indian case, called a 'communitarian-liberal' democracy,[24] which not only provides for individual rights and safeguards, but also for legal pluralism and group-based quotas in education and public employment. The constitution decrees Islam to be the state religion, but at least until the end of the 90s no additional significance to this stipulation was given; lawyers, judges and politicians have repeatedly underlined that this is an innocent stipulation that only relates to the religious character of state ceremonies.[25] Malaysia also has no provision that the Syariah is a source of law. On the contrary, article 160 of the Constitution, which includes a definition of 'law', does not refer to Islamic law at all. However the constitution grants the state the power to draw up Islamic legislation and to set up Islamic courts.

As Hamayotsu so aptly summarised: "the question of the official position of Islam was a source of debate at independence [...] though the debate was settled relatively peacefully thanks to the British colonial policy of privileging Islam and Malay identity and due to weak Islamists demands at that time".[26] The negotiating partners at the time of the Constitution's drafting wanted to preserve the status quo concerning the limited form of legal pluralism already practiced in Malaysia.[27] As a matter of fact, historical developments in

24 Randeria, "Legal pluralism and cultural difference: The Indian model of a communitarian-liberal democracy." See also S. Fenton, "Malaysia and capitalist modernisation: Plural and multicultural models," 136.

25 This remained the orthodox view until end of the 1990s and was affirmed in the judgment of the Supreme Court in the case of *Che Omar Bin Che Soh v. PP* of 1988: Article 3 of the Federal Constitution never aimed for an enlarged role for Islam in public law. See also Harding, "*Syariah* en nationaal recht in Maleisië," 306–7.

26 Hamayotsu, "Democracy and Religious Pluralism in Southeast Asia: Indonesia and Malaysia Compared," 8.

27 Harding stresses that the constitution was drafted at a time when Islam still played a peripheral role and no one within the country had yet conceived of an Islamic state; the rise of Malay nationalism and relations between the three major ethnic groups were more

Malaysia have led to the existence of three systems of family law (and in a limited sense also penal and land law). The Malaysian legal pluralism is rooted in a colonial legacy of co-existence of different normative or legal orders and a plural system of courts: one for non-Muslims, one for Muslims, and one for natives in Sabah and Sarawak. This legal pluralism is recognised by the constitution, as the constitution has brought Islamic and native (family) law and courts under the legislative powers of the thirteen member states in the Malaysian federation. The same applies to the organisation and procedure of the Islamic and native courts.[28] Constitutionally, Malaysian statutes (both secular and Islamic[29]) cannot be reviewed exclusively in the light of Islamic principles.[30] In the *Che Omar* ruling of 1988, the federal court ruled that the Syariah was not the supreme law of the land. Indeed, Islamic law is subject to the supremacy of the Constitution and federal law.[31] In theory, the supremacy of the Constitution means that religious law and religious legal practice are

---

pressing concerns at the time. The constitution consolidated the position of Islamic law as it was during colonisation. A. Harding, "*Syariah* en nationaal recht in Maleisië," 306–7.

28 The state legislatures are allowed to enact religious Islamic laws over matters enumerated in the Constitution (to Muslims only, with respect to a limited range of matters relating to marriage, inheritance and other personal laws) and to create Syariah courts. See article 74 of the Constitution, list II – *State list* and list IIA, *Supplement to the State list for the states of Sabah and Sarawak*, of the 9th schedule of the Constitution. confinder.richmond.edu/admin/docs/malaysia.pdf.

29 Some Islamic enactments stipulate, however, that the interpretation of those laws can be reviewed to adhere to *Hukum Syariah* ('Islamic principles'). For example, Section 245 (1) of Syariah Court Civil Procedure 1999 (Selangor) stipulates that 'Any provisions or interpretation of provisions under this enactment that are inconsistent with Islamic Law shall, to the extent of the inconsistency, be void.'

30 Most authors conclude that all in all, Malaysia is not a theocratic state: it can be, "best characterized as an intermediate hybrid along the secular-theocratic continuum". In the *Lina Joy* case the court describes Malaysia as a hybrid between a secular and theocratic state. The High Court decision in the case of *Lina Joy* dated from 18 April, 2001 and was only reported in 2004. The *Lina Joy* case was tried in the Federal Court for months; the Court said that the time it took before passing sentence in the appeal of Lina Joy, who had converted from Islam to Christianity, was due to the fact that the issue is 'sensitive and needs careful examination'. On 31 May, 2007 the Federal Court ruled in a 2–1 majority decision that only the *Syariah* court has the power to determine whether a person is still a Muslim. Such jurisprudence leaves the applicants without any legal remedy, given the fact that in many states, apostasy law provisions exist. See New Straits Times, 31 May, 2007, on the webpage: www.nst.com.my/Current_News/NST/Thursday/Frontpage/20070531073056/Article/index_html. (Last consulted 25 June, 2007). Neo, "Malay nationalism, Islamic supremacy and the constitutional bargain," 115.

31 Article 4 of the Constitution declares that the constitution is the supreme law of the land, so that incompatible legislation is void. Article 75 of the Constitution stipulates that in case of conflict between the federal law and state law, federal law shall be applicable.

subject to the constitutionality test; they can in theory be reviewed according to constitutional principles, including the fundamental liberties provisions in the Articles 5–13 of the Constitution.[32]Article 11 of the Constitution provides for the fundamental right to freedom of religion: "Every person has the right to profess and practice his religion and subject to clause 4, to propagate it." This clause 4 allows the states to issue a ban on proselytising among Muslims: "state law […] may control or restrict the propagation of any religious doctrine or belief among persons professing the religion of Islam".[33] Thus in principle, although the constitution declares that Islam is the religion of the state, people are free to belong to any religion of their choice. As we will see, however, serious threats to the freedom of religion can be identified today more than before. This is especially the case for the issue of conversion out of Islam and apostasy[34] and for jurisdictional conflicts in the case of interreligious marriages. According to Peletz, disputes over the change of religion of Muslims and interfaith custody cases: i.e., "custody disputes over children born to non-Muslim couples that are complicated by one parent's embrace of Islam" (or disputes about "the proper burial of those who have allegedly undergone late-life conversion to another religion") have in the last decades led to "highly controversial landmark decisions".[35] For example, one of the most famous Malaysian court cases, *Lina Joy v. Religious Council of the Federal Territories*, concerned a woman who sought state recognition of her religious conversion,[36] in an

32 See Chevallier-Govers, "The rule of law and legal pluralism in Malaysia," 92.

33 "there is a constitutionally backed prohibition to proselytize among the Muslims." Chevallier-Govers, "The rule of law and legal pluralism in Malaysia", 100.

34 In the Lina Joy case of 2007, the Federal Court affirmed that a Muslim who wants to leave Islam must first get the Syariah court to confirm this act of renunciation, but in some states apostasy is a criminal offence or there is no provision to give them this power. In several recent lawsuits, mostly concerning issues of conversion from Islam and apostasy, the federal high courts have declared themselves incompetent, claiming these cases fall within the jurisdiction of Islamic courts.

35 Peletz, "A tale of two courts," 149.

36 A person who has left the Islamic religion must submit proof of having done so. In Malaysia, a person's name is linked to his religion: an individual with a Muslim name and an individual whose birth certificate indicates that one of his parents had a Muslim name is supposed to be a Muslim. In addition, the National Registration Act requires that the word "Islam" be printed on the identity card of all those who are supposed to be Muslims. A former Muslim who has left Islam must therefore change his or her name from a Muslim name to a non-Muslim name and this change of name should also be made on official documents such as his identity card. As long as these formalities have not taken place, a former Muslim may be harassed by religious prosecutors for eating food during the month of fasting, he may encounter problems when trying to register a marriage with a non-Muslim and if teaching his children another religion. His rights in connection with child welfare decisions, custody and education, personal behaviour, and

almost decade-long procedure.[37] Since the late 90s, in contrast to the past, an increasingly heated public and political debate can be observed in Malaysia centring around the question of whether or not Malaysia is an 'Islamic' state. Several eminent politicians, including some moderate UMNO-politicians, have declared that Malaysia is indeed an Islamic state. Although UMNO-leaders are championing a progressive and modern form of Islam (*Islam Hadhari*), many commentators point to the ascendancy of Islamist conservatives in Malaysia and the government's continuing policy of institutionalising Islam and imposing more strict Islamic norms on the public sphere.[38]

---

funeral arrangements remain subject to Islamic law and remain under the jurisdiction of the Syariah courts. See also Chevallier-Govers, "The rule of law and legal pluralism in Malaysia," 98.

37 Moustafa, "The Politics of Religious Freedom in Malaysia," 484. During the *Shamala* case (2003–2004) the Article 11 coalition was created, an umbrella organisation of NGO's, lawyers, academics, and activists, formed to upheld constitutional supremacy and to defend freedom of religion. See section "Religious freedom and multiculturalism" in Basarudin, *Humanizing the Sacred*, 132–7. See also Kok Wah Loh, "Malaysia after Mahathir," 133: the article 11 coalition pointed out that the conflict between two legal jurisdictions (namely civil laws and the Syariah) was undermining constitutional safeguards and threatening ethnoreligious understanding. This effort in defense of the Federal Constitution was ironically deemed 'sensitive' by the prime minister.

38 This policy shows also the UMNO politicians' desire to counter and undercut the Islamic state political programme of the PAS party Neo, "Malay nationalism, Islamic supremacy," 106 and fn. 70; Meerschaut, *Law and Social Diversity*, Chapter 2, nr. 2.3.1.2. Neoh also refers to a Mahathir declaration in Parliament in 2002: 'Malaysia is not a moderate Islamic state but an Islamic fundamentalist state as its policy is to abide by the fundamental teachings of Islam [...] Malaysia [is] not only an Islamic state as acknowledged by other countries but also a model Islamic state', and to Badawi's parliamentary reply in 2007, in which he said that 'Malaysia is an Islamic state which is administered based on the principles of parliamentary democracy guided by the highest law of the land – the Federal Constitution. The Islamic principles that I mean can be seen from [the concept of] Islam Hadhari that I have introduced'. Neoh, "Islamic State and the Common Law in Malaysia: A Case Study of Lina Joy," 3. Neo also refers to a 1999 Seremban High Court case (the *Meor Atiqulrahman* case) in which the view was expressed that Article 3 imposed an obligation on the government to promote Islam and that the role of Islam was not limited only to 'rituals' and 'ceremonies'. The Barisan National, the national front ruling coalition with UMNO as major component party, advocate nevertheless, "rather a more liberal interpretation of Islam that emphasized the promotion of Islamic values in administration and in society writ large, rather than the establishment of an Islamic state, which PAS and other Muslim radicals advocated"; "Muslims were also reminded that pursuing development was compatible with being a good Muslim," Kok Wah Loh, "Malaysia after Mahathir," 127. However, although UMNO has been known for its moderate stance, see for the rise of Islamist conservatism in Malaysia during Abdullah Ahmed Badawi's premiership (2003–2009), Hamid & Ismail, "Islamist Conservatism and the Demise of Islam Hadhari in Malaysia," 159–80.

4 Legal Reforms in Islamic Law

Conventional accounts trace the Islamisation policy of the Malaysian federal government since the 80s to the rise of the *dakwah* (i.e. religious revival) movement, since the late 1970s.[39] Especially during the term in office of Prime Minister Mahathir Mohamed (1981–2003), the regime implemented a strategic and proactive promotion of Islamism to co-opt and undercut Islamist movements and parties.[40] Islamic institutions of banking, finance and education proliferated. Examples are the Institute of Islamic Understanding and the International Islamic University of Malaysia (IIUM). Yet, as Moustafa points out, many mosques and prayer houses were also either constructed or renovated, primary and secondary education curricula and radio and television content were adapted, "to include more material on Islamic civilisation, but it was in the field of law and legal institutions that the most consequential innovations were made."[41] Striking examples include the institutional

39 This was not only the case in Malaysia. Muslim movements agitating for the implementation of shari'a affected the Muslim world in general. In the Muslim world today, we see an even more visible and influential pro shari'a implementation movement, even in the once secular Turkish state. See Aljunied, "Demarginalizing the sharia," 127 and 133.

40 Peletz, "A tale of two courts," 155: "the government sought both to counter and co-opt the proselytizing activities of Islamist groups such as the Malaysian Islamic Youth Movement (ABIM) and other piety – dakwah organizations it perceived as a threat to its hold on power and to undercut the appeal of the opposition PanMalaysian Islamic Party, which has long depicted UMNO as having dubious religious credentials and being ethically bankrupt." For an essay which focuses on the pivotal role of ABIM, the Angkitan Belia Islam Malaysia – the largest Muslim youth movement in Malaysia and a civil society organisation that has been deeply involved in shari'a activism since its founding in 1971 – in agitating for more room for the Islamisation of the state and society in the last four decades, see Aljunied, "Demarginalizing the sharia," 127–46.

41 Moustafa, "Judging in God's name?," 161. See also Peletz, "A tale of two courts," 155. The reforms involved a significant upgrading and expansion of the Islamic judiciary, improving the infrastructure (adequate buildings and facilities; Peletz notices that in the period 2011–2013, we can see new more spacious and high-tech courthouses with computers with access to the e-syariah portal. Peletz, "A tale of two courts," 148) and increasing the number of better-trained staff and Syariah judges. These improvements were intended to make the Syariah legal apparatus more professional and efficient. See also Aljunied, "Demarginalizing the sharia," 135. Founded in 1983, the International Islamic University Malaysia (IIUM) provided an important educational dimension to these institutional reforms; later on, it also played a key role in terms of the further reform of the Syariah system. This university now has a law programme that combines secular and Islamic legal courses and offers academic specialisations in Islamic law. Awal, "Legal Education in Malaysia"; Ibrahim, "Recent Developments in the Syariah Law in Malaysia."

restructuring and upgrading of the Islamic judiciary and religious bureaucracy, and by substantive reforms in Islamic family, evidence, procedure and criminal law. Regarding the religious bureaucracy – elaborating on this would go beyond the reach of this chapter – we want to underscore that authorities were restructured and created with a monopoly on religious interpretation, backed by the power of the state.[42] These include the Islamic Religious Council (*Majlis Agama Islam*) and the office of the Mufti. The Mufti is empowered to issue *fatwas* that, upon publication, are binding for Muslims. Under Article 9 of the Syariah Criminal Offences Act of the federal territories (a provision which also exists in the Syariah criminal offences laws of other states), each person who acts, "in contempt of religious authority or defies, disobeys or disputes the orders or directions of the Yang di-Pertuan Agong as the Head of the Religion of Islam, the Majlis or the Mufti, expressed or given by way of fatwa", is guilty of an offence punishable with a maximum fine of 3000 ringgit or a maximum prison sentence of two years. Other articles of this act criminalise the communication of an opinion and the possession of materials that contain opinions contrary to a fatwa (articles 12–13).[43] Moreover, article 34 on Fatwa of the 505 Act Administration of Islamic law (federal territories) Act 1993 states that, "Upon publication in the Gazette, a fatwa shall be binding on every Muslim resident in the Federal Territories as a dictate of his religion and it shall be his religious duty to abide by and uphold the fatwa, unless he is permitted by Islamic Law to depart from the fatwa in matters of personal observance, belief, or opinion", and that, "A fatwa shall be recognised by all Courts in the Federal Territories as authoritative of all matters laid down therein".

42 In the meantime, "the Islamic bureaucracy has acquired a dynamic of its own," "perennially slanted towards defending the religious status quo, and enveloped by a false pretence of sanctity bordering on infallibility." This happened "at the expense of Islamic intellectual growth," as evidenced inter alia "by the priority placed on banning rather than debating unorthodox literature." Hamid & Ismail, "Islamist Conservatism and the Demise of Islam Hadhari in Malaysia," 170.

43 In classical jurisprudence fatwa's were always considered and served as non-binding opinions from religious scholars. Martinez indicates that no support can be found in the textual sources or the historical practice of the Islamic religion for the penalizing of such disobedience. As a result of the existence of such legislation some Muslims who were interviewed by her describe themselves as second-rank citizens who know no freedom. Martinez, "The Islamic state or the state of Islam in Malaysia," 482–3. Several action groups, lawyers, and academics such as Norani Othman and Patricia Martinez, both Muslim women and educated in Islamic law, raise serious questions about the constitutionality and the Islamic validity of this legislation.

4.1 *Some Notable Features of the 'New' Islamic Family Law*

In a comparative legal analysis of twelve countries regarding the implementation of Islamic norms, Otto speaks of 'a gradual trend towards liberalisation'.[44] In Malaysia, we also notice this trend to a certain degree. Islamic family law underwent significant changes since the 1980s.[45] Women's rights activists welcomed many of these changes as progressive[46] and, "Islamic family law in Malaysia was [even] considered one of the most progressive compared to other Muslim-majority countries".[47] These changes were carried out by way of a top-down codification of Islamic law in which a partial, more formal introduction of the classical *fiqh* took place.

Most member states opted for a legislative model that was elaborated under the auspices of the federal government. Surprisingly, the latter was more inspired by the Islamic reforms in other countries such as Pakistan and India, and by other schools of law, such as the *Hanafi* and *Maliki* school, which are not widely followed in Malaysia. The legal actors who were at the origins of this model came from a Malaysian elite with a common law education. The changes were thus introduced top-down. This model was characterised by the inclination to opt for progressive legal rules inspired by other schools, or for Islamic statutes introduced by other countries – legitimised by the use of the Islamic legal methods *ijtihād* (free interpretation or pragmatic interpretation of Islamic texts), *takhayyur* (free selection between rules and opinions of different Islamic schools of law) and *talfiq* (the combining of points of view of different schools of law and lawyers in a single legal rule). The will to modernise Islamic courts and rules of procedure and of evidence was very strong, as was

44 Otto, Dekker, and van Soest-Zuurdeeg, *Sharia en nationaal recht in twaalf moslimlanden*. See also www.law.emory.edu/ifl/ for a global "mapping" survey of regional socio-cultural profiles as well as country-specific legal, institutional and other aspects of the theory and practice of Islamic Family Law, under direction of Dr. Abdullahi A. An-Na'im, Professor of Law, Emory University, Atlanta, GA, USA.

45 Previously, each state had its own version of the Administration of Muslim Law Enactment. This involved a kind of omnibus legislation, which controlled all aspects of Islamic law, ranging from mosques, religious councils, muftis, and religious crimes to family law. The family law provisions of those laws, however, were limited to the organisation and the powers of the Syariah Courts. Their only substantial provision was that hukum syarak (equivalent to the traditional Islamic law) should be applied. See for more Siraj, "Women and the law: Significant developments in Malaysia," 565; Shah, *Marriage and Divorce. Law Reform within Islamic Framework*; Kamaruddin, *Islamic Family Law issues 2000*; Kamali, *Islamic Law in Malaysia. Issues and Developments*.

46 Moustafa, "Judging in God's name," 158–9.

47 See for a good summary of the progressiveness of Islamic Family Law (Federal Territories) Act 1984 and the conservatism underlying the following Sharia'h Islamic family law amendments: Mahmood, "The politics of Shari'ah Reform," 6–9, footnotes 25 and 26.

initially the clear aversion to extrajudicial repudiations, unequal divorce rights, polygamy[48] and arbitrariness in the judicial procedure.[49] As documented so accurately and meticulously by Horowitz, these reforms were an interesting example of hybridising and transposition. Certainly, many of the reforms were moving in a similar direction as their secular equivalents. Sometimes they were formulated in exactly the same manner: in fact the Islamic law statutes were often based on existing secular statutes in the same field and they were only modified if Islamic doctrine explicitly differed. This process of change has produced paradoxical and hybrid results: it turned out to be both more Islamic and more common law at the same time.

However, regressive reforms took place since 1994, caused by the influence of conservative Islamist views and by the growing political success of the Islamic opposition party in Malaysia, which has booked considerable electoral successes in some states since the 90s.[50] Women Muslim organisations in Malaysia such as Sisters in Islam have strongly criticised these legislative

48 Polygamy, although practised in a very small minority (5%) of marriages and declared illegal for Hindu and Buddhist men, is nevertheless still a very important symbolic issue. The reforms led to restrictions on men's ability to engage in polygamy by giving the Islamic courts the power to scrutinise applications for subsequent marriages in order to ensure that justice be done to all women and children. Since the new Islamic family Law 1984, polygamy has had to comply with five conditions: the proposed marriage has to be just and necessary; the applicant has to have the means to support all his wives and dependants; equal treatment of all his wives; the proposed marriage does not cause "darar syarie" (harm) to the existing wife; and the proposed marriage does not directly or indirectly lower the standard of living of the existing wife and dependants. However, subsequent amendments eased these restrictions. The condition that the subsequent marriage should not lower the standard of living enjoyed by existing wife and children, was deleted in 1994. The 2005 amendment to the IFL act of 1984 modified the first condition of polygamy from "just and necessary" to "just or necessary." Thanks to the campaigning of women's groups the (ultimately passed) Islamic Family Law Bill of 2006 states again the husband has to prove that his proposed marriage was both "necessary and just." See for more: i.a. Mahmood, "The politics of Sharia'ah Reform," 15 and footnotes 57 and 58.

49 A better and more uniform protection of married Muslim women's rights was sought in terms of the distribution of the marital property, their rights to initiate divorce and their rights after divorce. See for an excellent analysis of this legislative reform: Horowitz, (part I), 264, 268–9, 273 and (part II), 571. The direction taken by the reforms can be understood in light of the reformers' background (representing both the common law and the Islamic law tradition; a framework of lawyers familiar with both legal traditions), the power of the secular legal system running in parallel, the reformers' aim to create an authentic and comparable legal system, and the fact that they seized the opportunity to borrow from a variety of supposedly legitimate sources of rules and institutions. Horowitz, 569 (part II).

50 Otto, "The compatibility of syariah with the rule of law", 145.

amendments.[51] We hereby observe a tendency to reintroduce, introduce, or emphasise more orthodox, conservative, and patriarchal interpretations of Islamic legal sources.[52]

4.2 *Criminalising (and Control of) Muslim (Moral) Behaviour*

Since the late 1990s, Malaysian states have adopted, beside the separate Islamic Family law enactment and procedural enactments, separate Islamic criminal offences enactments.[53] Previously few offenses were formally designated as a Syariah offense by statute and, "such matters accounted for a negligible percentage of the cases on the docket".[54] Constitutionally, the power of the state to enforce Islamic criminal law is limited and it can only apply to persons professing Islam.[55] According to the 1965 Federal Act the punishment is limited, often

---

51 Anwar, "What Islam, whose Islam? Sisters in Islam and the struggle for women's rights." See about SIS, a very recent publication: Basarudin, *Humanizing the Sacred.* In its struggle to improve women's rights under Islamic law, SIS has been actively speaking out against misinterpretations of sources of Islam and unjust practices through letters, memoranda, and campaigns, as well as voicing support for various legal reforms: "the end goal is an across-the-board reform of family law that is based on equality and justice" (109–110). See about the amendments and SIS's struggle to review these amendments: section "Islamic family Law (federal territories) Act 2005 in Chapter 3, 128–131. SIS's lobbying paved the way for it to be reviewed. Since 2005 (by 2005 the bill had been adopted in 11 states), women's groups have continued to pressure the state for a favourable outcome.

52 The preservation or reintroduction of conservative and patriarchal interpretations of Islamic rules also causes very serious difficulties when both legal systems come into collision as a result of (one of) the spouse(s) changing religion. See inter alia: Nair and Chuan, "The Effects of Conversion to Islam of a Non-Muslim Spouse on the Custody of Minor Children-Thoughts and Trends from a Malaysia Perspective." Adil, Azam and Saidon, "Religion as a Determinant of Child Welfare in Custody Cases in Malaysia and Classical Islamic Law". Nowadays there is a political shift and willingness to review "State Syariah family law, particularly on divorce and alimony involving converts […] to provide better protection for the affected spouses and children." http://www.theborneopost.com/2017/05/31/states-syariah-family-law-to-be-reviewed-cm/, 31 May, 2017, consulted in June, 2017.

53 Previously, there existed, in each state, a sort of omnibus legislation aimed at the establishment of Syariah Courts (the chief Qāḍī, the Qāḍī and the Syariah Appeal Committee), and of a religious council (the Majlis Agama Islam, fronted by a mufti), in addition to substantive rules regarding Islamic family law, religious misdemeanors (minor moral transgressions by Muslims) and testimonies.

54 Peletz, "A Tale of two courts," 149.

55 Although criminal law is a federal matter (ninth schedule of the constitution, first list, fourth item), the authority to stipulate and punish criminal offences against the prescriptions of the religion has been granted to the states in the state list of the same ninth schedule (list II, point 1). The authority of the state legislature in the field of religious criminal offences may also not be related to matters set out in the federal list ("except in regard to matters included in the Federal List").

referred to as the 3/5/6 formula (3 years jail, a fine of 5000 RM and 6 strikes with the rotan stick).[56] Those new Islamic criminal law enactments contain many provisions which exert ample control on the public moral behaviour of Muslims. For example, state law requires Muslims to go to Friday prayers, to fast during Ramadan, to comply with alimentary regulations; furthermore drinking, gambling, adultery, interfaith marriages, lesbianism, sodomy, premarital sex, *khalwat* ('close proximity'), pimps, incest and prostitution face penalties, and some states also have apostasy laws.[57] Several authors note the increase since about 2000 of state-sanctioned religious policing with regard to the enforcement of these Islamic penal provisions.[58] Moreover, as already mentioned, fatwas of official, state appointed officials are binding. In addition, next to these criminal offences enactments, the states of Kelantan and Terengganu have adopted *ḥuḍūḍ* laws.[59] They are at this stage not yet implemented and have been judicially challenged as unconstitutional. Yet the passing of these bills on *ḥuḍūḍ* created unrest around the country and has been at the forefront

56 See also Chevallier-Govers, "The rule of law and legal pluralism in Malaysia," 93–94.

57 Liwat/sodomy, indecent acts and gambling are also punished in the penal code and other federal laws. See also Moustafa 2014: 152, note 2. In the Federal Territories, the Syariah Criminal Offences Act criminalizes failure to perform Friday prayers (Art 14), breaking one's fast during Ramadan (Art 15), gambling (Art 18), drinking (Art 19), and 'sexual deviance' (Arts 20–29). State-level enactments mirror most of these federal-level statutes.

58 In her 2001 article, Martinez writes that for at least three years now, the federal government has checked whether the standard sermon it prescribes is given, and it keeps an equally close eye on other activities in the mosque. For example, in October 2001, fifteen Muslims were prosecuted in the Syariah Court because they neglected a *Majlis* command concerning Friday prayers. Martinez, "The Islamic state or the state of Islam in Malaysia," 482. In 2006, Neo also noted the increase in state-sanctioned religious policing. Furthermore, she observes that Islamic laws seeking to regulate the activities of Muslims as well as their clothing have been more actively enforced in recent years. She also refers to a 2005 case in which Muslims were convicted for alcohol consumption, probably for the first time in Malaysia. Neo 2006: 106–108).

59 Kelantan Syariah Criminal Code (II) Enactment of 25 November, 1993 and Terengganu Syariah Criminal Offences (Hudud and Qisas) Bill of 8 July, 2002. These *ḥuḍūḍ* acts introduce traditional Islamic punishments, such as the amputation of hands for theft (albeit framed with fifteen exceptions), crucifixion for robbery and stoning for adultery, for which the traditional Islamic rules of evidence apply. The *ḥuḍūḍ* laws of Kelantan and Terengganu have, however, not been implemented yet. These *ḥuḍūḍ* laws have been judicially challenged as unconstitutional on the grounds that individual states have no legislative power to enact such laws, since they prescribe *ḥuḍūḍ* punishments for theft, robbery, criminal conspiracy, rape and manslaughter, which are actions punishable under federal law. Neo, "Malay nationalism, Islamic supremacy," 106. See also: Hamid, "The Hudud Controversy in Malaysia," 205–19.

of many harsh debates.[60] It is clear that such religious penal provisions cause much discussion and polemics in Malaysia among Muslims with regard to their religious freedom, to their freedom of opinion and of expression, and to the appropriate relationship between state and religion. The constitutional and even Islamic validity of such 'paternalistic' and 'authoritarian' legislation is strongly criticised, not only by non-Muslims, but also by Muslim intellectuals, academics, and action groups such as SIS (Sisters in Islam). Moreover, the drip-feeding of such authoritarian elements into penal statutes is not limited to Islamic provisions, but equally characterises the realm of secular law in Malaysia (e.g. the sodomy prohibition, the Internal Security Act (ISA), etc.). Consequently, we are not talking about the reintroduction of Islamic medieval practices and rules but about very modern (authoritarian) developments, caused by a variety of reasons. The reasons have to do with neoliberal globalisation, growing piety, the growth of ultra-conservative Islamism and the growing power of religious departments and courts.[61] Shariʿa legislation should, in this view, be seen as a thoroughly modern, post-colonial concept. It can only function if it finds itself being part of the centralisation of power in the nation-state, without which it does not exist.

5 Concluding Reflections

Tradition and modernity cannot be presented as binary opposites, and neither can Islamic law and Western law, or Islam and democracy. The experiences of diversity management in 'alternative modernities' can hold new perspectives for our thinking about the relation between religion and law, and religion and politics. In discussing the issue of the accommodation of religious law, one should *contextualise*. Answering questions on the compatibility of Islamic law, legal pluralism and democratic constitutionalism with a plain 'no' misses

60 Nowadays there is still discussion about it and debate following the tabling of private member's Bill by PAS president Abdul Hadi Awang to amend the Syariah Courts (Criminal Jurisdiction) Act, known in Malaysia by its Malay language acronym RUU355. RUU355 will raise these to a maximum punishment of 30 years' prison, a RM 100,000 fine and 100 strokes of the cane. http://www.straitstimes.com/asia/se-asia/all-eyes-on-syariah-bill-as-malaysias-parliament-reopens, 6 March, 2017, consulted June, 2017. https://asiancorrespondent.com/2017/02/malaysians-gather-pas-355-rally-support-controversial-syariahbill/#EHGFiilzJ50Ivkoy.97, 18 February, 2017.

61 Peletz, "A Tale of two courts", 156. Reactionary Islamist conservatives could be divided essentially in four groups in Malaysia: UMNO ultra-conservatives, opposition party Islamists, Islamist civil society groups and religious bureaucrats. Hamid & Ismail "Islamist Conservatism," 173.

out on a vital part of the real issue, overlooking the complexity and diversity of Islamic religion and Islamic legal practices. The contextual framing of the issue of Islamic law and legal pluralism is therefore absolutely necessary. In many countries such as Malaysia, legal pluralism is furthermore to be taken as an empirical reality (or as a *fait accompli*) in the same way as social diversity.[62] Moreover, the increasing popular call for a return to shariʿa, "is one of the most significant developments" the Muslim world is facing and challenged by today.[63]

The important reforms of Malaysian Islamic family law in the 1980s and 1990s have shown that interesting and creative contextual institutional and legal ways can be found for the interaction, articulation, and compromise between religion and state, and between legal pluralism (involving the accommodation of Islamic rules and courts) and equality. Nevertheless, the subsequent negative developments in the Malaysian Islamic legal field have also shown that political compromises have to be principled: they should be constitutional compatible with the most minimal interpretations of religious freedoms and equality[64] – and democratic – in the broadest sense, which means also giving space to the voices of minorities and vulnerable minorities within minorities such as women, and, "not through legislation driven from above with no public support nor public discussion". There should be a combination of liberalism in a traditional sense, with emphasis on individual rights and freedoms, legal pluralism, the coexistence of different normative systems against the background of constitutional and international principles and deliberative liberalism – which also includes the right of minorities to participate into the

62 Sparr, "Legal Pluralism and Sharia: Implementing Islamic Law in States and Societies," For Sparr, however, legal pluralism is not to be seen as a good solution for it: "legal pluralism is, after all, an empirical reality, and so are social diversity and multiculturalism in the nation-states of today." "[in] the case of Sharia – apart from the necessary reinterpretation – the best alternative solution is not legal pluralism; it is to encourage political participation and make representation more effective under an equal citizenship."

63 Aljunied, "Demarginalizing the sharia," 127. *"This has not only catalyzed fierce debate amongst those advocating its implementation and those opposed, but also between proponents of sharia who differ over its interpretation."* Osman and Hirst, *Sisters in Islam, Engendering Islamic Reform in Malaysia*, 191.

64 In the dissenting opinion in the Lina Joy case, the judge Malanjum rightly underscores the following: "Since constitutional issues are involved especially on the question of fundamental rights as enshrined in the Constitution, it is of critical importance that the civil superior courts should not decline jurisdiction by merely citing art 121 (1A). The article only protects the Shariah Court in matters within their jurisdiction, which does not include interpretation of the provisions of the Constitution. Hence, when jurisdictional issues arise, civil courts are not required to abdicate their constitutional function. Legislation criminalizing apostasy or limiting the scope of fundamental liberties … are constitutional issues in nature which only the civil courts have jurisdiction to determine."

shaping of public and political culture and into deliberations regarding the recognition of cultural diversity. Another aspect which usually drops out of the picture is, as underlined by, inter alia, Tamir Moustafa, Anver Emon and Asifah Quraishi-Landes, that the state incorporation of Islamic law, at least in the manner documented here, also subverts foundational concepts and principles of the Islamic legal tradition itself [up to a certain level], such as the *qāḍī's* hermeneutical autonomy and the legal diversity of Islamic legal schools and fiqh rules. Quraishi-Landes argues that by failing to take account of the important distinction between what is siyasa (*laws made by temporal rulers which are not derived from scripture*) and what fiqh, many Muslim-majority countries have created near-theocratic rule. As a scholar of comparative constitutional theory, she looks for themes and recurring principles across systems: (1) a separation between state lawmaking (siyasa) and non-state lawmaking (fiqh); (2) a legitimation of state lawmaking based upon service of the public good; and (3) respect in the field of siyasa for the five general purposes of shariʿa (protection of religion, life, intellect, family and property). For her these three themes, updated for modern sensibilities, should form the core elements of modern Islamic constitutional theory today. However today we can observe that the Islamisation policies in many Muslim countries has collapsed shariʿa into just fiqh, and used state power (today's siyasa) to bring fiqh into the political realm. Moreover, she underlines that so-called "sharia legislation," does not really legislate "sharia" at all, but it merely legislates one (or several) among many fiqh possibilities.[65] Moreover, as Moustafa stated in a recent article, for many lay Muslims, the state's selective codification of Islamic law is understood as the faithful implementation of divine command.[66] Islamic law is seen there, as in the Western world, as a codified, systemised system of law, strongly focused on criminal law, and denying the wealth of hermeneutical techniques and millennium-long questioning, searching and debating. The extensive

---

65 Quraishi-Landes, "How to create an Islamic government – not an Islamic state"; Quraishi-Landes, "Islamic constitutionalism: not secular. not theocratic. not impossible." Quraishi-Landes, "The Sharia Problem with Sharia Legislation."

66 Moustafa, "Islamic Law, Women's Rights, and Popular Legal Consciousness in Malaysia," 169. He examines in this article how lay Muslims in Malaysia understand foundational concepts in Islamic law. He shows, based on recent polling data, lay Muslim ignorance of core epistemological commitments in Islamic legal theory, such as its commitment to pluralism and the centrality of human agency in fiqh law-making. 168: "In contemporary Malaysia, lay Muslims tend to understand Islamic law as being purely divine, with a single 'correct' answer to any given question. The practical implications of these findings illustrate how popular misconceptions of Islamic law hinder the efforts of those working to reform family law codes while strengthening the hand of conservative actors wishing to maintain the status quo."

control over the public moral behaviour of Muslims, the legal problems they encounter when leaving their religion and especially the striking state's monopoly on religious interpretation raises the question whether Malaysia is, or is not, a country marked by a strong state establishment of the Islamic religion. Following Bader, we are of the opinion that such a strong establishment of a specific religion by the state – through massive state interference and control of established religions, including the checking of the standard sermon and the monitoring of other activities in mosques – can be seen as incompatible with even a minimalist interpretation of democratic constitutionalism.[67] Harding strikingly describes the syncretic legal system of Malaysia as an institutionally imperfect system. Not because it is a pluralistic legal system in which religious and other law is recognised and applied, but because the rule of law is seen as a competitive value system rather than as a basic condition.[68] Neither Islamic or civil judges show an active commitment to the Constitution and to international human rights: the courts in cases concerning Muslim dissidents and their freedom of religion outside or inside Islam do not show any sensitivity towards the rule of law, nor do they make use of the possibility of constitutional review;[69] or if they do, they apply that possibility very restrictively.[70] In the "apostasy cases", they are even ruling against the core of a constitutional state upholding the rule of law,[71] where the right to leave one's religion is a necessary

---

67 Bader defines a 'strong establishment' as the constitutional or legal establishment of a monopolistic religion, which always implies an administrative and political monism aimed at religious national monism. He refers to Greece, Serbia and Israel as examples. According to him, such 'strong establishment' is incompatible with the minimally required institutional differentiation and with the most minimalist interpretations of religious freedoms and equality. See Bader, *Religious Diversity and Democratic Institutional Pluralism*, 269.

68 Harding, "Global doctrine and Local Knowledge: Law in South East Asia," 44–45.

69 As an example for the statements in the text above, we can also refer to the serious blow by the government against this duty of the judiciary since '88, when Mahathir proceeded to remove several Supreme Court Judges.

70 With Chevallier-Govers, we can say that their rulings raise the following questions: why should the Syariah court be competent concerning the Faith of a non-Muslim? Ultimately, professing is a matter of inner feeling. It is not something that can be decided by a court. This goes far beyond the problem of distribution of jurisdiction. Chevallier-Govers, "The rule of law and legal pluralism in Malaysia", 98. Neo mentions that while previously there was no formal procedure by which a Muslim could renounce or change his religion, it was possible for a Muslim to be freed from the legal obligations of Islam and exempted from the jurisdiction of the Muslim courts. Neo, "Malay nationalism, Islamic supremacy," 113.

71 Since the case *Soon Singh v Pertubuhan Kebajikan Islam Malaysia* (PERKIM) [1999] 1 MLJ 489, the secular courts take the position that the authority to deal with the conversion from the Islamic religion belongs to the Syariah Courts (on the grounds of Article 121 (A) of the Constitution, as amended in 1988. See the following cases: *Daud bin Mamat* & Ors

and fundamental liberty.[72] The absence of effective exit opportunities is a fundamental criticism of the system of separate personal laws for Muslims: a democratic constitutional state has the minimal positive duty to protect the right of dissidents to leave their own churches or mosques and courts.[73]

2001: "[...] Returning to the current facts, as the plaintiffs are yet to be found guilty of the second charges of apostasy [...] for all intents and purposes I have to conclude that they still are Muslims. [...] Indisputably [...] then by virtue of Article 121(1A) of the Federal Constitution, my powers are curtailed. That being so, the plaintiffs being legally Muslims will still remain within the jurisdiction of the Syariah Court, and thus outside my jurisdictional purview.' And 'The act of exiting from a religion is not a religion, and hence could not be equated with the right to 'profess and practice' their religion. To seriously accept that exiting from a religion may be equated to the latter two interpretations would stretch the scope of Article 11(1) to ridiculous heights and rebel against the canon of construction. On that score, I reject the contention of the plaintiffs that their rights pursuant to Article 11 (1) had been infringed." *Lina Joy* 2004 (High Court 18 April, 2001); On 31 May, 2007, the Federal Court ruled in a 2–1 majority decision that only the Syariah Court has the power to determine whether a person is still a Muslim. In the *'Shamala case'*, in which a non-Muslim mother sought a declaration that the conversion of her two children by her husband without her consent was void, the High Court held that the lack of legal remedy, 'would not make the jurisdiction exercisable by the civil court', and that, 'it was for the parliament to provide the remedy'. *Kamariah case*: a case concerning apostasy, in which the Court of Appeals stated that: "Article 11 of the Federal Constitution (in relation to Islam) cannot be interpreted so widely as to revoke all legislation requiring a person of the Muslim faith to perform a requirement under Islam or prohibit him or her from committing an act forbidden by Islam or that prescribes a system of committing an act related to Islam. This was because the standing of Islam in the Federal Constitution was different from that of other religions. Firstly, only the Islamic faith is mentioned by name in the Federal Constitution as the religion of the Federation. Secondly, the Constitution itself empowers State Legislative Bodies (for states) to codify Islamic Law in matters mentioned in List II, State List, Schedule Nine of the Federal Constitution ('List II')."

72 Constitutional provisions give also rise to different interpretations. This is especially the case for article 121 A (1988 Amendment) and the equality provision. The article concerning equality before the law and non-discrimination on grounds of religion, gender, race, etc. explicitly exclude their application to the legislation concerning personal laws. The result is that a constitutional limitation to the principle of equality and non-discrimination is foreseen in an area in which gender discrimination has to be challenged and which poses the most serious threats to the individual rights *of women*. Since the constitution does not provide for cultural rights, it protects cultural diversity in family law via constitutional provisions concerning the legislative competences for the member states and via this exception to the anti-discrimination provision. This constitutional construction has however as negative consequence that it could be interpreted as protecting religious or native personal laws from invalidation on the ground of gender anti-discrimination. Family law is the site where the private and public spheres of life intersect. The federal constitution therefore can fail to protect vulnerable *groups* such as women against a legal system and social structures in which the equality between the sexes has an apparent place.

73 This statement is affirmed by Neoh's analysis of the majority judgment by the Federal court in the *Lina Joy case*. The author notes that the focus of the majority judgment was 'not on public order arguments contemplating the trade-off between rights and social

This did not happen in Malaysia. It remains to be seen if this authoritarian evolution of Western-style codification will predominate in a nation known for its pluralism and diversity. The quest for power, and attached to that, the denial of a creative and more authentic tradition of applying and interpreting Islamic law, could well prove to be a painful, yet hopefully temporary experience for the Malaysian society.[74]

Bibliography

Adil, Mohamed, Mohamed Azam and Rafeah Saidon. "Religion as a Determinant of Child Welfare in Custody Cases in Malaysia and Classical Islamic Law: A Comparative Overview." *Islam and Civilisational Renewal* (ICR) [S. l.] 8, no. 1: 35–46, June 2017. http://www.icrjournal.org/icr/index.php/icr/article/view/614.

Aljunied, Syed Muhd Khairudin. "Demarginalizing the sharia: Muslim activists and legal reforms in Malaysia." *ReOrient* 1, no. 2 (Spring 2016): 135.

Anwar, Z. "What Islam, whose Islam? Sisters in Islam and the struggle for women's rights." In *The Politics of Multiculturalism*, edited by R.W. Hefner, 227–253. Honolulu: University of Hawai'i Press, 2001.

Awal, Noor Aziah Mohd. "Legal Education in Malaysia: Where is it heading?" http://www.aals.org/international2004/Papers/Awal.pdf.

Basarudin, Azza. *Humanizing the Sacred: Sisters in Islam and the Struggle for Gender Justice in Malaysia*. Seattle: University of Washington Press, 2016.

Bader, V.M. "Religious Diversity and Democratic Institutional Pluralism." *Political Theory* 31, no. 2 (2003): 265–294.

Chevallier-Govers, Constance. "The rule of law and legal pluralism in Malaysia." *Islam and Civilisational Renewal* (ICR) [*S.l.*]. 2, no. 1 (October 2010). http://www.icrjournal.org/icr/index.php/icr/article/view/206.

---

responsibilities characteristics of typical constitutional rights adjudication within the common law system; the chief trust of his judgment rested on the imperative to protect Islam' [...] 'this decision in effect conditions the act of leaving the Islamic faith to another regulatory order other than constitutional and common law norms'. Neoh, "A Case Study of Lina Joy," 12–13.

74 With Hamid, we could say that "unfortunately if present manifestations of bureaucratic Islamism are to be taken as indicative of what an Islamist-driven Malaysia would look like, a rosy picture can hardly be imagined." Hamid, "Political Islam and Islamist Politics in Malaysia," 20. Malaysia is of course certainly not the only Muslim country, in which we see that the incorporation of Islamic law involves a wiping out of the complex and polyparadigmatic history of interpretations within Islamic law, to replace it with a homogeneous and essentialising system which pro-Syariah (salafist) voices are fighting for in the first place.

Fenton, S. "Malaysia and capitalist modernisation: Plural and multicultural models." *International Journal of Comparative Sociology* 45, no. 3–4 (2003): 135–147.

Hamayotsu, Kikue. Democracy and Religious Pluralism in Southeast Asia: Indonesia and Malaysia Compared, 2015. Accessed 14 March, 2018. https://www.bu.edu/cura/files/2015/10/Religious-Pluralism-and-Democracy-in-Southeast-Asia-Hamayotsu-093015.pdf.

Hamid, Ahmad Fauzi Abdul. "Political Islam and Islamist Politics in Malaysia." *Trends in Southeast Asia*, no. 2 (2013).

Hamid, A. F. A. "The Hudud Controversy in Malaysia: Religious Probity or Political Expediency?" *Southeast Asian Affairs*, no. 1 (2015): 205–219.

Hamid, Ahmad Fauzi Abdul & Ismail Muhamad Taiyuddin. "Islamist Conservatism and the Demise of Islam Hadhari in Malaysia." *Islam and Christian-Muslim Relations* 25, no. 2 (2014): 159–180.

Harding, A. J. *Law, Government and the Constitution in Malaysia*. London: Kluwer Law International, 1996.

Harding, A.J. "Comparative law and legal transplantation in South East Asia: Making sense of the 'Nomic Din'." In *Adapting Legal Cultures*, edited by D. Nelken en J. Feest, 199–223. Oxford/Portland, Hart Publishing, 2001.

Harding, A. "Global doctrine and Local Knowledge: Law in South East Asia." *The International and Comparative Law Quarterly* 51, no. 1 (January 2002): 35–53.

Harding, A. "Sharia en nationaal recht in Maleisië." In *Sharia en nationaal recht in twaalf moslimlanden*, edited by J.M. Otto, A.J. Dekker and L.J. van Soest-Zuurdeeg, 303–34. Amsterdam: Amsterdam University Press, 2006.

Hefner, R.W., ed. *The Politics of Multiculturalism. Pluralism and Citizenship in Malaysia, Singapore, and Indonesia*. Honolulu: University of Hawai'i Press, 2001.

Hooker, M.B. *Islamic Law in South-East Asia*. Singapore/Oxford/New York: Oxford University Press, 1984.

Horowitz, D.L. "The Qur'an and the Common Law: Islamic Law Reform and the Theory of Legal Chance." *American Journal of Comparative Law* 42: 233–293; 543–580.

Ismail, Siti Zubaidah. "At the Foot of the Sultan: The Dynamic Application of Shariah in Malaysia." *Electronic Journal of Islamic and Middle Eastern Law* (EJIMEL) 3 (2015): 69–81. http://www.ejimel.uzh.ch.

Kamali, Mohammad Hashim. *Islamic Law in Malaysia. Issues and Developments*. Kuala Lumpur, Ilmiah Publishers, 2000.

Kamaruddin, Z. *Islamic Family Law issues 2000*. Kuala Lumpur: International Islamic University Malaysia Press, 2001.

Kok Wah Loh, Francis. "Malaysia after Mahathir: Late democratization amidst development, the developmental state and developmentalism." In *Democracy or Alternative*

Political Systems in Asia: After the Strongmen, edited by Hsin-Huang Michael Hsiao, 114–36. London and New York: Routledge, 2014.

Ibrahim, Ahmad Mohammed. "Recent Developments in the Syariah Law in Malaysia." In *The administration of Islamic law in Malaysia*, edited by A. Ibrahim. Institute of Islamic Understanding Malaysia (2000).

Lepard, Brian D., Anver M. Emon, Mark S. Ellis and Benjamin Glahn. "Islamic Law and International Human Rights Law: Searching for Common Ground?" Oxford: Oxford University Press, 2012. https://doi.org/10.1093/ojlr/rwv034.

Mahmood, Shahirah. "The Politics of Shari'ah Reform and Its Implications for Muslim Women in Malaysia." *Intersections: Gender & Sexuality in Asia & the Pacific* 36, (September 2014).

Martinez, P. A. "The Islamic state or the state of Islam in Malaysia." *Contemporary South-East Asia* 23, no. 3 (2001): 482–483.

Meerschaut, Karen and Serge Gutwirth. "Legal Pluralism and Islam in the Scales of the European Court of Human Rights." In *Conflicts between Fundamental Rights*, edited by Eva Brems, 431–465. Antwerp, Oxford and Portland: Intersentia, 2008.

Meerschaut, Karen and Serge Gutwirth. "Continuities and ruptures in the governance of Islam in Malaysia." In *Colonial and Post-colonial Governance of Islam: Continuities and Ruptures*, edited by Marcel Maussen, Veit-Michael Bader and Annelies Moors, 175–198. Amsterdam: Amsterdam University Press, 2011.

Moustafa, Tamir. "Islamic Law, Women's Rights, and Popular Legal Consciousness in Malaysia." (2013), 178.

Moustafa, Tamir. "Judging in God's Name: State Power, Secularism, and the Politics of Islamic law in Malaysia." *Oxford Journal of Law and Religion*, no. 1 (2014): 152–167.

Moustafa, Tamir. "The Politics of Religious Freedom in Malaysia." *Maryland Journal of International Law* 29 (2014), 481–504. http://digitalcommons.law.umaryland.edu/mjil/vol29/iss1/17.

Nair, Heama Latha and Gan Ching Chuan. "The Effects of Conversion to Islam of a Non-Muslim Spouse on the Custody of Minor Children – Thoughts and Trends from a Malaysia Perspective." *Advanced Science Letters* 23, no. 1 (January 2017): 688–691. https://doi.org/10.1166/asl.2017.7298.

Neo, Jaclyn Ling-Chien. "Malay nationalism, Islamic supremacy and the constitutional bargain in the multi-ethnic composition of Malaysia." *International Journal on Minority and Group Rights* 13 (2006): 95–118.

Neoh, Joshua. "Islamic State and the Common Law in Malaysia: A Case Study of Lina Joy." *Global Jurist* 8, no. 2 (2008). https://doi.org/10.2202/1934-2640.1269.

Osmann, Ratna and Catherine Hirst. "Sisters in Islam: Engendering Islamic Law Reform in Malaysia." In *Muslim Secular Democracy: Voices from Within*, edited by Lily Zubaidah Rahim, 191–284. New York, Palgrave Macmillan, 2013.

Otto, J. M., A. Dekker and L. van Soest-Zuurdeeg. *Sharia en nationaal recht in twaalf moslimlanden*. Amsterdam University Press, 2006.

Otto, J. M. "The compatibility of sharia with the rule of law. Fundamental conflict: between civilizations? Within civilisations? Or between scholars?" In *Knowledge in Ferment. Dilemmas in Science, Scholarship and Society*, edited by A. in't Groen et al. Leiden: Leiden University Press, 2007.

Peletz, Michael G., *Islamic Modern. Religious Courts and Cultural Politics in Malaysia*, Princeton/Oxford: Princeton University Press, 2002.

Peletz, M. G. "The cultural politics of legitimacy." In *Remaking Muslim Politics: Pluralism Democratisation Contestation*, edited by R. W. Hefner, 240–273. Princeton: Princeton University Press, 2005.

Peletz, Michael G. "Malaysia's Syariah Judiciary as Global Assemblage: Islamization, Corporatization, and Other Transformations in Context." *Comparative Studies in Society and History* 55, no. 3 (2013): 603–633.

Peletz, Michael G. "A tale of two courts: Judicial transformation and the rise of a corporate Islamic governmentality in Malaysia." *American Ethnologist* 42 (2015): 144–160. https://anthrosource.onlinelibrary.wiley.com/doi/abs/10.1111/amet.12122.

Quraishi-Landes, Asifah. "The Sharia Problem with Sharia Legislation." *Ohio North University Law Review* 41 (2015): 545. https://law.wisc.edu/profiles/pubs.php?iEmployeeID=17.

Quraishi-Landes, Asifah. "Islamic constitutionalism: not secular. not theocratic. not impossible." *Rutgers Journal of Law & Religion* 16 (2015): 553–79.

Quraishi-Landes, Asifah. "How to create an Islamic government – not an Islamic state." Accessed 12 October, 2016. https://law.wisc.edu/profiles/pubs.php?iEmployeeID=17.

Randeria, S. "Legal pluralism and cultural difference: The Indian model of a communitarian-liberal democracy." Unpublished paper, presented at The International Francqui Colloquium by Marie-Claire Foblets, *The Response of State Law to the Expression of Cultural Diversity*, Brussels, 28 September–1 October, 2006.

Shah, Noriani Nik Badli. *Marriage and Divorce. Law Reform within Islamic Framework*. Kuala Lumpur: International Law Book Services, 2000.

Siraj, Mehrun. "Women and the law: Significant developments in Malaysia." *Law and Society Review* 28, no. 3 (1994): 565.

Sparr, Adel Elsayed. "Legal Pluralism and Sharia: Implementing Islamic Law in States and Societies." *E-International Relations*, 18 December, 2014. http://www.e-ir.info/2014/12/18/legal-pluralism-and-sharia-implementing-islamic-law-in-states-and-societies/.

Index

acceptable citizens 110
accommodation 73, 163, 218, 231–232, 246–247
Addis Ababa 141 n. 16, 143, 145–146, 151–152, 157–158, 160
agency 85, 99, 101, 211, 248 n. 66
agent-based approach 178
alternative dispute resolution 13, 15, 19–20, 30, 35–36
Angrezi Shariat 19
arbitration 8, 12–14, 16–20, 23–28, 30–32, 35–38, 99
Arbitration Act 1996 (UK) 8, 12, 18, 20, 23, 27, 30–31, 36–37
Arbitration and Mediation Services (Equality) Bill 14, 28, 30, 37
Archbishop of Canterbury 12, 17
autonomy 7, 64, 85, 91–93, 96–99, 121, 160, 248

Beersheba 94, 100, 103
British Muslims 7–8, 45–46, 54, 58–59, 61

cases (UK)
  Dukali v Lamrani 49–50, 53
  El Gamal v Al Maktoum 51 n. 28
  Hudson v Leigh 47, 49–50, 52
  Radwan v Radwan 50 n. 22
  Sharbatly v Shagroon 53 n. 34
Christian 7–8, 12, 29, 44, 47, 49, 51–52, 59, 61, 64, 67, 78–79, 90, 93 n. 40, 140, 142, 155–157, 177, 179–180, 200 n. 5, 201, 205–206, 212
citizenship 29, 63, 65–68, 80, 82, 102 n. 77, 247 n. 62
Civil Code (Switzerland) 111, 132
Civil Code (Turkey) 121, 125, 127, 130–131
civilising mission 3, 109
clan-based justice
  clan-based justice and reconciliation (al-qaḍāʾ wa-ṣ-ṣulḥ al-ashāʾirī) 174
codification 88, 89 n. 26, 143, 233, 242, 251
cohabitation 43, 125, 221 n. 113
consensus 147, 149, 161, 175, 188 n. 35
conservatives 110–111, 113, 132, 239, 246 n. 61
constitution 5–6, 24, 68, 70–72, 75, 78, 82, 111, 113, 125, 141, 144–148, 153, 157–164, 177, 199–200, 202, 210–211, 214 n. 80, 215, 218–222, 233, 235–238, 239 nn. 37, 38, 244 n. 55, 247 n. 64, 249, 250 nn. 71, 72
contextualisation 246
counter-hegemonic 3, 110, 113
court
  Constitutional Court (Indonesia) 199 n. 1, 203, 217, 219–220, 222–224
  Constitutional Court (Turkey) 124, 129
  Court of Cassation (Turkey) 73, 76–80, 82, 91, 124, 131
  European Court of Human Rights 63, 66, 77
  Federal Shariat Court (Pakistan) 113–114, 119
  Shariʿa courts 13, 35–36
  Supreme Court (Indonesia) 61, 145, 149–150, 152–153, 157, 160–162, 201 n. 10, 210–211, 212 n. 70, 213–215, 217, 224, 236 n. 25, 249 n. 69
criminal law 30, 32, 96, 119, 230, 241, 244–245, 248
cultural revolution 121
customary law 2, 6–7, 84, 88, 89 n. 26, 111, 139 n. 4, 144, 164, 177, 200 n. 5

Dakwah 240
daʿwa 128, 188
Dire Dawa 141 n. 16, 145, 151–152, 157–158
discrimination 7, 29–30, 37, 58, 70–72, 75, 79–82, 96–97, 112, 120, 142, 149
dispute resolution, *also see* alternative dispute resolution 13–16, 18–20, 22, 28, 30, 35–36, 146, 151
divorce, *also see* Islamic divorce 13, 16–17, 19–22, 35, 36, 49–50, 53, 61, 69, 95–96, 111–112, 117–120, 122, 127–128, 130–132, 159, 243, 244 n. 42
Dodecanese 63, 65, 68–69, 81
domestic violence 8–9, 13, 20, 22, 32–36

England and Wales 7, 23, 43–45, 49–50, 59–61
English law 13–14, 17–21, 23–24, 31, 35–38, 46, 49–50, 55, 58
equality 1, 4, 6, 14, 18, 28, 30, 37, 70, 73–74, 79–80, 96, 120, 126, 129, 145–146, 154 n. 75, 157, 159, 162, 164, 202, 206 n. 37, 210, 214, 230 n. 2, 233 n. 13, 244 n. 41, 247, 249 n. 67, 250 n. 72
Ethiopia 3, 6, 140–145, 147–148, 152, 157–158, 160–161, 163

faskh 21
fatāwa, fatwā 112
fiqh 154–155, 157, 201, 204–207, 233, 235, 242, 248
forced marriage 13, 114, 126–127, 178, 195
forum shopping 75, 145, 151, 176 n. 10

gender 28–30, 59, 73, 96, 112, 120, 126, 130, 145, 154–157, 159, 162, 164, 179–180, 187 n. 32, 204, 205 n. 34, 214, 233 n. 13, 250 n. 72
Greece 7, 63–66, 68–71, 72 n. 17, 73–75, 76 n. 25, 77–78, 80–81, 249 n. 67

Hanafi school *see* Islamic law
Harar 141 n. 16, 142, 151, 154
hegemony/hegemonial 98, 109 n. 3, 133
hermeneutical 248
House of Lords (UK) 13, 28–29, 32, 35
ḥuḍūḍ 245
human rights 4, 7, 63, 66, 68–82, 147, 164, 201–203, 206–207, 209, 212, 214–216, 218–222, 224–225, 230, 232 n. 13, 233, 249
hybrid laws 133

identity 5–6, 12, 54, 63, 65–66, 74, 82, 93, 111, 121, 163, 195, 234, 236, 238 n. 36
ijtihād 97, 119–120, 155, 242
imam 53–56, 116, 123–124, 130
imam nikahı 123, 125, 130–131
interlegality 132, 141
ʿirḍ 7, 174–175, 191
ISIS 129
Islam Hadhari 239
Islamic divorce, *also see* divorce 13, 16–17, 19, 21, 35–36
Islamic law, *also see* Shariʿa
  Hanafi school 19, 27 n. 130
  Islamic family law 140–141, 144, 156, 160, 204, 207–208, 225, 231–233, 242, 243 n. 48, 244, 247
  Maliki school 242
  Muslim law 20 n. 67, 71, 75, 77–78, 91, 110–112, 114–122, 125, 127, 132–133, 242 n. 45
  school of law 19, 27 n. 130, 201
Islamic legal practices 2, 230, 247
Islamic Religious Council 241
Islamic state 199 n. 4, 224, 230, 233, 236, 239
Islamism, Islamists 129, 133, 240, 246, 251 n. 74

Jerusalem 84 n. 1, 89–90, 92–94, 100–103
Jewish 12, 44, 94, 98, 209 n. 52
jihād 128
judicial decrees 99
judicial review 25, 38, 160, 164, 199 n. 1, 203, 219–220, 222–224
jurisdictional conflicts 238
jurisprudence 78 n. 32, 89 n. 29, 117, 119, 154, 201, 233, 235, 237 n. 30, 241 n. 43

Kadis 140, 142–143, 145, 150–157, 159, 162–164
Kemalism 5, 110, 121, 125, 132–133
khulʿ 17, 20–21, 119
Kulturkampf 120

law of evidence 8, 152, 154
legal diversity 248
legal instrumentalism 111
legal pluralism
  Muslim legal pluralism 3, 110–111, 132–133
  state-recognised legal pluralism 140–141, 159
  strong legal pluralism 110, 120, 133
  unofficial legal pluralism 110
  weak legal pluralism 110, 141
legal positivists 110
legislation 4–5, 13–14, 30, 72, 94–97, 99, 112, 120, 145, 147, 158, 176–178, 231, 234–236, 237 n. 31, 241 n. 43, 242 n. 45, 244 n. 53, 246, 247–248, 250 n. 71
liberalisation 206, 242

Majlis Agama Islam 241, 244 n. 53
Malaysia 3, 5, 231–240, 242–247, 248 n. 66, 249, 251
Maliki school *see* Islamic law
marriage
  celebrant marriage 60 n. 43
  Child Marriage 115–117, 124–128
  interfaith marriages 5, 156–158, 199–210, 212–214, 217–218, 219 n. 103, 221–225, 245
  interreligious marriages 157, 238
  marriage formalities 46, 54
  marriage law 5, 7, 43, 57, 73, 95, 199 n. 1, 200–201, 203–205, 208–212, 213 n. 75, 214–218, 219 n. 103, 220–224
  Muslim marriage 8, 47, 59, 114, 120
  nikah marriage, *also see* nikāḥ 46, 54–55, 57–58, 61
  non-marriage 8, 46–54, 57–59, 61
  registration 4, 8, 44–47, 54–56, 59–61, 111, 113–114, 118–119, 122, 132, 200, 201 n. 10, 202, 211, 213, 215, 216 n. 89, 217, 222–223
  religious marriage 8, 35, 44–48, 59, 60 n. 43, 123–124, 130, 146, 158, 202, 212–213, 215
  void marriage 8, 44–48
Marriage Act 1949 (UK) 43, 45, 51, 53, 59, 61
mediation 8, 12–17, 19–24, 28, 30–31, 33–34, 36–37
Mejelle 87–88, 89 nn. 28, 29, 94
MFLO 112–113, 115–119
migrants 65–66, 68–69, 81
millet system 64, 90–91, 96, 132
Minorities 2, 66, 78, 81, 184, 247
moderate Islam 203 n. 20, 231
modernists 110–112
modernity 1, 109, 121, 231 n. 6, 235, 246
mubāra'a 119
Mufti 7, 64, 67, 69–70, 72–82, 91–92, 241, 242 n. 45, 244 n. 53

Nakba 93
nation building 109
nation state 110–111, 132, 176
national identity 93, 111, 121
native 88, 97, 200 n. 5, 231, 234, 237, 250 n. 72
natural justice 19, 97
nikāḥ, *also see* marriage 114, 131
  hidden nikāḥ 131
normative vacuum 109

OLFR (Ottoman Law of Family Rights) 4, 87, 89–91, 94–96
One Law for All 29
Ottomans 92, 132

Pakistan, Pakistani 3–5, 9, 15, 65, 110–121, 132–133, 242
Pakistanisation 133
parallel justice 2, 30, 181
plurality 113, 140–141, 165
polygamy 4–5, 72, 95–97, 100, 111–112, 116–118, 122, 127–130, 132, 158, 243
polygyny 156, 158–159
post-modern 111
power elites 2–3, 5, 109
pragmatism 173, 181
Purdah 234

Qur'an 117, 119, 159

rationalist approach 173, 197
religious freedom 54, 67, 74, 147, 202, 211, 214, 220, 222, 224, 246–247, 249 n. 67
religious laws 2, 29, 91, 140, 144, 203, 208 n. 48, 209, 218–220, 223–224
resistance 3, 5, 97–98, 100, 103–104, 110, 132, 142
rule of law 1–2, 75, 79–80, 173, 185, 194, 196–197, 232 n. 9, 233, 235–236, 249

Salafists 110, 113, 120, 132
school of law *see* Islamic law
second wife 128–129
secular 2, 9, 29, 110–111, 121–122, 124, 129, 132, 144, 147–148, 156, 159, 162, 199, 221, 232–233, 235 n. 23, 237, 240 nn. 39, 41, 243, 246, 249 n. 71
secularism 121, 147–149, 206 n. 37, 232 n. 9
Serban 234
Shafi'i 234
sharaf 7, 174–175, 189
Shari'a, *also see* Islamic law
  Shari'a law 12–13, 20, 29, 72–73

Shari'a courts *see* court
siyasa 248
social engineering 5, 109–110, 121, 130, 132
spirituality 15, 202
state ceremonies 236
state-justice 173, 184
Sufi 15
sujets de droits 133
Sunna 117, 206 n. 37, 207
Sunni 19, 27–28, 65, 89, 121, 132, 155, 157, 160, 201, 234
Supreme Muslim Council 92–94
syariah 230, 232–234, 235 n. 23, 236–237, 238 n. 34, 239 nn. 36, 37, 240 n. 41, 241, 242 n. 45, 244, 245 nn. 57, 58, 59, 246 n. 60, 249 nn. 70, 71, 250 n. 71
Syncretism 249

Takhayyur 242
tanẓīmāt 86–87
testimony 8, 28, 37, 152, 154–156, 211
Thrace 7, 63–81
traditionalists 110, 115
Treaty of Lausanne 7, 63, 66, 68–79, 81
tribunal 8–9, 12–14, 17 n. 39, 18–20, 23–28, 30–32, 35–37, 189, 191–192
Turkish Institute of Statistics (TurkStat) 129

'ulama 110, 132
Usul al-fiqh 233

vigilante justice 7, 174, 178, 197

weak state structures 1, 181
women's rights 12, 36, 114, 117–118, 126, 162, 232, 242, 243 n. 49, 244 n. 51

www.ingramcontent.com/pod-product-compliance
Lightning Source LLC
LaVergne TN
LVHW010641300926
849161LV00005B/1012
* 9 7 8 9 0 0 4 3 9 8 2 1 4 *